Complete Book of

BETTER HOMES AND GARDENS ® BOOKS
Des Moines, Iowa

BETTER HOMES AND GARDENS® BOOKS
An Imprint of Meredith® Books

Complete Book of Baking
Editor: Shelli McConnell
Recipe Developers and/or Recipe Writers:
    Maureen M. Fischer, Connie Hay, Lisa Mannes,
    Marla Mason, Diane Nelson, Janet Sadlack,
    Joyce Trollope
Text Writer: Marty Schiel
Copy Editor: Jennifer Speer Ramundt
Associate Art Director: Lynda Haupert
Test Kitchen Product Supervisor: Marilyn Cornelius
Food Stylists: Lynn Blanchard, Pat Godsted,
    Jennifer Peterson, Janet Pittman
Photographers: Mike Dieter, Scott Little, Kathy Sanders
Electronic Production Coordinator: Paula Forest
Production Manager: Douglas Johnston

❧

Vice President and Editorial Director: Elizabeth P. Rice
Executive Editor: Kay M. Sanders
Art Director: Ernest Shelton
Managing Editor: Christopher Cavanaugh
Test Kitchen Director: Sharon Stilwell

❧

President, Book Group: Joseph J. Ward
Vice President, Retail Marketing: Jamie L. Martin
Vice President, Direct Marketing: Timothy Jarrell

Meredith Corporation
Chairman of the Executive Committee: E.T. Meredith III
Chairman of the Board and Chief Executive Officer:
    Jack D. Rehm
President and Chief Operating Officer: William T. Kerr

WE CARE!

All of us at Better Homes and Gardens® Books are dedicated to providing you with the information and ideas you need to create tasty foods. We welcome your comments and suggestions. Write us at: Better Homes and Gardens® Books, Cookbook Editorial Department, RW240, 1716 Locust St., Des Moines, IA 50309-3023

Our seal assures you that every recipe in the *Complete Book of Baking* has been tested in the Better Homes and Gardens® Test Kitchen. This means that each recipe is practical and reliable, and meets our high standards of taste appeal. We guarantee your satisfaction with this book for as long as you own it.

If you would like to order additional copies of any of our books, call 1-800-678-2803 or check with your local bookstore.

Back to Baking

It's true—what goes around comes around. Despite the frantic pace of life these days and the incredible array of convenience foods at our fingertips, we're heading back into the kitchen and getting back to baking from scratch.

We're getting back to the luscious aromas that once drew us irresistibly to Mom's or Grandma's kitchen and the freshly baked breads, pies, cakes, and cookies that always seemed to be popping out of the oven at just the right time. Back to the simple satisfaction of making something that can be shared with family and friends. Back to the wholesomeness that can be created only when you start from scratch.

Whether you learned everything you need to know about baking while growing up or you're an apprentice to the trade, you'll love the Complete Book of Baking.

Go ahead, throw away those bits of paper with scribbled notes that you never can seem to find when you need them. We've collected some of the best tried-and-true recipes and blended them with our top test kitchen secrets (some of which even Grandma didn't know) to take the mystery out of baking, yet leave in all the taste that you remember.

Sprinkled throughout the book are Delicious Memories, personal favorites of Meredith employees, editors, designers, and freelance writers that we're sure will become your favorites as well. Also, there are cherished recipes from around the world and recipes designed to be easy enough that children can get involved in baking.

What are you waiting for? Get back to baking, and make your own delicious memories. Baking definitely is better the second time around and, with Better Homes and Gardens® Complete Book of Baking, it's a whole lot easier, too.

Contents

Unique Features of This Book

Baker's Bonus

Idea-packed, useful tips are scattered throughout the book.

Delicious Memories

Cherished recipes from some of our staff members are topped with delightful remembrances.

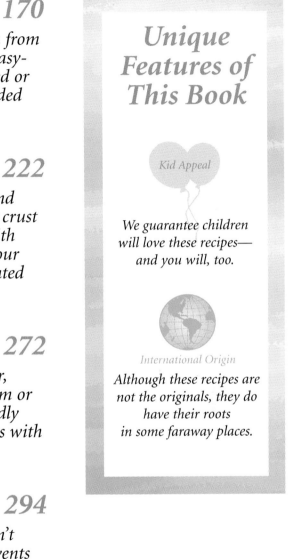

Unique Features of This Book

Kid Appeal

We guarantee children will love these recipes— and you will, too.

International Origin

Although these recipes are not the originals, they do have their roots in some faraway places.

Before You Begin
The Essence of Baking

For many would-be bakers, mastering the art of baking has been an elusive dream. Not any more. Everything you need to know to make your culinary dreams a reality is right here.

❧

You wouldn't build a house without a good set of plans, an understanding of the materials and techniques, or the right tools. Baking is no different.

❧

This book is full of tempting recipes to help you plan your baking. But before you get started, thoroughly read this chapter. It's full of information about common ingredients, measuring methods, mixing techniques, equipment, and bakeware that can help make your baking successful.

❧

And, just to make sure you're never caught unprepared, we've included a section on emergency substitutions. You never know when you'll run out of something essential in the middle of mixing up that special cake for a birthday supper.

Expressions of Interest

Many common baking terms are used throughout this cookbook. Some helpful definitions follow.

Bake: Cooking food, covered or uncovered, using the indirect, dry heat of an oven.

Beat: Briskly whipping or stirring an ingredient or mixture with a spoon, wire whisk, or electric mixer until smooth.

Blend: Processing an ingredient or mixture in an electric blender.

Boil: Heating liquids over heat on top of the stove (or in the microwave) until bubbles form and rise in a steady pattern, breaking on the surface.

Dash: An ingredient measure that equals about half of ⅛ teaspoon.

Dissolve: Stirring a dry substance in a liquid, such as yeast or gelatin in water, until no solids remain. Heating the liquid sometimes is necessary.

Fold: Gently mixing ingredients using a spatula. Cut down through the mixture, cut across the bottom of the bowl, then lift up and over close to the surface. Turn the bowl frequently for even distribution.

Garnish: Adding visual interest to a finished product by decorating it with small pieces of food, icing, nuts, fruits, or edible flowers.

Glaze: Brushing a mixture on a food to give it a glossy appearance or hard finish.

Grind: Using a food grinder or food processor to cut an ingredient into fine pieces.

Knead: Working dough with the heel of your hand in a pressing and folding pattern.

Melt: Heating a solid ingredient, such as butter, until it is a liquid.

Mix: Stirring ingredients, usually with a spoon, until they are thoroughly combined.

Peel: Removing the outer layer or skin from a fruit or vegetable.

Process: Preparing an ingredient or mixture in a food processor.

Simmer: Heating liquids over low heat on top of the stove (or in the microwave) until bubbles form slowly and burst below the surface.

Whip: Beating an ingredient or mixture lightly and rapidly using a wire whisk, rotary beater, or electric mixer to incorporate air and increase the volume.

Citrus Fruits

Juicing: Let fruit sit at room temperature about 30 minutes. Roll each piece on the counter with the palm of your hand a few times. This will encourage more juice to flow. Cut fruit in half crosswise. Hold a citrus juicer atop a measuring cup or a bowl, or use a freestanding juicer. Press each half of fruit into juicer, turning fruit back and forth until all juice is out. Discard pulp and seeds that collect in the juicer.

Sectioning: Cut a thin slice from each end of the fruit. With a very sharp utility knife or a serrated knife for peeling citrus fruits, cut from the top of the fruit down, cutting off the peel and the white membrane. (Or, cut around the fruit in a spiral.) Working over a bowl to catch juices, cut between one fruit section and the membrane to center of fruit. Turn knife and slide it up the other side of the section next to membrane; repeat. Remove any seeds from the sections.

Eggs

There are several techniques involved in the preparation of eggs.

Separating eggs: Over a bowl carefully crack an egg into an egg separator. Gently raise the separator, allowing the white to fall into the bowl. Place the egg yolk in a second bowl. To ensure that no yolk accidentally spills into the egg white, spoiling the entire batch, pour the white into a third bowl. Separate the remaining egg whites into the first bowl, transferring each to the third bowl before separating another. Even the smallest amount of egg yolk can prevent the whites from beating properly.

Slightly beating eggs: Use a fork to beat the whole egg until the white and yolk are thoroughly combined and no streaks remain.

Beating egg whites to soft peaks: Place egg whites in a clean glass or metal bowl; do not use a plastic bowl. Beat egg whites with an electric mixer or rotary beater until they form soft peaks (tips that curl over when beaters are lifted) or stiff peaks (tips that stand straight when beaters are lifted).

continued

Beating egg yolks: Place the egg yolks in a mixing bowl. Beat with an electric mixer on high speed about 5 minutes or until thick and the color of lemons.

High Altitude Baking

Baking at high altitudes requires some special adjustments to standard recipes.

If you live more than 3,000 feet above sea level, use the chart, below, to adjust the cake ingredients listed. Try the smaller amounts first, then make any necessary adjustments next time around.

For both cakes and cookies, increase the oven temperature about 20 degrees and decrease the baking time slightly to keep cakes from expanding too much and cookies from drying out.

For cakes leavened by air, such as angel food, beat the egg whites only to soft peaks. Otherwise your cakes may expand too much (because the air pressure is less). If you're making a cake that contains a large amount of fat or chocolate, you may need to reduce the shortening by 1 to 2 table-spoons and add an egg to prevent the cake from falling. The leavening, sugar, and liquid in cakes leavened with baking powder or baking soda may need adjustment, too (see chart, below).

Cookies, biscuits, and muffins are more stable than cakes and need little adjustment at high altitudes. If you feel it is necessary, experiment by slightly reducing the sugar and baking powder and increasing the liquid.

If you're working with a yeast dough, allow unshaped dough to rise according to recipe directions; punch dough down. Repeat rising step once more before shaping dough. If dough seems dry, add more liquid and reduce the amount of flour the next time you make the recipe. Because flours tend to be drier at high altitudes, they sometimes absorb more liquid.

For more information on cooking at high altitudes, contact your county extension agent or Colorado State University (Bulletin Room, Fort Collins, CO 80523; 303/491-7334). Please use this number only for questions related to high altitude cooking.

Toasting Coconut, Nuts, and Seeds

Spread the coconut, nuts, or seeds in a thin layer in a shallow baking pan. Bake in a 350° oven for 5 to 10 minutes or until light golden brown, stirring once or twice.

Additional Baking and Preparation Techniques

Caramelizing sugar: Some wonderful garnishes are made from caramelized sugar and, if you follow directions closely, it's not hard. Place the sugar in a heavy skillet or saucepan. Heat the sugar over medium-high heat, without stirring, until it begins to melt; shake skillet occasionally. Reduce heat to low; cook and stir frequently until the sugar is golden brown and completely melted.

Dissolving unflavored gelatin: Dissolving gelatin prevents rubbery lumps from forming in the final product. Place 1 envelope of unflavored gelatin in a small saucepan. Stir in at least ¼ cup water or other liquid, such as fruit juice. Let the mixture stand 5 minutes to soften gelatin; cook and stir over low heat until gelatin is dissolved. If the gelatin has been combined with at least ¼ cup sugar, it is not necessary to let it stand; just combine it with a liquid and heat. Once dissolved, the gelatin can be combined with other ingredients.

High Altitude Adjustments

Ingredient	3,000 feet	5,000 feet	7,000 feet
Liquid: add for each cup	1 to 2 tablespoons	2 to 4 tablespoons	3 to 4 tablespoons
Baking powder: decrease for each teaspoon	⅛ teaspoon	⅛ to ¼ teaspoon	¼ teaspoon
Sugar: decrease for each cup	0 to 1 tablespoons	0 to 2 tablespoons	1 to 3 tablespoons

Preheating the oven: This is essential to achieve the best results in baking. All recipe timings in this cookbook are based on a preheated oven. After preheating the oven, double-check the internal temperature with an oven thermometer. If the appearance or texture of a baked product does not seem correct, check the oven manufacturer's instructions for preheating your oven.

Sieving berries: In a blender container or food processor bowl, blend or process berries until smooth. Place a sieve over a bowl. Pour the puréed berries into the sieve. With the back of a wooden spoon, stir and press the fruit through the sieve. Discard the remaining seeds.

Whipping cream: For the best volume, first chill the bowl and beaters about 30 minutes in the refrigerator (10 minutes in the freezer) and use chilled cream. Use an electric mixer or rotary beater to beat the cream just until it mounds slightly and soft peaks form when the beaters are lifted. If you overbeat the whipping cream it will turn to butter, so watch it closely.

Measuring Up

Baking is both an art and a science. To satisfy the scientific aspects, you must be correct and consistent when measuring ingredients. Not all ingredients are measured the same way.

Liquids

Measuring cups: Use a glass or clear plastic measuring cup to measure liquids because it's important to see the contents. Place the cup on a level surface; bend down so that your eye is level with the mark you wish to read. Fill the cup up to that mark. Don't lift the cup to eye level—your hand is not as steady as a countertop!

Measuring spoons: Use a measuring spoon that is the exact capacity you wish to measure. Measure over a separate, empty small bowl in case the liquid overflows. Pour the liquid just to the top of the spoon.

Dry Ingredients

Use a measuring cup or spoon that is the exact capacity you wish to measure, and make sure it's dry.

Flours: Stir flour before measuring. There's no need to sift it first anymore, unless you're using cake flour; then sifting is recommended. Using a spoon, lightly sprinkle flour into the measuring cup. Then, using the straight edge of a metal spatula or knife, level off the measure.

Sugars: Spoon sugar into measuring cup, then level it off with the straight edge of a metal spatula or knife. For brown sugar, press it firmly into measuring cup so that it holds the shape of the measure when turned out.

Spices: Lightly fill the spoon just to top with spice. A dash is less than ⅛ teaspoon, which is the smallest amount you can measure accurately using a standard measuring spoon. It's often used when calling for salt, or another dry seasoning. Just shake or sprinkle ingredient into palm of your hand, and add it to suit your taste.

Solid Shortening or Softened Butter or Margarine

Use a measuring cup that is the exact capacity you wish to measure, and make sure it's dry. Then use a rubber spatula to press the shortening, margarine, or butter firmly into the cup. Level it off with the straight edge of a metal spatula or knife.

Stick butter or margarine: An entire stick equals ½ cup or ¼ pound; an eighth of a stick equals 1 tablespoon. Use a sharp knife to cut off the amount needed, following the wrapper markings for assistance.

Tools of the Trade

Using the right equipment is another way to guarantee your baking experience will be both enjoyable and successful.

Electric mixers make life in the kitchen a whole lot easier. Portable (hand-held) electric mixers are perfect for light jobs and short mixing periods, like whipping cream. For heavy-duty jobs and long mixing periods, a freestanding electric mixer works best, and it leaves you free to proceed with another part of the recipe. Some heavy-duty brands with dough hooks even take the effort out of kneading bread.

Food processors can blend, chop, and purée like a blender, but also slice and shred. Some brands even can mix batters and knead bread and pastry doughs (check your owner's manual to see what your model can do).

continued

Bakeware is made in an range of materials—aluminum, tin, stainless steel, black steel, and pottery. Both the material and the finish affect the final product. Shiny bakeware reflects heat, slowing the browning process. On the other hand, dark and dull-finish bakeware absorb more heat, increasing the amount of browning.

Here are some rules of thumb.

Shiny bakeware, including aluminum, tin, and stainless steel, will result in thinner cake crusts and softer-set cookies that spread more.

Dark or dull-finish bakeware, including dull aluminum or tin and glass, will give you heavier cake crusts, piecrusts that are evenly browned underneath as well as on top, crisp and nicely browned bread crusts, and crisper cookies. Black steel pans give breads a crisp dark crust and often are used for French bread sticks to give them their distinctive crunch.

Essential bakeware includes:
✦ Baking pans: 9x9x2 inch, 11x7x1½ inch, and 13x9x2 inch
✦ Baking sheets: 14x9 inch
✦ Cake pans (round): 8x1½ inch and 9x1½ inch
✦ Casserole dishes in various sizes
✦ Custard cups: 6 ounces each
✦ Fluted tube pan: 10 inch
✦ Glass baking dishes: 1½ quarts, 2 quarts, and 8x8x2 inch
✦ Jelly-roll pan: 15x10x1 inch
✦ Loaf pans: 8x4x2 inch and 9x5x3 inch
✦ Muffin pan
✦ Pie plate: 9 or 10 inch
✦ Pizza pan or stone

✦ Rectangular pans: 12x7x1½ inch and 13x9x2½ inch
✦ Springform pan: 8 or 9 inch
✦ Square pan: 8x8x2 inch or 9x9x2 inch
✦ Tube pan: 10 inch

Basic Truths

Perfect baking is not the result of some mysterious ritual known only to lucky initiates. The secrets to baking success lie in understanding the properties of the ingredients used and how those ingredients interact, then making sure that you use the freshest and purest ingredients possible. A dash of your own imagination ensures that whatever you bake will be deliciously unique.

Flour
Flours are essential to many baked products. Many cereals, roots, and seeds are milled to make flour, although wheat is by far the most popular and contains gluten necessary to give baked goods their structure. Some flours are made from soft wheats, some from hard wheats, and others are a combination of the two. Each type of flour gives a different flavor and crumb texture to baked products.

All-purpose flour is a blend of soft and hard wheat flours and, as the name says, is used as a multipurpose flour in a range of baked goods. However, different manufacturers use varying proportions of hard and soft wheats so the protein level in all-purpose flours ranges from 9 to 15 grams per cup.

When baking yeast breads, use a bread flour or an all-purpose flour with at least 2¾ grams of protein per ¼ cup because high-protein flours tend to produce more evenly textured yeast breads. To find out how much protein an all-purpose flour contains, get the amount of protein in grams per cup from the nutrition information on the flour bag. Popular brands of all-purpose flour have the following amounts of protein per cup:

King Arthur: 3¼ grams
Robin Hood: 3¼ grams
Pillsbury: 2¾ grams
Gold Medal: 2¾ grams
White Lily: 2¼ grams

All-purpose flour may be bleached or unbleached; unbleached all-purpose flour has a higher nutritional value. Store it in an airtight container at room temperature.

Cake flour is made from soft wheat and produces a tender, delicate crumb because the gluten is less elastic. Many bakers use it for angel food and chiffon cakes. All the recipes in this cookbook were perfected using all-purpose flour. If you would like to use cake flour instead, sift it before measuring, then use 1 cup plus 2 tablespoons cake flour for every 1 cup all-purpose flour.

Self-rising flour is an all-purpose flour that contains baking powder, baking soda, and salt. You can use it as a substitute for all-purpose flour in quick bread recipes, but be sure to omit the salt, baking powder, and baking soda from the recipe.

Bread flour contains more gluten and protein than all-purpose flour, making it ideal for baking breads.

When rubbed between your fingers, it feels a bit more granular than all-purpose flour. When used instead of all-purpose flour, you usually need less.

Specialty flours, such as whole wheat, rye, oat, graham, and soy, generally are combined with all-purpose flour in baked products because none has sufficient gluten to provide the right amount of elasticity on its own.

Whole wheat or graham flours are more minimally processed than plain flour and, therefore, retain more of their nutrients.

Rye flour is a traditional ingredient in many breads, cakes, and pastries of northern and eastern Europe. The gluten in rye flour adds stickiness to the dough, but lacks the elasticity of wheat flour gluten. Using a large proportion of rye flour to wheat flour results in a more compact product.

Oat flour can be made by grinding rolled oats to a fine powder in a food processor.

Soy flour is a creamy, strongly flavored flour that is a rich source of protein and iron and contains no gluten. Baked products made with soy flour brown more quickly, so you may have to reduce the baking temperature depending on the amount used.

Sweeteners

Sweeteners are essential for adding flavor, tenderness, and a bit of browning to baked goods. They may be either granular, as in granulated white or brown sugar, or liquid, as in honey or corn syrup.

Granulated, or white, sugar is the most common sweetener used in baking. It is made from sugarcane or sugar beets.

Brown sugar is less refined than granulated sugar. It is soft, moist, and has a distinctive flavor and color that comes from molasses that clings to fine sugar crystals. Brown sugar is available in both light and dark varieties; dark brown sugar has the stronger flavor. Recipes in this cookbook were tested using light brown sugar, unless specified otherwise.

You can substitute granulated sugar measure for measure for brown sugar, except in products where color and flavor might be important, such as a caramel sauce. In baked products that use baking powder or baking soda, add ¼ teaspoon more baking soda for each cup of brown sugar used in place of granulated sugar.

Powdered sugar, also known as confectioner's sugar, is granulated sugar that has been milled to a fine powder, then mixed with cornstarch to prevent lumping. Sift powdered sugar before using, and do not substitute it for granulated sugar.

Honey is made by bees from all sorts of flower nectars. It is sweeter than sugar and adds moisture, sweetness, and a characteristic flavor to baked goods. Because it caramelizes more quickly and at lower temperatures than sugar, honey causes baked goods to brown more quickly. Although it is available in whipped forms, the recipes in this cookbook refer to pure, unwhipped honey.

Corn syrup is a heavy syrup that has half the sweetness of sugar. It is available in light and dark varieties. Like dark brown sugar, dark corn syrup has the stronger flavor.

Fats and Oils

Fats and oils are added to baked products for flavor and tenderness. Fats generally are solid at room temperature and have the ability to incorporate air; oils are liquid and cannot incorporate air. Success of a recipe depends on using a specified fat or oil.

Butter and margarine cannot necessarily be used interchangeably. Butter is made from milk's natural sweet cream and must contain 80 percent butterfat. Margarine that has been made to resemble butter has 80 percent vegetable oil or animal fat; margarine-type products may have as little as 40 percent oil or fat.

In baking, if you choose margarine instead of butter, results may vary. Be sure to use a stick product that has at least 60 percent oil or fat. Do not use stick or tub products labeled "spreads." These products, and those labeled "extra light," contain only about 40 percent oil or fat and are mostly water, so they do not work well in baking. Use only butter or shortening when making piecrust or pastry, crumb crusts, crumb toppings, butter creams, pound cakes, or shortbreads and other "butter" cookies.

Hydrogenated vegetable shortening is referred to as shortening in this book. Made by processing oils such as
continued

soy or palm to create a light, creamy texture, shortening is solid at room temperature.

Cooking oils and flavored oils cannot be used interchangeably with solid fats because they are unable to hold air when beaten. Mildly flavored vegetable oils generally are made from corn, soybeans, sunflower seeds, or peanuts and have a pale color. Nut oils, such as walnut oil, have a pronounced nutty flavor and can be darker in color.

Leavening Agents

Leavening agents add lightness to a baked product by "raising" it. Common leavens include yeast, baking powder, and baking soda. Steam, which forms when the liquid in the batter heats up, also can cause a product to expand.

Yeast is a microscopic single-cell organism that ferments sugars to produce carbon dioxide. These bubbles of carbon dioxide are trapped in the dough and cause the product to rise. Yeast also adds a distinctive flavor and aroma to the final product. All recipes in this cookbook were tested using active dry yeast. In some yeast bread recipes you may use quick-rising, active, dry yeast as a substitute (see page 60). Be sure the liquid is the right temperature to dissolve yeast. If it's too hot, the yeast will die; if it's too cool the yeast won't activate properly.

Baking soda also creates carbon dioxide and is used in conjunction with acidic ingredients such as buttermilk, sour cream, brown sugar, or fruit juices to create the bubbles that make the product rise. The soda and acid begin to react as soon as a liquid is added, so any product that uses only soda as the leaven should be baked immediately. Using too much baking soda gives baked product a soapy taste.

Baking powder is a combination of a dry acid, baking soda, and a starch. It has the ability to release carbon dioxide in two stages; first, when liquid ingredients are added and second, when mixture is heated. If you don't use a lot of it, buy it in small cans as it loses its raising ability fairly quickly. Using too much baking powder gives the baked product a bitter taste.

Eggs

Eggs are used in baked products to add color and flavor and to thicken the mixture, bind ingredients, emulsify the fats, and form a structure.

You should use eggs labeled "large" for all the recipes in this cookbook. A fresh egg will have a firm yolk and a thick white. Store eggs in the refrigerator in the carton to keep them fresh.

Dairy Products

Milk and milk products are used in baking to provide moisture, flavor, color, and to activate the leavening agents. Because whole, low-fat, and skim milk vary only in fat content, you can use them interchangeably in baking. Whole milk will, however, result in a richer flavor than skim milk.

Buttermilk is skim milk to which a bacterial culture has been added. It is low in fat, thick, and creamy, with a mildly acidic taste. Sour milk, made from milk and lemon juice or vinegar, can be substituted for buttermilk (see page 307).

Whipping cream contains between 30 and 49 percent fat and can be beaten to form peaks that retain their shape. To speed up whipping, chill the bowl and beaters first.

Light cream or table cream contains 10 to 30 percent fat, which is not sufficient for whipping. Half-and-half, a mixture of milk and cream, can be used instead of light cream.

Evaporated milk is milk that has had 60 percent of its water removed. It is sold in cans and can be stored at room temperature until opened. Do not use evaporated milk as a substitute for other milk products unless you reconstitute it using 2 parts evaporated milk to 3 parts water (e.g. ½ cup evaporated milk to ¾ cup water).

Sweetened condensed milk is milk that has had about 50 percent of its water removed and, like evaporated milk, is sold in cans and can be stored at room temperature until opened. Because it also has about 40 percent added sugar, it is not a suitable substitute for other milks.

Nonfat dry milk has both the fat and water removed. Mix nonfat milk powder with water according to package directions to form milk. Some of the recipes in this cookbook call for it as a dry ingredient to add richness to baked products.

In a Pinch

There's no doubt that you'll get the best baking results when you use the specified ingredients. There's also no doubt that sooner or later you'll be caught short of something.

If you can't borrow that cup of sugar or few squares of unsweetened chocolate from your neighbor, here are some handy substitutions. You may notice a change in flavor or texture, so use these substitutions only in a pinch.

Ingredient	Substitution
1 cup cake flour	1 cup minus 2 tablespoons all-purpose flour
1 cup self-rising flour	1 cup all-purpose flour plus 1 teaspoon baking powder, ½ teaspoon salt, and ¼ teaspoon baking soda
1 cup sugar	1 cup packed brown sugar
1 teaspoon baking powder	½ teaspoon cream of tartar plus ¼ teaspoon baking soda
1 cup buttermilk	1 tablespoon lemon juice or vinegar plus enough milk to make 1 cup (let stand 5 minutes before using), or 1 cup milk plus 1¾ teaspoons cream of tartar, or 1 cup yogurt
1 cup half-and-half or light cream	1 tablespoon melted butter or margarine plus enough milk to make 1 cup
1 cup milk	½ cup evaporated milk plus ½ cup water, or 1 cup water plus ⅓ cup nonfat dry milk powder
1 cup corn syrup	1 cup sugar plus ¼ cup liquid
1 cup honey	1¼ cups sugar plus ¼ cup liquid
1 teaspoon apple pie spice	½ teaspoon ground cinnamon plus ¼ teaspoon ground nutmeg, ⅛ teaspoon ground allspice, and dash ground ginger
1 teaspoon pumpkin pie spice	½ teaspoon ground cinnamon plus ¼ teaspoon ground ginger, ¼ teaspoon ground allspice, and ⅛ teaspoon ground nutmeg
1 ounce semisweet chocolate	½ ounce unsweetened chocolate plus 1 tablespoon sugar, or 3 tablespoons semisweet chocolate pieces
4 ounces sweet baking chocolate	¼ cup unsweetened cocoa powder plus ⅓ cup sugar and 3 tablespoons shortening
1 ounce unsweetened chocolate	3 tablespoons unsweetened cocoa powder plus 1 tablespoon shortening or cooking oil

Giant Cinnamon Rolls (see recipe, page 58)

The Bread Basket

Bread is a fundamental food in nearly every cuisine and has been since the first loaf of unleavened bread was baked thousands of years ago. That's not to say bread hasn't changed; in fact it's hard to imagine daily life without it. What would a hamburger be without a bun? A pizza without a crust? Cream cheese and lox without a bagel?

❧

Every kind of bread is here. Muffins, coffee cakes, and nut breads to accompany a cup of coffee and biscuits and scones for a formal cup of tea. There are savory yeast breads to wrap sandwiches, and buns to toast and serve with hearty soups. Don't miss the selection of buttery croissants and pastries sure to tempt the fussiest sweet tooth.

When Size Matters

Any of these recipes can be adjusted to make whatever size popovers you desire. For all sizes, fill the prepared custard cups or popover pans half full with the batter, and bake in a 400° oven. Remember that the wider the cup or pan, the less the popovers will "pop" because there's nothing to hold up the center.

Regular: Use 6-ounce custard cups, a heavy cast-iron or steel popover pan, or a 2½-inch muffin pan. Grease each cup with ½ teaspoon shortening. Bake the popovers about 40 minutes or until done.

Mini: Use a 1¾-inch muffin pan. Grease each cup with ⅛ teaspoon shortening. Bake about 25 minutes or until done.

A Bit of Ginger Popovers

To make one large popover, prepare recipe as directed, except use a 10-inch ovenproof skillet instead of the pie plates. Place the 2 tablespoons butter or margarine in the skillet. Place skillet in a cold oven, then preheat oven to 400° (allow 8 to 10 minutes). Pour batter into preheated pan. Bake about 25 minutes or until done.

2 **tablespoons butter or margarine**
3 **eggs**

½ **cup half-and-half or light cream**
2 **tablespoons cooking oil**
½ **teaspoon grated orange peel**
½ **cup all-purpose flour**
1 **teaspoon grated gingerroot**
¼ **teaspoon salt**
4 **to 5 cups mixed berries**
¼ **cup sifted powdered sugar**

1 Using 1 teaspoon butter for each cup, grease the bottoms and sides of six 4¼-inch pie pans. Place the pie pans on a 15x10x1-inch baking pan. Set the baking pan aside.

2 In a medium mixing bowl use a wire whisk or rotary beater to beat eggs, half-and-half, cooking oil, and orange peel together until combined. Add flour, gingerroot, and salt. Beat until mixture is smooth.

3 Place baking pan in a 400° oven for 1 to 2 minutes or until the butter in pie pans is melted. Remove from oven. Immediately pour ¼ cup of the batter into each of the pie pans. Return to the oven, and bake for 15 to 20 minutes or until edges are puffed and centers appear dry.

4 To serve, transfer each popover to a serving plate. Spoon berries into centers of the popovers. Sprinkle with powdered sugar. Makes 6.

Nutrition facts per popover: *239 calories, 5 g protein, 21 g carbohydrate, 15 g total fat (6 g saturated fat), 131 mg cholesterol, 169 mg sodium, 5 g fiber. Daily values: 13% vitamin A, 43% vitamin C, 4% calcium, 8% iron.*

Popovers

1 **tablespoon shortening or nonstick spray coating**
2 **eggs**
1 **cup milk**
1 **tablespoon cooking oil**
1 **cup all-purpose flour**
¼ **teaspoon salt**

1 Using ½ teaspoon shortening for each cup, grease the bottom and sides of six 6-ounce custard cups or the cups of a popover pan. Or, spray cups with the nonstick coating. Place the custard cups on a 15x10x1-inch baking pan. Set pan aside.

2 In a medium mixing bowl use a wire whisk or rotary beater to beat eggs, milk, and cooking oil together until combined. Add flour and salt. Beat until smooth.

3 Fill the prepared cups half full with batter. Bake in a 400° oven about 40 minutes or until firm.

4 Immediately after removing popovers from oven, use tines of a fork to prick each popover to let steam escape. Turn off oven. For crisper popovers, return popovers to oven 5 to 10 minutes or until desired crispness is reached. Remove popovers from cups and serve immediately. Makes 6.

Nutrition facts per popover: *154 calories, 5 g protein, 17 g carbohydrate, 7 g total fat (2 g saturated fat), 74 mg cholesterol, 131 mg sodium, 1 g fiber. Daily values: 5% vitamin A, 0% vitamin C, 5% calcium, 7% iron.*

Pierce each popover with a fork to allow the steam to escape. The steam helps a popover rise during baking, but will make it soggy if allowed to remain inside.

Mexican Skillet Popover

If you have a food processor, use it to blend the eggs, milk, flour, chili powder, and salt. Then, using a spoon, stir in the cooked onion and chili peppers and bake as directed.

2 **tablespoons butter or margarine**
2 **tablespoons finely chopped onion**
2 **eggs**
1 **cup milk**
1 **cup all-purpose flour**
½ **teaspoon chili powder**
¼ **teaspoon salt**
¼ **cup canned chopped green chili peppers**
¾ **cup shredded Monterey Jack cheese or cheddar cheese (3 ounces)**
½ **cup taco sauce, heated**

Baker's Bonus

Letting Off Steam

Popovers pop even though you don't add a leavening agent such as baking powder. Steam that forms inside them when they bake is what causes them to rise.

To make sure your popovers have plenty of puff:

✦ *Use large eggs.*

✦ *Stir the batter while filling the cups to keep it well mixed, and do not add more cheese or meat than the recipe directs.*

✦ *Grease the pans properly to make the popovers easy to remove.*

✦ *Don't open the oven door during baking. The cool air that gets in can cause the popovers to fall.*

✦ *Prevent overbrowning by placing the oven shelf in the lower part of the oven so the tops of the custard cups (or popover pan) are in the center.*

✦ *Bake the popovers for the time indicated or until firm; do not underbake.*

✦ *Prick each popover with a fork to let steam escape after removing them from the oven so they don't get soggy. To crisp popovers, shut off the oven, return the popovers to the oven for 5 to 10 minutes more, and remove them from their pans while warm.*

✦ *Serve popovers hot from the oven. If there are leftovers, place them in a freezer bag and freeze up to 3 months. Reheat frozen popovers in a shallow baking pan in a 400° oven for 10 to 15 minutes or until warm.*

1 Place 1 tablespoon butter in a 10-inch ovenproof skillet. Place skillet in a cold oven, then preheat oven to 400° (allow about 10 minutes); do not brown the butter.

2 Meanwhile, in a small skillet cook onion in remaining 1 tablespoon butter until tender but not brown. In a medium mixing bowl use a wire whisk or rotary beater to beat eggs and milk together until combined. Add flour, chili powder, and salt. Beat until mixture is smooth. Stir cooked onion and chili peppers into egg mixture.

Remove skillet from oven and immediately pour in egg mixture. Return skillet to the oven and bake about 40 minutes or until firm.

3 To serve, cut popover into wedges. Top with cheese and drizzle with taco sauce. Makes 6 servings.

Nutrition facts per serving: *213 calories, 9 g protein, 19 g carbohydrate, 11 g total fat (6 g saturated fat), 97 mg cholesterol, 359 mg sodium, 1 g fiber. Daily values: 14% vitamin A, 13% vitamin C, 15% calcium, 10% iron.*

Nutty Popovers

To turn these crispy popovers into a delectable dessert, simply split them open, fill with ice cream, and drizzle on the hot fudge sauce.

1 **tablespoon shortening or nonstick spray coating**
¼ **cup very finely chopped walnuts, hazelnuts (filberts), almonds, or pecans**
2 **eggs**
1 **cup milk**
1 **tablespoon nut-flavored cooking oil (such as walnut, hazelnut, almond, or pecan) or cooking oil**
1 **cup all-purpose flour**
¼ **teaspoon salt**

1 Using ½ teaspoon shortening for each cup, grease bottom and sides of six 6-ounce custard cups or cups of a popover pan. Or, spray each cup with nonstick coating. Sprinkle 1 teaspoon of the nuts into each cup so that bottoms and sides of cups are evenly coated. Place custard cups on a 15x10x1-inch baking pan. Set pan aside.

2 In a medium mixing bowl use a wire whisk or rotary beater to beat eggs, milk, and cooking oil together until combined. Add flour, the remaining nuts, and the salt. Beat until mixture is well blended.

3 Fill the prepared cups half full with batter. Bake in a 400° oven about 40 minutes or until firm.

4 Immediately after removing the popovers from oven, use the tines of a fork to prick each popover to let the steam escape. Turn off the oven. For crisper popovers, return the popovers to the oven for 5 to 10 minutes or until desired crispness is reached. Remove popovers from cups and serve immediately. Makes 6.

Nutrition facts per popover: *168 calories, 6 g protein, 18 g carbohydrate, 8 g total fat (2 g saturated fat), 74 mg cholesterol, 131 mg sodium, 1 g fiber. Daily values: 5% vitamin A, 0% vitamin C, 5% calcium, 8% iron.*

Notes

———————————————

———————————————

———————————————

———————————————

———————————————

———————————————

———————————————

Provolone and Pepper Popovers

What a combination! These packed-with-punch popovers taste great when served with beef, lamb, or pork.

1 **tablespoon shortening or nonstick spray coating**
2 **eggs**
1 **cup milk**
1 **tablespoon cooking oil**
1 **cup all-purpose flour**
¼ **teaspoon salt**
¼ **cup finely shredded provolone cheese (1 ounce)**
1 **to 2 teaspoons cracked black pepper**

1 Using ½ teaspoon shortening for each cup, grease the bottom and sides of six 6-ounce custard cups or the cups of a popover pan. Or, spray cups with the nonstick coating. Place the custard cups on a 15x10x1-inch baking pan. Set pan aside.

2 In a medium mixing bowl use a wire whisk or rotary beater to beat eggs, milk, and cooking oil together until combined. Add flour and salt. Beat until mixture is smooth. Fold in provolone cheese and black pepper.

3 Fill the prepared cups half full with batter. Bake in a 400° oven about 40 minutes or until firm.

4 Immediately after removing from oven, use the tines of a fork to prick each popover to let the steam escape. Turn off the oven. For crisper popovers, return the popovers to the oven for 5 to 10 minutes or until desired crispness is reached. Remove popovers from cups and serve immediately. Makes 6.

Nutrition facts per popover: *171 calories, 7 g protein, 17 g carbohydrate, 8 g total fat (3 g saturated fat), 77 mg cholesterol, 172 mg sodium, 1 g fiber. Daily values: 6% vitamin A, 1% vitamin C, 8% calcium, 8% iron.*

Provolone and Pepper Popovers, top, and Nutty Popovers, bottom

Best-Ever Buttermilk Biscuits

Slather these fresh-from-the-oven biscuits with jam for breakfast or cover them with gravy for your evening meal.

- 2 **cups all-purpose flour**
- 1 **tablespoon baking powder**
- 2 **teaspoons granulated sugar**
- ½ **teaspoon cream of tartar**
- ¼ **teaspoon salt**
- ¼ **teaspoon baking soda**
- ½ **cup shortening**
- ⅔ **cup buttermilk**

1 In a mixing bowl combine flour, baking powder, sugar, cream of tartar, salt, and baking soda. Cut in shortening until mixture resembles coarse crumbs. Make a well in center, then add buttermilk all at once. Using a fork, stir just until moistened.

2 Turn dough out onto a lightly floured surface. Quickly knead by folding and pressing gently 10 to 12 strokes or until dough is nearly smooth. Pat or lightly roll to ½-inch thickness. Cut dough with a floured 2½-inch biscuit cutter.

3 Place biscuits 1 inch apart on an ungreased baking sheet. Bake in a 450° oven for 10 to 12 minutes or until golden. Remove biscuits from baking sheet and serve warm. Makes 10 to 12.

Nutrition facts per biscuit: 185 calories, 3 g protein, 20 g carbohydrate, 11 g total fat (3 g saturated fat), 1 mg cholesterol, 211 mg sodium, 1 g fiber. Daily values: 0% vitamin A, 0% vitamin C, 10% calcium, 8% iron.

To Make Ahead

Prepare and bake biscuits as directed, cool completely. Place biscuits in a freezer container or bag and freeze up to 3 months. To serve, wrap frozen biscuits in foil and bake in a 300° oven 20 to 25 minutes or until warm.

Kid Appeal

Applesauce Biscuits

- 2 **cups all-purpose flour**
- 2 **teaspoons baking powder**
- 2 **teaspoons granulated sugar**
- ½ **teaspoon ground allspice**
- ¼ **teaspoon baking soda**
- ¼ **teaspoon salt**
- ¼ **teaspoon ground cinnamon**
- ½ **cup shortening**
- ⅓ **cup buttermilk**
- ¼ **cup applesauce**

1 In a medium mixing bowl stir together flour, baking powder, sugar, allspice, baking soda, salt, and cinnamon. Using a pastry blender, cut in shortening until mixture resembles coarse crumbs. Make a well in the center of dry mixture. In a small mixing bowl combine buttermilk and applesauce; add to dry mixture all at once. Using a fork, stir just until moistened.

2 Turn dough out onto a lightly floured surface. Quickly knead dough by gently folding and pressing 10 to 12 strokes or until dough is nearly smooth. Pat or lightly roll dough to ½-inch thickness. Cut dough with a floured 2½-inch biscuit cutter.

Use a pastry blender with a rocking motion to make uniform, coarse crumbs of the shortening. When the biscuits are baked, these layers of fat contribute to the flakiness of the biscuits.

To knead, gently fold the dough in half toward you. Then press the two edges together with the heal of your hand. Give the dough a quarter turn and repeat the process.

3 Place biscuits 1 inch apart on an ungreased baking sheet. Bake in a 450° oven 10 to 12 minutes or until golden. Remove biscuits from the baking sheet and serve warm. Makes 10 to 12.

Nutrition facts per biscuit: *187 calories, 3 g protein, 20 g carbohydrate, 11 g total fat (3 g saturated fat), 0 mg cholesterol, 167 mg sodium, 1 g fiber. Daily values: 0% vitamin A, 0% vitamin C, 6% calcium, 8% iron.*

To Make Ahead

Prepare and bake biscuits as directed, cool completely. Place biscuits in a freezer container or bag and freeze up to 3 months. To serve, wrap frozen biscuits in foil and bake in a 300° oven 20 to 25 minutes or until warm.

Orange and Raisin Biscuits

 2 cups all-purpose flour
 ½ cup raisins or currants
 4 teaspoons granulated sugar
 2 teaspoons baking powder
 1 teaspoon finely shredded
     orange peel
 ½ teaspoon ground cinnamon
 ¼ teaspoon baking soda
 ¼ teaspoon salt
 ½ cup shortening
 ⅔ cup buttermilk

1 In a medium mixing bowl combine flour, raisins, sugar, baking powder, orange peel, cinnamon, baking soda, and salt. Cut in shortening until mixture resembles coarse crumbs. Make a well in the center of dry mixture. Add

Baker's Bonus

Biscuit Essentials

There are as many hints to preparing light, tender, and flaky biscuits and scones as there are bakers. While making them is easy, you'll need to remember some basic techniques:

 ◆ *Use only chilled butter or margarine.*
 ◆ *Stir dry ingredients well to distribute the leavening agent.*
 ◆ *Mix the butter or margarine and flour only until the mixture resembles coarse crumbs.*
 ◆ *Stir in the liquid just until moistened.*
 ◆ *Lightly knead the dough by folding and pressing; 10 to 12 strokes should be enough to distribute the moisture.*
 ◆ *Cut out as many as possible from a single rolling of the dough (additional rolling and flour will make them tough and dry). Cutting the dough into squares will eliminate the need to reroll it.*
 ◆ *Place biscuits or scones close together on the baking sheet for a soft crust; for a crispy crust, place them about 1 inch apart.*
 ◆ *Remove from the oven when top and bottom crusts are an even golden brown.*
 ◆ *Store in foil or a sealed plastic bag at room temperature for 2 to 3 days; freeze in heavy foil up to 3 months.*
 ◆ *Reheat foil-wrapped biscuits in a 300° oven for 10 to 12 minutes; reheat frozen biscuits for 20 to 25 minutes.*

buttermilk all at once to dry mixture. Using a fork, stir just until moistened.

2 Turn the dough out onto a lightly floured surface. Quickly knead dough by gently folding and pressing for 10 to 12 strokes or until the dough is nearly smooth. Pat or lightly roll dough to ½-inch thickness. Cut dough with a floured 2½-inch biscuit cutter.

3 Place biscuits 1 inch apart on an ungreased baking sheet. Bake in a 450° oven for 10 to 12 minutes or until golden brown. Remove biscuits from the baking sheet and serve warm. Makes 10 to 12.

Nutrition facts per biscuit: *210 calories, 3 g protein, 26 g carbohydrate, 11 g total fat (3 g saturated fat), 1 mg cholesterol, 174 mg sodium, 1 g fiber. Daily values: 0% vitamin A, 1% vitamin C, 7% calcium, 9% iron.*

To Make Ahead

Prepare and bake biscuits as directed, cool completely. Place biscuits in a freezer container or bag and freeze up to 3 months. To serve, wrap frozen biscuits in foil; bake in a 300° oven and heat 20 to 25 minutes or until warm.

Lemon Burst Biscuits

Lemon Burst Biscuits

Buttermilk, mayonnaise, and lemon peel add a tangy burst to these tender, cakey biscuits.

2   cups all-purpose flour
1   tablespoon granulated sugar
2   teaspoons baking powder
2   teaspoons finely shredded
     lemon peel
¼   teaspoon baking soda
¼   teaspoon salt
½   cup shortening
⅓   cup buttermilk
⅓   cup mayonnaise or salad
     dressing
     Lemon Glaze (optional)

1 In a medium mixing bowl stir together flour, sugar, baking powder, lemon peel, baking soda, and salt. Using a pastry blender, cut in shortening until mixture resembles coarse crumbs. Make a well in the center of dry mixture. In a small mixing bowl combine the buttermilk and mayonnaise; add to dry mixture all at once. Using a fork, stir just until moistened.

2 Turn the dough out onto a lightly floured surface. Quickly knead dough by folding and pressing gently for 10 to 12 strokes or until the dough is nearly smooth. Pat or lightly roll dough to ½-inch thickness. Cut dough with a floured 2½-inch biscuit cutter, dipping the cutter into flour between cuts.

3 Place biscuits 1 inch apart on an ungreased baking sheet. Bake in a 450° oven for 10 to 12 minutes or until golden. Remove the biscuits from the baking sheet and cool slightly. If desired, drizzle Lemon Glaze over the biscuits just before serving. Serve warm. Makes 10 to 12.

Lemon Glaze: In a mixing bowl stir together 1 cup sifted powdered sugar, ½ teaspoon finely shredded lemon peel, ¼ teaspoon vanilla, and 1 tablespoon milk. Stir in additional milk, 1 teaspoon at a time, until glaze is smooth and of drizzling consistency.

Nutrition facts per biscuit: 236 calories, 3 g protein, 19 g carbohydrate, 17 g total fat (4 g saturated fat), 3 mg cholesterol, 201 mg sodium, 1 g fiber. Daily values: 0% vitamin A, 0% vitamin C, 6% calcium, 7% iron.

Orange Burst Biscuits: Prepare Lemon Burst Biscuits as directed, except substitute 2 teaspoons finely shredded orange peel for the lemon peel and ¼ cup orange juice for the mayonnaise. In the glaze, substitute ½ teaspoon finely shredded orange peel for the lemon peel.

To Make Ahead
Prepare and bake biscuits as directed, cool completely. Do not glaze. Place biscuits in a freezer container or bag and freeze up to 3 months. Before serving, wrap frozen biscuits in foil and bake in a 300° oven 20 to 25 minutes or until warm. Glaze as directed.

Baker's Bonus

Totally Stuffed

Biscuits and scones are the ideal quick bread for so many occasions. Savory biscuits can add a quick dash of sophistication to soups and stews, be filled to make kid-size sandwiches, or even made small to be used as the base for hors d'oeuvres. Few things are as luscious as a sweet biscuit or scone topped with some berry jam and lots of whipped cream to accompany a cup of tea or coffee.

Favorite fillings for adults
   Prosciutto and grainy mustard
   Smoked salmon, asparagus, and cream cheese
   Pastrami and sun-dried tomatoes
   Herbed roast chicken and avocado
   Ham and chutney
   Tapenade, feta, and roasted red peppers

Favorite fillings for kids
   Egg salad
   Tuna salad
   Peanut butter, honey, and bananas
   Any flavor chip dip with ham, chicken, turkey, and shredded carrot or
      sprouts
   Tomato and cheese

Fresh Dill Biscuits

Add flecks of orange color and a bit of vegetable flavor by adding ¼ cup finely shredded carrot with the buttermilk.

- **2 cups all-purpose flour**
- **2 teaspoons baking powder**
- **2 teaspoons granulated sugar**
- **1 tablespoon snipped fresh dill or ½ teaspoon dried dillweed**
- **¼ teaspoon baking soda**
- **¼ teaspoon salt**
- **½ cup shortening**
- **½ cup buttermilk**
- **¼ cup dairy sour cream**

1 In a medium mixing bowl stir together flour, baking powder, sugar, dill, baking soda, and salt. Using a pastry blender, cut in shortening until mixture resembles coarse crumbs. Make a well in the center of dry mixture. In a small mixing bowl combine the buttermilk and sour cream; add to dry mixture all at once. Using a fork, stir just until moistened.

2 Turn the dough out onto a lightly floured surface. Quickly knead dough by folding and pressing gently for 10 to 12 strokes or until the dough is nearly smooth. Pat or lightly roll dough to ½-inch thickness. Cut dough with a floured 2½-inch biscuit cutter.

3 Place biscuits 1 inch apart on an ungreased baking sheet. Bake in a 450° oven for 10 to 12 minutes or until golden brown. Remove biscuits from the baking sheet and serve warm. Makes 10 to 12.

Nutrition facts per biscuit: 195 calories, 3 g protein, 19 g carbohydrate, 12 g total fat (3 g saturated fat), 3 mg cholesterol, 174 mg sodium, 1 g fiber. Daily values: 1% vitamin A, 0% vitamin C, 7% calcium, 7% iron.

To Make Ahead

Prepare and bake biscuits as directed, cool completely. Place biscuits in a freezer container or bag and freeze up to 3 months. To serve, wrap frozen biscuits in foil and bake in a 300° oven 20 to 25 minutes or until warm.

Wild Rice and Bacon Biscuits

If cooked bacon pieces are an item you keep in the cupboard, substitute ¼ cup of them for the bacon slices and cook the onion in 3 tablespoons butter or margarine.

- **¼ cup wild rice**
- **4 slices bacon**
- **2 tablespoons finely chopped green onion**
- **1 cup all-purpose flour**
- **1 cup whole wheat flour**
- **1 tablespoon baking powder**
- **½ teaspoon cream of tartar**
- **⅓ cup chilled butter or margarine**
- **⅔ cup milk**

1 Run cold water over uncooked rice in a strainer for 30 seconds, lifting rice with fingers to rinse well. In a small saucepan combine the rice and 1 cup water. Bring to boiling, then reduce heat. Cover and simmer for 40 to 50 minutes or until tender. Drain rice in a strainer, then run cold water over rice until cooled. Drain well. Chop cooked rice; set aside.

2 In a skillet cook bacon over medium heat until crisp. Drain bacon, reserving 3 tablespoons of the drippings.* Crumble bacon and set aside. Cook green onion in reserved drippings over medium heat until tender.

3 In a medium mixing bowl stir together all-purpose flour, whole wheat flour, baking powder, and cream of tartar. Using a pastry blender, cut in butter until mixture resembles coarse crumbs. Add drained rice, onion mixture, and cooked bacon; toss until well mixed. Make a well in center of dry mixture, then add milk all at once. Using a fork, stir just until moistened.

4 Turn dough out onto a lightly floured surface. Quickly knead dough by folding and pressing gently for 10 to 12 strokes. Pat or lightly roll dough to ½-inch thickness. Cut dough with a floured 2½-inch biscuit cutter, dipping cutter into flour between cuts.

5 Place biscuits 1 inch apart on an ungreased baking sheet. Bake in a 450° oven for 10 to 12 minutes or until golden. Remove biscuits from baking pan and serve warm. Makes 10.

Note: If necessary, add cooking oil to equal 3 tablespoons.

Nutrition facts per biscuit: *204 calories, 5 g protein, 22 g carbohydrate, 11 g total fat (7 g saturated fat), 29 mg cholesterol, 256 mg sodium, 2 g fiber. Daily values: 10% vitamin A, 2% vitamin C, 10% calcium, 8% iron.*

Shortcut

Prepare Wild Rice and Bacon Biscuits as directed, except increase milk to 1 cup. Do not knead, roll, or cut dough. Drop dough from a tablespoon into mounds 1 inch apart on a greased baking sheet. Bake and serve as directed above. Makes 10 to 12.

To Make Ahead

Prepare and bake biscuits as directed, cool completely. Place biscuits in a freezer container or bag and freeze up to 3 months. To serve, wrap frozen biscuits in foil and bake in a 300° oven 20 to 25 minutes or until warm.

Pesto and Cheese Ladder Loaf

Every bite is worth savoring. Homemade pesto forms the center of this elegant, but easy loaf.

1 **cup lightly packed fresh basil**
   leaves (about 1 ounce)
¼ **cup toasted pine nuts, broken**
   walnuts, or slivered almonds
1 **clove garlic**
⅓ **cup grated Parmesan or**
   Romano cheese
1 **tablespoon all-purpose flour**
2 **cups all-purpose flour**
2 **tablespoons grated Parmesan**
   or Romano cheese
1 **tablespoon baking powder**
2 **teaspoons granulated sugar**
½ **cup shortening**
½ **cup shredded provolone or**
   Swiss cheese (2 ounces)
⅔ **cup milk**

1 For pesto, in a food processor bowl combine basil, nuts, and garlic. Cover and process until finely chopped. (When necessary, stop and scrape sides.) Add ⅓ cup Parmesan cheese. Cover and process until combined. Stir in 1 tablespoon flour. Set aside.

2 In a large mixing bowl stir together 2 cups flour, 2 tablespoons Parmesan cheese, baking powder, and sugar. Using a pastry blender, cut in shortening until mixture resembles coarse crumbs. Add provolone cheese; toss until combined. Make a well in the center of the dry mixture; then add milk all at once. Using a fork, stir just until moistened.

3 Turn dough out onto a well-floured surface. Quickly knead dough by folding and pressing gently for 10 to 12 strokes or until dough is nearly smooth. On a sheet of waxed paper, pat or lightly roll dough to a 15x9-inch rectangle, flouring hands or rolling pin, if necessary.

4 Invert dough onto an ungreased baking sheet. Remove waxed paper. Spread filling lengthwise down center third of dough. On the long sides, make 3-inch cuts from the edges toward the center at 1-inch intervals. Starting at one end, alternately fold opposite strips of dough at an angle across pesto, pinching into narrow points at center. Bake in a 425° oven for 15 to 20 minutes or until golden. Serve warm. Makes 12 servings.

Nutrition facts per serving: *209 calories, 6 g protein, 18 g carbohydrate, 13 g total fat (4 g saturated fat), 7 mg cholesterol, 210 mg sodium, 1 g fiber. Daily values: 2% vitamin A, 0% vitamin C, 16% calcium, 9% iron.*

Use kitchen shears to make the 3-inch cuts from the edges toward the center. Alternately fold opposite strips at an angle across pesto. To seal, slightly press each strip where it overlaps another.

Big Fat Deal

It does make a difference whether you use butter or margarine in your baking.

With quick breads and coffee cakes, to ensure best results, use only butter, margarine, or a stick spread that contains at least 60% vegetable oil. Do not use an "extra light" spread that contains only about 40% oil.

Dried Cherry Scones

Soaking the dried cherries or fruit bits in cherry brandy or apricot nectar makes them plump and keeps them soft when they're baked in the scones.

½ **cup dried tart red cherries or mixed dried fruit bits**
2 **tablespoons cherry brandy or apricot nectar**
2 **cups all-purpose flour**
3 **tablespoons granulated sugar**
1 **tablespoon baking powder**
¼ **teaspoon salt**
6 **tablespoons chilled butter or margarine**
¼ **cup chopped walnuts or pecans, toasted (optional)**
1 **beaten egg**

⅓ **cup half-and-half, light cream, or milk**
1 **beaten egg**
1 **tablespoon half-and-half, light cream, or milk**
2 **teaspoons granulated sugar**

1 In a small bowl combine dried cherries or fruit bits and cherry brandy or apricot nectar. Let stand 15 minutes.

2 Meanwhile, in a medium mixing bowl stir together flour, 3 tablespoons sugar, baking powder, and salt. Using a pastry blender, cut in butter until mixture resembles coarse crumbs. If desired, add walnuts or pecans; toss until mixed. Make a well in center of dry mixture.

3 In a small mixing bowl stir together the egg and ⅓ cup half-and-half. Add the egg mixture and cherry mixture to dry mixture all at once. Using a fork, stir just until moistened.

4 Turn dough out onto a lightly floured surface. Quickly knead dough by folding and pressing gently for 12 to 15 strokes or until the dough is nearly smooth. Pat or lightly roll dough to ½-inch thickness. Cut dough into desired shapes (circles, squares, diamonds, or hearts) with a floured 2½- to 3-inch cutter, dipping cutter into flour between cuts.

5 Place scones 1 inch apart on an ungreased baking sheet. Brush tops with half-and-half. Sprinkle with 2 teaspoons sugar. Bake in a 400° oven 12 to 15 minutes or until golden. Remove from baking sheet, and cool on a wire rack 5 minutes. Serve warm. Makes 10 to 12.

Nutrition facts per scone: 224 calories, 4 g protein, 27 g carbohydrate, 10 g total fat (5 g saturated fat), 43 mg cholesterol, 243 mg sodium, 1 g fiber. Daily values: 11% vitamin A, 0% vitamin C, 10% calcium, 9% iron.

Dried Apple Scones: Prepare Dried Cherry Scones as directed above, except substitute ½ cup snipped dried apples for the cherries and 2 tablespoons Apple Jack, apple juice, or apple cider for cherry brandy or apricot nectar. Makes 10 to 12.

Shortcut

Prepare Dried Cherry Scones or Dried Apple Scones as directed, except increase half-and-half, light cream, or milk from ⅓ cup to ½ cup. Do not knead, roll, or cut dough. Drop dough from a tablespoon into mounds 1 inch apart on an ungreased baking sheet. Brush tops with half-and-half, light cream, or milk and sprinkle with sugar. Bake and serve as directed above. Makes 10 to 12.

To Make Ahead

Prepare and bake scones as directed, cool completely. Place scones in a freezer container or bag and freeze up to 3 months. Before serving, wrap frozen scones in foil and bake in a 300° oven 20 to 25 minutes or until warm.

Bran-Raisin Scones (see recipe, page 28)

Dried Cherry Scones

Lemon-Almond Scones

For a different twist, omit the glaze. Then, before baking, brush the scones with milk and sprinkle them with almonds.

- **2 cups all-purpose flour**
- **2 tablespoons brown sugar**
- **2 teaspoons baking powder**
- **1 teaspoon finely shredded lemon peel**
- **¼ teaspoon salt**
- **¼ cup chilled butter or margarine**
- **¼ cup almond paste (about ¼ of an 8 ounce can)**
- **1 beaten egg**
- **⅓ cup milk**
- **½ cup sifted powdered sugar**
- **2 to 3 teaspoons lemon juice**
- **¼ cup toasted sliced almonds**

1 In a medium mixing bowl stir together flour, brown sugar, baking powder, lemon peel, and salt. Using a pastry blender, cut in butter or margarine and almond paste until mixture resembles coarse crumbs. Make a well in center of dry mixture. In a small mixing bowl combine egg and milk; add to dry mixture all at once. Using a fork, stir just until moistened.

2 Turn dough out onto a lightly floured surface. Quickly knead dough by folding and pressing gently for 10 to 12 strokes or until the dough is nearly smooth. Pat or lightly roll dough to ½-inch thickness. Cut dough into desired shapes (circles, squares, diamonds, or hearts) with a floured 2- to 2½-inch

cutter, dipping cutter into flour between cuts.

3 Place the scones 1 inch apart on an ungreased baking sheet. Bake in a 400° oven for 10 to 12 minutes or until golden. Remove the scones from the baking sheet and cool on a wire rack for 5 minutes.

4 Meanwhile, for glaze, in a small mixing bowl stir the powdered sugar and enough lemon juice to reach drizzling consistency. Brush glaze over scones and sprinkle with almonds. Serve warm. Makes ten 2½-inch or twenty 2-inch scones.

Nutrition facts per scone: 208 calories, 5 g protein, 29 g carbohydrate, 8 g total fat (3 g saturated fat), 34 mg cholesterol, 185 mg sodium, 1 g fiber. Daily values: 5% vitamin A, 1% vitamin C, 9% calcium, 2% iron.

Shortcut

Prepare Lemon-Almond Scones as directed, except increase milk to 2/3 cup. Do not knead, roll, or cut dough. Drop dough from a tablespoon into mounds 1 inch apart on an ungreased baking sheet. Bake and serve as directed above.

To Make Ahead

Prepare and bake scones as directed, cool completely. Do not glaze. Place scones in a freezer container or bag and freeze up to 3 months. Before serving, wrap the frozen scones in foil and bake in a 300° oven for 20 to 25 minutes or until warm. Glaze and sprinkle with almonds as directed.

Bran-Raisin Scones

If you're a fan of the popular combination of bran and raisin cereal, then these hearty scones are for you. (Pictured on page 27.)

- **1 beaten egg**
- **⅔ cup buttermilk**
- **1 cup whole bran cereal**
- **1¼ cups all-purpose flour**
- **3 tablespoons granulated sugar**
- **2 teaspoons baking powder**
- **½ teaspoon ground cinnamon**
- **¼ teaspoon salt**
- **⅓ cup shortening**
- **⅔ cup raisins, chopped, or ⅔ cup chopped pitted dates**

1 In a small bowl stir together egg, buttermilk, and cereal. Let stand about 3 minutes or until liquid is absorbed. In a large mixing bowl stir together flour, sugar, baking powder, cinnamon, and salt. Using a pastry blender, cut in shortening until mixture resembles coarse crumbs. Add raisins or dates, then toss until mixed. Make a well in center of dry mixture, then add bran mixture all at once. Using a fork, stir just until moistened.

2 Turn dough out onto a lightly floured surface. Quickly knead dough by folding and pressing gently for 5 to 6 strokes.* Pat or lightly roll dough into a 7-inch circle about ¾-inch thick. Using a sharp knife, cut the circle into 12 wedges.

3 Place wedges 1 inch apart on an ungreased baking sheet. Bake in a 400° oven about 10 minutes or until golden brown. Remove scones from baking sheet and serve warm. Makes 12.

Note: Do not overknead; it will cause this dough to be sticky.

Nutrition facts per scone: 311 calories, 3 g protein, 25 g carbohydrate, 24 g total fat (6 g saturated fat), 18 mg cholesterol, 206 mg sodium, 3 g fiber. Daily values: 10% vitamin A, 6% vitamin C, 7% calcium, 13% iron.

Shortcut

Prepare Bran-Raisin Scones as directed, except increase buttermilk to 1 cup. Do not knead, roll, or cut dough. Drop dough from a tablespoon in mounds 1 inch apart on an ungreased baking sheet. Bake in a 400° oven about 13 minutes or until golden brown.

To Make Ahead

Prepare and bake scones as directed, cool completely. Place scones in a freezer container or bag and freeze for up to 3 months. Before serving, wrap frozen scones in foil and bake in a 300° oven 20 to 25 minutes or until warm.

Anise Scones

Go beyond the basics and complement these licorice-flavored scones with Citrus Butter (see page 44).

2 cups all-purpose flour
3 tablespoons granulated sugar
2 teaspoons baking powder

1 tablespoon aniseed, crushed
½ teaspoon baking soda
½ teaspoon salt
⅓ cup butter or margarine
1 8-ounce carton dairy sour cream
1 beaten egg yolk
1 slightly beaten egg white
2 tablespoons chopped pecans or walnuts
Powdered Sugar (optional)

1 Grease a baking sheet; set aside. In a large mixing bowl stir together flour, granulated sugar, baking powder, aniseed, baking soda, and salt. Using a pastry blender, cut in butter or margarine until mixture resembles coarse crumbs. Make a well in the center of the dry mixture. In a small mixing bowl combine sour cream and egg yolk; add to dry mixture all at once. Using a fork, stir just until moistened.

2 Turn the dough out onto a lightly floured surface. Quickly knead dough by folding and pressing gently for 10 to 12 strokes or until the dough is nearly smooth. Divide dough in half. On the prepared baking sheet, pat or lightly roll a portion of dough into a 5½- to 6-inch circle. Repeat with the remaining portion of dough. Using a sharp knife, cut each circle into 6 wedges; do not separate wedges.

3 Brush dough circles with beaten egg white, then sprinkle with nuts. Bake in a 400° oven for 15 to 18 minutes or until golden. Remove from baking sheet. Cool on a wire rack for 5 min-

utes. If desired, sift powdered sugar over tops. Separate scones and serve warm. Makes 12.

Nutrition facts per scone: 171 calories, 3 g protein, 19 g carbohydrate, 9 g total fat (5 g saturated fat), 39 mg cholesterol, 264 mg sodium, 1 g fiber. Daily values: 9% vitamin A, 0% vitamin C, 7% calcium, 8% iron.

Coconut Scones: Prepare Anise Scones as directed, except substitute ¾ cup shredded coconut, toasted, for the 1 tablespoon aniseed.

To Make Ahead

Prepare and bake scones as directed, cool completely. Place scones in a freezer container or bag and freeze for up to 3 months. Before serving, wrap frozen scones in foil and bake in a 300° oven 20 to 25 minutes or until warm.

After cutting the flattened dough circles into wedges, leave the wedges nestled together to produce soft scones. To get crisper sides, pull the wedges apart about 1-inch.

Onion and Walnut Pizza-Style Scone

2 tablespoons butter or
   margarine
½ cup coarsely chopped walnuts
1 teaspoon brown sugar
1 medium white onion, thinly
   sliced and separated into
   rings
2 cups all-purpose flour
¼ cup finely chopped walnuts
1 tablespoon baking powder
⅛ teaspoon salt
¼ cup olive oil or cooking oil
⅔ cup chicken broth or milk
¾ cup shredded provolone cheese
   (3 ounces)
¾ cup shredded mozzarella
   cheese (3 ounces)

1 To toast walnuts, in a large skillet melt 1 tablespoon of the butter. Add the ½ cup coarsely chopped walnuts; cook and stir over medium heat about 5 minutes or just until toasted. Remove walnuts from skillet and set aside.

2 Melt remaining butter and brown sugar in the skillet. Add onion. Reduce heat and cook, covered, 10 minutes or until tender, stirring occasionally.

3 In a large mixing bowl combine flour, ¼ cup finely chopped walnuts, baking powder, and salt. Make a well in center. In a small mixing bowl combine olive oil and chicken broth; add all at once to dry mixture. Using a fork, stir just until moistened.

4 Turn dough out onto a lightly floured surface. Quickly knead dough by folding and pressing gently 5 or 6 strokes. Place dough on a large ungreased baking sheet; pat dough into a 10-inch circle. Bake in a 400° oven for 5 minutes.

5 Drain liquid from onions, then spread onions evenly over prebaked crust. Sprinkle with toasted walnuts and provolone and mozzarella cheeses. Bake in the 400° oven for 20 to 23 minutes or until golden. Cool on the baking sheet on a wire rack for 5 minutes. Cut into wedges and serve warm. Makes 12 appetizer servings.

Nutrition facts per serving: 225 calories, 7 g protein, 18 g carbohydrate, 14 g total fat (4 g saturated fat), 14 mg cholesterol, 272 mg sodium, 1 g fiber. Daily values: 4% vitamin A, 1% vitamin C, 16% calcium, 8% iron.

Honey Scones

2 cups all-purpose flour
3 tablespoons granulated sugar
2 teaspoons baking powder
¼ teaspoon baking soda
¼ teaspoon salt
⅓ cup butter or margarine
¼ cup half-and-half, light cream,
   or milk
2 tablespoons honey
1 beaten egg yolk
   Powdered Sugar

1 Grease a baking sheet; set aside. In a bowl combine flour, sugar, baking powder, soda, and salt. Cut in butter until mixture resembles coarse crumbs. Make a well in center.

2 In a mixing bowl combine half-and-half, honey, and egg yolk. Add all at once to dry mixture. Using a fork, stir just until moistened.

3 Turn dough out onto a lightly floured surface. Quickly knead dough by folding and pressing gently for 10 to 12 strokes or until the dough is nearly smooth. Divide dough in half.

4 On prepared baking sheet, pat 1 portion of dough to ½-inch thickness. Repeat with remaining dough. Using a sharp knife, cut each circle into 6 wedges; do not separate wedges.

5 Bake in a 375° oven 15 to 18 minutes or until golden. Remove from baking sheet and cool on a wire rack. Sift with powdered sugar. Separate scones and serve warm. Makes 12.

Nutrition facts per scone: 151 calories, 2 g protein, 22 g carbohydrate, 6 g total fat (4 g saturated fat), 33 mg cholesterol, 186 mg sodium, 1 g fiber. Daily values: 8% vitamin A, 0% vitamin C, 5% calcium, 7% iron.

To Make Ahead

Prepare and bake scones as directed, cool completely. Place scones in a freezer container or bag and freeze for up to 3 months. Before serving, wrap frozen scones in foil and bake in a 300° oven 20 to 25 minutes or until warm.

Onion and Walnut Pizza-Style Scone

Sweet Pepper Scones

Try this savory scone late in the summer when the baskets at the farmer's markets are overflowing with sweet peppers. During their peak season you can get a pepper of each color for the off-season price of just one.

⅔ **cup finely chopped red, yellow, and/or green sweet pepper**
¼ **cup olive oil or cooking oil**
1¾ **cups all-purpose flour**
¼ **cup grated Parmesan cheese**
2½ **teaspoons baking powder**
⅛ **teaspoon salt**
1 **beaten egg**
⅓ **cup milk**
1 **tablespoon milk**
1 **tablespoon grated Parmesan cheese**

1 In a medium skillet cook the sweet pepper in oil over medium heat about 5 minutes or until nearly tender. Set aside until cooled.

2 In a medium mixing bowl stir together flour, ¼ cup Parmesan cheese, baking powder, and salt. Make a well in center of dry mixture.

3 In a small mixing bowl combine beaten egg, ⅓ cup milk, and pepper-oil mixture. Add milk mixture all at once to dry mixture. Using a fork, stir just until moistened.

4 Turn dough out onto a lightly floured surface. Quickly knead dough by folding and pressing gently for 10 to 12 strokes or until dough begins to hold together. Pat or lightly roll dough into an 8-inch circle about ½ inch thick. Using a sharp knife, cut circle into 8 to 10 wedges.

5 Place wedges 1 inch apart on an ungreased baking sheet. Brush tops with remaining milk, then sprinkle with the 1 tablespoon Parmesan cheese. Bake in a 400° oven for 10 to 12 minutes or until golden. Remove scones from baking sheet and cool on a wire rack for 5 minutes. Serve warm. Makes 8 to 10.

Nutrition facts per scone: 188 calories, 5 g protein, 21 g carbohydrate, 9 g total fat (2 g saturated fat), 31 mg cholesterol, 234 mg sodium, 1 g fiber. Daily values: 6% vitamin A, 18% vitamin C, 15% calcium, 10% iron.

Shortcut

Prepare Sweet Pepper Scones as directed, except increase ⅓ cup milk to ⅔ cup. Do not knead, roll, or cut dough. Drop dough from a tablespoon into mounds 1 inch apart on a greased baking sheet. Do not brush tops with milk. Sprinkle tops with the 1 tablespoon Parmesan cheese. Bake and serve as directed.

To Make Ahead

Prepare and bake scones as directed, cool completely. Place scones in a freezer container or bag and freeze for up to 3 months. Before serving, wrap frozen scones in foil and bake in a 300° oven 20 to 25 minutes or until warm.

Lemon-Poppy Seed Muffins

Make any excuse for a cup of tea or coffee instantly elegant with these delicate muffins.

1⅓ **cups all-purpose flour**
⅔ **cup granulated sugar**
2 **teaspoons poppy seed**
¾ **teaspoon baking powder**
¼ **teaspoon baking soda**
1 **beaten egg**
⅓ **cup butter or margarine, melted**
2 **teaspoons finely shredded lemon peel**
3 **tablespoons lemon juice**
½ **cup buttermilk**

1 Grease twelve 1¾-inch muffin cups or line with paper bake cups; set aside.

2 In a medium mixing bowl stir together the flour, sugar, poppy seed, baking powder, and baking soda. Make a well in the center of dry ingredients; set aside.

3 In another medium mixing bowl combine the egg, butter, lemon peel, and lemon juice. Add buttermilk and stir until combined. Add egg mixture all at once to the dry ingredients. Stir just until moistened (batter should be slightly lumpy).

4 Spoon batter into prepared muffin cups, filling each two-thirds full. Bake in a 400° oven about 15 minutes or until lightly golden. (Bake 2½-inch muffins 20 to 25 minutes; bake giant muffins at 375° about 25 minutes.) Cool in muffin cups on a wire rack for 5 minutes. Then remove muffins from muffin cups. Serve warm. Cover and store any leftovers at room temperature or in the refrigerator for up to 3 days. Makes about 30.

Nutrition facts per muffin: *59 calories, 1 g protein, 9 g carbohydrate, 2 g total fat (1 g saturated), 13 mg cholesterol, 47 mg sodium, 0 g fiber. Daily values: 2% vitamin A, 1% vitamin C, 1% calcium, 2% iron.*

To Make Ahead

Prepare and bake muffins as directed, cool completely. Place muffins in a freezer container or bag and freeze up to 3 months. Before serving, wrap the frozen muffins in foil and bake in a 300° oven 15 to 18 minutes or until muffins are warm.

Almond-Apricot Crunch Muffins

Sugar and spice make these streusel-topped muffins particularly nice.

2 tablespoons granulated sugar
4 teaspoons all-purpose flour
4 teaspoons butter or margarine
2 tablespoons chopped almonds
or pecans
1½ cups all-purpose flour
¼ cup packed brown sugar

2 teaspoons baking powder
½ teaspoon ground cinnamon
¼ teaspoon baking soda
2 slightly beaten egg whites
⅔ cup apricot nectar or apple juice
¼ cup cooking oil
⅔ cup finely snipped dried apricots or dried apples

1 Line twelve 2½-inch muffin cups with paper bake cups; set aside.

2 For topping, in a small mixing bowl stir together the sugar and 4 teaspoons flour. Cut in butter until crumbly. Stir in almonds; set aside.

3 In a large mixing bowl combine the 1½ cups flour and the brown sugar; stir in baking powder, cinnamon, and baking soda. Make a well in the center of dry ingredients. In another bowl combine egg whites, apricot nectar, and oil. Add egg mixture all at once to dry ingredients. Stir just until moistened (batter should be lumpy). Fold in snipped apricots. Fill prepared muffin cups two-thirds full. Sprinkle the topping evenly over the batter in each cup.

4 Bake in a 400° oven about 20 minutes or until golden. Remove from pans; serve warm. Cover and store any leftovers at room temperature or in the refrigerator for up to 3 days. Makes 12.

Nutrition facts per muffin: *167 calories, 3 g protein, 25 g carbohydrate, 7 g total fat (2 g saturated), 3 mg cholesterol, 112 mg sodium, 1 g fiber. Daily values: 8% vitamin A, 8% vitamin C, 5% calcium, 9% iron.*

To Make Ahead

Prepare and bake muffins as directed; cool completely. Place in a freezer container or bag and freeze for up to 3 months. Before serving, wrap frozen muffins in foil and reheat in a 300° oven 15 to 18 minutes or until warm.

Eye-Openers

Think about it. Which would you rather have, several steaming hot spiced Oat-Bran Apple Muffins or a bowl of cold cereal? Would you prefer a warm, yeasty piece of Berry-Cheesy Coffee Cake or a dish of plain hot oatmeal?

There's no better way to start any day than with some warm fresh bread. If you can't agree on a favorite, why not make two or three different kinds, and freeze some for next week?

To make sure that you don't have to get up at the crack of dawn, we've done the hard work and picked the best and easiest breads for your breakfast or brunch. So roll over and grab a few more minutes sleep. Then get up, put the coffee on, and pop some bread in the oven. The day will look a whole lot better!

Pineapple Upside-Down Muffins

¼ cup packed brown sugar
2 tablespoons butter or
  margarine, melted
1 8-ounce can crushed pineapple
  (juice pack), drained
12 maraschino cherries, halved
1¾ cups all-purpose flour
⅓ cup granulated sugar
2 teaspoons baking powder
¼ teaspoon salt
1 beaten egg
¾ cup milk
¼ cup cooking oil

1 Grease twelve 2½-inch muffin cups; set aside.

2 In a small mixing bowl combine brown sugar and butter. Divide sugar mixture evenly among muffin cups. Divide pineapple and cherries evenly among the cups. Set muffin cups aside.

3 In a medium mixing bowl stir together flour, sugar, baking powder, and salt. Make a well in the center of dry ingredients; set aside.

4 In another medium mixing bowl combine the egg, milk, and oil. Add egg mixture all at once to the dry ingredients. Stir just until moistened (batter should be lumpy).

5 Spoon batter into the prepared muffin cups, filling each three-fourths full. Bake in a 400° oven for 20 to 25 minutes or until golden. Cool in muffin cups on a wire rack for 5 minutes.

To remove muffins from muffin cups, invert them onto the wire rack. Serve warm. Cover and store any leftovers in the refrigerator up to 3 days. Makes 12.

Nutrition facts per muffin: 182 calories, 3 g protein, 27 g carbohydrate, 7 g total fat (2 g saturated), 24 mg cholesterol, 140 mg sodium, 1 g fiber. Daily values: 3% vitamin A, 2% vitamin C, 7% calcium, 7% iron.

Peach-Streusel Muffins

1 8-ounce can peach slices
  (juice pack)
3 tablespoons all-purpose flour
3 tablespoons granulated sugar
2 tablespoons butter
  (no substitutes)
1¾ cups all-purpose flour
⅓ cup granulated sugar
2 teaspoons baking powder
1 teaspoon ground cinnamon
¼ teaspoon salt
1 beaten egg
½ cup milk
¼ cup cooking oil

1 Grease twelve 2½-inch muffin cups or line with paper bake cups; set aside.

2 Drain peaches, reserving ¼ cup juice; set juice aside. Chop ½ cup of the peaches; set aside. Reserve remaining peaches for another use.

3 In a small mixing bowl stir together the 3 tablespoons flour and the 3 tablespoons sugar. Cut in butter until mixture resembles coarse crumbs. Set sugar mixture aside.

4 In a medium mixing bowl combine the 1¾ cups flour, the ⅓ cup sugar, baking powder, cinnamon, and salt. Make a well in the center; set aside.

5 In another mixing bowl combine the egg, milk, oil, and reserved peach juice. Add egg mixture all at once to dry ingredients. Stir just until moistened (batter should be lumpy).

6 Spoon about half of the batter into the prepared muffin cups, filling each one-fourth full. Place a few peach pieces on top of the batter in each cup. Spoon remaining batter into muffin cups, filling each two-thirds full. Sprinkle the sugar mixture evenly over the muffins. Bake in a 400° oven for 20 to 25 minutes or until golden. Cool in muffin cups for 5 minutes. Then remove muffins from muffin cups. Serve warm. Cover and store any leftovers in the refrigerator for up to 3 days. Makes 12.

Nutrition facts per muffin: 176 calories, 3 g protein, 25 g carbohydrate, 7 g total fat (2 g saturated), 24 mg cholesterol, 136 mg sodium, 1 g fiber. Daily values: 3% vitamin A, 1% vitamin C, 7% calcium, 7% iron.

To Make Ahead

Prepare and bake muffins as directed, cool completely. Place muffins in a freezer container or bag and freeze up to 3 months. To serve, wrap frozen muffins in foil and bake in a 300° oven 15 to 18 minutes or until warm.

Pineapple Upside-Down Muffins

A Soft Touch

Use your microwave to quickly soften butter, margarine, or cream cheese without melting it. These timings were achieved in a 600- to 700-watt oven, so if your oven has a lower wattage, you may need to increase the cooking time slightly.

For butter or margarine, place ½ cup in a microwave-safe container. Cook, uncovered, on 10% power (low) for 1 to 1½ minutes or until softened.

For cream cheese, place 3 ounces in a microwave-safe container. Cook, uncovered, on 100% power (high) for 15 to 30 seconds (45 to 60 seconds for 8 ounces) or until softened.

Notes

Kid Appeal

Chocolaty Cheesecake Muffins

Who says you can't indulge your chocolate craving for breakfast?

   1   **3-ounce package cream cheese, softened**
   2   **tablespoons granulated sugar**
   1   **egg yolk**
1½   **cups all-purpose flour**
   ½   **cup granulated sugar**
   ¼   **cup unsweetened cocoa powder**
   2   **teaspoons baking powder**
   ¼   **teaspoon salt**
   1   **egg**
   ¾   **cup milk**
   ¼   **cup cooking oil**
   ½   **cup chopped walnuts**
   2   **teaspoons powdered sugar**

1 Grease twelve 2½-inch muffin cups or line with paper bake cups; set aside.

2 In a small mixing bowl beat the cream cheese, the 2 tablespoons sugar, and the egg yolk with an electric mixer on medium speed until blended. Set cream cheese mixture aside.

3 In a medium mixing bowl stir together the flour, the ½ cup sugar, cocoa powder, baking powder, and salt. Make a well in the center of the dry ingredients; set aside.

4 In another medium mixing bowl combine the whole egg, milk, and oil. Add the egg mixture all at once to the dry ingredients. Stir just until moistened (batter should be lumpy). Fold in the walnuts.

5 Spoon half of the batter into prepared muffin cups (about 1 tablespoon in each muffin cup). Spoon about 1½ teaspoons cream cheese mixture on top of the batter in each cup. Spoon remaining batter into muffin cups, filling each two-thirds full.

6 Bake in a 400° oven about 20 minutes or until tops are dry. Cool in muffin cups on a wire rack for 5 minutes. Then remove muffins from muffin cups. Sift powdered sugar over top of each muffin. Serve warm or cool. Cover and store any leftovers in the refrigerator for up to 3 days. Makes 12.

Nutrition facts per muffin: 218 calories, 4 g protein, 25 g carbohydrate, 12 g total fat (3 g saturated), 45 mg cholesterol, 141 mg sodium, 1 g fiber. Daily values: 7% vitamin A, 0% vitamin C, 9% calcium, 8% iron.

To Make Ahead

Prepare and bake muffins as directed; cool completely. Place muffins in a freezer container or bag and freeze for up to 3 months. Before serving, wrap the frozen muffins in foil and bake in a 300° oven for 15 to 18 minutes or until warm.

Oat Bran-Apple Muffins

Try some healthy muffins that taste so great you'll never believe how good they are for you.

2 tablespoons brown sugar
1 tablespoon whole wheat flour
1 teaspoon butter or margarine, melted
¼ teaspoon ground cinnamon
¾ cup oat bran
½ cup whole wheat flour
½ cup whole bran cereal
¼ cup packed brown sugar
2½ teaspoons baking powder
½ teaspoon ground cinnamon
¼ teaspoon salt
1 beaten egg
¾ cup milk
¼ cup cooking oil
1 small apple peeled and finely chopped (about ½ cup)

1 Grease twelve 2½-inch muffin cups or line with paper bake cups; set aside.

2 In a small mixing bowl combine the 2 tablespoons brown sugar, the 1 tablespoon whole wheat flour, butter, and the ¼ teaspoon cinnamon. Set brown sugar mixture aside.

3 In a medium mixing bowl stir together oat bran, the ½ cup whole wheat flour, bran cereal, the ¼ cup brown sugar, baking powder, the ½ teaspoon cinnamon, and salt. Make a well in the center of the dry ingredients; set aside.

4 In another medium mixing bowl combine the egg, milk, and oil. Add egg mixture all at once to the dry ingredients. Stir just until moistened (batter should be lumpy). Fold in the chopped apple.

5 Spoon batter into the prepared muffin cups, filling each three-fourths full. Sprinkle about 1 teaspoon of the brown sugar mixture evenly over the batter in each cup. Bake in a 400° oven about 15 minutes or until lightly browned. Cool in muffin cups on a wire rack for 5 minutes. Then remove muffins from muffin cups. Serve warm. Cover and store any leftovers in the refrigerator up to 3 days. Makes 12.

Nutrition facts per muffin: 130 calories, 3 g protein, 19 g carbohydrate, 6 g total fat (1 g saturated), 20 mg cholesterol, 179 mg sodium, 3 g fiber. Daily values: 6% vitamin A, 3% vitamin C, 8% calcium, 9% iron.

To Make Ahead

Prepare and bake muffins as directed, cool completely. Place muffins in a freezer container or bag and freeze for up to 3 months. Before serving, wrap the frozen muffins in foil and reheat in a 300° oven for 15 to 18 minutes or until warm.

Stir just until the ingredients are moistened. Overmixing can cause peaks, tunnels, and a tough texture in muffins and quick breads.

Because each muffin batter has different leavening and may need more or less space than another, spoon batter into the cups to the level described in the recipe. Using a spoon or your fingers for a dry topping, sprinkle the mixture evenly over the batter in the cups.

Wheat and Shallot Muffins

Cooking spray is a quick and easy way to grease the muffin cups.

1¼ **cups all-purpose flour**
½ **cup whole wheat flour**
2 **tablespoons granulated sugar**
2 **teaspoons baking powder**
¼ **teaspoon salt**
¼ **teaspoon pepper**
1 **beaten egg**
¾ **cup milk**
¼ **cup butter or margarine, melted**
¼ **cup finely chopped shallots or thinly sliced green onions (2 to 3 shallots or 2 green onions)**

1 Grease twelve 2½-inch muffin cups; set aside.

2 In a medium mixing bowl stir together the all-purpose flour, whole wheat flour, sugar, baking powder, salt, and pepper. Make a well in the center of dry ingredients; set aside.

3 In another medium mixing bowl combine the egg, milk, butter, and shallots. Add egg mixture all at once to the dry ingredients. Stir just until moistened (batter should be lumpy).

4 Spoon batter into the prepared muffin cups, filling each two-thirds full. Bake in a 400° oven for 15 to 20 minutes or until golden. Cool in muffin cups on a wire rack for 5 minutes. Then remove muffins from muffin cups. Serve warm. Cover and store any leftovers at room temperature or in the refrigerator for up to 3 days. Makes 12.

Nutrition facts per muffin: *122 calories, 3 g protein, 16 g carbohydrate, 5 g total fat (3 g saturated), 29 mg cholesterol, 157 mg sodium, 1 g fiber. Daily values: 9% vitamin A, 0% vitamin C, 6% calcium, 6% iron.*

To Make Ahead

Prepare and bake muffins as directed, cool completely. Place muffins in a freezer container or bag and freeze for up to 3 months. Before serving, wrap the frozen muffins in foil and reheat in a 300° oven for 15 to 18 minutes or until warm.

Cheese 'n' Jalapeño Corn Muffins

If you like playing with fire, make these muffins with both the ground red pepper and the chili peppers. Then serve with a spicy bowl of chili and lots of water to cool things off.

1 **cup all-purpose flour**
¾ **cup yellow cornmeal**
3 **tablespoons granulated sugar**
2½ **teaspoons baking powder**
¼ **teaspoon salt**
⅛ **teaspoon ground red pepper (optional)**
1 **beaten egg**
¾ **cup milk**
⅓ **cup cooking oil**
½ **cup shredded cheddar or Monterey Jack cheese (2 ounces)**
2 **tablespoons canned chopped jalapeño or green chili peppers**

1 Grease twelve 2½-inch muffin cups; set aside.

2 In a medium mixing bowl stir together the flour, cornmeal, sugar, baking powder, salt, and ground red pepper (if desired). Make a well in the center of dry ingredients; set aside.

3 In another medium mixing bowl combine the egg, milk, and oil. Add egg mixture all at once to the dry ingredients. Stir just until moistened. Fold in cheese and peppers.

4 Spoon batter into prepared muffin cups, filling each two-thirds full. Bake in a 400° oven for 20 to 23 minutes or until golden. Cool in muffin cups on a wire rack for 5 minutes. Then remove muffins from muffin cups. Serve warm. Cover and store any leftovers at room temperature or in the refrigerator for up to 3 days. Makes 10 to 12.

Nutrition facts per muffin: *198 calories, 5 g protein, 22 g carbohydrate, 10 g total fat (3 g saturated), 29 mg cholesterol, 195 mg sodium, 1 g fiber. Daily values: 4% vitamin A, 7% vitamin C, 12% calcium, 8% iron.*

To Make Ahead

Prepare and bake muffins as directed; cool completely. Place muffins in a freezer container or bag and freeze up to 3 months. To serve, wrap frozen muffins in foil and bake in a 300° oven 15 to 18 minutes or until warm.

Wheat and Shallot Muffins

Cheese 'n' Jalapeño Corn Muffins

Quick Bread Quirks

Like cakes, quick breads require precise amounts of ingredients to achieve the final product. Liquids are used to activate the leavening agents, flours provide structure, fats tenderize, leavens add volume, and flavorings round out the flavor. To make this mixture work, you need to be accurate in your measurements.

Always remember to avoid mixing the batter too much. When you add the liquid to the dry ingredients, stir until the dry ingredients are just moistened; the batter will be lumpy. If you overmix, the baked product will be tough and have tunnels throughout.

If the texture of your bread is soggy and the middle has sunk, it means there was too much liquid in proportion to the dry ingredients, insufficient leavening, the batter stood too long before baking, or it's underdone. A coarse texture indicates too much fat and leavening. Too much sugar will give you a thick, dark brown crust, while too much leavening will result in a bitter (baking powder) or soapy (baking soda) aftertaste.

Coconut Quick Bread

Toasted coconut has a rich, nutty flavor. To toast coconut, spread the desired amount in a thin layer in a shallow baking pan. Bake it in a 350° oven for 5 to 10 minutes or until lightly golden brown, stirring once or twice.

1¾ **cups all-purpose flour**
1 **cup toasted coconut**
1 **cup granulated sugar**
1½ **teaspoons baking powder**
½ **teaspoon ground allspice**
¼ **teaspoon baking soda**
¼ **teaspoon salt**
1 **beaten egg**
½ **cup milk**
¼ **cup coconut milk**
¼ **cup cooking oil**

½ **teaspoon vanilla**
½ **cup chopped walnuts or macadamia nuts**

1 Grease one 8x4x2-inch loaf pan or four 4½x2½x1½-inch loaf pans; set pan(s) aside.

2 In a medium mixing bowl stir together flour, coconut, sugar, baking powder, allspice, baking soda, and salt. Make a well in the center of dry mixture; set aside.

3 In another medium mixing bowl combine the egg, milk, coconut milk, cooking oil, and vanilla. Add egg mixture all at once to the dry mixture. Stir just until moistened (batter should be lumpy). Fold in nuts.

4 Pour batter into the prepared pan(s). Bake in 350° oven for 55 to 60 minutes for large loaf pan (about 35 minutes for small loaves) or until a wooden toothpick inserted near the center comes out clean. Cool in the pan(s) for 10 minutes on a wire rack. Then remove bread from pan(s) and cool completely on the wire rack. Wrap and store overnight before slicing. Store at room temperature up to 3 days or in the refrigerator up to 1 week. Makes 1 large loaf or 4 smaller loaves (16 servings).

Nutrition facts per serving: *183 calories, 3 g protein, 25 g carbohydrate, 9 g total fat (2 g saturated), 14 mg cholesterol, 103 mg sodium, 0 g fiber. Daily values: 1% vitamin A, 0% vitamin C, 4% calcium, 6% iron.*

Peach Quick Bread: Prepare Coconut Quick Bread as directed, except add ¼ cup snipped dried peaches and omit the walnuts.

Chocolate-Coconut Quick Bread: Prepare Coconut Quick Bread as directed, except substitute ½ cup chopped almonds for the walnuts. After the almonds have been folded in, divide the batter in half. Stir ¼ cup cocoa powder into one half of the batter. Spoon half of the white batter into the baking pan. Using teaspoons, drop half of the chocolate batter onto the white batter. Spoon the remaining white batter on top of the chocolate batter. Using teaspoons, drop the remaining chocolate batter on top of the white batter. With a knife, cut through the batter to swirl the chocolate and white batters together.

To Make Ahead

Prepare and bake bread as directed; cool completely. Place bread in a freezer container or bag and freeze up to 3 months. Before serving, thaw wrapped bread overnight in the refrigerator.

Wheat and Honey-Nut Bread

Feeling fruity instead of nutty? Prepare the bread as directed, except stir ¾ cup snipped, pitted prunes into the batter in place of the ¾ cup nuts.

1¼ **cups all-purpose flour**
¾ **cup whole wheat flour**
¼ **cup granulated sugar**
2 **teaspoons baking powder**
½ **teaspoon baking soda**
¼ **teaspoon salt**
1 **beaten egg**
1 **cup milk**
¼ **cup honey**
¼ **cup cooking oil**
¾ **cup chopped hazelnuts (filberts), walnuts, or pecans**
1 **teaspoon honey**
1 **tablespoon finely chopped hazelnuts (filberts), walnuts, or pecans**

1 Grease an 8x4x2-inch loaf pan or a 5-cup mold; set aside.

2 In a medium mixing bowl stir together the all-purpose flour, whole wheat flour, sugar, baking powder, baking soda, and salt. Make a well in the center of dry mixture. Set the dry mixture aside.

3 In another medium mixing bowl combine egg, milk, ¼ cup honey, and cooking oil. Add egg mixture all at once to dry mixture. Stir just until moistened. Fold in the ¾ cup nuts.

4 Pour batter into prepared pan. Bake in a 350° oven for 45 to 50 minutes for loaf pan (55 to 60 minutes for 5-cup mold) or until a wooden toothpick inserted near the center comes out clean (if necessary, cover loosely with foil the last 10 minutes to prevent overbrowning). Cool in the pan on a wire rack for 10 minutes. Then remove the bread from the pan. Cool completely on a wire rack.

5 Lightly brush the 1 teaspoon honey over center top of loaf. Sprinkle with the 1 tablespoon finely chopped nuts. Wrap and store overnight before slicing. Store at room temperature up to 3 days or in the refrigerator for up to 1 week. Makes 1 loaf (12 to 14 servings).

Nutrition facts per serving: 215 calories, 5 g protein, 27 g carbohydrate, 10 g total fat (1 g saturated), 19 mg cholesterol, 171 mg sodium, 2 g fiber. Daily values: 2% vitamin A, 0% vitamin C, 8% calcium, 8% iron.

To Make Ahead

Prepare and bake bread as directed, except do not brush with the honey or sprinkle with the nuts. Place bread in a freezer container or bag and freeze for up to 3 months. Before serving, thaw the wrapped bread overnight in the refrigerator. Brush bread with honey and top with nuts.

Notes

Pumpkin Bread, top, and Old-Fashioned Banana Bread, bottom

Old-Fashioned Banana Bread

When a friend and I were about 10, we baked this recipe for a 4-H Club demonstration. We spent our summer making it three or four times a week, and our once-enthusiastic families grew pretty tired of it. Now, more than 20 years later, the bread is a top request once again, and my friend is married to my brother!
—Marilyn Cornelius—

 2 **cups all-purpose flour**
1½ **teaspoons baking powder**
 ½ **teaspoon baking soda**
 ½ **cup butter or margarine**
 1 **cup granulated sugar**
 2 **eggs**
 1 **cup mashed bananas**
 2 **tablespoons milk**
 1 **teaspoon lemon juice**

1 Grease one 9x5x3-inch loaf pan or three 5½x3x2-inch loaf pans; set aside.

2 In a bowl combine flour, baking powder, and soda. Set aside. In a bowl beat butter with an electric mixer on medium speed 30 seconds. Add sugar; beat until fluffy. Add eggs, one at a time, beating well. Add bananas, milk, and lemon juice. Beat until mixed. Add flour mixture; beat until combined. Pour batter into prepared pan(s).

3 Bake in a 350° oven 45 to 50 minutes for larger pan (35 to 40 minutes for smaller pans) or until a wooden toothpick inserted near center comes out clean. Cool bread in pan(s) 10 minutes. Remove from pan(s); cool. Cover and store at room temperature overnight before slicing. Store at room temperature up to 3 days or in refrigerator up to 1 week. Makes 1 large loaf or 3 smaller loaves (16 servings).

Nutrition facts per serving: *174 calories, 3 g protein, 27 g carbohydrate, 7 g total fat (4 g saturated), 42 mg cholesterol, 141 mg sodium, 1 g fiber. Daily values: 6% vitamin A, 2% vitamin C, 3% calcium, 5% iron.*

To Make Ahead

Prepare and bake bread as directed; cool completely. Place bread in a freezer container or bag and freeze for up to 3 months. Before serving, thaw the wrapped bread overnight in the refrigerator.

Pumpkin Bread

There is something to be said about the way you slice your bread. The first time I took my husband, Tim, to my grandparents house, I remember slicing a loaf of freshly baked Pumpkin Bread. Mom always sliced everything paper thin, so that's how I sliced the bread. Grandpa threw his arms in the air and said, "Darn it, give 'im a piece." To this day, I slice the bread thin and Tim slices the bread thick, like Grandpa and every time, we laugh.
—Shelli McConnell—

 3 **cups granulated sugar**
 1 **cup cooking oil**
 4 **eggs**
3⅓ **cups all-purpose flour**
 2 **teaspoons baking soda**
1½ **teaspoons salt**
 1 **teaspoon ground cinnamon**
 1 **teaspoon ground nutmeg**
 ⅔ **cup water**
 1 **16-ounce can pumpkin**

1 Grease three 8x4x2-inch or two 9x5x3-inch loaf pans; set aside.

2 In a large mixing bowl beat together sugar and oil using an electric mixer on medium speed. Add eggs and beat well; set aside. In a bowl, combine flour, soda, salt, cinnamon, and nutmeg. Add dry ingredients and water alternately to sugar mixture, beating on low speed after each addition just until combined. Beat in pumpkin.

3 Pour batter into prepared pans. Bake in a 350° oven 50 minutes for smaller pans (55 minutes for larger pans) or until done. Cool in pans 10 minutes. Remove from pans; cool. Cover; store at room temperature up to 3 days or chill up to 1 week. Makes 3 small or 2 large loaves (48 servings).

Nutrition facts per serving: *127 calories, 1 g protein, 19 g carbohydrate, 5 g total fat (1 g saturated), 18 mg cholesterol, 100 mg sodium, 0 g fiber. Daily values: 21% vitamin A, 0% vitamin C, 0% calcium, 3% iron.*

To Make Ahead

Prepare and bake bread as directed; cool completely. Place bread in a freezer container or bag and freeze up to 3 months. To serve, thaw the wrapped bread overnight in the refrigerator.

Buttering Up

If you're going to put butter on a nice warm muffin or piece of nut bread, why not give that butter some added flavor first. Each of these recipes for flavored butter makes enough so you can enjoy some now and save some for later.

Store the leftovers, covered, for up to 2 weeks in the refrigerator or up to 2 months in the freezer.

Fruit-Nut Butter: *Place 1 cup nuts (almonds, pecans, or walnuts) in a blender container or food processor bowl. Cover and blend or process until finely chopped. Transfer nuts to a small mixing bowl.*

Place ½ cup butter or margarine, cut up and softened, and ½ cup fruit preserves (peach, apricot, strawberry, cherry, or raspberry) in the blender container or food processor bowl. Cover and blend or process until combined, stopping to scrape down the sides as necessary. Add preserves mixture to the nuts in the bowl; mix well. Cover and chill for at least 1 hour before serving. Makes 1½ cups.

Citrus Butter: *In a small mixing bowl beat ½ cup softened butter or margarine, 1 tablespoon powdered sugar, ½ teaspoon finely shredded citrus peel (orange, lemon, or lime), and 1 teaspoon freshly squeezed citrus juice with an electric mixer until smooth. Cover and chill. Let stand at room temperature about 30 minutes before serving. Makes ⅔ cup.*

Chocolate-Nut Butter: *Melt ¼ cup semisweet chocolate pieces and 1 tablespoon butter or margarine; cool. Mix ½ cup butter or margarine, ½ cup chopped pecans, ½ teaspoon vanilla, and chocolate mixture; chill. Let stand at room temperature 1 hour before serving. Makes ¾ cup.*

Hazelnut-Cream Cheese Butter: *In a small bowl combine ½ cup softened butter or margarine and ½ cup softened cream cheese. Beat in 1 to 2 tablespoons hazelnut liqueur to taste. (You also could use almond-flavor liqueur or honey).*

Parmesan-Garlic Butter: *In a small mixing bowl beat ½ cup softened butter or margarine, ⅓ cup grated Parmesan cheese, and ¼ teaspoon garlic powder with an electric mixer until smooth. Stir in 2 tablespoons snipped fresh parsley. Cover and chill. Bring to room temperature before serving. Makes ⅔ cup.*

Herb Butter: *In a small bowl combine ½ cup softened butter or margarine and ½ teaspoon each dried thyme and dried marjoram, crushed, or 1 teaspoon dried basil, crushed. For an unbeatable fresh taste, substitute 1 tablespoon snipped fresh herb for each teaspoon of dried.*

Kid Appeal

Peanut Butter-Streusel Coffee Cake

Whether you serve it as a morning pick-me-up or an afternoon snack, there's nothing like the taste of peanut butter and chocolate to make the world look a whole lot brighter.

¼ cup all-purpose flour
¼ cup packed brown sugar
2 tablespoons peanut butter
1 tablespoon butter
  (no substitutes)
¼ cup miniature semisweet
  chocolate pieces
¼ cup peanut butter
2 tablespoons butter or
  margarine
1 cup all-purpose flour
½ cup packed brown sugar
½ cup milk
1 egg
1 teaspoon baking powder
¼ teaspoon baking soda
¼ teaspoon salt
¼ cup miniature semisweet
  chocolate pieces

1 Grease an 8x8x2-inch baking pan; set aside.

2 For streusel topping, in a small mixing bowl combine the ¼ cup flour, the ¼ cup brown sugar, the 2 tablespoons peanut butter, and the 1 tablespoon butter. Stir together until crumbly. Stir in the ¼ cup chocolate pieces. Set topping aside.

3 In a large mixing bowl beat the ¼ cup peanut butter and the 2 tablespoons butter with an electric mixer on medium to high speed for 30 seconds or until combined.

4 Add about half of the 1 cup flour, the ½ cup brown sugar, half of the milk, the egg, baking powder, baking soda, and salt. Beat with an electric mixer on low speed until thoroughly combined, scraping the sides of the bowl constantly. Add the remaining flour and remaining milk. Beat on low to medium speed just until combined. Stir in the ¼ cup chocolate pieces.

5 Spread batter evenly in the prepared pan. Sprinkle with the streusel topping. Bake in a 375° oven for 25 to 30 minutes or until a wooden toothpick inserted near the center comes out clean. Cool on a wire rack for 15 minutes. Cut into squares. Serve warm. Cover any leftovers and store at room temperature or in the refrigerator up to 3 days. Makes 1 cake (9 servings).

Nutrition facts per serving: *269 calories, 6 g protein, 36 g carbohydrate, 13 g total fat (4 g saturated), 35 mg cholesterol, 243 mg sodium, 1 g fiber. Daily values: 5% vitamin A, 0% vitamin C, 6% calcium, 10% iron.*

To Make Ahead

Prepare and bake coffee cake as directed; cool completely. Place coffee cake in an airtight container or bag and freeze for up to 3 months. Before serving, wrap the frozen coffee cake in foil and bake in a 300° oven about 25 minutes or until warm.

Pear-Streusel Coffee Cake

If you don't have any ripe pears, use one 8- or 8½-ounce can pear or peach halves (juice pack), drained, reserving juice. Add water to reserved juice to make ½ cup liquid and use that liquid in place of the pear nectar. Thinly slice fruit.

⅔	**cup packed brown sugar**
⅔	**cup all-purpose flour**
1	**teaspoon ground cinnamon**
¼	**teaspoon ground ginger**
⅓	**cup butter (no substitutes)**
3	**cups all-purpose flour**
1	**cup granulated sugar**
1	**tablespoon baking powder**
¼	**teaspoon salt**
1	**cup butter or margarine**
2	**beaten eggs**
½	**cup milk**
½	**cup pear nectar**
2	**medium pears, peeled, halved, cored, and thinly sliced**
1	**recipe Powdered Sugar Icing (see page 151) (optional)**

1 Grease a 13x9x2-inch baking pan. Set the pan aside.

2 For streusel topping, in a small mixing bowl combine brown sugar, ⅔ cup flour, cinnamon, and ginger. Cut in the ⅓ cup butter until mixture resembles coarse crumbs. Set topping aside.

3 Combine the 3 cups flour, sugar, baking powder, and salt. Cut in the 1 cup butter until mixture resembles fine crumbs. Set dry mixture aside.

4 Combine eggs, milk, and pear nectar. Add egg mixture all at once to the dry mixture. Stir just until moistened (batter should be lumpy).

5 Spread half of the batter evenly in the prepared pan. Arrange pear slices on top of batter. Drop remaining batter, by small spoonfuls, over fruit. Sprinkle with streusel topping. Bake in a 350° oven 30 minutes or until a wooden toothpick inserted near center comes out clean. Cool on a wire rack 15 minutes. If desired, drizzle with Powdered Sugar Icing. Serve warm. Cover and chill any leftovers up to 3 days. Makes 1 cake (15 servings).

Nutrition facts per serving: *359 calories, 4 g protein, 48 g carbohydrate, 17 g total fat (10 g saturated), 73 mg cholesterol, 289 mg sodium, 1 g fiber. Daily values: 16% vitamin A, 1% vitamin C, 8% calcium, 12% iron.*

Papaya Coffee Cake: Prepare Pear Coffee Cake as directed, except substitute 1 papaya peeled, seeded, and sliced for the pears, and substitute papaya nectar for the pear nectar.

To Make Ahead

Prepare and bake coffee cake as directed; cool completely. Do not glaze. Place in a freezer container or bag and freeze up to 3 months. To serve, wrap frozen cake in foil; bake in a 300° oven 25 minutes or until warm. Drizzle with icing and serve as directed.

Take a Break

Whenever you need a break, coffee cakes are a delightful choice for a tasty treat. They're an all-American concoction, closely related to biscuits, scones, muffins, quick breads, and creamed cakes, and use many of the same simple preparation techniques.

Neither too sweet nor rich and best served warm, coffee cake should stand for 20 to 30 minutes after you take it out of the oven before you cut it. And, as the name says, nothing goes better with it than a cup of freshly brewed coffee.

To make good coffee, start with fresh beans or ground coffee and fresh cold water. Use ¾ cup cold water and 1 to 2 tablespoons ground coffee for each 6-ounce cup.

For drip coffee, line a coffee basket with a filter, and measure the ground coffee into the lined basket. If you have an electric drip coffeemaker, pour cold water into the water compartment, place the pot on the heating element, let the water run through the basket, and coffee drip into the pot. If you have a nonelectric drip coffeemaker, pour boiling water over the ground coffee in the lined basket, and let coffee drip into the pot.

Don't let the coffee stand on the warming plate for a long time or it will develop a bitter flavor. Always wash the coffeemaker after each use.

Almond-Cherry-Streusel Coffee Cake

If you have a 12-ounce jar of cherry, apricot, strawberry, or raspberry preserves on the shelf in your pantry, you can substitute it for the pie filling.

- ½ **cup all-purpose flour**
- 3 **tablespoons granulated sugar**
- 3 **tablespoons butter (no substitutes)**
- ¼ **cup sliced almonds**
- 2 **cups all-purpose flour**
- 2 **teaspoons baking powder**
- ¼ **teaspoon baking soda**
- ¼ **teaspoon salt**
- ½ **cup butter or margarine, softened**
- ⅔ **cup granulated sugar**
- 1 **beaten egg**
- 1 **8-ounce carton dairy sour cream**
- 1 **teaspoon vanilla**
- ¼ **teaspoon almond extract**
- ½ **cup milk**
- 1 **20-ounce can cherry, apricot, strawberry, or raspberry pie filling**

1 Grease a 9-inch springform pan. Set the pan aside.

2 In a medium mixing bowl stir together the ½ cup flour and the 3 tablespoons sugar. Using a pastry blender, cut in the 3 tablespoons butter until mixture resembles coarse crumbs. Stir in almonds. Set sugar mixture aside.

3 In another medium mixing bowl stir together the 2 cups flour, baking powder, baking soda, and salt. Set flour mixture aside.

4 In a large mixing bowl beat the ½ cup butter and the ⅔ cup sugar with an electric mixer on medium speed until fluffy. Beat in egg, sour cream, vanilla, and almond extract until fluffy. Add flour mixture and milk alternately, beating just until blended after each addition.

5 Spread two-thirds of the batter evenly into the prepared pan. Spread pie filling on top of batter. Dollop remaining batter on top of filling. Sprinkle sugar mixture over batter in the pan. Bake in a 350° oven about 1 hour or until a wooden toothpick inserted near the center comes out clean. Cool in pan on a wire rack for 10 minutes. Serve warm. Cover any leftovers in the refrigerator for up to 3 days. Makes 1 cake (12 servings).

Nutrition facts per serving: *369 calories, 5 g protein, 55 g carbohydrate, 15 g total fat (9 g saturated), 54 mg cholesterol, 258 mg sodium, 1 g fiber. Daily values: 13% vitamin A, 0% vitamin C, 9% calcium, 11% iron.*

To Make Ahead
Prepare and bake the coffee cake as directed; cool completely. Place coffee cake in a freezer container or bag and freeze for up to 3 months. Before serving, wrap the frozen coffee cake in foil and bake in a 300° oven about 25 minutes or until warm.

Almond-Cherry-Streusel Coffee Cake

Apple Coffee Cake

For a tart apple coffee cake with a bit of pucker power, use Granny Smith or Jonathan apples.

2 **cups all-purpose flour**
⅔ **cup granulated sugar**
2½ **teaspoons baking powder**
½ **teaspoon ground cinnamon**
¼ **teaspoon salt**
¼ **teaspoon ground nutmeg**
½ **cup butter or margarine**
½ **cup milk**
1 **beaten egg**
2 **cups thinly sliced, peeled cooking apples (about 2 apples)**
½ **recipe Powdered Sugar Icing (see page 151)**

1 Grease a 9x9x2-inch baking pan. Set the pan aside.

2 In a large mixing bowl stir together the flour, sugar, baking powder, cinnamon, salt, and nutmeg. Cut in butter until mixture resembles coarse crumbs. Set dry mixture aside.

3 In a medium mixing bowl stir together milk and egg. Add egg mixture all at once to dry mixture. Stir just until moistened.

4 Spread half of the batter evenly in the prepared pan. Arrange apple slices on top of the batter. Dollop remaining batter, by small spoonfuls, on top of the apple slices. Bake in a 350° oven about 40 minutes or until a wooden toothpick inserted near the center comes out clean. Cool slightly. Drizzle icing over the top. Serve warm. Cover and store leftovers at room temperature or in refrigerator for up to 3 days. Makes 1 cake (9 servings).

Nutrition facts per serving: 294 calories, 4 g protein, 45 g carbohydrate, 11 g total fat (7 g saturated), 52 mg cholesterol, 279 mg sodium, 1 g fiber. Daily values: 11% vitamin A, 2% vitamin C, 10% calcium, 10% iron.

Peach Coffee Cake: Prepare the Apple Coffee Cake recipe as directed, except substitute 2 cups sliced peaches for the cooking apples.

Shortcut

If you do not have time to slice apples or peaches, substitute one 21-ounce can of your favorite pie filling, such as apple, apricot, pineapple, raspberry, or blackberry, for the sliced fruit.

To Make Ahead

Prepare and bake the coffee cake as directed; cool completely. Do not ice. Place the coffee cake in a freezer container or bag and freeze for up to 3 months. Before serving, wrap the frozen coffee cake in foil and bake in a 300° oven about 25 minutes or until warm. Glaze and serve as directed.

Blueberry Tea Cake

Serve fresh or frozen raspberries alongside this delicious tea cake for even more fruit flavor.

½ **cup granulated sugar**
½ **cup all-purpose flour**
1½ **teaspoons ground cinnamon**
¼ **cup butter (no substitutes)**
2½ **cups all-purpose flour**
1 **package active dry yeast**
1 **cup milk**
½ **cup butter or margarine**
⅓ **cup granulated sugar**
¼ **teaspoon salt**
2 **eggs**
2 **cups fresh or frozen blueberries**

1 Grease a 13x9x2-inch baking pan; set aside.

2 For sugar topping, in a medium mixing bowl stir together the ½ cup sugar, the ½ cup flour, and ½ teaspoon of the cinnamon. Cut in the ¼ cup butter until mixture resembles coarse crumbs; set aside.

3 In a large bowl combine 1½ cups of the flour, the yeast, and the remaining 1 teaspoon cinnamon. Set the flour mixture aside.

4 In a medium saucepan heat and stir milk, the ½ cup butter or margarine, the ⅓ cup sugar, and salt just until warm (120° to 130°) and butter almost melts. Add milk mixture to flour mixture. Then add eggs. Beat with an electric mixer on low to medium speed for

30 seconds, scraping the sides of the bowl constantly. Then beat on high speed for 3 minutes. Using a wooden spoon, stir in as much of the remaining flour as you can.

5 Cover and let dough rest for 10 minutes. Spread the dough into the prepared pan. Spoon blueberries on top of the dough. Sprinkle sugar topping over fruit. Cover and let rise until double (about 60 minutes).

6 Bake in a 350° oven for 40 minutes or until golden brown. Cool on a wire rack. Serve warm or cool. Cover and store any leftovers at room temperature or in refrigerator and use within 3 days. Makes 1 cake (12 servings).

Nutrition facts per serving: 297 calories, 5 g protein, 41 g carbohydrate, 13 g total fat (8 g saturated), 68 mg cholesterol, 183 mg sodium, 2 g fiber. Daily values: 13% vitamin A, 5% vitamin C, 3% calcium, 11% iron.

Overnight Version: Prepare sugar topping; cover and refrigerate. Prepare dough as directed and spread into prepared pan. Cover and refrigerate for 4 to 24 hours. To serve, spoon berries on top of dough. Sprinkle sugar topping over berries. Cover and let stand for 20 minutes. Bake and serve as directed.

To Make Ahead

Prepare and bake the tea cake as directed; cool completely. Place tea cake in a freezer container or bag and freeze for up to 3 months. Before serving, wrap the frozen tea cake in foil and bake in a 300° oven about 25 minutes or until warm.

Berry-Cheesy Coffee Cake

If your mornings are too hectic for yeast-leavened coffee cakes, you haven't tried this one. It's easy. Prepare the batter the night before and let it rise overnight in the refrigerator. Then let the dough stand at room temperature for 20 minutes before baking. It only takes about 45 minutes from start to finish in the morning!

⅓ **cup granulated sugar**
2 **tablespoons cornstarch**
⅓ **cup water**
1½ **cups fresh or frozen blueberries or raspberries**
1 **tablespoon lemon juice**
2 **3-ounce packages cream cheese, softened**
½ **cup granulated sugar**
1 **tablespoon lemon juice**
1 **package active dry yeast**
¼ **cup warm water (105° to 115°)**
3 **tablespoons butter or margarine**
2 **tablespoons granulated sugar**
¼ **teaspoon salt**
2 **cups all-purpose flour**
3 **tablespoons milk**
1 **egg**
Streusel Topping

1 Grease a 12-inch pizza pan. For fruit filling, in a saucepan combine the ⅓ cup sugar, cornstarch, and the ⅓ cup water. Stir in berries. Cook and stir until mixture is thickened and bubbly. Remove from heat; stir in 1 tablespoon lemon juice. Cool.

2 For cheese filling, in a bowl combine cream cheese, the ½ cup sugar, and 1 tablespoon lemon juice. Beat until smooth; set aside.

3 Dissolve yeast in ¼ cup warm water. Let stand 5 to 10 minutes to soften. Meanwhile, combine the 3 tablespoons butter, the 2 tablespoons sugar, and salt. Beat with an electric mixer on medium speed until fluffy. Add ½ cup of the flour, the milk, egg, and softened yeast; beat well. Stir in enough remaining flour to make a smooth dough.

4 Divide dough in half. On a well-floured surface, roll half of the dough into a 12-inch circle. Transfer dough to prepared pan. Spread cheese filling over dough to within ½ inch of the edges. Spread fruit filling evenly over cheese filling. Roll remaining half of dough into a 12-inch circle. Set dough circle atop filling. Press edges to seal.

5 Sprinkle Streusel Topping over dough. Cover; let rise in a warm place 30 minutes. Bake in a 375° oven 20 to 25 minutes until golden. Serve warm. Cover and chill any leftovers up to 3 days. Makes 1 cake (12 servings).

Streusel Topping: Combine 3 tablespoons all-purpose flour, 2 tablespoons granulated sugar, and ½ teaspoon ground cinnamon. Cut in 2 tablespoons butter (no substitutes) until coarse crumbs.

Nutrition facts per serving: 264 calories, 4 g protein, 39 g carbohydrate, 11 g total fat (6 g saturated), 47 mg cholesterol, 145 mg sodium, 1 g fiber. Daily values: 11% vitamin A, 5% vitamin C, 2% calcium, 9% iron.

Orange Moravian Sugar Bread

Orange Moravian Sugar Bread

It may be necessary to regularly reflour the handle of the wooden spoon that you use to make the holes in the dough.

1 cup Sourdough Starter
(see page 82)
3½ cups all-purpose flour
1 package active dry yeast
½ cup granulated sugar
½ cup milk
¼ cup butter or margarine
½ teaspoon salt
2 slightly beaten eggs
2 teaspoons finely shredded
orange peel (set aside)
2 tablespoons orange juice
¾ cup flaked coconut
¾ cup packed brown sugar
⅓ cup butter or margarine
1 teaspoon ground cinnamon

1 Bring the Sourdough Starter to room temperature. Lightly grease a 13x9x2-inch baking pan; set aside.

2 In a large mixing bowl combine 1½ cups of the flour and yeast; set aside.

3 In a small saucepan heat and stir the sugar, milk, the ¼ cup butter, and salt just until warm (120° to 130°) and butter almost melts. Add milk mixture to flour mixture. Then add Sourdough Starter, eggs, and orange juice. Beat with an electric mixer on low speed for 30 seconds, scraping sides of bowl. Beat on high speed 3 minutes. Using a wooden spoon, stir in coconut, orange peel, and the remaining flour.

4 Spread dough evenly in the prepared baking pan. Cover and let rise in a warm place until nearly double (about 1 hour).

5 In a small saucepan heat and stir the brown sugar, the ⅓ cup butter, and cinnamon until melted and smooth. Poke holes in the dough with the floured handle of a wooden spoon. Pour brown sugar mixture evenly over dough in the pan. Bake in a 375° oven about 25 minutes or until bread is golden. Cool slightly on a wire rack. Serve warm. Cover and store any leftovers at room temperature or in the refrigerator for up to 3 days. Makes 1 cake (12 servings).

Nutrition facts per serving: *356 calories, 6 g protein, 57 g carbohydrate, 12 g total fat (7 g saturated), 60 mg cholesterol, 202 mg sodium, 2 g fiber. Daily values: 10% vitamin A, 3% vitamin C, 3% calcium, 17% iron.*

To Make Ahead

Prepare and bake bread as directed; cool completely. Place bread in a freezer container or bag and freeze for up to 3 months. Before serving, wrap bread in foil and bake in a 300° oven about 25 minutes or until warm.

Baker's Bonus

Acerbic Wit

You don't have to have some sort of culinary green thumb to cultivate a healthy sourdough starter. Just remember to feed it regularly, and you can keep it on hand indefinitely to add a bit of tang to your favorite breads and coffee cakes.

If you do not use the sourdough starter for 10 days, stir in 1 teaspoon granulated sugar or honey. Add more sugar or honey every 10 days until you use starter.

Your starter may thicken over time. There is no need to adjust your recipes to compensate; however, you may find yourself needing the lesser amount of recommended flour when a range is given in yeast bread recipes.

After you use the sourdough starter, replenish it as necessary with whole wheat or all-purpose flour, warm water, and granulated sugar or honey, adding these amounts:

Amount Starter Used	Amount Flour	Amount Warm Water	Amount Sugar or Honey
½ cup	⅓ cup	⅓ cup	½ teaspoon
1 cup	¾ cup	¾ cup	1 teaspoon
1½ cups	1 cup	1 cup	1½ teaspoons

Then cover the starter with cheesecloth. Let it stand at room temperature until bubbly (about 1 day). Refrigerate in a covered, plastic container for later use. Bring the desired amount to room temperature.

Coffee-Chocolate Tea Ring

Two favorite flavor combinations—chocolate and coffee or chocolate and peanut butter—in this tea ring; it's your choice.

1 recipe Sweet Roll Dough
   (see page 57)
1 teaspoon instant coffee crystals
¾ cup milk chocolate pieces or
   semisweet chocolate pieces
   (4 ounces)
2 tablespoons butter or
   margarine
¾ cup chopped walnuts or pecans
2 recipes Chocolate Powdered
   Sugar Icing (see page 151)

1 Line a baking sheet with foil. Lightly grease foil. Set baking sheet aside.

2 Prepare Sweet Dough as directed, except add instant coffee crystals to the milk mixture to dissolve. While dough is resting, in a small saucepan, combine chocolate pieces and butter. Heat and stir until melted; set aside.

3 Do not divide Sweet Dough into 2 portions as directed in the Sweet Dough recipe. Instead, roll dough into a 14x10-inch rectangle. Spread rectangle with melted chocolate mixture to within 1 inch of the long edges. Sprinkle nuts evenly over chocolate. Tightly roll up, jelly-roll style, starting from one of the long sides. Seal with fingertips as you roll.

4 Place dough on prepared pan, seam side down. Form dough into a circle, tucking ends together. Using a sharp knife, make 12 evenly spaced slits two-thirds of the way through dough. Alternating sides, pull cut-edge pieces out, twisting slightly to form "heart" shapes around bread. Cover; let rise until double (30 to 40 minutes).

5 Bake in a 375° oven about 30 to 35 minutes or until bread sounds hollow when you tap the top with your fingers (if necessary, cover loosely with foil the last 15 minutes of baking to prevent overbrowning). Immediately remove bread from pan. Cool on a wire rack. Drizzle with Chocolate Powdered Sugar Icing. Place tea ring in an airtight container and store at room temperature for up to 3 days. Makes 1 ring (12 to 16 servings).

Nutrition facts per serving: *418 calories, 9 g protein, 64 g carbohydrate, 15 g total fat (6 g saturated), 53 mg cholesterol, 180 mg sodium, 2 g fiber. Daily values: 9% vitamin A, 0% vitamin C, 6% calcium, 17% iron.*

Peanut Butter-Chocolate Tea Ring: Prepare Coffee-Chocolate Tea Ring as directed, except omit coffee crystals in dough. Prepare filling as directed, except reduce chocolate pieces to ½ cup. Stir ¼ cup peanut butter into the melted chocolate mixture and substitute chopped peanuts for the walnuts.

To Make Ahead
Prepare and bake tea ring as directed. Do not ice. Place tea ring in a freezer container or bag and freeze for up to 3 months. Before serving, thaw at room temperature for 2 hours. Drizzle with Chocolate Powdered Sugar Icing and serve as directed.

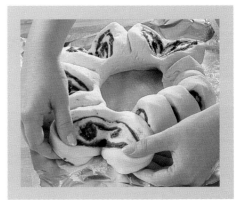

Make the cuts in the dough ring from the outside toward the center. Working with two adjoining pieces of dough, fold them away from their center cut to form a heart shape. Repeat around the ring for a total of six heart shapes.

Date Twist

The best way to crack Brazil nuts is to cook them slightly first. In a saucepan, combine nuts with enough cold water to cover them. Bring water to boiling, and boil nuts 3 minutes. Drain and cover nuts with cold water again. Let nuts stand 1 minute, then drain again. Use a hand-held nutcracker or hammer to open shells.

3¾ to 4¼ cups all-purpose flour
 2 packages active dry yeast
 1 cup milk
 ¼ cup granulated sugar
 ¼ cup butter or margarine
 1 teaspoon salt
 1 egg
 1 cup snipped dates or prunes

½ **cup chopped Brazil nuts or
    walnuts**
1 **beaten egg yolk**
1 **tablespoon water**

1 Grease 2 baking sheets. In a large mixing bowl combine 1½ cups of the flour and yeast. Set baking sheets and flour mixture aside.

2 In a medium saucepan heat and stir milk, sugar, butter, and salt just until warm (120° to 130°) and butter almost melts. Add milk mixture to flour mixture. Then add egg. Beat with an electric mixer on low to medium speed 30 seconds, scraping bowl. Then beat on high speed 3 minutes. Using a wooden spoon, stir in dates, nuts, and as much of the remaining flour as you can.

3 Turn dough out onto a lightly floured surface. Knead in enough of the remaining flour to make a moderately soft dough that is smooth and elastic (6 to 8 minutes total). Shape dough into a ball. Place in a lightly greased bowl, turning once to grease surface. Cover and let rise in a warm place until double (about 1 hour).

4 Punch dough down. Turn dough out onto a lightly floured surface. Divide dough into quarters. Cover and let rest for 10 minutes.

5 Roll each quarter of dough into a 26-inch rope. Place 2 ropes, side by side, on each of the prepared baking sheets (ropes will extend beyond ends of baking sheet). Working from center to ends, twist 2 ropes together. Shape

Baker's Bonus

The Proof Is in Your Microwave

Part of the reason that baking yeast breads can be time consuming is the proofing process (the time it takes to raise). But you can cut that process in half if you use your microwave oven.

Before you start, check your owner's manual to see if it recommends using your oven to proof breads. Or, test your oven by placing 2 tablespoons of cold stick margarine (do not use corn oil margarine) in a custard cup in the center of the oven. Cook it, uncovered, on 10% power (low) for 4 minutes. If the margarine doesn't melt completely, you can use your oven to proof yeast dough; if it does melt, you will have to proof your breads conventionally.

While kneading your dough, place 3 cups water in a microwave-safe 4-cup measure. Cook on 100% power (high) for 6½ to 8½ minutes or until boiling. Move the measure to the back of the oven.

For the first rise, place the kneaded dough in a microwave-safe, greased bowl, turning the dough once to coat it. Cover the bowl with waxed paper, and place it in the oven with the hot water. Heat dough and water on 10% power (low) for 13 to 15 minutes or until dough has nearly doubled (allow 15 to 20 minutes for rich yeast breads, which have eggs and a higher amount of sugar). Punch dough down; shape dough as directed. (For shapes other than a loaf, you'll have to do the second proofing step conventionally).

For the second rise, place the shaped loaves into microwave-safe 8x4x2- or 9x5x3-inch loaf dishes. Place the dishes in the microwave oven with the hot water. Cover with waxed paper; heat on low for 6 to 8 minutes or until nearly doubled (allow 10 to 14 minutes for rich yeast breads). Bake according to the recipe.

each twist into a figure 8, tucking ends under in center. Cover; let rise until nearly double (about 40 minutes).

6 In a small mixing bowl use a fork to beat the egg yolk and water. Brush loaves with some of the egg mixture. Bake in 350° oven for 25 to 30 minutes or until bread sounds hollow when you tap the top with your fingers (if necessary, cover loosely with foil the last 15 minutes of baking to prevent overbrowning). Remove bread from baking sheets and cool on a wire rack. Makes 2 loaves (24 servings).

Nutrition facts per serving: *143 calories, 3 g protein, 22 g carbohydrate, 5 g total fat (2 g saturated), 24 mg cholesterol, 117 mg sodium, 1 g fiber. Daily values: 4% vitamin A, 0% vitamin C, 2% calcium, 7% iron.*

To Make Ahead

Prepare and bake twists as directed; cool completely. Place twists in a freezer container or bag and freeze for up to 3 months. Before serving, thaw the wrapped twists at room temperature for 2 hours.

Almond-Apricot Bread

Almond-Apricot Bread

*Serve this apricot delight
with Fruit-Nut Butter using peach
preserves (see page 44).*

3¼   **to 3¾ cups all-purpose flour**
1   **package active dry yeast**
¾   **cup milk**
¼   **cup granulated sugar**
¼   **cup butter or margarine**
½   **teaspoon salt**
2   **eggs**
1   **egg yolk**
1   **teaspoon finely shredded
      lemon peel**
3   **tablespoons apricot preserves**
⅔   **cup ground almonds or
      walnuts**
½   **cup finely snipped dried
      apricots or dried peaches**
3   **tablespoons granulated sugar**
1   **egg white**
¼   **teaspoon lemon juice**
1   **egg**
1   **tablespoon water**

1 In a large mixing bowl stir together 1½ cups of the flour and the yeast. Set flour mixture aside.

2 In a medium saucepan heat and stir the milk, the ¼ cup sugar, butter, and salt just until warm (120° to 130°) and butter almost melts. Add milk mixture to flour mixture. Then add the 2 whole eggs and the egg yolk (reserve and chill egg white). Beat with an electric mixer on low to medium speed 30 seconds, scraping sides of the bowl. Beat on high speed 3 minutes. Using a wooden spoon, stir in lemon peel and as much of the remaining flour as you can.

3 Turn the dough out onto a lightly floured surface. Knead in enough of the remaining flour to make a moderately soft dough that is smooth and elastic (6 to 8 minutes total). Shape the dough into a ball. Place dough in a lightly greased bowl, turning once to grease the surface of the dough. Cover and let rise in a warm place until double (1 to 1½ hours).

4 For filling, in a small saucepan heat apricot preserves just until melted. Remove the saucepan from heat and stir in the almonds, apricots, the 3 tablespoons sugar, the egg white, and lemon juice; set aside.

5 Punch dough down. Turn dough out onto a lightly floured surface. Divide dough in half. Cover and let rest for 10 minutes.

6 Lightly grease 2 baking sheets. In a small mixing bowl, using a fork, beat the 1 whole egg and water. Set baking sheets and egg mixture aside.

7 Roll each half of the dough into a 12x10-inch rectangle. Cut each rectangle into three 10x4-inch strips (6 strips total). Spread 3 tablespoons of the apricot filling down the center of each strip. Brush edges of the rectangles with some of the egg mixture. Fold long sides of dough over filling. Press edges to seal.

8 To shape the bread, place 3 filled ropes, seam sides down, 1 inch apart on one of the prepared baking sheets. Starting in the middle, loosely braid the ropes by bringing left rope underneath center rope; lay it down. Bring right rope under new center rope; lay it down. Repeat to end. On the other end, braid by bringing outside ropes alternately over center rope to the center. Press ends together to seal. Tuck ends under. Braid the remaining 3 ropes on the second baking sheet. Cover and let rise in a warm place until nearly double (45 to 60 minutes).

9 Brush loaves with some more of the egg mixture. Bake in a 350° oven about 30 minutes or until bread sounds hollow when you tap the top with your fingers (if necessary, cover loosely with foil the last 15 minutes of baking to prevent overbrowning). Remove from baking sheets and cool on wire racks. Place loaves in an airtight container or bag and store at room temperature or in the refrigerator for up to 3 days. Makes 2 loaves (16 servings).

Nutrition facts per serving: *202 calories, 6 g protein, 29 g carbohydrate, 7 g total fat (3 g saturated), 62 mg cholesterol, 119 mg sodium, 2 g fiber. Daily values: 10% vitamin A, 0% vitamin C, 3% calcium, 11% iron.*

To Make Ahead

Prepare and bake bread as directed; cool completely. Place bread in a freezer container or bag and freeze for up to 3 months. Before serving, thaw bread at room temperature for 2 to 3 hours.

International Origin

Stollen

A traditional German bread, Stollen is full of dried fruits, nuts, and candied fruits and peels.

- **4 to 4½ cups all-purpose flour**
- **1 package active dry yeast**
- **¼ teaspoon ground cardamom**
- **1¼ cups milk**
- **½ cup butter or margarine**
- **¼ cup granulated sugar**
- **½ teaspoon salt**
- **1 egg**
- **1 cup raisins or currants**
- **¼ cup diced mixed candied fruits and peels**
- **¼ cup chopped blanched almonds**
- **1 tablespoon finely shredded orange peel**
- **1 tablespoon finely shredded lemon peel**
- **1 cup sifted powdered sugar**
- **2 tablespoons hot water**
- **½ teaspoon butter or margarine**

1 In a large mixing bowl combine 2 cups of the flour, the yeast, and cardamom; set aside.

2 In a saucepan heat and stir milk, ½ cup butter, the sugar, and salt until warm (120° to 130°) and butter almost melts. Add milk mixture to flour mixture. Then add egg. Beat with an electric mixer on low to medium speed for 30 seconds, scraping the sides of the bowl constantly. Then beat on high

speed for 3 minutes. Using a wooden spoon, stir in raisins, candied fruits and peels, almonds, orange peel, lemon peel, and as much of the remaining flour as you can.

3 Turn dough out onto a lightly floured surface. Knead in enough of the remaining flour to make a moderately soft dough that is smooth and elastic (3 to 5 minutes total). Shape dough into a ball. Place dough in a lightly greased bowl; turning once to grease the surface of the dough. Cover and let rise in a warm place until double (about 1¾ hours).

4 Punch dough down. Turn out onto a lightly floured surface. Divide dough into thirds. Cover and let rest 10 minutes. Grease 3 baking sheets; set aside.

5 Roll a portion of the dough into a 10x6-inch oval. Without stretching, fold a long side over to within 1 inch of the opposite side; press edges lightly to seal. Place on a prepared baking sheet. Repeat with remaining dough. Cover and let rise until nearly double (about 1 hour).

6 Bake in a 375° oven for 18 to 20 minutes or until golden and sounds hollow when you tap the top with your fingers (if necessary, cover loosely with foil the last 10 minutes of baking to prevent overbrowning). Immediately remove bread from baking sheets. Cool on wire racks 30 minutes.

7 In a small mixing bowl stir together the powdered sugar, hot water, and the ½ teaspoon butter. Brush tops of the

warm loaves with some of the powdered sugar mixture. Serve warm or cool. Place any cooled bread in an airtight container or bag and store at room temperature for up to 3 days. Makes 3 loaves (48 servings).

Nutrition facts per serving: *83 calories, 7 g protein, 14 g carbohydrate, 3 g total fat (1 g saturated), 10 mg cholesterol, 25 mg sodium, 0 g fiber. Daily values: 2% vitamin A, 0% vitamin C, 1% calcium, 1% iron.*

To Make Ahead
Prepare and bake bread as directed; cool completely. Do not glaze. Place bread in a freezer container or bag and freeze for up to 3 months. Before serving, wrap the frozen bread in foil. Bake in a 300° oven about 25 minutes or until warm. Glaze as directed.

Delicious Memories

Butterscotch Rolls

The perfect ending to a long winter's day was coming home from school to the aroma of Mom's fresh, hot, sticky buns. Take it from me, the best way to eat them is layer by layer, saving the sweetest, stickiest, middle piece for last.
—Tom Wierzbicki—

- **1 package active dry yeast**
- **1½ cups warm water (105° to 115°)**
- **½ cup milk**
- **3 tablespoons granulated sugar**
- **3 tablespoons butter or margarine**
- **1 teaspoon salt**

5¾ to 6¼ cups all-purpose flour
½ cup butter or margarine
1 cup packed brown sugar
1 cup chopped walnuts or pecans

1 In a large mixing bowl dissolve yeast in warm water. Let stand for 5 to 10 minutes to soften.

2 Meanwhile, in a medium saucepan heat and stir the milk, sugar, the 3 tablespoons butter, and salt until lukewarm (105° to 115°). Add milk mixture to softened yeast. Add 3 cups of the flour. Beat with an electric mixer on low to medium speed for 30 seconds, scraping the sides of the bowl. Beat on high speed for 3 minutes. Using a wooden spoon, stir in as much of the remaining flour as you can.

3 Turn dough out onto a lightly floured surface. Knead in enough of the remaining flour to make a moderately soft dough that is smooth and elastic (6 to 8 minutes). Shape dough into smooth ball. Place dough in a lightly greased bowl, turning once to grease the surface of the dough. Cover and let rise in a warm place until double (about 45 minutes).

4 For filling, melt the ½ cup butter. Add brown sugar; stir until dissolved. Stir in nuts. Cool slightly; set aside.

5 Punch dough down. Turn dough out onto a lightly floured surface. Divide dough in half. Cover and let rest for 15 minutes. Grease a 13x9x2-inch baking pan; set aside.

6 Roll each half of the dough into a 12x8-inch rectangle. Sprinkle each rectangle with half of the filling. Tightly roll up, jelly-roll style, starting from one of the long sides. Cut each roll into 1½-inch-wide slices. Place slices in prepared pan. Cover and let rise in a warm place until nearly double (about 45 minutes).

7 Bake in 350° oven for 30 to 35 minutes or until golden (if necessary, cover loosely with foil the last 10 minutes of baking to prevent overbrowning). Cool in pan for 5 minutes. Invert rolls onto a serving plate. Serve warm. Place any cooled rolls in an airtight container and store at room temperature for up to 3 days. Makes 16.

Nutrition facts per roll: *323 calories, 6 g protein, 47 g carbohydrate, 13 g total fat (5 g saturated), 22 mg cholesterol, 356 mg sodium, 2 g fiber. Daily values: 7% vitamin A, 0% vitamin C, 3% calcium, 16% iron.*

To Make Ahead

Prepare and bake rolls as directed; cool completely. Place rolls in a freezer container or bag and freeze for up to 3 months. Before serving, wrap the frozen rolls in foil and bake in a 300° oven about 25 minutes or until warm.

Sweet Roll Dough

This simple dough serves as the basis for many of the delicious pastries in this chapter.

4 to 4½ cups all-purpose flour
1 package active dry yeast
1 cup milk
⅓ cup granulated sugar
¼ cup butter or margarine
½ teaspoon salt
¼ teaspoon ground ginger, nutmeg, cinnamon, finely shredded orange peel, or finely shredded lemon peel (optional)
2 eggs

1 In a large mixing bowl stir together 2 cups of the flour and the yeast. Set flour mixture aside.

2 In a medium saucepan heat and stir milk, sugar, butter, salt, and, if desired, a spice or peel just until warm (120° to 130°) and butter almost melts. Add milk mixture to flour mixture. Then add the eggs. Beat with an electric mixer on low to medium speed for 30 seconds, scraping the sides of the bowl constantly. Then beat on high speed for 3 minutes. Using a wooden spoon, stir in as much of the remaining flour as you can.

3 Turn the dough out onto a lightly floured surface. Knead in enough of the remaining flour to make a moderately soft dough that is smooth and elastic (6 to 8 minutes total). Shape the dough into a ball. Place dough in a lightly greased bowl, turning once to grease the surface. Cover and let rise in a warm place until double (about 1 hour). Or, cover dough with oiled waxed paper, then with plastic wrap, and refrigerate 6 to 24 hours.

4 Shape dough according to the recipe. If dough has been chilled, let it stand at room temperature for 20 minutes before proceeding with the recipe.

Kid Appeal

Giant Cinnamon Rolls

6¼ **to 6¾ cups all-purpose flour**
  2 **packages active dry yeast**
  2 **cups milk**
  ¼ **cup granulated sugar**
  ¼ **cup butter or margarine**
1½ **teaspoons salt**
  1 **egg**
  ½ **cup packed brown sugar**
  ½ **cup granulated sugar**
  ¼ **cup all-purpose flour**
  1 **tablespoon ground cinnamon**
  ½ **cup butter or margarine**
  1 **cup chopped nuts or 1 cup**
     raisins (optional)
  3 **cups sifted powdered sugar**
  3 **tablespoons butter or**
     margarine, melted
1½ **teaspoons vanilla**
  2 **to 3 tablespoons milk**

1 In a large mixing bowl stir together 3 cups of the flour and the yeast. Set flour mixture aside.

2 In a medium saucepan heat and stir milk, the ¼ cup sugar, the ¼ cup butter, and salt just until warm (120° to 130°) and butter almost melts. Add milk mixture to flour mixture. Then add egg. Beat with an electric mixer on low to medium speed for 30 seconds, scraping the sides of the bowl. Then beat on high speed for 3 minutes. Using a wooden spoon, stir in as much of the remaining flour as you can.

3 Turn the dough out onto a lightly floured surface. Knead in enough of the remaining flour to make a moderately soft dough that is smooth and elastic (3 to 5 minutes total). Shape the dough into a ball. Place dough in a lightly greased bowl, turning once to grease the surface of the dough. Cover and let rise in a warm place until double (45 to 60 minutes).

4 For filling, in a small mixing bowl combine the ½ cup brown sugar, the ½ cup sugar, the ¼ cup flour, and cinnamon. Cut in the ½ cup butter until mixture resembles coarse crumbs. If desired, stir in nuts. Set aside.

5 Punch dough down. Turn dough out onto a lightly floured surface. Cover and let rest 10 minutes. Grease a 13x9x2-inch baking pan; set aside.

6 Roll dough into a 24x16-inch rectangle. Sprinkle rectangle with the filling. Tightly roll up, jelly-roll style, starting from one of the long sides. Seal with fingertips as you roll.

7 Cut dough crosswise into twelve 2-inch pieces. Place pieces, cut sides down, in prepared pan. Cover and let rise in a warm place until dough has nearly doubled in size (about 30 to 40 minutes). Or, cover with oiled waxed paper, then with plastic wrap. Chill in the refrigerator for 2 to 24 hours.

8 If rolls have been chilled, let them stand, covered, for 20 minutes at room temperature. Uncover and puncture any surface bubbles with a greased wooden toothpick. Bake in a 350° oven for 25 to 35 minutes or until golden brown. Cool in pan for 10 minutes. Remove rolls from pan and cool slightly on a wire rack.

9 For frosting, in a medium mixing bowl stir together the powdered sugar, the 3 tablespoons melted butter, vanilla, and enough milk (2 to 3 tablespoons) to make the frosting easy to spread. Spread warm cinnamon rolls with frosting. Place any cooled rolls in an airtight container and store at room temperature up to 3 days. Makes 12.

Nutrition facts per roll: *616 calories, 11 g protein, 95 g carbohydrate, 22 g total fat (10 g saturated), 59 mg cholesterol, 447 mg sodium, 2 g fiber. Daily values: 16% vitamin A, 1% vitamin C, 7% calcium, 25% iron.*

To Make Ahead

Prepare and bake rolls as directed; cool completely. Do not frost. Place rolls in a freezer container or bag and freeze for up to 3 months. Before serving, wrap the frozen rolls in foil and bake in a 300° oven about 25 minutes or until warm. Frost as directed.

Gooey Caramel-Pecan Rolls

Have plenty of napkins on hand for these irresistible sticky rolls.

1 **recipe Sweet Roll Dough**
    (see page 57)
⅓ **cup butter or margarine**
⅔ **cup packed brown sugar**
3 **tablespoons light corn syrup**
1 **cup chopped pecans**
½ **cup packed brown sugar**
2 **tablespoons granulated sugar**
1 **teaspoon ground cinnamon**
3 **tablespoons butter or**
    margarine, melted

1 Prepare Sweet Roll Dough as directed. While dough is resting, in a medium saucepan melt butter. Stir in the ⅔ cup brown sugar and light corn syrup. Cook and stir just until blended. Pour syrup into a 13x9x2-inch baking pan and sprinkle pecans evenly over the top; set aside.

2 For filling, in a small mixing bowl stir together the ½ cup brown sugar, granulated sugar, and cinnamon. Set aside.

3 Punch dough down. Turn the dough out onto a lightly floured surface. Cover and let rest for 10 minutes. Roll dough into an 18x10-inch rectangle. Brush dough with the 3 tablespoons melted butter. Sprinkle filling over the rectangle. Tightly roll up rectangle, jelly-roll style, starting from one of the long sides. Seal with fingertips as you roll.

4 Cut roll into 12 pieces. Place pieces, cut sides down, in the prepared pan. Cover and let rise in a warm place until nearly double (about 30 minutes). Or, cover rolls with oiled waxed paper, then with plastic wrap. Chill in the refrigerator for 2 to 24 hours.

5 If chilled, let rolls stand, covered, for 20 minutes at room temperature. Uncover and puncture any surface bubbles with a greased wooden toothpick. Bake in a 375° oven for 20 to 25 minutes or until golden. Cool in pan for 5 minutes. Invert rolls onto a wire rack or serving platter. Serve warm. Place any cooled rolls in an airtight container and store at room temperature for up to 3 days. Makes 12.

Nutrition facts per roll: *445 calories, 7 g protein, 68 g carbohydrate, 17 g total fat (7 g saturated), 61 mg cholesterol, 213 mg sodium, 2 g fiber. Daily values: 11% vitamin A, 0% vitamin C, 5% calcium, 20% iron.*

Miniature Gooey Caramel-Pecan Rolls: Prepare Gooey Caramel-Pecan Rolls as directed, except place the syrup mixture in a 15½x10½x2-inch baking pan. Or, divide the syrup mixture between one 13x9x2-inch baking pan and one 8x8x2-inch baking pan; set aside. Divide dough into 4 equal portions. Roll each portion of the dough into a 12x6-inch rectangle. Using ¼ cup melted butter or margarine instead of 3 tablespoons, brush tops of rectangles. Sprinkle each rectangle with one-fourth of the filling.

Tightly roll up rectangles, jelly-roll style, starting from one of the long sides. Seal with fingertips as you roll. Slice the dough into 1-inch pieces. Place pieces, cut sides down, in prepared pans. Let rise and bake as directed. Makes 48.

Butterscotch Rolls: Prepare Gooey Caramel-Pecan Rolls as directed, except substitute one 4-serving-size package instant butterscotch pudding mix for the brown sugar, granulated sugar, and cinnamon.

To Make Ahead

Prepare and bake rolls as directed; cool completely. Place rolls in a freezer container or bag and freeze for up to 3 months. Before serving, wrap the frozen rolls in foil and bake in a 300° oven about 25 minutes or until warm.

To easily cut the dough roll, place a piece of heavy duty thread or a double length of regular thread under the roll where you want to make your cut. Bring the thread up around the sides, crisscross it at the top, and quickly pull the ends in opposite directions.

Kolaches

My grandma's recipe said to "soak 1 cent worth of yeast in ½ cup of milk and then add 3 tablespoons sugar and 1 sifter of flour". It then said to "stretch and work the dough until blisters appear." Our modern interpretation of Grandma's recipe may read a bit differently, but it gives the same old-fashioned good taste.
—Linda Fillenworth—

4 to 4½ cups all-purpose flour
1 package active dry yeast
1 cup milk

Baker's Bonus

Quick on the Rise

Baking bread doesn't have to take all day. In fact, by using quick-rising yeast, you can cut the dough's rising time by a third.

The yeast bread and roll recipes in this cookbook were tested using active dry yeast. With the exception of the sourdough starter on page 82 and any yeast dough requiring a refrigerated rise, you can substitute quick-rising yeast for active dry yeast. The directions remain the same, but the rising time will be less. The first rising time can be shortened to 10 to 15 minutes; the second may need to be shortened as well.

¾ cup butter or margarine
½ cup granulated sugar
½ teaspoon salt
4 egg yolks
1 teaspoon finely shredded lemon peel
Apricot Filling
2 tablespoons butter or margarine, melted, or milk
Powdered sugar

1 In a large mixing bowl combine 2 cups of the flour and yeast; set aside.

2 In a medium saucepan heat and stir the 1 cup milk, the ¾ cup butter, sugar, and salt just until warm (120° to 130°) and butter almost melts. Add milk mixture to the flour mixture. Then add the egg yolks. Beat with an electric mixer on low to medium speed for 30 seconds, scraping the sides of the bowl. Beat on high speed 3 minutes. Stir in the lemon peel and as much of the remaining flour as you can.

3 Turn dough out onto a lightly floured surface. Knead in enough of the remaining flour to make a moderately soft dough that is smooth and elastic (6 to 8 minutes total). Place dough in a lightly greased bowl, turning once to grease the surface. Cover and let rise in a warm place until double (1 to 1½ hours).

4 Meanwhile, prepare Apricot Filling. Set filling aside to cool.

5 Punch down dough. Turn dough out onto a lightly floured surface. Divide dough in half. Cover; let rest 10 minutes. Grease 2 baking sheets.

6 Shape each half of the dough into 12 balls, pulling the edges under to make smooth tops. Place the balls 3 inches apart on the prepared baking sheets. Flatten each ball to 2½ inches in diameter. Cover and let rise in a warm place until nearly double (about 35 minutes).

7 Using your thumb, make an indentation in the center of each dough circle. Spoon about 2 teaspoons of the Apricot Filling into each indentation. Lightly brush the edges of the dough with the 2 tablespoons melted butter or milk. Bake in a 375° oven for 12 to 15 minutes or until golden brown. Remove from baking sheets and cool on wire racks. Lightly sift powdered sugar over the tops. Place in an airtight container and store in the refrigerator for up to 2 days. Makes 24.

Apricot Filling: In a small saucepan combine 1 cup snipped dried apricots and enough water to cover apricots by 1 inch. Bring mixture to boiling. Reduce heat. Cover and simmer 10 to 15 minutes or until apricots are very soft. Drain, reserving 2 tablespoons of the cooking liquid. In a blender container or food processor bowl place apricots, reserved liquid, ¼ cup granulated sugar, 1 teaspoon lemon juice, ¼ teaspoon ground cinnamon, and ⅛ teaspoon ground nutmeg. Cover and blend or process until smooth, stopping to scrape down sides as necessary.

Nutrition facts per roll: 182 calories, 3 g protein, 25 g carbohydrate, 8 g total fat (5 g saturated), 54 mg cholesterol, 120 mg sodium, 1 g fiber. Daily values: 16% vitamin A, 0% vitamin C, 2% calcium, 8% iron.

Kolaches

Boysenberry
Sweet Rolls
(see recipe, page 62)

Boysenberry Sweet Rolls

Substitute a favorite preserve—such as pineapple—for the boysenberry to suit your mood or the occasion. (Pictured on page 61.)

**1 recipe Sweet Roll Dough
       (see page 57)**
**2 tablespoons butter or
       margarine, melted, or
       1 egg plus 1 tablespoon
       water or milk**
**½ cup boysenberry preserves
       Granulated sugar**
**1 recipe Powdered Sugar Icing
       (see page 151)**

1 Prepare Sweet Roll Dough as directed. Grease 2 baking sheets; set aside.

2 Punch dough down. Turn dough out onto a lightly floured surface. Divide dough into fourths. Cover and let rest 10 minutes. Divide each fourth into 6 equal pieces. Roll each piece into a 14-inch rope. Coil each rope loosely into a circle on the prepared baking sheets, tucking the ends under. Cover and let rise in a warm place until double (30 to 40 minutes).

3 Using your thumb, make an indentation in the center of each roll. Brush rolls with some of the melted butter. (Or, in a small mixing bowl use a fork to beat the egg and the 1 tablespoon water; brush over rolls.) Spoon 1 tea-spoon of the preserves in each indentation. Sprinkle with additional sugar.

4 Bake in a 350° oven for 15 to 20 minutes or until golden brown. Remove from baking sheets and cool slightly on wire racks. Drizzle Powdered Sugar Icing over rolls. Serve warm. Place any cooled rolls in a single layer in an airtight container and store in refrigerator up to 2 days. Makes 24.

***Nutrition facts per roll:** 169 calories, 3 g protein, 31 g carbohydrate, 4 g total fat (2 g saturated), 26 mg cholesterol, 86 mg sodium, 1 g fiber. Daily values: 4% vitamin A, 0% vitamin C, 1% calcium, 7% iron.*

Lemon Pockets

**1 cup Sourdough Starter
       (see page 82)**
4½ to 5 cups all-purpose flour
1 package active dry yeast
¾ cup milk
¼ cup butter or margarine
½ cup granulated sugar
¾ teaspoon salt
2 eggs
2 beaten eggs
1 cup granulated sugar
2 tablespoons all-purpose flour
**¼ cup lemon juice
       Powdered sugar**

1 Bring Sourdough Starter to room temperature. In a large mixing bowl stir together 1½ cups of the flour and the yeast; set aside.

2 In a small saucepan heat and stir the milk, butter, the ½ cup sugar, and salt until warm (120° to 130°) and butter almost melts. Add milk mixture to flour mixture. Then add 2 eggs and Sourdough Starter. Beat with an electric mixer on low to medium speed for 30 seconds, scraping the sides of the bowl constantly. Then beat on high speed for 3 minutes. Using a wooden spoon, stir in as much of the remaining flour as you can.

3 Turn the dough out onto a lightly floured surface. Knead in enough of the remaining flour to make a moderately soft dough that is smooth and elastic (3 to 5 minutes total). Shape the dough into a ball. Place dough in a lightly greased bowl, turning once to grease the surface of the dough. Cover and let rise in a warm place until double (about 1½ hours).

4 Meanwhile, for filling, in a small saucepan heat and stir the 2 beaten eggs, the 1 cup sugar, the 2 tablespoons flour, and lemon juice. Cook and stir over medium heat just until mixture is thickened and bubbly. Remove from heat. Cover surface with plastic wrap. Cool without stirring.

5 Punch dough down. Turn the dough out onto a lightly floured surface. Divide dough into fourths. Cover and let rest for 10 minutes. Grease 2 baking sheets; set aside.

6 Roll each portion of the dough into a 12x8-inch rectangle. Cut each rectangle into six 4-inch squares. Using a scant tablespoon for each square, divide filling evenly among the squares. Fold opposite corners to the center, pinching with fingers to seal dough. Place pockets 2 inches apart on prepared baking sheets. Cover and let rise in a warm place until nearly double (25 to 35 minutes).

7 Bake in a 375° oven for 12 to 15 minutes or until golden brown. Remove pockets from baking sheets. Cool on wire racks. Sprinkle with powdered sugar. Serve warm or cool. Place any cooled pockets in an airtight container and store in the refrigerator for up to 2 days. Makes 24.

Nutrition facts per pocket: 181 calories, 4 g protein, 34 g carbohydrate, 3 g total fat (2 g saturated), 41 mg cholesterol, 101 mg sodium, 1 g fiber. Daily values: 3% vitamin A, 1% vitamin C, 1% calcium, 9% iron.

Shortcut

For a simple filling, substitute one 20-ounce can of your favorite pie filling in place of the homemade lemon filling.

To Make Ahead

Prepare and bake pockets as directed; cool completely. Place pockets in a single layer in a freezer container or bag and freeze for up to 3 months. Before serving, thaw pockets overnight in the refrigerator.

Mango Ladder Loaf

Mangoes vary in size, shape, and color, but all are ripe when the flesh yields slightly to finger pressure.

1	**recipe Sweet Roll Dough (see page 57)**
⅓	**cup granulated sugar**
2	**tablespoons all-purpose flour**
½	**teaspoon ground cinnamon**
4	**cups thinly sliced, peeled mangoes**
¼	**cup butter or margarine, softened**
1½	**recipes Powdered Sugar Icing (see page 151)**

1 Prepare Sweet Roll Dough as directed. Grease 2 baking sheets; set aside.

2 In a large mixing bowl stir together the sugar, flour, and cinnamon. Add the mangoes and toss to coat the fruit; set aside.

3 Punch dough down. Turn the dough out onto a lightly floured surface. Divide dough in half. Cover and let rest for 10 minutes. Roll each half of the dough into a 12x9-inch rectangle. Transfer each rectangle to a prepared baking sheet. Spread each rectangle with 2 tablespoons of the butter. Spread half of the filling in a 3-inch-wide strip down the center of each rectangle to within 1 inch of the ends.

4 On the long sides, make 3-inch cuts from the edges toward the center at 1-inch intervals. Starting at an end, alternately fold opposite strips of dough, at an angle, across the filling. Slightly press ends together in center to seal. Cover and let rise in a warm place until nearly double (45 to 60 minutes).

5 Bake in a 350° oven about 25 minutes or until golden. Remove loaves from oven. Drizzle with Powdered Sugar Icing. Serve warm or cool. Place any cooled loaves in an airtight container or bag and store in the refrigerator for up to 2 days. Makes 2 loaves (16 servings).

Nutrition facts per serving: 301 calories, 5 g protein, 55 g carbohydrate, 7 g total fat (4 g saturated), 43 mg cholesterol, 144 mg sodium, 3 g fiber. Daily values: 32% vitamin A, 30% vitamin C, 3% calcium, 12% iron.

Peach or Pear Ladder Loaf: Prepare the Mango Ladder Loaf as directed, except substitute 4 cups sliced peaches or pears for the mangoes.

Shortcut

Use one 20-ounce can of pie filling (your favorite flavor) as a substitute for the homemade filling.

To Make Ahead

Prepare loaves as directed except omit last rise and do not bake. Immediately freeze the loaves on the greased baking sheets. After frozen, wrap in heavy foil and freeze up to 3 months. To bake, unwrap loaves. Allow loaves to come to room temperature and rise (about 3 hours). Bake as directed.

Orange Bowknots

Orange Bowknots

*These mouthfuls of citrusy sunshine
will brighten any day.*

- **4 to 4½ cups all-purpose flour**
- **2 packages active dry yeast**
- **½ cup milk**
- **⅓ cup granulated sugar**
- **⅓ cup butter or margarine**
- **½ teaspoon salt**
- **2 eggs**
- **2 tablespoons finely shredded orange peel (set aside)**
- **½ cup orange juice**
- **Orange Icing**

1 In a large mixing bowl combine 2 cups of the flour and yeast; set aside.

2 In a medium saucepan heat and stir the milk, sugar, butter, and salt until warm (120° to 130°) and butter almost melts. Add milk mixture to flour mixture. Then add eggs and orange juice. Beat with an electric mixer on low to medium speed for 30 seconds, scraping the sides of the bowl. Beat on high speed for 3 minutes. Using a wooden spoon, stir in orange peel and as much of the remaining flour as you can.

3 Turn dough out onto a lightly floured surface. Knead enough of the remaining flour to make a moderately soft dough that is smooth and elastic (6 to 8 minutes total). Shape dough into a ball. Place dough in a lightly greased bowl, turning once to grease surface. Cover and let rise in a warm place until double (about 1 hour).

4 Punch dough down. Turn dough out onto a lightly floured surface. Divide dough in half. Cover and let rest for 10 minutes. Grease 2 baking sheets; set aside.

5 Roll each half of the dough into a 12x10-inch rectangle. Cut each rectangle into twelve 10-inch strips. Tie each strip into a loose knot. Place the knots 3 inches apart on the prepared baking sheets. Cover and let rise in a warm place until nearly double (about 30 minutes).

6 Bake in a 375° oven for 10 to 12 minutes or until lightly browned. Remove from baking sheets and place on wire racks. Drizzle with Orange Icing. Serve warm or cool. Place any cooled bowknots in a single layer in an airtight container or bag and store at room temperature for up to 3 days. Makes 24.

Orange Icing: In a small mixing bowl stir together 1½ cups sifted powdered sugar, 1 teaspoon finely shredded orange peel, and enough orange juice (2 to 3 tablespoons) to make the icing easy to drizzle.

Nutrition facts per bowknot: *141 calories, 3 g protein, 25 g carbohydrate, 3 g total fat (2 g saturated), 25 mg cholesterol, 78 mg sodium, 1 g fiber. Daily values: 3% vitamin A, 6% vitamin C, 1% calcium, 7% iron.*

Lemon Bowknots: Prepare Orange Bowknots as directed, except substitute 1 tablespoon finely shredded lemon peel for the orange peel and ¼ cup lemon juice plus ¼ cup water for the orange juice. Drizzle bowknots with Lemon Icing.

Lemon Icing: In a small mixing bowl stir together 1½ cups sifted powdered sugar, 2 teaspoons lemon juice, and enough milk (1 to 2 tablespoons) to make the icing easy to drizzle.

To Make Ahead

Prepare and bake bowknots as directed; cool completely. Do not ice. Place bowknots in a single layer in a freezer container or bag and freeze for up to 3 months. Before serving, thaw the bowknots at room temperature about 2 hours. Ice and serve as directed.

Setting Some Aside

Assuming you're lucky enough to have some leftover bread, you can keep it fresh by storing it properly.

Completely cool the bread, then place it in an airtight container or bag. Store it in a cool, dry place for 2 to 3 days. Do not refrigerate unfilled yeast bread because it will grow stale more quickly.

To freeze up to 3 months, place completely cooled, unfrosted bread in a freezer container or bag. Thaw the wrapped bread at room temperature for 2 hours. Frost sweet yeast breads after thawing.

Old-Fashioned Potato Bread

1½ cups water
1 medium potato, peeled and cubed
1 cup buttermilk
3 tablespoons granulated sugar
2 tablespoons butter or margarine
2 teaspoons salt
6 to 6½ cups all-purpose flour
2 packages active dry yeast
All-purpose flour

1 In a saucepan combine the water and potato. Bring to boiling. Cover and cook 12 minutes or until potato is very tender. Do not drain. Mash potato in the water. Measure the potato-water mixture. If necessary, add additional water to make 1¾ cups total.

2 Return potato mixture to saucepan. Add buttermilk, sugar, butter, and salt. Heat or cool and stir as necessary until warm (120° to 130°); set aside.

3 In a large mixing bowl combine 2 cups of the flour and yeast. Add the potato mixture. Beat with an electric mixer on low to medium speed for 30 seconds, scraping the sides of the bowl. Then beat on high speed 3 minutes. Using a wooden spoon, stir in as much of the remaining flour as you can.

4 Turn the dough out onto a lightly floured surface. Knead in enough of the remaining flour to make a moderately soft dough that is smooth and elastic (6 to 8 minutes total). Shape dough into a ball. Place dough in a lightly greased bowl, turning once to grease the surface of the dough. Cover and let rise in a warm place until double (45 to 60 minutes).

5 Punch dough down. Turn dough out onto a lightly floured surface. Divide dough in half. Cover and let rest for 10 minutes. Lightly grease two 8x4x2-inch loaf pans; set aside.

6 Shape each half of the dough into a loaf by gently pulling dough into a loaf shape, tucking edges beneath. Lightly dip the tops of the loaves in the additional flour. Place loaves in prepared loaf pans, flour sides up. Cover and let rise in a warm place until nearly double (about 30 minutes).

7 Bake in a 375° oven 35 to 40 minutes or until bread sounds hollow when you tap top with your fingers (if necessary, cover loosely with foil the last 15 minutes of baking to prevent overbrowning). Remove bread from pans; cool on wire racks. Cover and store at room temperature for up to 3 days. Makes 2 loaves (32 servings).

Nutrition facts per serving: *99 calories, 3 g protein, 20 g carbohydrate, 1 g total fat (1 g saturated), 2 mg cholesterol, 150 mg sodium, 1 g fiber. Daily values: 0% vitamin A, 0% vitamin C, 1% calcium, 7% iron.*

To Make Ahead

Prepare and bake bread as directed; cool completely. Place bread in freezer container or bag and freeze for up to 3 months. Before serving, thaw bread at room temperature for 2 hours.

International Origin

French Bread

Serve this traditional crusty bread with olive oil instead of butter. Pour the olive oil onto a plate, break a piece of bread off, and dip the bread into the olive oil. Add a glass of good red wine, and you have a terrific bread course.

5½ to 6 cups all-purpose flour
2 packages active-dry yeast
1½ teaspoons salt
2 cups warm water
Cornmeal
1 slightly beaten egg white
1 tablespoon water

1 In a large bowl combine 2 cups of the flour, yeast, and salt. Add warm water to flour mixture. Beat with an electric mixer on low to medium speed 30 seconds, scraping bowl. Beat on high speed 3 minutes. Stir in as much of the remaining flour as you can.

2 Turn dough out onto a floured surface. Knead in enough of the remaining flour to make a stiff dough that is smooth and elastic (8 to 10 minutes total). Shape dough into a ball. Place dough in a lightly greased bowl, turning once to grease surface. Cover and let rise in a warm place until double (about 1 hour).

3 Punch dough down. Turn out onto a lightly floured surface. Divide dough in half. Cover and let rest for 10 minutes. Lightly grease a large baking sheet; sprinkle with cornmeal. In a small mixing bowl, using a fork, beat the egg white and the 1 tablespoon water. Set the baking sheet and egg mixture aside.

4 Roll each half of the dough into a 15x10-inch rectangle. Tightly roll up, jelly-roll style, starting from one of the long sides. Seal with fingertips as you roll. Taper ends. Place loaves, seam sides down, on the prepared baking sheet. Brush loaves with some of the egg white mixture. Cover and let rise in a warm place until nearly double (30 to 40 minutes).

5 Using a very sharp knife, make 4 or 5 diagonal cuts, about ¼ inch deep, across top of each loaf. Bake in a 375° oven for 20 minutes. Brush loaves again with some of the egg white mixture. Then bake for 15 to 20 minutes

more or until bread sounds hollow when you tap the top with your fingers (if necessary, cover loosely with foil the last 10 minutes of baking to prevent overbrowning). Remove loaves from baking sheet and cool on wire racks. Place in an airtight container or bag and store at room temperature for up to 3 days. Makes 2 loaves (30 servings).

Nutrition facts per serving: *80 calories, 3 g protein, 17 g carbohydrate, 0 g total fat (0 g saturated), 0 mg cholesterol, 109 mg sodium, 1 g fiber. Daily values: 0% vitamin A, 0% vitamin C, 0% calcium, 7% iron.*

Poppy Seed French Bread: Prepare French Bread as directed, except sprinkle 1 to 2 teaspoons poppy seed on the top of the dough after the second time it's brushed with egg white mixture.

Baguettes: Prepare French Bread as directed, except divide dough into 4

equal portions. Shape each portion into a ball. Cover and let rest for 10 minutes. Roll each dough portion into a 14x8-inch rectangle. Tightly roll up, jelly-roll style, starting from one of the long sides. Seal with fingertips as you roll. Taper ends. Place loaves, seam side down, on prepared baking sheet. Brush, let rise, and slash as directed. Bake in a 375° oven for 15 minutes. Brush loaves again with some of the egg white mixture. Continue baking for 10 minutes more or until bread tests done. Remove from baking sheet. Cool on wire racks. Makes 4 baguettes (30 servings).

To Make Ahead

Prepare and bake bread as directed; cool completely. Place bread in a freezer container or bag and freeze for up to 3 months. Before serving, thaw bread at room temperature for 2 hours.

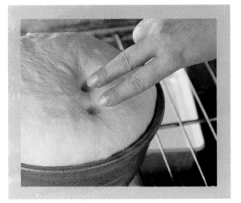

Besides a visual test, you can tell if the dough has doubled and is ready for shaping by pressing two fingers ½ inch into the dough. Remove your fingers; if the indentations remain, the dough has doubled in size and is ready to be punched down.

Tightly roll up the dough starting from a long side. Pinch with your fingertips occasionally to seal. Pinch to seal the seam. Taper the ends.

Use a serrated or other sharp knife to make approximately four or five slits in the top of the loaf. Cut them about ¼ inch deep. Slits are for decoration, so make crisscrosses or other patterns.

Wild Rice Bread

To get 1 cup cooked wild rice, start with ⅓ cup dry. Rinse rice well. In a small saucepan, bring ¾ cup water to boiling. Add rice. Simmer, covered, over low heat about 40 minutes. Drain, if necessary.

- 4¼ **to 4¾ cups all-purpose flour**
- 2 **packages active dry yeast**
- 1 **tablespoon snipped fresh parsley or 1 teaspoon dried parsley, crushed**
- 1 **teaspoon snipped fresh thyme or ¼ teaspoon dried thyme, crushed**
- 1 **cup cooked wild rice**
- 1 **cup water**
- ¼ **cup dry white wine or water**
- 3 **tablespoons butter or margarine**
- 2 **tablespoons granulated sugar**
- 1 **teaspoon instant chicken bouillon granules**
- ¼ **teaspoon salt**

1 In a large mixing bowl stir together 2 cups of the flour, the yeast, parsley, thyme, and wild rice; set aside.

2 In a medium saucepan heat and stir water, wine, butter, sugar, bouillon, and salt just until warm (120° to 130°), butter almost melts, and bouillon dissolves. Add water mixture to flour mixture. Beat with an electric mixer on low speed 30 seconds, scraping sides of bowl. Then beat on high speed 3 minutes. Sir in as much of the remaining flour as you can.

3 Turn the dough out onto a lightly floured surface. Knead in enough of the remaining flour to make a moder-ately soft dough that is smooth and elastic (6 to 8 minutes total). Shape dough into a ball. Place in a lightly greased bowl, turning once to grease surface. Cover; let rise in a warm place until double (45 minutes to 1 hour).

4 Punch dough down. Turn out onto a lightly floured surface. Divide in half. Cover and let rest for 10 minutes. Lightly grease a baking sheet; set aside.

5 Shape each half of the dough into a 6-inch round loaf, tucking edges beneath. Place the loaves 3 inches apart on the prepared baking sheet. Cover; let rise in a warm place until nearly double (30 to 40 minutes).

6 Using a sharp knife, cut an X in the top of each loaf. Bake in a 375° oven about 40 minutes or until bread sounds hollow when you tap top with your fingers (if necessary, cover loosely with foil during the last 10 minutes of baking to prevent overbrowning). Remove bread from pans and cool on wire racks. Place in an airtight container or bag and store at room temperature or in refrigerator up to 3 days. Makes 2 loaves (32 servings).

Nutrition facts per serving: *76 calories, 2 g protein, 14 g carbohydrate, 1 g total fat (1 g saturated), 3 mg cholesterol, 55 mg sodium, 1 g fiber. Daily values: 1% vitamin A, 0% vitamin C, 0% calcium, 5% iron.*

To Make Ahead

Prepare and bake bread as directed; cool completely. Place bread in a freezer container or bag and freeze for up to 3 months. Before serving, thaw bread at room temperature for 2 hours.

Things You Knead to Know

Kneading is the process used to develop the gluten that gives bread its structure. If you use the proper technique for kneading, knead the dough for the suggested time, and get a feel for the different levels of "stiffness," you'll make baking yeast breads look easy.

- ✦ *Before you start kneading, set a timer for the suggested time.*
- ✦ *Soft dough is used for breads that don't require kneading, such as batter breads. It is very sticky.*
- ✦ *Moderately soft dough is used for most sweet breads. It is slightly sticky and may be kneaded on a floured surface.*
- ✦ *Moderately stiff dough is used for most savory breads. It kneads easily on a floured surface, is not sticky, and yields slightly to the touch.*
- ✦ *Stiff dough is used for breads with chewy textures, such as French breads. It kneads easily on a lightly floured surface, is firm to the touch, and holds its shape after it is kneaded.*

Wild Rice Bread, top, and Honey-Grain Bread (see recipe, page 70), bottom

Honey-Grain Bread

To give the loaf a shiny top, beat 1 egg and 1 tablespoon of water with a fork. Brush the loaves with some of the egg mixture before baking. (Pictured on page 69.)

3 to 3½ cups all-purpose flour
2 packages active dry yeast
½ teaspoon ground cinnamon
2 cups water
¼ cup honey
¼ cup butter or margarine
¼ teaspoon salt
2½ cups whole wheat flour
1½ cups muesli

1 In a large mixing bowl stir together 2 cups of the all-purpose flour, the yeast, and cinnamon; set aside.

2 In a small saucepan heat and stir water, honey, butter, and salt just until warm (120° to 130°) and butter almost melts. Add honey mixture to the flour mixture. Beat with an electric mixer on low to medium speed for 30 seconds, scraping the sides of the bowl constantly. Then beat on high speed for 3 minutes. Using a wooden spoon, stir in whole wheat flour, muesli, and as much of the remaining all-purpose flour as you can.

3 Turn the dough out onto a lightly floured surface. Knead in enough of the remaining all-purpose flour to make a moderately soft dough that is smooth and elastic (6 to 8 minutes total). Shape the dough into a ball.

Place dough in a lightly greased bowl, turning once to grease the surface. Cover and let rise in a warm place until double (about 45 minutes).

4 Punch dough down. Turn dough out onto a lightly floured surface. Divide dough in half. Cover and let rest for 10 minutes. Lightly grease two 8x4x2-inch loaf pans; set aside.

5 Shape each half into a loaf by gently pulling into a loaf shape, tucking edges beneath. Place the shaped loaves in the prepared pans. Cover and let rise in a warm place until nearly double in size (about 30 minutes).

6 Bake in a 375° oven for 30 to 35 minutes or until bread sounds hollow when you tap the top with your fingers (if necessary, cover loosely with foil the last 10 minutes of baking to prevent overbrowning). Remove loaves from pans and cool on wire racks. Place in an airtight container or bag and store at room temperature for up to 3 days. Makes 2 loaves (32 servings).

Nutrition facts per serving: *114 calories, 3 g protein, 21 g carbohydrate, 2 g total fat (1 g saturated), 4 mg cholesterol, 44 mg sodium, 2 g fiber. Daily values:1% vitamin A, 0% vitamin C, 1% calcium, 7% iron.*

To Make Ahead

Prepare and bake bread as directed; cool completely. Place bread in a freezer container or bag and freeze for up to 3 months. Before serving, thaw bread at room temperature for 2 hours.

Shallot-Sage Bread

1 tablespoon butter or margarine
⅔ cup shallots, finely chopped (8 shallots), or green onions
6½ to 7 cups all-purpose flour
2 packages active dry yeast
1 tablespoon snipped fresh sage or 1 teaspoon dried sage, crushed
2 cups water
3 tablespoons butter or margarine
2 tablespoons granulated sugar
½ teaspoon salt

1 In a skillet melt the 1 tablespoon butter; cook shallots 2 to 3 minutes or until translucent. Set aside. In a large mixing bowl stir together 2 cups of the flour, the yeast, and sage; set aside.

2 Heat and stir water, butter, sugar, and salt just until warm (120° to 130°) and butter almost melts. Add shallots and water mixture to flour mixture. Beat with an electric mixer on low speed 30 seconds, scraping bowl. Beat on high speed 3 minutes. Stir in much of the remaining flour as you can.

3 Turn dough out onto a lightly floured surface. Knead in enough of the remaining flour to make a moderately soft dough that is smooth and elastic (6 to 8 minutes total). Shape into a ball. Place dough in a lightly greased bowl, turning once. Cover; let rise in a warm place until double (about 1 hour).

4 Punch dough down. Turn dough out onto a lightly floured surface. Divide in half. Cover; let rest 10 minutes. Grease 2 baking sheets; set aside.

5 Shape each half of the dough into a 6-inch round loaf, tucking edges beneath. Using a sharp knife or kitchen shears, make 3, evenly spaced, 3-inch cuts toward center of rounds. Place rounds on prepared baking sheets. Cover; let rise in a warm place until nearly double (30 to 40 minutes).

6 Bake in a 375° oven about 40 minutes or until done (if necessary, cover loosely with foil during the last 10 minutes of baking to prevent over-browning). Remove bread from pans; cool on wire racks. Cover and store at room temperature for up to 3 days. Makes 2 loaves (32 servings).

Nutrition facts per serving: 104 calories, 3 g protein, 19 g carbohydrate, 2 g total fat (1 g saturated), 4 mg cholesterol, 49 mg sodium, 1 g fiber. Daily values: 5% vitamin A, 0% vitamin C, 0% calcium, 8% iron.

To Make Ahead
Prepare and bake bread as directed; cool completely. Place bread in a freezer container or bag and freeze for up to 3 months. Before serving, thaw bread at room temperature for 2 hours.

Rye Bread

3¾ **to 4¼ cups all-purpose flour**
2 **packages active dry yeast**
2 **cups water**
¼ **cup packed brown sugar**
¼ **cup butter or margarine**

Cover browned bread with foil to reflect some of the dry heat from the surface. This prevents overbrowning while allowing the inside to complete cooking. Breads with some sugar and butter are more likely to overbrown and need this preventative measure.

¾ **teaspoon salt**
2 **cups rye flour**
1 **tablespoon caraway seed**

1 In a bowl combine 2½ cups of the all-purpose flour and yeast; set aside.

2 Heat and stir water, brown sugar, butter, and salt just until warm (120° to 130°) and butter almost melts. Add water mixture to flour mixture. Beat with an electric mixer 30 seconds, scraping bowl. Beat on high speed 3 minutes. Stir in rye flour, caraway seed, and as much remaining all-purpose flour as you can.

3 Turn dough out onto a lightly floured surface. Knead in enough of the remaining all-purpose flour to make a moderately soft dough that is smooth and elastic (6 to 8 minutes total). Shape the dough into a ball. Place dough in a lightly greased bowl, turning once. Cover; let rise in a warm place until double (about 1 hour).

4 Punch dough down. Turn dough out onto a lightly floured surface. Divide dough in half. Cover and let rest for 10 minutes. Lightly grease 2 8x4x2-inch loaf pans.

5 Shape each half of dough into a loaf by gently pulling dough into a loaf, tucking edges beneath. Place each shaped loaf in a prepared loaf pan. Cover; let rise in a warm place until nearly double (30 to 40 minutes).

6 Bake in a 375° oven about 40 minutes or until done (if necessary, cover with foil during the last 10 minutes of baking to prevent overbrowning). Remove from pans; cool on wire racks. Cover and store at room temperature for up to 3 days. Makes 2 loaves (32 servings).

Nutrition facts per serving: 93 calories, 2 g protein, 17 g carbohydrate, 2 g total fat (1 g saturated), 4 mg cholesterol, 66 mg sodium, 1 g fiber. Daily values: 10% vitamin A, 0% vitamin C, 0% calcium, 5% iron.

Orange-Rye Bread: Prepare Rye Bread as directed, except add 1 tablespoon finely shredded orange peel to the liquid ingredients.

To Make Ahead
Prepare bread as directed; cool completely. Place in a freezer container or bag and freeze for up to 3 months. Before serving, thaw bread at room temperature for 2 hours.

Delicious
Memories

Peda Bread

My husband and I once belonged to a gourmet dinner group where the hosts put together the menu, assigning one recipe to each participating couple and preparing the rest themselves. Though none of us had tried any of the recipes ahead of time, the meals were surprisingly successful. I made this bread for one of our dinners, and it has been a favorite ever since. When I'm entertaining, I make the dough a day ahead and pop it in the refrigerator to rise. Then I only have to bake it to have fresh, homemade bread at dinnertime.
—Lynda Haupert—

- **2 packages active dry yeast**
- **½ cup lukewarm water (105° to 115°)**
- **1¾ cup lukewarm milk (105° to 115°)**
- **2 tablespoons granulated sugar**
- **1 teaspoon salt**
- **3 tablespoons olive oil**
- **6 to 6¼ cups all-purpose flour Olive oil**
- **1 egg yolk**
- **1 tablespoon water**
- **4 tablespoons sesame seed**

1 In a large bowl dissolve yeast in warm water. Let stand 5 to 10 minutes.

2 Stir in milk, sugar, salt, and the 3 tablespoons olive oil. Add 2½ cups of the flour. Beat with an electric mixer 30 seconds, scraping bowl. Then beat on medium speed for 5 minutes. Stir in 3 cups more of the flour.

3 Turn dough out onto a lightly floured surface. Knead in enough remaining flour to make a moderately stiff dough that is smooth and elastic (8 to 10 minutes total). Cover dough with plastic wrap; let rest 20 minutes. Grease 2 baking sheets; set aside.

4 On a floured surface, knead dough to collapse air bubbles. Then pinch off 2 small (about ½ cup each) portions of dough. Set small portions aside.

5 Divide remaining dough in half. Knead each half into a smooth ball. For each loaf, shape into a 10-inch round, tucking edges beneath. Pulling your fingers in opposition, make a hole 4 inches in diameter in the center of each. Place a small portion of dough in the center of the hole and flatten it gently to fill the hole.

6 Brush loaves lightly with some of the additional olive oil. Cover with plastic wrap and refrigerate for 2 to 12 hours. When ready to bake, remove the loaves from the refrigerator. Uncover the loaves and let them stand at room temperature for 10 minutes.

7 Meanwhile, in a small mixing bowl, Beat the egg yolk and the 1 tablespoon water. Brush loaves with some egg mixture. Sprinkle with sesame seed.

8 Bake in a 350° oven 30 to 35 minutes or until crust is a deep golden brown and bread sounds hollow when you tap top with your fingers (if necessary, cover loosely with foil the last 10 minutes of baking to prevent over-browning). Cool bread slightly before cutting. Place any cooled bread in an airtight container or bag and store at room temperature for up to 3 days. Makes 2 loaves (32 servings).

Nutrition facts per serving: *116 calories, 3 g protein, 18 g carbohydrate, 3 g total fat (1 g saturated), 8 mg cholesterol, 74 mg sodium, 1 g fiber. Daily values: 1% vitamin A, 0% vitamin C, 1% calcium, 7% iron.*

To Make Ahead

Prepare and bake bread as directed; cool completely. Place bread in a freezer container or bag and freeze for up to 3 months. Before serving, thaw bread at room temperature for 2 hours.

Kid Appeal

Whole Wheat Pizza Roll

- **1½ to 2 cups all-purpose flour**
- **1 package active dry yeast**
- **1 cup milk**
- **1 tablespoon shortening**
- **½ teaspoon salt**
- **1 cup whole wheat flour**
- **8 ounces bulk sweet or hot Italian sausage**
- **1 cup finely chopped red or green sweet pepper**
- **½ cup chopped onion (1 medium)**
- **1 cup shredded mozzarella cheese (4 ounces)**
- **2 tablespoons snipped parsley**
- **1 teaspoon dried Italian seasoning, crushed**

1 **egg white**
1 **tablespoon water**
1 **tablespoon grated Parmesan
cheese**

1 In a bowl combine 1 cup of the all-purpose flour and yeast; set aside.

2 In a small saucepan heat and stir the 1 cup milk, shortening, and salt just until warm (120° to 130°) and shortening almost melts. Add milk mixture to the flour mixture. Beat with an electric mixer on low to medium speed 30 seconds, scraping sides of bowl. Then beat on high speed 3 minutes. Stir in the whole wheat flour and as much of the all-purpose flour as you can.

3 Turn the dough out onto a lightly floured surface. Knead in enough of the remaining all-purpose flour to make a moderately soft dough that is smooth and elastic (6 to 8 minutes total). Place dough in a lightly greased bowl, turning once to grease surface. Cover and let rise in a warm place until double (30 to 45 minutes).

4 For filling, in a skillet cook sausage, sweet pepper, and onion until sausage is brown. Drain well. Stir in mozzarella cheese, parsley, and Italian seasoning; set aside.

5 Punch dough down. Turn dough out onto a lightly floured surface. Divide in half. Cover; let rest 10 minutes. Grease 2 baking sheets; set aside.

6 On a lightly floured surface, roll each half of the dough into a 10x8-inch rectangle. Spread each rectangle

with half of the filling to within 1 inch of the edges. Tightly roll up, jelly-roll style, starting with one of the long sides. Seal with fingertips as you roll.

7 Place rolls, seam sides down, on prepared baking sheets. Form rolls into a crescent shape. Using a sharp knife, make cuts about 1 inch apart on top of loaves, cutting deep enough to expose 1 layer of filling. Cover; let rise in a warm place until nearly double (about 30 minutes).

8 Meanwhile, in a small mixing bowl, beat egg white and water. Brush tops of rolls with egg mixture. Sprinkle with Parmesan cheese. Bake in a 375° oven about 30 minutes or until golden. Remove from baking sheets and cool slightly on wire racks. Serve warm. Place any cooled leftovers in an airtight container or bag and store in the refrigerator for up to 3 days. Makes 2 loaves (20 servings).

Nutrition facts per serving: 222 calories, 11 g protein, 25 g carbohydrate, 8 g total fat (3 g saturated), 22 mg cholesterol, 345 mg sodium, 2 g fiber. Daily values: 9% vitamin A, 24% vitamin C, 10% calcium, 12% iron.

Pepper and Fennel Batter Bread

2½ **cups all-purpose flour**
1 **package active dry yeast**
1 **to 2 teaspoons coarsely ground
black pepper**
1 **to 2 teaspoons fennel seed,
crushed**
1 **cup cream-style cottage cheese**

¼ **cup water**
¼ **cup butter or margarine**
2 **teaspoons granulated sugar**
½ **teaspoon salt**
2 **eggs**

1 Grease a 1½-quart casserole. In a bowl combine 1 cup of the flour, yeast, pepper, and fennel. Set aside.

2 In a small saucepan heat and stir cottage cheese, water, butter, sugar, and salt just until warm (120° to 130°) and butter almost melts. Add cottage cheese mixture to flour mixture. Add eggs. Beat with an electric mixer on low to medium speed 30 seconds, scraping bowl. Beat on high speed 3 minutes. Sir in the remaining flour (batter will be sticky). Spoon batter into prepared casserole. Cover; let rise in a warm place until nearly double (50 to 60 minutes).

3 Bake in a 375° oven for 25 to 30 minutes or until golden. Remove from casserole; cool on a wire rack. Serve warm or cool. Cover cooled bread and store at room temperature for up to 3 days. Makes 1 loaf (12 servings).

Nutrition facts per serving: 157 calories, 6 g protein, 20 g carbohydrate, 6 g total fat (3 g saturated), 48 mg cholesterol, 210 mg sodium, 1 g fiber. Daily values: 5% vitamin A, 0% vitamin C, 21% calcium, 9% iron.

To Make Ahead

Prepare and bake bread as directed; cool completely. Place bread in a freezer container or bag and freeze up to 3 months. Before serving, thaw bread at room temperature for 2 hours.

Daily Breads

A day without bread is like a day without sunshine—there's just something missing. To make sure that you never have to face the prospect, we've gathered six kinds of special whole wheat breads on the next four pages. There's one for every taste and every sandwich.

Whole Wheat and
Carrot Bread

Whole Wheat and
Corn Flour Bread

Three-Seed
Bread

Four-Grain
Bread

Whole Wheat and
Tomato-Herb Bread

Four-Grain
Bread

Three-Seed
Bread

Four-Grain
Bread

Four-Grain
Bread

Whole Wheat and
Corn Flour Bread Sticks

Basic Whole Wheat Bread

3 to 3½ cups all-purpose flour
1 package active dry yeast
1¾ cups water
¼ cup packed brown sugar or
   3 tablespoons honey
3 tablespoons butter or
   margarine
1 teaspoon salt
2 cups whole wheat flour
   Half-and-half, light cream, or
   milk
   Toasted wheat germ (optional)

1 In a large mixing bowl stir together 2 cups of the all-purpose flour and the yeast; set aside.

2 In a saucepan heat and stir water, brown sugar, butter, and salt just until warm (120° to 130°) and butter almost melts. Add to flour mixture. Beat with an electric mixer on low to medium speed 30 seconds, scraping bowl. Then beat on high speed 3 minutes. Using a wooden spoon, stir in whole wheat flour and as much of the remaining all-purpose flour as you can.

3 Turn dough out onto a lightly floured surface. Knead in enough of the remaining all-purpose flour to make a moderately stiff dough that is smooth and elastic (6 to 8 minutes total). Shape into a ball. Place in a lightly greased bowl, turning dough once. Cover; let rise in a warm place until double in size (about 1 hour).

4 Punch dough down. Turn out onto a lightly floured surface. Divide dough in half. Cover and let rest 10 minutes. Meanwhile, lightly grease two 8x4x2-inch loaf pans.

5 Shape each portion of dough into a loaf by patting or rolling. To pat dough, gently pull it into a loaf shape, tucking edges underneath. To shape dough by rolling, on a lightly floured surface, roll each half into a 12x8-inch rectangle. Roll up tightly, starting with a narrow edge. Seal with your fingertips as you roll. Place the shaped loaves in the prepared pans. Cover and let rise in a warm place until nearly double in size (about 45 minutes).

6 Brush tops of loaves with half-and-half. If desired, sprinkle with toasted wheat germ. Bake in a 375° oven 40 to 45 minutes or until bread sounds hollow when you tap the top with your fingers (if necessary, cover loosely with foil the last 15 minutes of baking to prevent overbrowning). Immediately remove bread from pans. Cool on wire racks. Makes 2 loaves (32 servings).

Nutritional facts per serving: 80 calories, 1 g total fat (1 g saturated), 3 mg cholesterol, 79 mg sodium, 15 g carbohydrate, 1 g fiber, 2 g protein. Daily values: 0% vitamin A, 0% vitamin C, 0% calcium, 5% iron.

Three-Seed Bread: Prepare Basic Whole Wheat Bread as directed, except stir in ⅓ cup sunflower nuts, 2 tablespoons poppy seed, and 2 tablespoons toasted sesame seed with whole wheat flour. Knead and let rise as directed.

Punch dough down. Turn out onto a lightly floured surface. Divide dough in half. Cover; let rest for 10 minutes. Meanwhile, grease 2 baking sheets. Shape each portion into an oval or round loaf. Place on prepared baking sheets. Slightly flatten each loaf. Cover; let rise in a warm place until nearly double in size (about 45 minutes).

Brush tops of loaves with half-and-half. Sprinkle with additional sunflower nuts, poppy seed, and toasted sesame seed (about 2 teaspoons total). If desired, using a very sharp knife, cut a long slit or an X in center of loaves. Bake in a 375° oven 35 to 40 minutes or until done (if necessary, cover with foil last 15 minutes of baking to prevent overbrowning). Cool as directed.

Four-Grain Bread: In a medium mixing bowl combine ¼ cup bulgur, ¼ cup steel cut oats or cracked rye, ¼ cup millet, ¼ cup buckwheat groats or cracked wheat, and 2 cups boiling water. Cover and let stand 5 minutes; drain well. Prepare Basic Whole Wheat Bread as directed, except reduce water to 1¼ cups, increase salt to 1½ teaspoons, and reduce whole wheat flour to 1½ cups. Stir in the drained grain mixture with the whole wheat flour.

Knead, shape, and let rise as directed for the Three-Seed Bread. (Or, shape into small loaves as directed for Whole Wheat and Tomato-Herb Bread.) Brush tops of loaves with half-and-half. If desired, sprinkle with additional bulgur. Using a very sharp knife or kitchen shears, cut or snip slits in top of loaves to create texture. Bake as directed for Three-Seed Bread.

Whole Wheat and Carrot Bread: Make a carrot purée by peeling 12 ounces of carrots (3 to 4 medium) and cutting them into 2-inch pieces. Cook, covered, in $\frac{1}{3}$ cup boiling water for 15 to 20 minutes or until very tender. Cool slightly (do not drain). Place cooked carrots and water in a food processor bowl or blender container. Cover; process or blend until smooth. You should have $\frac{3}{4}$ cup carrot purée.

Prepare Basic Whole Wheat Bread as directed, except reduce water to 1 cup and stir in the $\frac{3}{4}$ cup carrot purée; heat mixture as directed. Knead dough and let rise as directed.

Punch dough down. Turn dough out onto a lightly floured surface. Divide dough in half. Cover and let rest 10 minutes. Thoroughly flour two $1\frac{1}{2}$- to 2-quart tightly woven baskets or wooden bowls. Shape each half of dough into a ball. Place each ball in a prepared basket or bowl. Sprinkle tops with 1 tablespoon all-purpose flour. Cover; let rise in a warm place until nearly double (about 45 minutes).

Grease 2 baking sheets. Invert each basket onto a prepared baking sheet. Bake in a 375° oven 35 to 40 minutes or until done (if necessary, cover with foil last 15 minutes of baking to prevent overbrowning). Cool as directed.

Whole Wheat and Tomato-Herb Bread: Prepare Basic Whole Wheat Bread as directed, except reduce water to $1\frac{1}{2}$ cups and add one 6-ounce can tomato paste, 1 tablespoon snipped fresh basil, and 1 tablespoon snipped fresh oregano (or $1\frac{1}{2}$ teaspoons dried Italian seasoning, crushed) to the water before heating. Knead dough and let rise as directed.

Punch dough down. Turn dough out onto a lightly floured surface. Divide dough in half. Cut each half into 5 pieces, making 10 pieces total. Shape into balls. Cover and let rest 10 minutes. Grease a large baking sheet. Shape each ball into a 5-inch loaf; taper ends. Place loaves 2 inches apart on prepared baking sheet. Cover and let rise in a warm place until nearly double (about 35 minutes).

Brush tops of loaves with half-and-half. Sprinkle with $\frac{1}{2}$ teaspoon crushed dried Italian seasoning. With a very sharp knife, cut a slit or an X down the center of each loaf. Bake in a 375° oven 30 minutes or until done (if necessary, cover loosely with foil the last 15 minutes of baking to prevent overbrowning). Cool as directed.

Whole Wheat and Corn Flour Bread: Prepare Basic Whole Wheat Bread as directed, except reduce whole wheat flour to $1\frac{1}{2}$ cups. Stir in $\frac{1}{2}$ cup masa harina (corn flour) with whole wheat flour. Knead and let rise as directed for Whole Wheat and Tomato-Herb Bread.

Punch down dough. Turn out onto a lightly floured surface. Divide dough in half. Cover and let rest 10 minutes. Grease 2 baking sheets and sprinkle with cornmeal. To make a twisted loaf, divide each half into two 15-inch-long ropes. Twist 2 ropes together and seal the ends. Place twists on prepared baking sheets. Cover and let rise in a warm place until double (about 45 minutes). (Or, to make bread sticks, roll each half of dough into a 10x8-inch rectangle. Cut each rectangle into twenty $\frac{1}{2}$-inch-wide strips. Brush strips with half-and-half; sprinkle with cornmeal. Twist each strip and place on a lightly greased baking sheet).

Brush dough with half-and-half; sprinkle with 2 teaspoons cornmeal. Bake loaves as directed for Whole Wheat and Tomato-Herb Bread (Bake bread sticks in a 375° oven for 15 to 18 minutes or until lightly browned). Cool as directed.

Rising to the Top

Those who are privy to bread-making particulars know the fundamental rules for achieving a light, delicate texture, a crisp crust, and a tender crumb. The rules are not difficult and definitely are satisfying.

♦ Check the temperature of the heated liquid mixture with a thermometer to make sure it's just right; if it's too hot or too cold, your bread won't rise.

♦ Use just enough flour when kneading the bread to make the dough the proper stiffness or your bread will be heavy and compact. Never use more than the maximum amount specified in the recipe.

♦ Knead dough by folding it over and pushing down with the heel of your hand, curving your fingers over the dough. Give the dough a quarter turn, fold it over, and push down again. Continue this fold-push-turn procedure until the dough is smooth and elastic.

♦ Proof (raise) your dough in a draft-free area between 80° and 85° just until double for the first rise and just until nearly double for the second rise. To use your oven for proofing, place the bowl of dough in an unheated oven; set a large pan of hot water underneath on the oven's lower rack.

♦ Don't let the dough rise above the top of the pan because the dough needs room to rise more as it bakes.

Use an oven thermometer to check the temperature of your oven before baking. If it is too low, your bread is likely to be heavy and have a thick crust.

♦ Bake several long, individual or round loaves of bread at the same time on an extra-large (17x14-inch) baking sheet. If you don't have one, shape the loaves on two smaller baking sheets; let them rise as directed. Put one in the refrigerator, and bake the other. Don't bake the two smaller sheets at the same time as it inhibits the air circulation in the oven and the loaves won't bake evenly.

♦ Check bread for doneness by tapping top of loaf with your fingers. If it sounds hollow, bread is done. (Check rolls and coffee cakes for golden brown tops.)

♦ Brush the top of baked bread with butter or margarine when you take it out of the oven for a soft and shiny crust. Brush with milk, water, or beaten egg before baking for a glossy, crispy crust.

*Notes*_____

_____

_____

_____

Wheat and Oat Brown-and-Serve Rolls

½ **cup cracked wheat**
1 **cup boiling water**
5¾ **to 6¼ cups all-purpose flour**
1 **package active dry yeast**
1 **cup milk**
¼ **cup packed brown sugar**
¼ **cup butter or margarine**
½ **teaspoon salt**
2 **eggs**
1 **cup quick-cooking rolled oats**
   Butter or margarine, melted (optional)

1 Combine cracked wheat and boiling water. Let stand 10 minutes. Do not drain. In a large mixing bowl stir together 1½ cups of the flour and the yeast; set aside.

2 Heat and stir milk, brown sugar, the ¼ cup butter, and salt just until warm (120° to 130°) and butter melts. Add milk mixture to flour mixture. Add eggs. Beat with an electric mixer 30 seconds, scraping bowl. Beat on high speed 3 minutes. Stir in cracked wheat mixture and rolled oats. Stir in as much remaining flour as you can.

3 Turn dough out onto a floured surface. Knead in enough remaining flour to make a moderately soft dough that is smooth and elastic (6 to 8 minutes). Shape dough into a ball. Place in a lightly greased bowl, turning once. Cover and let rise in a warm place until double (about 1 hour).

4 Punch dough down. Turn dough out onto a lightly floured surface. Divide dough into 24 portions. Cover and let rest for 10 minutes. Grease 2 baking sheets; set aside.

5 Shape each portion into a smooth ball, tucking edges under. Place balls, smooth sides up, on prepared baking sheets. Using kitchen shears, on top of each ball make 5 snips from outside edge to center, creating a flower shape. Cover; let rise in a warm place until nearly double (about 30 minutes).

6 Bake in a 325° oven 10 minutes. Do not brown. Cool on wire racks. Place in a freezer container and freeze for up to 3 months. Before serving, thaw rolls in container at room temperature for 10 minutes. Place rolls on ungreased baking sheets and bake in a 375° oven 10 to 12 minutes or until golden. If desired, brush tops with melted butter. Serve warm. Place any cooled rolls in an airtight container or bag and store at room temperature up to 3 days. Makes 24 rolls.

Nutrition facts per roll: 156 calories, 5 g protein, 27 g carbohydrate, 3 g total fat (2 g saturated), 24 mg cholesterol, 76 mg sodium, 1 g fiber. Daily values: 3% vitamin A, 0% vitamin C, 1% calcium, 10% iron.

Butter Rosettes

5½ **to 6 cups all purpose flour**
2 **packages active dry yeast**
1 **cup water**
½ **cup milk**
½ **cup butter or margarine**
2 **tablespoons granulated sugar**

Tie the 12-inch rope in a single, loose knot. Tuck the top end under the roll. Then bring the bottom end up and tuck it into the center of the roll.

¾ **teaspoon salt**
2 **eggs**
1 **egg yolk**
1 **tablespoon water**

1 In a large mixing bowl combine 2 cups of the flour and yeast; set aside.

2 In a saucepan heat and stir water, milk, butter, sugar, and salt just until warm (120° to 130°) and butter melts. Add milk mixture to flour mixture. Add 2 whole eggs. Beat with an electric mixer 30 seconds, scraping bowl. Beat on high speed 3 minutes. Stir in as much remaining flour as you can.

3 Turn dough out onto a floured surface. Knead in enough remaining flour to make a moderately soft dough that is smooth and elastic (6 to 8 minutes total). Shape into a ball. Place dough in a lightly greased bowl, turning once to grease the surface of the dough. Cover and let rise in a warm place until double (about 1 hour).

4 Punch dough down. Turn out onto a lightly floured surface. Divide dough in half. Cover and let rest for 10 minutes. Grease 2 baking sheets.

5 Divide each half of the dough into 12 pieces. To shape rolls, roll each piece into a 12-inch rope, and tie it in a loose knot. Tuck top end under roll. Then bring bottom end up and tuck it into center of roll. Place rolls 3 inches apart on prepared baking sheets. Cover; let rise in a warm place until double in size (for 30 to 40 minutes).

6 Beat egg yolk and 1 tablespoon water. Brush over rolls. Bake in a 375°oven 12 minutes or until golden. Remove from baking sheets; cool on wire racks. Cover; store at room temperature up to 3 days. Makes 24.

Nutrition facts per roll: 146 calories, 4 g protein, 22 g carbohydrate, 5 g total fat (3 g saturated), 37 mg cholesterol, 114 mg sodium, 1 g fiber. Daily values: 5% vitamin A, 0% vitamin C, 1% calcium, 9% iron.

Shortcut

Prepare the dough and place it in the greased bowl. Cover with oiled waxed paper and then plastic wrap. Place in the refrigerator 2 to 24 hours. When you're ready to use it, let stand at room temperature 20 minutes.

To Make Ahead

Prepare and bake rolls as directed; cool completely. Place rolls in a single layer in a freezer container or bag and freeze for up to 3 months. To serve, thaw rolls at room temperature for 2 hours.

Soft Pretzels

4 to 4½ cups all-purpose flour
1 package active dry yeast
1½ cups milk
¼ cup granulated sugar
2 tablespoons cooking oil
1 teaspoon salt
2 tablespoons salt
3 quarts boiling water
1 egg white
1 tablespoon water
  Sesame seed, poppy seed, or
    coarse salt
  Cheddar Sauce (optional)

1 In a large mixing bowl combine 1½ cups of the flour and yeast, set aside.

2 In a medium saucepan heat and stir milk, sugar, oil, and the 1 teaspoon salt just until warm (120° to 130°) and butter almost melts. Add milk mixture to the flour mixture. Beat with an electric mixer on low to medium speed for 30 seconds, scraping sides of bowl. Beat on high speed for 3 minutes. Using a wooden spoon, stir in as much of the remaining flour as you can.

3 Turn dough out onto a lightly floured surface. Knead in enough of the remaining flour to make a moderately soft dough that is smooth and elastic (6 to 8 minutes total). Shape the dough into a ball. Place dough in a lightly greased bowl, turning once to grease the surface of the dough. Cover and let rise in a warm place until double in size (about 1¼ hours).

4 Punch dough down. Turn dough out onto a lightly floured surface.

Cover and let rest for 10 minutes. Grease 2 baking sheets; set aside.

5 Roll dough into a 12x10-inch rectangle. Cut rectangle into twenty 12x½-inch strips. Gently pull each strip into a rope about 16 inches long. Shape into a pretzel. Place pretzels ½ inch apart on prepared baking sheets. Bake in a 475° oven for 4 minutes. Remove from oven. Reduce oven temperature to 350°.

6 Meanwhile, in a large saucepan dissolve the 2 tablespoons salt in the boiling water. Reduce heat. Lower pretzels, 4 or 5 at a time, into simmering water. Simmer for 2 minutes, turning once. Remove with a slotted spoon and drain on paper towels. Let stand on towels only a few seconds. (If left too long, they will stick.) Place pretzels ½ inch apart on well-greased baking sheets.

7 In a small mixing bowl use a fork to beat the egg white and water. Brush tops of the pretzels with some of the egg mixture. Lightly sprinkle tops of pretzels with sesame seed.

8 Bake in the 350° oven 20 to 25 minutes or until golden. Remove pretzels from baking sheets and cool on wire racks. If desired, serve with Cheddar Sauce. Cover and store at room temperature up to 3 days. Makes 20.

Nutrition facts per pretzel: *119 calories, 3 g protein, 21 g carbohydrate, 2 g total fat (0 g saturated), 1 mg cholesterol, 226 mg sodium, 1 g fiber. Daily values: 1% vitamin A, 0% vitamin C, 2% calcium, 7% iron.*

Shape each pretzel by crossing one end over the other to form a circle, overlapping about 4 inches from the ends. Take one end of dough in each hand and twist once at the crossover point. Lay each end across to the circle's opposite edge. Moisten ends, tuck under, and press to seal.

Cheddar Sauce: In a small saucepan melt 1 tablespoon butter or margarine. Stir in 4 teaspoons all-purpose flour and a dash ground red pepper. Add ½ cup milk all at once. Cook and stir over medium heat until mixture thickens and is bubbly. Cook and stir 1 minute. Stir in ½ cup shredded cheddar cheese (2 ounces) until melted.

Whole Wheat Soft Pretzels: Prepare Soft Pretzels as directed, except substitute 1½ cups whole wheat flour for 1½ cups of the stirred-in all-purpose flour.

To Make Ahead

Prepare and bake pretzels as directed; cool completely. Place pretzels in a freezer container or bag and freeze for up to 3 months. Before serving, thaw pretzels overnight in the refrigerator.

Bagels

By broiling, boiling, and baking, you'll be able to achieve a distinctive crusty outside and a chewy inside— the trademark texture of real bagels.

  4 to 4 ½ cups all-purpose flour
  1 package active dry yeast
1½ cups warm water (120° to 130°)
  2 tablespoons granulated sugar
1½ teaspoons salt
  1 tablespoon granulated sugar
  1 beaten egg

1 In a large mixing bowl combine 2 cups of the flour and the yeast. Add the warm water, the 2 tablespoons sugar, and salt. Beat with an electric mixer on low to medium speed 30 seconds, scraping bowl. Beat on high speed 3 minutes. Stir in as much of the remaining flour as you can.

2 Turn dough out onto a floured surface. Knead in enough remaining flour to make a moderately soft dough that is smooth and elastic (6 to 8 minutes total). Cover; let rest 10 minutes. Grease 2 baking sheets; set aside.

3 Working quickly, divide dough into 12 portions. Shape each portion into a smooth ball. Cover; let rest 5 minutes. With a floured finger, punch a 2-inch hole in center of each, keeping a uniform shape. Place bagels 2 inches apart on prepared baking sheets. Reshape so holes are 2 inches in diameter. Cover; let rise 20 minutes (start timing after first bagel is shaped).

4 Broil raised bagels 5 inches from heat 3 to 4 minutes or until bagels look set, turning once (tops should not brown). Meanwhile, in a 12-inch skillet or 4½-quart Dutch oven, bring 6 cups water and the 1 tablespoon sugar to boiling. Reduce heat; simmer bagels, 4 or 5 at a time, 7 minutes, turning once. Drain on paper towels. Let stand on towels only a few seconds. (If left too long, they will stick.)

5 Place drained bagels 2 inches apart on prepared baking sheets. Brush bagels with beaten egg. Bake in a 375° oven 20 to 25 minutes or until tops are golden. Remove from baking sheets; cool on wire racks. Place in an airtight container and store at room temperature for up to 2 days. Makes 12 bagels.

Nutrition facts per bagel: 160 calories, 5 g protein, 33 g carbohydrate, 1 g total fat (0 g saturated), 18 mg cholesterol, 273 mg sodium, 1 g fiber. Daily values: 0% vitamin A, 0% vitamin C, 0% calcium, 12% iron.

Egg Bagels: Prepare Bagels as directed, except reduce warm water to 1¼ cups. Add 2 egg yolks to the flour mixture along with the warm water.

Onion Bagels: Prepare Bagels as directed, except omit brushing with egg. Cook ½ cup finely chopped onion in 3 tablespoons butter or margarine until tender but not brown. Brush bagels with onion mixture after the first 15 minutes of baking.

Flour your hands to shape bagels. With your finger, punch a hole in the center of each ball. Using four fingers, gently pull the dough to make a 2-inch hole. While pulling, try to keep each bagel uniform in shape.

Poppy Seed or Sesame Bagels: Prepare Bagels as directed, except before baking, sprinkle with 2 teaspoons poppy seed or toasted sesame seed.

Light Rye Bagels: Prepare Bagels as directed, except substitute 1¼ cups rye flour for 1¼ cups of the stirred-in all-purpose flour. Stir in 1 teaspoon caraway seed with the rye flour.

Whole Wheat Bagels: Prepare Bagels as directed, except substitute 1½ cups whole wheat flour for 1½ cups of the stirred-in all-purpose flour.

To Make Ahead
Prepare bagels as directed; cool completely. Place bagels in a freezer container or bag and freeze for up to 3 months. Before serving, thaw bagels at room temperature for several hours.

Sourdough Starter

To make sure you get the right fermentation process going, don't use quick-rising yeast to make this starter.

  1 **package active dry yeast**
2½ **cups lukewarm water
      (105° to 115°)**
  2 **cups all-purpose flour**
  1 **tablespoon granulated sugar
      or honey**

1 In a large mixing bowl dissolve yeast in ½ cup of the lukewarm water. Stir in remaining water, the flour, and sugar. Stir until smooth. Cover the bowl with 100% cotton cheesecloth. Let stand at room temperature (75° to 85°) for 5 to 10 days or until the mixture has a sour, fermented aroma, stirring 2 or 3 times each day. (Fermentation time depends upon the room temperature; a warmer room speeds fermentation.)

2 When mixture has fermented, transfer to a 1-quart covered plastic container. If you haven't used starter within 10 days, stir in 1 teaspoon granulated sugar or honey. Repeat every 10 days until starter is used.

3 To use Sourdough Starter, bring the desired amount to room temperature. For every 1 cup of starter used, stir ¾ cup all-purpose flour, ¾ cup water, and 1 teaspoon granulated sugar or honey into the remaining starter. Cover and let the remaining starter stand at room temperature at least 1 day or until bubbly. Then refrigerate for later use. Makes about 2 cups.

Cheesy Vegetable-Sourdough Twist

Test Kitchen home economist Kay Cargill says this bread is just "dandy" toasted.

  1 **cup Sourdough Starter
      (at left)**
5½ **to 6 cups all-purpose flour**
  1 **package active dry yeast**
  3 **tablespoons granulated sugar**
1½ **teaspoons salt**
1½ **cups warm water (120° to 130°)**
  3 **tablespoons cooking oil**
  1 **cup shredded cheddar cheese
      (4 ounces)**
  ½ **cup finely chopped red sweet
      pepper**
  ⅓ **cup finely shredded carrot**
  ⅓ **cup thinly sliced green onion**

1 Bring Sourdough Starter to room temperature.

2 In a large mixing bowl combine 2½ cups of the flour, the yeast, sugar, and salt. Add water, oil, and Sourdough Starter. Beat with an electric mixer on low to medium speed 30 seconds, scraping sides of bowl. Then beat on high speed 3 minutes. Using a wooden spoon, stir in cheese, red sweet pepper, carrot, green onion, and as much of the remaining flour as you can.

3 Turn the dough out onto a lightly floured surface. Knead in enough of the remaining flour to make a moderately soft dough that is smooth and elastic (6 to 8 minutes total). Shape the dough into a ball. Place dough in a lightly greased bowl, turning once to grease the surface of the dough. Cover and let rise in a warm place until double (45 to 60 minutes).

4 Punch dough down. Turn dough out onto a lightly floured surface. Divide dough into fourths. Cover and let rest for 10 minutes. Lightly grease two 8x4x2- or 9x5x3-inch loaf pans; set aside.

5 Shape each fourth of the dough into a 12-inch rope. Twist 2 of the ropes together. Place twist in a prepared loaf pan, tucking under ends. Repeat with remaining 2 ropes in the other pan. Cover; let rise in a warm place until nearly double (about 30 minutes).

6 Bake in a 375° oven for 35 to 40 minutes or until bread sounds hollow when you tap the top with your fingers (if necessary, cover with foil the last 10 minutes to prevent overbrowning). Remove loaves from pans and cool on wire racks. Place in an airtight container or bag and store at room temperature or in the refrigerator for up to 3 days. Makes 2 loaves (32 servings).

Nutrition facts per serving: 113 calories, 3 g protein, 19 g carbohydrate, 3 g total fat (1 g saturated), 4 mg cholesterol, 123 mg sodium, 1 g fiber. Daily values: 6% vitamin A, 5% vitamin C, 2% calcium, 7% iron.

To Make Ahead

Prepare and bake bread as directed; cool completely. Place bread in a freezer container or bag and freeze for up to 3 months. Before serving, thaw bread at room temperature for 2 hours.

*Cheesy Vegetable-
Sourdough Twist*

Sourdough Bread

Traditional sourdough bread has a chewy texture and a distinctive tang that makes it perfect plain, for toast, or as a base for a fresh herb bread.

**1 cup Sourdough Starter
      (see page 82)**
5½ to 6 cups all-purpose flour
1 package active dry yeast
1½ cups water
3 tablespoons granulated sugar
**3 tablespoons butter or
      margarine**
**1 teaspoon salt
      Cornmeal**

1 Bring Sourdough Starter to room temperature. In a large mixing bowl stir together 2½ cups of the flour and the yeast; set aside.

2 In a small saucepan heat and stir water, sugar, butter, and salt just until warm (120° to 130°) and butter almost melts. Add water mixture to flour mixture. Add Sourdough Starter. Beat with an electric mixer on low to medium speed for 30 seconds, scraping the sides of the bowl constantly. Beat on high speed for 3 minutes. Using a wooden spoon, stir in as much of the remaining flour as you can.

3 Turn the dough out onto a lightly floured surface. Knead in enough of the remaining flour to make a moderately stiff dough that is smooth and elastic (8 to 10 minutes total). Shape dough into a ball. Place dough in a lightly greased bowl, turning once to grease the surface of the dough. Cover and let rise in a warm place until double (45 to 60 minutes).

4 Punch dough down. Turn out onto a lightly floured surface. Divide in half. Cover and let rest 10 minutes. Lightly grease a large baking sheet. Sprinkle with cornmeal; set aside.

5 Shape each half of the dough into a ball. Flatten balls slightly to 6 inches in diameter. Place dough rounds 3 inches apart on the prepared baking sheet. Using a sharp knife, cut crisscross slashes about ¼ inch deep across the tops of the loaves. Cover and let rise in a warm place until nearly double in size (about 30 minutes).

6 Bake in a 375° oven for 30 to 35 minutes or until the bread sounds hollow when you tap the top with your fingers (if necessary, cover loosely with foil the last 15 minutes of baking to prevent overbrowning). Cool on wire racks. Place in an airtight container and store at room temperature up to 3 days. Makes 2 loaves (32 servings).

Nutrition facts per serving: 99 calories, 3 g protein, 19 g carbohydrate, 1 g total fat (1 g saturated), 3 mg cholesterol, 79 mg sodium, 1 g fiber. Daily values: 0% vitamin A, 0% vitamin C, 0% calcium, 7% iron.

To Make Ahead

Prepare and bake bread as directed; cool completely. Place bread in a freezer container or bag and freeze for up to 3 months. Before serving, thaw bread overnight in the refrigerator.

Wheat Germ Sourdough Bread

To bring the Sourdough Starter to room temperature more quickly, set the measuring cup in a bowl of warm water for a few minutes.

**1 cup Sourdough Starter
      (see page 82)**
5¼ to 5¾ cups all-purpose flour
1 package active dry yeast
1½ cups water
3 tablespoons granulated sugar
**3 tablespoons butter or
      margarine**
1 teaspoon salt
½ cup toasted wheat germ

1 Bring Sourdough Starter to room temperature. In a large mixing bowl stir together 2½ cups of the flour and the yeast; set aside.

2 In a small saucepan heat and stir the water, sugar, butter, and salt just until warm (120° to 130°) and butter almost melts. Add water mixture to flour mixture. Add Sourdough Starter. Beat with an electric mixer on low to medium speed 30 seconds, scraping the sides of the bowl. Then beat on high speed for 3 minutes. Using a wooden spoon, stir in the wheat germ and as much of the remaining flour as you can.

3 Turn the dough out onto a lightly floured surface. Knead in enough of the remaining flour to make a moderately soft dough that is smooth and elastic (6 to 8 minutes total). Shape dough into a ball. Place dough in a lightly greased bowl, turning once to grease the surface dough. Cover and let rise in a warm place until double (45 to 60 minutes).

4 Punch dough down. Turn dough out onto a lightly floured surface. Divide dough in half. Cover and let rest for 10 minutes. Grease 2 baking sheets; set aside.

5 Shape each half of the dough by gently pulling it into a round loaf, tucking edges beneath. Place each round loaf onto a prepared baking sheet. Flatten each loaf slightly to 6 inches in diameter. Cover and let rise in a warm place until nearly double in size (about 30 minutes).

6 Bake in a 375° oven for 30 to 35 minutes or until bread sounds hollow when you tap the top with your fingers (if necessary, cover loosely with foil the last 10 minutes of baking to prevent overbrowning). Remove bread from pans and cool on wire racks. Place in an airtight container or bag and store at room temperature for up to 3 days. Makes 2 loaves (32 servings).

Nutrition facts per serving: *101 calories, 3 g protein, 19 g carbohydrate, 2 g total fat (1 g saturated), 3 mg cholesterol, 79 mg sodium, 1 g fiber. Daily values: 0% vitamin A, 0% vitamin C, 0% calcium, 8% iron.*

To Make Ahead

Prepare and bake bread as directed; cool completely. Place bread in a freezer container or bag and freeze for up to 3 months. Before serving, thaw bread at room temperature for 2 hours.

Fig-Sourdough Coffee Cake

If you would like to reduce the calories, use a reduced-fat or fat-free sour cream.

½ **cup Sourdough Starter (see page 82)**
1 **8-ounce carton dairy sour cream**
½ **cup peach preserves**
1 **teaspoon honey**
1¼ **cups all-purpose flour**
¾ **cup granulated sugar**
1 **teaspoon baking powder**
¼ **teaspoon baking soda**
¼ **teaspoon salt**
⅓ **cup butter or margarine**
1 **beaten egg**
1 **teaspoon vanilla**
1 **cup finely chopped dried figs or dried dates**

1 Bring Sourdough Starter to room temperature. Grease a 9x9x2-inch baking pan; set aside.

2 For topping, in a small bowl stir together sour cream, peach preserves, and honey. Cover and refrigerate.

3 In a large mixing bowl stir together flour, sugar, baking powder, baking soda, and salt. Using a pastry blender, cut in butter until mixture resembles fine crumbs. Set dry mixture aside.

4 In a small mixing bowl stir together the Sourdough Starter, egg, and vanilla. Add sourdough mixture to dry mixture. Stir just until moistened. Fold in the figs.

5 Spread batter evenly in prepared baking pan. Bake in a 350° oven about 35 minutes or until a wooden toothpick inserted near the center comes out clean. Cool on a wire rack for 15 minutes. Serve warm or cool with a dollop of topping. Place any cooled coffee cake in an airtight container and store in the refrigerator for up to 3 days. Makes 1 loaf (9 servings).

Nutrition facts per serving: *373 calories, 5 g protein, 62 g carbohydrate, 13 g total fat (8 g saturated), 53 mg cholesterol, 229 mg sodium, 3 g fiber. Daily values: 13% vitamin A, 1% vitamin C, 9% calcium, 12% iron.*

Fig and Nut Coffee Cake: Prepare Fig-Sourdough Coffee Cake as directed, except fold in ½ cup chopped hazelnuts (filberts) or pecans in with the figs.

Fig and Cranberry Coffee Cake: Prepare Fig-Sourdough Coffee Cake as directed, except increase the granulated sugar to 1 cup and fold in ¾ coarsely chopped cranberries with the figs.

To Make Ahead

Prepare and bake coffee cake as directed; cool completely. Remove cake from pan and place in a freezer container or bag and freeze for up to 3 months. Before serving, thaw coffee cake at room temperature for 2 hours. Or, to reheat, wrap the frozen coffee cake in foil and bake in a 300° oven about 25 minutes or until warm.

Gouda Cheese Roll-Up

Gouda Cheese Roll-Up

For a more shallow loaf, use a 9-inch loaf pan.

1 **cup Sourdough Starter (see page 82)**
3½ **to 4 cups all-purpose flour**
1 **package active dry yeast**
3 **tablespoons granulated sugar**
¾ **teaspoon salt**
1½ **cups warm water (120° to 130°)**
3 **tablespoons cooking oil**
2 **cups rye flour**
1 **cup shredded Gouda cheese (4 ounces)**
½ **cup finely chopped toasted pecans**
  Butter or margarine, melted (optional)

1 Bring Sourdough Starter to room temperature.

2 In a large mixing bowl stir together 2 cups of the flour, the yeast, sugar, and salt. Add the warm water, oil, and the Sourdough Starter. Beat with an electric mixer on low to medium speed for 30 seconds, scraping the sides of the bowl constantly. Then beat on high speed for 3 minutes. Using a wooden spoon, stir in the rye flour and as much of the remaining all-purpose flour as you can.

3 Turn the dough out onto a lightly floured surface. Knead in enough of the remaining all-purpose flour to make a moderately soft dough that is smooth and elastic (6 to 8 minutes total). Shape the dough into a ball. Place dough in a lightly greased bowl, turning once to grease the surface. Cover and let rise in a warm place until double (about 1 hour).

4 Punch dough down. Turn dough out onto a lightly floured surface. Divide dough in half. Cover and let rest 10 minutes. Lightly grease two 8x4x2-inch loaf pans. In a small mixing bowl stir together cheese and nuts. Set pans and cheese mixture aside.

5 Roll each half of the dough into a 12x8-inch rectangle. Sprinkle each rectangle with half of the cheese mixture. Tightly roll up each rectangle, jelly-roll style, starting from a short side. Seal with fingertips as you roll. Place rolls, seam sides down, in prepared pans. Cover and let rise in a warm place until nearly double (45 to 60 minutes).

6 Bake in a 375° oven for 35 to 40 minutes or until bread sounds hollow when you tap the top with your fingers (if necessary, cover loosely with foil the last 10 minutes of baking to prevent overbrowning). Remove loaves from pans and cool on wire racks. Place in an airtight container or bag and store in the refrigerator for up to 3 days. Makes 2 loaves (32 servings).

Nutrition facts per serving: *135 calories, 4 g protein, 19 g carbohydrate, 5 g total fat (2 g saturated), 9 mg cholesterol, 115 mg sodium, 1 g fiber. Daily values: 1% vitamin A, 0% vitamin C, 4% calcium, 6% iron.*

Wheat and Havarti Cheese Roll-Up: Prepare Gouda Cheese Roll-Up as directed, except substitute 2 cups whole wheat flour for rye flour, and substitute 1 cup shredded Havarti cheese (4 ounces) for Gouda cheese.

To Make Ahead

Prepare and bake bread as directed; cool completely. Place bread in a freezer container or bag and freeze for up to 3 months. Before serving, thaw bread overnight in the refrigerator.

Lofty Loaves

Most baking procedures, including those for yeast breads, must be adapted for high altitudes. Not only are flours drier at high altitudes, so they absorb more liquid, but the higher the altitude, the faster the bread dough may rise. Because this can cause the final loaf to be coarse in texture, only let the dough rise until nearly double. If you want to give the yeast flavor more time to develop, punch the dough down once, and let it rise a second time.

Conventional Wisdom

There's no great secret to converting conventional yeast bread recipes for use in your bread machine. Just follow these tips:

♦ *Reduce the amount of flour to 2 cups for a 1-pound machine or 3 cups for a 1½-pound machine.*

♦ *Reduce all ingredients by the same proportion, including the yeast (one package equals about 2¼ teaspoons). If a range is given for flour, use the lower amount to figure the reduction proportion. For example, for a 1½-pound bread machine, a recipe calling for 4½ to 5 cups flour and 1 package yeast would be decreased by ⅓ to 3 cups flour and 1½ teaspoons yeast.*

♦ *If the bread uses two or more types of flour, add the flour amounts together and use that total as the basis for reducing the recipe. The total amount of flour used should be only 2 or 3 cups, depending on the size of your machine.*

♦ *Use bread flour instead of all-purpose flour or add 1 to 2 tablespoons gluten flour (available at health food stores) to the all-purpose flour. Rye breads usually need 1 tablespoon of gluten flour even when bread flour is used.*

♦ *Make sure the liquids in the recipe are at room temperature before starting.*

♦ *Measure the ingredients as you would for any other recipe, but add them in the order specified by the bread machine manufacturer.*

♦ *Add dried fruits or nuts at the raisin-bread cycle, if your machine has one. If it does not, add them according to the manufacturer's directions.*

♦ *Do not use light-color dried fruits, such as apricots and light raisins, because the preservatives added to them can inhibit yeast performance. Choose another fruit or use the dough cycle and lightly knead in the fruit by hand before shaping the loaves.*

(Note: When making the dough only, it may be necessary to knead in a little more flour after removing the dough from the bread machine and before shaping it. Knead in just enough additional flour to make the dough easy to handle. If necessary, let the dough rest 5 minutes before shaping it. The dough is extremely elastic and letting it rest makes it easier to shape.)

♦ *For breads containing whole wheat or rye flour, use the whole-wheat cycle, if your machine has one. For sweet or rich breads, use the light-color setting or sweet-bread cycle, if your machine has one. Watch the bread carefully because with some machines, using the sweet-bread cycle may result in a product that is slightly underdone or gummy in the center.*

♦ *The first time you try a new bread in your machine, watch and listen carefully. Check the dough after the first 3 to 5 minutes of kneading. If your machine works excessively hard during the mixing cycle, if the dough looks dry and crumbly, or if two or more balls of dough form, add 1 to 2 tablespoons of extra liquid. If the dough looks extremely soft and is unable to form a ball, add more flour, 1 tablespoon at a time, until a ball does form. For future reference, record how much additional liquid or flour was added.*

Quick-Method Croissants

Our easy-mix method saves you time without sacrificing the taste and texture of your croissants.

1½	**cups cold butter (no substitutes)**
3	**cups all-purpose flour**
1½	**cups all-purpose flour**
1	**package active dry yeast**
1¼	**cups milk**
¼	**cup granulated sugar**
¼	**teaspoon salt**
1	**egg**
¼	**to ½ cup all-purpose flour**
1	**egg**
1	**tablespoon water or milk**

1 Cut butter into ½-inch slices. In a medium mixing bowl stir butter slices into the 3 cups flour until slices are coated and separated. Chill butter mixture while preparing the dough.

2 For dough, in a large mixing bowl combine the 1½ cups flour and the yeast; set aside. In a medium saucepan heat and stir the milk, sugar, and salt just until warm (120° to 130°). Add milk mixture to flour mixture. Add 1 egg. Beat with an electric mixer on low to medium speed 30 seconds, scraping the sides of the bowl. Beat on high speed 3 minutes. Using a wooden spoon, stir in the chilled flour-butter mixture until flour is well moistened (butter will remain in large pieces).

3 Sprinkle a pastry cloth or surface with ¼ cup of the remaining flour.

Turn dough out onto the floured surface. With floured hands, gently knead the dough for 8 strokes. Using a well-floured rolling pin, roll dough into a 21x12-inch rectangle (if necessary, sprinkle surface of the dough with enough remaining flour to prevent sticking). Fold dough crosswise into thirds to form a 7x12-inch rectangle. Loosely wrap in plastic wrap and chill 1 to 1½ hours in the refrigerator or 20 to 30 minutes in the freezer or until dough is firm but not excessively stiff.

4 On a well-floured surface, roll dough into a 21x12-inch rectangle. Fold dough crosswise into thirds again and give dough a quarter-turn. Then roll, fold, and turn twice more, flouring surface as needed (it is not necessary to chill dough between each rolling). Place dough in a plastic bag. Seal bag, leaving room for dough to expand. Chill dough for 4 to 24 hours.

5 Cut dough crosswise into fourths. Wrap and return 3 portions to refrigerator until ready to use. To shape croissants, on a lightly floured surface, roll the fourth portion of dough into a 16x8-inch rectangle. Cut rectangle crosswise in half to form two squares. Then cut each square diagonally in half to form two triangles. (You will have 4 triangles total from each rectangle.) Loosely roll up each triangle, starting from an 8-inch side and rolling toward opposite point.

6 Repeat cutting and shaping with remaining 3 portions. Place croissants, points down, 4 inches apart on ungreased baking sheets. Curve ends. Cover; let rise in a warm place until double (about 1 hour).

7 Beat 1 egg with the 1 tablespoon water. Lightly brush croissants with egg mixture. Bake in a 375° oven 15 minutes or until golden. Remove from baking sheets. Cool slightly. Serve warm or cool. Cover; chill any cooled croissants for up to 3 days. Makes 16.

Nutrition facts per serving: *306 calories, 5 g protein, 30 g carbohydrate, 18 g total fat (11 g saturated), 74 mg cholesterol, 225 mg sodium, 1 g fiber. Daily values: 18% vitamin A, 0% vitamin C, 3% calcium, 11% iron.*

Wheat Croissants: Prepare Quick-Method Croissants, except use 2 cups all-purpose flour and 1 cup whole wheat flour for the 3 cups all-purpose flour.

To Make Ahead

Prepare dough as directed to the point of dividing dough into fourths. Place in a freezer container or bag and freeze up to 3 months. Before using, thaw overnight in the refrigerator. Continue as directed in the recipes.

For light and flaky croissants, it's important to keep the butter in separate pieces so it will make layers in the dough. After thoroughly coating the butter pieces with flour, chill the mixture while preparing the yeast dough.

On a well-floured surface, use a well-floured rolling pin to roll dough into a 21x12-inch rectangle. The pastry still will be rough after first rolling; it will get smoother with each fold and roll.

Then fold dough crosswise into thirds to form a 12x7-inch rectangle.

Peach-Filled Croissants, top left, and Chocolate-Cherry Croissants, top right and bottom

Peach-Filled Croissants

1 recipe Quick-Method Croissant dough (see page 88)
1 cup dried peaches or dried apricots
1 5½-ounce can peach nectar or apricot nectar
¼ cup water
1 tablespoon orange liqueur (optional)
¼ cup granulated sugar
⅓ cup finely chopped pecans or almonds

1 Prepare Quick-Method Croissant dough as directed; set aside.

2 For filling, in a small saucepan combine dried peaches, nectar, and water. Bring mixture to a boil; reduce heat. Cover; simmer 20 to 25 minutes or until nearly all liquid is absorbed. Do not drain; cool. In a blender container or food processor bowl, combine cooked fruit mixture, orange liqueur (if desired), and sugar. Cover; blend or process until smooth; set aside.

3 Cut dough crosswise into fourths. Wrap and return 3 portions to the refrigerator until ready to use. To shape croissants, on a lightly floured surface, roll the fourth portion of dough into a 16x8-inch rectangle. Cut the rectangle crosswise in half to form 2 squares. Then cut the square diagonally in half to form 2 triangles. (You will have 4 triangles from each rectangle. Spoon about 1 tablespoon fruit mixture onto each dough triangle on an 8-inch side. Loosely roll up each triangle, rolling towards opposite point. Sprinkle with 1 teaspoon pecans. Repeat cutting, filling, and shaping with remaining 3 portions of dough.

4 Place croissants, points down, 4 inches apart on ungreased baking sheets. Cover; let rise in a warm place until nearly double (about 1 hour).

5 Bake in a 375° oven 15 minutes or until golden. Remove from baking sheets; cool slightly. Serve warm. Cover any cooled croissants and chill for up to 3 days. Makes 16.

Nutrition facts per croissant: 367 calories, 6 g protein, 41 g carbohydrate, 20 g total fat (11 g saturated), 87 mg cholesterol, 231 mg sodium, 2 g fiber. Daily values: 21% vitamin A, 2% vitamin C, 3% calcium, 15% iron.

Chocolate-Cherry Croissants

1 recipe Quick-Method Croissant dough (see page 88)
1 cup milk chocolate pieces, semisweet chocolate pieces, or semisweet mint-flavored chocolate pieces (6 ounces)
½ cup coarsely chopped maraschino cherries
1 egg
1 tablespoon water
Powdered sugar (optional)
Melted chocolate (optional)

1 Prepare Quick-Method Croissant dough as directed except, substitute ¼ cup unsweetened cocoa powder for ¼ cup of the flour added to the yeast. Cut dough crosswise into fourths. Wrap and return 3 portions to the refrigerator until ready to use. To shape croissants, on a lightly floured surface, roll the fourth portion of dough into a 16x8-inch rectangle. Then cut it into four 4x8-inch rectangles. Spoon about 1 tablespoon of the chocolate pieces and 1 teaspoon of the maraschino cherry pieces onto the center of each dough rectangle.

2 In a small mixing bowl use a fork to beat the egg and water. Brush edges of each dough rectangle with some of the egg mixture. Fold short sides of each rectangle over filling, overlapping in center. Pinch edges together to seal. Repeat cutting, filling, and shaping with remaining 3 portions of dough.

3 Place bundles, seam sides down, 4 inches apart on ungreased baking sheets. Cover; let rise in a warm place until nearly double (about 1 hour). Brush croissants again with some of the egg mixture. Bake in a 375° oven about 15 minutes or until lightly browned on bottom. Remove from baking sheets. Cool slightly on a wire rack. If desired, sprinkle with powdered sugar and drizzle with melted chocolate. Serve warm. Cover any cooled croissants and store in the refrigerator for up to 3 days. Makes 16.

Nutrition facts per croissant: 374 calories, 7 g protein, 39 g carbohydrate, 22 g total fat (13 g saturated), 87 mg cholesterol, 240 mg sodium, 1 g fiber. Daily values: 19% vitamin A, 0% vitamin C, 5% calcium, 13% iron.

Blueberry Croissants

1 recipe Quick-Method Croissant
   dough (see page 88)
½ cup blueberry preserves
1 cup fresh or frozen blueberries
1 egg
1 tablespoon water

1 Prepare Quick-Method Croissant dough as directed.

2 Cut dough crosswise into fourths. Wrap and return three portions to the refrigerator until ready to use.

3 To shape croissants, on a lightly floured surface, roll the fourth portion of dough into a 16x8-inch rectangle. Cut rectangle crosswise in half to form two squares. Then cut each square diagonally in half to form two triangles. (You will have four triangles total from each rectangle.)

4 Spoon 2 teaspoons of the preserves along an 8-inch side of each triangle. Add 3 or 4 blueberries. Loosely roll up each triangle, starting from the 8-inch side with the preserves and rolling toward the opposite point.

5 Repeat cutting, filling, and shaping with the remaining 3 portions of dough. Place croissants, points down, 3 to 4 inches apart on ungreased baking sheets. Curve the ends to form crescent shapes. Cover and let rise in a warm place until nearly double (about 1 hour).

Add filling along the 8-inch side of the triangle. Loosely roll up the dough starting from the 8-inch side and rolling toward the opposite point. If the croissant is rolled too tightly, there will not be enough room for the dough to rise and expand and it may tear.

6 In a small mixing bowl use a fork to beat the egg and water. Lightly brush croissants with the egg mixture. Bake in a 375° oven about 15 minutes or until golden. Cool slightly on wire racks. Serve warm. Cover and refrigerate any leftovers and use within 3 days. Makes 16.

Nutrition facts per croissant: 343 calories, 6 g protein, 39 g carbohydrate, 19 g total fat (11 g saturated), 87 mg cholesterol, 231 mg sodium, 1 g fiber. Daily values: 18% vitamin A, 2% vitamin C, 3% calcium, 13% iron.

Quick-Method Danish Pastry

Danish pastries definitely look more difficult than they really are, especially when you use this super-simple method.

1½ cups cold butter
     (no substitutes)
3 cups all-purpose flour
1½ cups all-purpose flour
1 package active dry yeast
1¼ cups half-and-half, light cream,
     or milk
¼ cup granulated sugar
¼ teaspoon salt
1 egg
¼ to ½ cup all-purpose flour

1 Cut butter into ½-inch slices. In a medium mixing bowl stir butter slices into the 3 cups flour until slices are coated and separated; chill.

2 For dough, in a large mixing bowl stir together the 1½ cups flour and yeast. In a medium saucepan, heat and stir the half-and-half, sugar, and salt just until warm (120° to 130°). Add half-and-half mixture to flour mixture. Add egg. Beat with an electric mixer on low to medium speed for 30 seconds, scraping the sides of the bowl constantly. Beat on high speed for 3 minutes. Using a wooden spoon, stir in the chilled flour-butter mixture until the flour is well moistened (butter will remain in large pieces).

3 Sprinkle a pastry cloth or surface with ¼ cup of the remaining flour. Turn dough out onto the floured surface. With floured hands, gently knead dough for 8 strokes. Using a well-floured rolling pin, roll dough into a 21x12-inch rectangle (if necessary, sprinkle surface of dough with enough remaining flour to prevent sticking). Fold dough crosswise into thirds to form a 7x12-inch rectangle. Loosely wrap in plastic wrap and chill for 1 to 1½ hours in the refrigerator or for 20 to 30 minutes in the freezer or until dough is firm but not excessively stiff.

4 On a well-floured surface, roll dough into a 21x12-inch rectangle. Fold dough crosswise into thirds again and give dough a quarter-turn. Then roll, fold, and turn twice more, flouring surface as needed (it is not necessary to chill dough between each rolling). Place dough in a plastic bag. Seal bag, leaving room for dough to expand. Chill dough 4 to 24 hours. Fill, shape, and bake as directed in recipes.

To Make Ahead

Prepare dough as directed, except divide in half. Place in a freezer container or bag; freeze up to 3 months. Before using, thaw overnight in refrigerator. Continue as directed in recipes.

Cheese and Lemon Danish

These 10 rich cheese pastries easily will serve 20.

1 **recipe Quick-Method Danish Pastry dough (at left)**
1 **8-ounce package cream cheese, softened**
1 **tablespoon dairy sour cream**
⅓ **cup granulated sugar**
1 **tablespoon all-purpose flour**

1 **egg yolk**
1 **teaspoon butter or margarine**
1 **teaspoon finely shredded lemon peel**
½ **teaspoon vanilla**
1 **whole egg**
1 **tablespoon water**
1 **recipe Powdered Sugar Icing (see page 151) (optional)**

1 Prepare Quick-Method Danish Pastry dough as directed; set aside.

2 For filling, in a medium mixing bowl beat cream cheese, sour cream, sugar, flour, egg yolk, butter, lemon peel, and vanilla with an electric mixer on medium speed for 3 minutes or until well mixed. Set aside.

3 To shape pastries, on a lightly floured surface, roll the chilled dough into a 20x12-inch rectangle. Cut rectangle into twenty 12x1-inch strips. Twist ends of each strip in opposite directions 3 or 4 times. Place 1 twisted strip on an ungreased baking sheet; form it into a wide U shape. Then coil 1 end of the strip to the center to form a snail shape. Tuck the end underneath. Coil the opposite end of the U-shape strip to the center so the 2 coils nearly touch. Tuck the second end under in the same manner as the first. Repeat with remaining strips, placing them 4 inches apart on baking sheets.

4 Spoon 1 tablespoon of the filling onto the center of each coil. Cover and let rise in a warm place until nearly double (30 to 45 minutes).

Chill Out

Chilling croissant and Danish pastry dough thoroughly is a snap in the freezer. If a recipe calls for 1 hour of chilling in the refrigerator, put it in the freezer for 20 minutes instead. Thorough chilling is important to relax the dough, keep the butter firm (making rolling easier), and reduce shrinking during rolling and baking.

You can freeze dough for up to 1 month (do not shape before freezing) by tightly wrapping it in foil or placing it in freezer bags. Thaw dough in the refrigerator overnight or for up to 24 hours. Use as directed.

5 In a small mixing bowl use a fork to beat the whole egg and water. Lightly brush dough portions of pastries with the egg mixture. Bake in a 375° oven for 18 to 20 minutes or until golden. Remove from baking sheets. Cool slightly on wire racks. If desired, drizzle with Powdered Sugar Icing. Serve warm. Cover cooled pastries and store in the refrigerator for up to 3 days. Makes 10.

Nutrition facts per pastry: 313 calories, 6 g protein, 28 g carbohydrate, 20 g total fat (12 g saturated), 105 mg cholesterol, 223 mg sodium, 1 g fiber. Daily values: 22% vitamin A, 0% vitamin C, 3% calcium, 11% iron.

Getting Flaky

When you're talking fantastic croissants and Danish pastries, the flakier the better. Here's how you do it:

✦ *Use only butter for the lightest and most airy pastry.*

✦ *Take the time to evenly roll and fold the dough to the size indicated in the recipe; this ensures proper rising and an even appearance.*

✦ *Chill the dough thoroughly. It should feel firm and cold to the touch.*

✦ *Keep the dough cold (below 75°) while you're working with it so the butter stays firm and sealed into the dough. If it softens, the pastries will become compact and the butter may leak out during baking.*

✦ *Always preheat the oven to ensure a constant temperature for proper proofing (rising).*

International Origin

Strawberry Turnovers

Fresh fruit out of season? Use 1 cup of your favorite canned pie filling instead.

1 **recipe Quick-Method Danish Pastry dough (see page 92)**
½ **cup strawberry preserves or peach preserves**
½ **cup chopped strawberries**
1 **egg**
1 **tablespoon water**
 Sifted powdered sugar

1 Prepare Quick-Method Danish Pastry dough as directed; set aside.

2 To shape turnovers, cut the chilled dough crosswise in half. On a lightly floured surface, roll each half of dough into a 12-inch square. Cut each square of dough into nine 4-inch squares (18 squares total).

3 Spoon about 2 teaspoons of the preserves onto the center of each square. Top with several pieces of the chopped strawberries.

4 In a small mixing bowl use a fork to beat the egg and water. Brush edges of dough squares with some of the egg mixture. Fold squares in half to form rectangles; seal with tines of a fork.

5 Place the rectangles 4 inches apart on ungreased baking sheets. Cover and let rise in a warm place until nearly double (45 to 60 minutes).

6 Brush turnovers with some more of the egg mixture. Bake in a 375° oven about 15 minutes or until golden. Remove turnovers from baking sheets. Cool slightly on wire racks. Sprinkle powdered sugar over warm turnovers. Serve warm or cool. Makes 18.

Nutrition facts per turnover: *305 calories, 5 g protein, 34 g carbohydrate, 17 g total fat (10 g saturated), 78 mg cholesterol, 205 mg sodium, 1 g fiber. Daily values: 16% vitamin A, 4% vitamin C, 3% calcium, 11% iron.*

ALLSPICE

GER

CINNAMON

*Strawberry
Turnovers*

Setting Some Aside

Consider yourself lucky if you have leftover croissants or Danish. To store baked croissants and Danish, place them in an airtight container or bag and keep them in the refrigerator for up to 3 days. (Storing baked croissants or Danish at room temperature is not recommended because of the high butter content). Allow them to stand at room temperature about 25 minutes before serving.

To freeze, place them in a freezer container or bag and freeze for up to 2 months. To serve, wrap frozen croissants or Danish in foil and bake in a 400° oven for 5 to 8 minutes or until warm.

Pecan Pinwheels

Nutty cinnamon-spice pinwheels drizzled with a coffee glaze just cry out for a steaming mug of freshly brewed coffee or a cappuccino.

1 **recipe Quick-Method Danish Pastry dough (see page 92)**
1 **cup pecans, finely chopped**
⅔ **cup packed brown sugar**
½ **teaspoon ground cinnamon**
⅓ **cup butter or margarine, softened**
1 **egg**

1 **tablespoon water**
½ **teaspoon instant coffee crystals**
1 **cup sifted powdered sugar**

1 Prepare Quick-Method Danish Pastry dough as directed; set aside. Grease 24 muffin cups; set aside.

2 For topping, in a small mixing bowl stir together the pecans, brown sugar, and cinnamon; set aside.

3 To shape pinwheels, cut the chilled dough crosswise in half. On a lightly floured surface, roll each half of dough into a 12-inch square. Spread each square with half of the softened butter. Sprinkle each square with half of the topping. Tightly roll up, jelly-roll style, starting from one of the sides. Seal with fingertips as you roll. Cut each roll into 12 pieces.

4 Place pieces, cut sides down, in the prepared muffin cups. Cover and let rise in a warm place until nearly double (45 to 60 minutes).

5 In a small mixing bowl use a fork to beat the egg and water. Lightly brush the tops of the pinwheels with the egg mixture. Bake in a 375° oven about 20 minutes or until golden. Invert pinwheels onto wire racks. Cool slightly.

6 Meanwhile, in a small mixing bowl stir together 1 tablespoon hot water and coffee crystals until coffee is dissolved. Stir into powdered sugar. If necessary, stir in additional water to make the frosting easy to drizzle. Drizzle over warm pinwheels. Serve

warm. Cover and refrigerate any leftovers and use within 3 days. Makes 24.

Nutrition facts per pastry: 298 calories, 4 g protein, 30 g carbohydrate, 18 g total fat (9 g saturated), 74 mg cholesterol, 183 mg sodium, 1 g fiber. Daily values: 15% vitamin A, 0% vitamin C, 2% calcium, 9% iron.

Apple-Maple Claws

If you line the baking sheets with foil, cleanup will be quicker and you'll have more time to enjoy the pastries.

1 **recipe Quick-Method Danish Pastry dough (see page 92)**
1½ **cups chopped, peeled apples**
2 **tablespoons granulated sugar**
½ **teaspoon ground cinnamon**
¼ **cup butter or margarine**
½ **cup powdered sugar**
2 **tablespoons all-purpose flour**
2 **teaspoons vanilla**
1 **teaspoon maple flavoring**
1 **egg**
1 **tablespoon water**
Maple Glaze

1 Prepare Quick-Method Danish Pastry dough as directed; set aside.

2 For filling, in a medium saucepan combine apples and sugar. Heat slowly until liquid accumulates. Bring mixture to boiling. Reduce heat; cover and simmer for 8 to 10 minutes or until apples are tender. Uncover and simmer for 2 to 3 minutes more or until most of the liquid evaporates. Stir in cinnamon. Mash apples slightly, leaving some chunks; set aside.

3 In a medium mixing bowl beat butter, powdered sugar, flour, vanilla, and maple flavoring with an electric mixer on medium speed for 2 to 3 minutes or until light and fluffy; set aside.

4 To shape claws, cut chilled dough crosswise in half. On a lightly floured surface, roll each half into a 12-inch square. Cut each square into three 4-inch-wide strips (6 strips total).

5 Spread about 1 tablespoon of the maple mixture down the center of each strip. Spoon about 2 tablespoons of the apple mixture on top of the maple mixture. Fold the strips lengthwise in half to cover the filling. Pinch the edges to seal.

6 Cut each strip into three 4-inch-long pieces. Make 4 or 5 evenly spaced cuts in each piece, snipping from the sealed edge almost to the folded edge. Place 2 inches apart on ungreased baking sheets, curving slightly to separate slits. Cover and let rise in a warm place until nearly double in size (45 to 60 minutes).

7 In a small mixing bowl use a fork to beat egg and water. Lightly brush dough with egg mixture. Bake in a 375° oven 15 minutes or until golden. Remove pastries and cool slightly on wire racks. Drizzle with Maple Glaze. Serve warm. Cover any cooled claws and store in the refrigerator up to 3 days. Makes 18.

Maple Glaze: In a small mixing bowl combine 1 cup sifted powdered sugar, ¼ teaspoon maple flavoring, and enough milk (1 to 2 tablespoons) to make a glaze that is easy to drizzle.

Nutrition facts per pastry: *351 calories, 6 g protein, 39 g carbohydrate, 20 g total fat (12 g saturated), 96 mg cholesterol, 234 mg sodium, 1 g fiber. Daily values: 19% vitamin A, 0% vitamin C, 3% calcium, 11% iron.*

Shortcut

Use ¾ cup canned sliced apples in place of the fresh apples (do not cook canned apples). Just stir together canned apples, granulated sugar, and cinnamon and continue as directed.

Make four or five evenly spaced cuts in each piece with a knife or kitchen shears, cutting from the sealed edge almost to the folded edge. Transfer pastries to an ungreased baking sheet and slightly curve each one.

Fatten 'em Up

So you don't want shriveled, tough, dry fruit in your fruit bread, but you forgot to soak the dried fruit? Don't worry, plumping dried fruit in the microwave takes next to no time at all.

Place the amount of fruit needed for your recipe in a 1-quart microwave-safe casserole. Add the same amount of water (or fruit juice or liqueur). Cook, covered, on 100% power (high) until boiling, stirring once. Allow 1½ to 2½ minutes for ½ cup dried currants or raisins, 2 to 3 minutes for ½ cup mixed dried fruit or 1 cup dried apricots, and 3 to 5 minutes for 1 cup dried apples, currants, raisins, figs, mixed fruit, peaches, or prunes. Drain fruit well.

Notes

Banana Split Cake
(see recipe, page 101)

All-Occasion Cakes

*What wonderful memories cakes can evoke,
including memories of those birthdays when
someone went to the extra work of baking
your favorite cake for a party or cupcakes for
you to share with your classmates.*

❦

*And everyone seems to love cake.
A cake you've made from scratch will add
a special touch to any occasion.*

❦

*No matter what your preference—a more
traditional layered cake, a sponge, creamed,
chiffon, or angel food cake, or a more
contemporary flourless nut torte—there is a
recipe in this chapter that you won't be
able to resist. To top them off, we have every
imaginable frosting and glaze. Try one
today. It'll be a piece of cake.*

Best Butter Cake

2⅔ cups all-purpose flour
  1 tablespoon baking powder
  ¼ teaspoon salt
  1 cup butter (no substitutes), softened
  2 cups granulated sugar
  2 teaspoons vanilla
  4 eggs
  1 cup milk
  1 recipe desired flavor Butter Frosting (see page 150)

1 Grease and lightly flour three 9x1½-inch or 8x1½-inch round baking pans. In a medium mixing bowl stir together flour, baking powder, and salt. Set pans and flour mixture aside.

2 In a large mixing bowl beat butter with an electric mixer on medium to high speed for 30 seconds. Add sugar and vanilla and beat until fluffy. Add eggs, one at a time, beating on medium speed after each addition until combined. Alternately add flour mixture and milk, beating on low to medium speed just until combined.

3 Pour batter into the prepared pans. Bake in a 350° oven for 30 to 35 minutes or until a wooden toothpick inserted near the center of each cake comes out clean. Cool cakes in pans on wire racks for 10 minutes. Remove cakes from pans and completely cool on the wire racks. Frost with desired Butter Frosting. Cover and store at room temperature for up to 3 days. Makes 12 servings.

Nutrition facts per serving: *674 calories, 6 g protein, 109 g carbohydrate, 25 g total fat (15 g saturated), 134 mg cholesterol, 403 mg sodium, 1 g fiber. Daily values: 25% vitamin A, 0% vitamin C, 11% calcium, 11% iron.*

To Make Ahead

Prepare and bake cakes as directed; cool completely. Place cakes on a baking sheet and freeze until firm. Once firm, place cakes in 2 gallon freezer bags and freeze up to 3 months. Before serving, thaw at room temperature for several hours. Frost as directed.

Devil's Food Layer Cake

1¼ cups boiling water
  ¾ cup unsweetened cocoa powder
2¼ cups all-purpose flour
  1 teaspoon baking soda
  ½ teaspoon baking powder
  ¼ teaspoon salt
  ¾ cup butter or margarine, softened
  1 cup granulated sugar
  ¾ cup packed brown sugar
1½ teaspoons vanilla
  3 eggs
    Creamy Bittersweet Frosting

1 In a small mixing bowl gradually whisk boiling water into cocoa powder until powder is dissolved. Cool to room temperature.

2 Meanwhile, grease and lightly flour two 9x1½-inch round baking pans. In a medium mixing bowl stir together flour, baking soda, baking powder, and salt. Set pans and flour mixture aside.

3 In a large mixing bowl beat butter with an electric mixer on medium to high speed for 30 seconds. Add granulated sugar, brown sugar, and vanilla and beat until fluffy. Add eggs, one at a time, beating on medium speed after each addition until combined. Alternately add flour mixture and cooled cocoa mixture, beating on low to medium speed after each addition just until combined.

4 Pour batter into the prepared pans. Bake in a 350° oven for 30 to 35 minutes or until a wooden toothpick inserted near the center of each cake comes out clean. Cool cakes in pans on wire racks for 10 minutes. Remove cakes from pans and completely cool on the wire racks. Frost with Creamy Bittersweet Frosting. Cover and store cake in the refrigerator for up to 3 days. Let stand at room temperature for 30 minutes before serving. Makes 16 servings.

Creamy Bittersweet Frosting: In a heavy medium saucepan combine 1½ cups whipping cream and ¼ cup light corn syrup. Bring to a simmer over medium-low heat; remove from heat. Stir in one 12-ounce package semisweet chocolate pieces and 1 teaspoon vanilla; let stand 2 minutes. Whisk mixture until smooth and melted. Chill about 1½ hours or until the mixture is easy to spread, stirring occasionally. Beat with an electric mixer on medium to high speed until fluffy.

Nutrition facts per serving: *438 calories, 5 g protein, 54 g carbohydrate, 24 g total fat (11 g saturated), 94 mg cholesterol, 238 mg sodium, 0 g fiber. Daily values: 19% vitamin A, 0% vitamin C, 7% calcium, 16% iron.*

To Make Ahead

Prepare and bake cakes as directed; cool completely. Place cakes on a baking sheet; freeze until firm. Once firm, place cakes in 2-gallon freezer bags and freeze for up to 3 months. Before serving, thaw at room temperature for several hours. Frost as directed.

Kid Appeal

Banana Split Cake

Banana split lovers will find this cake, with its strawberry, pineapple, and hot fudge fillings, every bit as satisfying as the real thing. (Pictured on page 98.)

　2　**cups all-purpose flour**
1½　**teaspoons baking powder**
　¾　**teaspoon baking soda**
　½　**teaspoon salt**
　½　**cup shortening**
1½　**cups granulated sugar**
　1　**teaspoon vanilla**
　2　**eggs**
　1　**cup mashed bananas**
　　　(3 medium)
　½　**cup buttermilk or sour milk**
　1　**11- to-12-ounce jar fudge**
　　　ice-cream topping

　1　**Sweetened Whipped Cream**
　1　**cup sliced fresh strawberries**
　1　**8¼-ounce can crushed**
　　　pineapple, well drained
　½　**cup chopped peanuts**
　　　Strawberries, halved (optional)

1 Grease and lightly flour two 9x1½-inch round baking pans. Combine flour, baking powder, soda, and salt. Set pans and flour mixture aside.

2 Beat shortening with an electric mixer 30 seconds. Add sugar and vanilla; beat until combined. Add eggs, one at a time, beating on medium speed after each addition until combined. Add bananas; beat until well blended. Alternately add flour mixture and buttermilk, beating on low to medium speed just until combined.

3 Pour batter into prepared pans. Bake in a 350° oven 30 to 35 minutes or until a wooden toothpick inserted near center comes out clean. Cool in pans for 10 minutes. Remove cakes from pans; cool on wire racks.

4 In a small saucepan, heat and stir fudge ice-cream topping over low heat just until warm (not hot).

5 To assemble, cut each cake layer horizontally into 2 even layers. Place bottom half of the first cake layer on a serving plate; spread with one-third of the Sweetened Whipped Cream; top with sliced strawberries. Add the top half of the first cake layer; spread with half of the warm fudge topping, letting it drizzle down the sides. Sprinkle with half of the peanuts. Add the bottom half of the second cake layer; spread with one-third of the Sweetened Whipped Cream; top with drained pineapple. Add the top half of the second cake layer; spread with remaining warm fudge topping, letting it drizzle down the sides. Sprinkle with the remaining peanuts. Pipe or dollop with remaining Sweetened Whipped Cream and garnish with halved strawberries.

6 Serve immediately or chill up to 2 hours. Cover any leftovers and store in the refrigerator. Serves 12.

Sweetened Whipped Cream: Combine 1 cup whipping cream and 1 tablespoon granulated sugar. Beat with an electric mixer on low to medium speed just until soft peaks form.

Nutrition facts per serving: *494 calories, 7 g protein, 67 g carbohydrate, 24 g total fat (10 g saturated), 63 mg cholesterol, 261 mg sodium, 2 g fiber. Daily values: 11% vitamin A, 19% vitamin C, 9% calcium, 2% iron.*

Shortcut

Substitute a 2-layer-size banana cake mix for the banana cake recipe and 6 ounces frozen whipped dessert topping, thawed, for the Sweetened Whipped Cream.

To Make Ahead

Prepare and bake cakes as directed; cool. Place on a baking sheet and freeze until firm. Once firm, place in 2-gallon freezer bags and freeze up to 3 months. Before serving, thaw at room temperature several hours. Cut and fill as directed.

Cream of the Cakes

Chances are that when you consider baking a cake, it's a creamed cake that springs to mind. No doubt your mother and grandmother baked luscious yellow cakes, rich and buttery pound cakes, fabulous fruitcakes, or fluffy buttermilk cakes and handed the recipes down to you.

What these cakes have in common is the method of "creaming" or beating the fat and sugar together until the mixture is fluffy; this traps air, which helps leaven the cake. While some of these recipes use that traditional technique, others have been adapted to an easy one-bowl process that saves time and dirty dishes.

There are other things to keep in mind.

◆ Beat fat and sugar until well combined or cake's texture may be coarse. With freestanding electric mixers use lower speed in recommended range; the higher speed is for portable electric mixers.

◆ Don't overbeat the egg whites or the cake will be dry.

◆ Check oven temperature carefully. If it's too hot, the cake may develop tunnels and cracks; if it's too cool, texture may be coarse.

◆ Don't overbake. Check cake at lower end of baking time range. It is done when a wooden toothpick inserted near center comes out clean. If it is not done, return to oven for full baking time.

Blackberry Jam Cake with Penuche Frosting

Enjoy an old-fashioned spice cake with a tender crumb and rich caramel-like frosting.

1⅓ **cups all-purpose flour**
 1 **teaspoon ground cinnamon**
 ½ **teaspoon baking soda**
 ½ **teaspoon ground nutmeg**
 ¼ **teaspoon ground cloves**
 ½ **cup butter or margarine, softened**
 ½ **cup granulated sugar**
 ½ **cup packed brown sugar**
 2 **eggs**
 ½ **cup buttermilk**
 ½ **cup blackberry jam**
 ½ **cup chopped pecans**
   Penuche Frosting
   Edible flowers (optional)

1 Grease and lightly flour two 8x1½-inch round baking pans. In a small mixing bowl stir together flour, cinnamon, baking soda, nutmeg, and cloves. Set pans and flour mixture aside.

2 In a large mixing bowl beat the butter with an electric mixer on medium to high speed about 30 seconds or until softened. Add granulated sugar and brown sugar to butter and beat until fluffy. Add eggs, one at a time, beating on medium speed after each addition until combined. Alternately add flour mixture and buttermilk, beating on low to medium speed after each addition just until combined. Stir in jam and pecans.

3 Pour batter into the prepared pans. Bake in a 350° oven for 30 to 35 minutes or until a wooden toothpick inserted near the center of each cake comes out clean. Cool cakes in pans on wire racks for 10 minutes. Remove cakes from pans and completely cool on wire racks. Frost with Penuche Frosting. If desired, garnish with edible flowers. Cover cake and store at room temperature for up to 3 days. Makes 12 servings.

Penuche Frosting: In a medium saucepan melt ½ cup butter or margarine; stir in 1 cup packed brown sugar. Cook and stir until bubbly. Remove from the heat. Add ¼ cup milk; beat vigorously until smooth. Add 3½ cups sifted powdered sugar; beat by hand until the frosting is easy to spread. Immediately frost cake.

Nutrition facts per serving: 495 calories, 3 g protein, 80 g carbohydrate, 19 g total fat (10 g saturated), 77 mg cholesterol, 240 mg sodium, 1 g fiber. Daily values: 16% vitamin A, 0% vitamin C, 4% calcium, 10% iron.

To Make Ahead

Prepare and bake cakes as directed; cool completely. Place the cakes on a baking sheet and freeze until firm. Once firm, place cakes in 2-gallon freezer bags and freeze for up to 3 months. Before serving, thaw at room temperature for several hours. Frost as directed.

**Blackberry Jam Cake with
Penuche Frosting**

Hazelnut Spice Cake

- 2 **cups all-purpose flour**
- 2 **teaspoons baking powder**
- 1 **teaspoon ground cinnamon**
- ½ **teaspoon baking soda**
- ½ **teaspoon ground nutmeg**
- ¼ **teaspoon ground cloves**
- ½ **cup butter or margarine, softened**
- 1 **cup packed brown sugar**
- 1 **teaspoon vanilla**
- 3 **eggs**
- ½ **cup dairy sour cream**
- ½ **cup milk**
- 1 **cup chopped, toasted hazelnuts (filberts), almonds, or pecans**
- 2 **teaspoons finely shredded orange peel or lemon peel**
- 1 **recipe Chocolate or Orange Butter Frosting (see page 150)**

1 Grease and flour two 9x1½-inch or 8x1½-inch round baking pans. In a medium mixing bowl stir together flour, baking powder, cinnamon, baking soda, nutmeg, and cloves. Set pans and flour mixture aside.

2 In a large mixing bowl beat butter with an electric mixer on medium to high speed for 30 seconds. Add brown sugar and vanilla and beat until fluffy. Add eggs, one at a time, beating well on medium speed after each addition. Combine sour cream and milk. Alternately add flour mixture and sour cream mixture to butter mixture, beating on low to medium speed just until combined. Stir in orange peel and ½ cup of the chopped nuts.

3 Pour batter into prepared pans. Bake in a 350° oven 30 to 35 minutes or until cakes test done. Cool in pans 10 minutes. Remove from pans; cool on wire racks. Frost with Chocolate or Orange Butter Frosting. Sprinkle top edge of cake with remaining ½ cup nuts. Cover and store at room temperature up to 3 days. Makes 12 servings.

Nutrition facts per serving: 492 calories, 6 g protein, 70 g carbohydrate, 22 g total fat (10 g saturated), 93 mg cholesterol, 276 mg sodium, 1 g fiber. Daily values: 17% vitamin A, 1% vitamin C, 11% calcium, 13% iron.

To Make Ahead
Prepare and bake cakes as directed; cool completely. Place cakes on a baking sheet and freeze until firm. Once firm, place cakes in 2-gallon freezer bags and freeze up to 3 months. Before serving, thaw at room temperature several hours. Frost as directed.

Use shortening on a pastry brush, paper towel, or piece of waxed paper to grease the bottom and sides of the cake pan. When baking in a fluted pan, be sure to get the shortening into all crevices. Add one or two tablespoons of flour to the well-greased pan. Tilt and tap the pan to evenly distribute the flour. Dump out any extra flour.

To test the cake for doneness, insert a wooden toothpick into the cake near the center. The toothpick should come out clean. If toothpick is doughy, bake the cake a few minutes longer, then test in another spot near the center.

Maple-Nut-Pumpkin Cake

- 2½ **cups all-purpose flour**
- 1½ **teaspoons ground cinnamon**
- 1 **teaspoon baking powder**
- ¾ **teaspoon baking soda**
- ½ **teaspoon ground nutmeg**
- ½ **teaspoon ground allspice**
- ¼ **teaspoon ground cloves**

½ **cup shortening**
1½ **cups granulated sugar**
¼ **cup maple-flavored syrup**
½ **teaspoon vanilla**
2 **eggs**
1 **cup canned pumpkin**
¾ **cup milk**
1 **cup chopped walnuts or pecans**
Maple Glaze

1 Grease and lightly flour a 10-inch tube pan. Combine flour, cinnamon, baking powder, soda, nutmeg, allspice, and cloves. Set aside.

2 Beat shortening with an electric mixer on medium to high speed 30 seconds. Add sugar, maple syrup, and vanilla; beat until combined. Add eggs, one at a time, beating after each addition until combined. Add pumpkin and milk; beat until combined. Add flour mixture and beat just until combined. Stir in nuts.

3 Pour batter into prepared pan. Bake in a 350° oven 50 to 55 minutes or until cake tests done. Cool in pan for 15 minutes. Remove cake and cool on wire rack. Drizzle with Maple Glaze. Cover and store at room temperature for up to 3 days. Makes 18 servings.

Maple Glaze: Combine 1 cup sifted powdered sugar, 2 tablespoons maple-flavored syrup, and 1 tablespoon melted butter or margarine. Stir until smooth. If necessary, add enough milk (1 to 3 teaspoons) to make the glaze easy to drizzle.

Nutrition facts per serving: 279 calories, 4 g protein, 42 g carbohydrate, 11 g total fat (3 g saturated), 26 mg cholesterol, 94 mg sodium, 1 g fiber. Daily values: 32% vitamin A, 1% vitamin C, 4% calcium, 9% iron.

To Make Ahead

Prepare and bake cake as directed; cool completely. Place on a baking sheet; freeze until firm. Once firm, place cake in a freezer bag; freeze up to 3 months. Before serving, thaw at room temperature several hours. Glaze as directed.

Delicious Memories

Chocolate-Cream Cheese Cake

This recipe is one of the first memories I have of baking a cake as a home economist in the Better Homes and Gardens® Test Kitchen. I was intrigued by the use of frosting both in and on the cake.
—Maryellyn Krantz—

2¼ **cups all-purpose flour**
1 **teaspoon baking powder**
1 **teaspoon baking soda**
2 **3-ounce packages cream cheese, softened**
½ **cup butter or margarine, softened**
1 **teaspoon vanilla**
6½ **cups sifted powdered sugar**
⅓ **cup milk**
4 **ounces unsweetened chocolate, melted and cooled**

¼ **cup butter or margarine, softened**
3 **eggs**
1¼ **cups milk**

1 Grease and lightly flour two 9x1½-inch round baking pans. Combine flour, baking powder, and soda. Set pans and flour mixture aside.

2 Beat together the cream cheese and the ½ cup butter. Beat in vanilla. Alternately beat in powdered sugar and the ⅓ cup milk; blend in melted chocolate. Remove 2 cups chocolate mixture for frosting; cover and chill.

3 Add the ¼ cup butter to remaining chocolate mixture and beat until well blended. Add eggs, one at a time, beating on medium speed after each addition until combined. Alternately add flour mixture and 1¼ cups milk, beating on low to medium speed after each addition just until combined.

4 Pour batter into prepared pans. Bake in a 350° oven 30 minutes or until cakes test done. Cool in pans on wire racks 10 minutes. Remove cakes from pans and completely cool on wire racks. Allow reserved frosting to stand at room temperature for 30 minutes before frosting cake. Cover and store in the refrigerator for up to 3 days. Makes 12 servings.

Nutrition facts per serving: 521 calories, 7 g protein, 76 g carbohydrate, 23 g total fat (13 g saturated), 102 mg cholesterol, 366 mg sodium, 1 g fiber. Daily values: 21% vitamin A, 0% vitamin C, 8% calcium, 14% iron.

Pistachio Cake With White Chocolate Buttercream

Look no further when you want something different to serve for your next special occasion. You'll find shelled pistachio nuts at specialty food stores and some supermarkets.

1⅔ **cups all-purpose flour**
4 **teaspoons baking powder**
½ **teaspoon baking soda**
¾ **cup butter or margarine, softened**
2 **cups granulated sugar**
1 **teaspoon vanilla**
1 **teaspoon almond extract**
1 **cup buttermilk**
6 **egg whites (reserve yolks for White Chocolate Buttercream)**

1½ **cups chopped pistachio nuts, toasted**
2 **teaspoons finely shredded orange peel**
White Chocolate Buttercream
1 **cup chopped pistachio nuts, toasted**

1 Grease and lightly flour three 8x1½-inch round baking pans. Stir together flour, baking powder, and baking soda. Set pans and flour mixture aside.

2 Beat butter with an electric mixer on medium to high speed 30 seconds. Add sugar, vanilla, and almond extract to butter and beat until fluffy. Alternately add flour mixture and buttermilk, beating on low to medium speed just until combined.

3 Thoroughly wash beaters. In a medium mixing bowl beat egg whites until stiff peaks form (tips stand straight). Gently fold beaten egg whites into batter. Fold in the 1½ cups pistachio nuts and the orange peel.

4 Pour batter into prepared pans. Bake in a 350° oven 30 to 35 minutes or until a wooden toothpick inserted near the center of each cake comes out clean. Cool in pans on wire racks 10 minutes. Remove cakes from pans and completely cool on wire racks. Frost with White Chocolate Buttercream. Press remaining pistachio nuts on sides of cake. Cover and store cake in the refrigerator for up to 3 days. Let stand at room temperature for 30 minutes before serving. Makes 12 servings.

White Chocolate Buttercream: In a medium mixing bowl combine ½ cup granulated sugar and 2 tablespoons all-purpose flour; add the 6 reserved egg yolks. Beat mixture with a wire whisk until combined; set aside. In a heavy, medium saucepan heat 1½ cups milk over medium heat just to boiling. Remove from heat. Gradually beat hot milk into egg mixture with the wire whisk; return entire mixture to saucepan. Cook over medium heat until bubbly, whisking constantly. Cook for 2 minutes more. Remove from heat. Add 6 ounces chopped white baking bar, 1½ teaspoons vanilla, and ½ teaspoon almond extract. Let stand 1 minute; stir until smooth. Transfer mixture to a bowl. Cover surface with plastic wrap to prevent a skin from forming; cool to room temperature. In a medium mixing bowl beat 1 cup softened butter (no substitutes) on medium to high speed until fluffy. Add cooled baking bar mixture, one-fourth at a time, beating on low speed after each addition until blended.

Nutrition facts per serving: *753 calories, 13 g protein, 74 g carbohydrate, 47 g total fat (22 g saturated), 182 mg cholesterol, 466 mg sodium, 3 g fiber. Daily values: 43% vitamin A, 4% vitamin C, 17% calcium, 20% iron.*

To Make Ahead

Prepare and bake cakes as directed; cool completely. Place cake layers on baking sheets; freeze until firm. Once firm, place cakes in 2-gallon freezer bags and freeze up to 3 months. Before serving, thaw at room temperature for several hours. Frost as directed.

Pistachio Cake with White Chocolate Buttercream

Sour Cream Pound Cake

Whenever our family was invited to a covered dish dinner my mother would take a crock of baked beans and this cake. It always was one of the first cakes to disappear from the dessert table. And it is so easy to transport, my mother once made it for a friend to take on a trip to England.
—Mary Williams—

1 **cup butter (no substitutes)**
6 **eggs**
1 **8-ounce carton dairy sour cream**
3 **cups all-purpose flour**
½ **teaspoon salt**
½ **teaspoon baking powder**
¼ **teaspoon baking soda**
¼ **teaspoon ground nutmeg**
3 **cups granulated sugar**
1 **teaspoon finely shredded lemon peel**
   Lemon Glaze

1 Allow butter, eggs, and sour cream to stand at room temperature for 30 minutes. Grease and lightly flour a 10-inch tube pan. In medium mixing bowl stir together flour, salt, baking powder, baking soda, and nutmeg. Set pan and flour mixture aside.

2 In a very large mixing bowl beat butter with an electric mixer on medium to high speed about 30 seconds or until softened. Gradually add sugar, 2 tablespoons at a time, beating on medium to high speed about 6 minutes or until well combined. Add eggs, one at a time, beating on low to medium speed for 1 minute after each addition, scraping bowl often. Alternately add flour mixture and sour cream, beating on low to medium speed just until combined. Fold in lemon peel.

3 Pour batter into prepared pan. Bake in a 325° oven 1 to 1¼ hours or until a wooden toothpick inserted near center of cake comes out clean. Cool in pan on a wire rack 15 minutes. Loosen sides of cake from pan. Remove cake from pan and completely cool on the wire rack. Drizzle with Lemon Glaze. Cover and store at room temperature up to 3 days. Makes 18 servings.

Lemon Glaze: In a bowl stir together 1 cup sifted powdered sugar, ½ teaspoon finely shredded lemon peel, and enough lemon juice (1 to 2 tablespoons) to make glaze easy to drizzle.

Nutrition facts per serving: 362 calories, 5 g protein, 54 g carbohydrate, 15 g total fat (8 g saturated), 104 mg cholesterol, 227 mg sodium, 1 g fiber. Daily values: 15% vitamin A, 1% vitamin C, 3% calcium, 8% iron.

To Make Ahead

Prepare and bake cake as directed; cool completely. Place the cake on a baking sheet and freeze until firm. Once firm, place cake in a 2-gallon freezer bag and freeze up to 3 months. Before serving, thaw at room temperature for several hours. Glaze as directed.

Cinnamon-Date Pound Cake with Caramel-Date Sauce

3 **cups all-purpose flour**
2 **teaspoons ground cinnamon**
1 **teaspoon baking powder**
¼ **teaspoon baking soda**
1½ **cups butter, softened (no substitutes)**
2 **cups packed brown sugar**
¼ **cup granulated sugar**
2 **teaspoons vanilla**
5 **eggs**
1 **cup milk**
1½ **cups chopped pitted dates**
1 **cup chopped almonds**
   Powdered sugar
   Caramel-Date Sauce
   Vanilla ice cream (optional)

1 Grease and lightly flour a 10-inch tube pan. Combine flour, cinnamon, baking powder, and baking soda. Set pan and flour mixture aside.

2 In a very large mixing bowl beat butter with an electric mixer on medium to high speed for 30 seconds. Combine brown sugar and granulated sugar. Gradually add sugar mixture to butter, 2 tablespoons at a time, beating on medium to high speed 6 minutes or until very light and fluffy. Add vanilla. Add eggs, one at a time, beating 1 minute after each addition, scraping bowl. Alternately add flour mixture and milk, beating on low to medium speed after each addition until combined. Stir in dates and nuts.

3 Pour batter into prepared pan. Bake in a 325° oven for 1½ hours to 1¾ hours or until cake tests done. Cool in pan on a wire rack 10 minutes. Loosen sides of cake from pan. Remove from pan and completely cool on wire rack. Sift powdered sugar over cake top. Serve with Caramel-Date Sauce and, if desired, ice cream. Cover any leftover cake and store at room temperature for up to 3 days. Refrigerate any remaining sauce. Makes 18 servings.

Caramel-Date Sauce: In a heavy, small saucepan combine 1 cup packed brown sugar, ½ cup butter or margarine, 2 tablespoons light corn syrup, and ¼ teaspoon ground cinnamon. Bring to a boil over medium heat, stirring constantly. Boil 1 minute or until sugar dissolves. Gradually whisk in ½ cup whipping cream; return mixture to a boil. Remove from heat. Stir in ½ cup chopped pitted dates and 1 teaspoon vanilla. Serve warm.

Nutrition facts per serving: *520 calories, 6 g protein, 66 g carbohydrate, 28 g total fat (15 g saturated), 124 mg cholesterol, 282 mg sodium, 3 g fiber. Daily values: 25% vitamin A, 0% vitamin C, 9% calcium, 17% iron.*

To Make Ahead

Prepare and bake cake as directed; cool completely. Place cake on a baking sheet and freeze until firm. Once firm, place cake in a 2-gallon freezer bag and freeze to 3 months. Before serving, thaw at room temperature several hours. Sauce can be made ahead, cooled, and chilled for up to 2 days. Reheat to serve.

Delicious Memories

Chocolate Pound Cake

Every time I go home my mother has made this cake for snacking. She just stores it in her plastic cake saver, and all of us (including the grandkids) help ourselves to a slice as we feel like it. I guess it's my family's substitute for cookies in a cookie jar!
—Mary Williams—

1	cup butter (no substitutes)
5	eggs
3	cups all-purpose flour
½	cup unsweetened cocoa powder
½	teaspoon baking powder
¼	teaspoon salt
2½	cups granulated sugar
2	teaspoons vanilla
1¼	cups milk
1	ounce semisweet chocolate, grated
	Chocolate Glaze (optional)

1 Allow butter and eggs to stand at room temperature for 30 minutes. Grease and lightly flour bottom and halfway up the sides of a 10-inch tube pan. In a medium mixing bowl stir together flour, unsweetened cocoa powder, baking powder, and salt. Set pan and flour mixture aside.

2 In a very large mixing bowl beat butter with an electric mixer on medium to high speed about 30 seconds or until softened. Gradually add sugar, beating on medium to high speed about 10 minutes or until well combined. Add vanilla. Add eggs, one at a time, beating on low to medium speed for 1 minute after each addition, scraping bowl often. Alternately add flour mixture and milk, beating on low to medium speed just until combined. Fold in grated chocolate.

3 Pour batter into prepared pan. Bake in a 325° oven about 1½ hours or until a wooden toothpick inserted near the center of the cake comes out clean. Cool cake in pan on a wire rack 15 minutes. Loosen sides of cake from pan. Remove cake from pan and completely cool on the wire rack. If desired, drizzle with Chocolate Glaze. Cover and store at room temperature for up to 3 days. Makes 18 servings.

Chocolate Glaze: Stir together 1½ cups sifted powdered sugar, 2 tablespoons unsweetened cocoa powder, 2 tablespoons butter, melted, and enough water (2 to 3 tablespoons) to make the glaze easy to drizzle.

Nutrition facts per serving: *249 calories, 3 g protein, 32 g carbohydrate, 13 g total fat (7 g saturated), 88 mg cholesterol, 169 mg sodium, 0 g fiber. Daily values: 13% vitamin A, 0% vitamin C, 5% calcium, 4% iron.*

To Make Ahead

Prepare and bake cake as directed; cool completely. Place cake on a baking sheet and freeze until firm. Once firm, place cake in a 2-gallon freezer bag and freeze up to 3 months. Before serving, thaw at room temperature several hours. Glaze as directed.

Orange-Poppy Seed Cake

Orange-Poppy Seed Cake

This recipe goes together in a snap and produces a wonderfully moist and flavorful cake. Serve it at your next weekend brunch.

3 **cups all-purpose flour**
2 **cups granulated sugar**
¼ **cup poppy seed**
2 **teaspoons baking powder**
¼ **teaspoon salt**
1 **cup cooking oil**
3 **eggs**
¾ **cup milk**
2 **teaspoons finely shredded orange peel**
½ **cup orange juice**
Easy Orange Glaze (optional)

1 Grease and lightly flour a 10-inch fluted tube pan. Set pan aside.

2 In a large mixing bowl stir together flour, sugar, poppy seed, baking powder, and salt. Add oil, eggs, milk, 2 teaspoons orange peel, and the orange juice. Beat with an electric mixer on low to medium speed about 60 seconds or until well combined.

3 Pour batter into prepared pan. Bake in a 350° oven for 50 to 55 minutes or until a wooden toothpick inserted near center of cake comes out clean. Cool cake in pan on a wire rack for 10 minutes. Remove cake from pan. If desired, prepare Easy Orange Glaze and drizzle over warm cake or pass with cake. Cover; store at room temperature for up to 3 days. Serves 18.

Easy Orange Glaze: In a small bowl combine 1 cup sifted powdered sugar and 3 to 4 teaspoons orange juice. Whisk until smooth.

Nutrition facts per serving: *316 calories, 4 g protein, 44 g carbohydrate, 14 g total fat (2 g saturated), 36 mg cholesterol, 87 mg sodium, 1 g fiber. Daily values: 2% vitamin A, 7% vitamin C, 7% calcium, 8% iron.*

To Make Ahead

Prepare, bake, and glaze cake as directed; cool completely. Place the cake on a baking sheet and freeze until firm. Once firm, place cake in a 2-gallon freezer bag and freeze for up to 3 months. Before serving, thaw at room temperature for several hours.

Embellishments

If you have neither all the ingredients on hand nor the time to start from scratch, why not spruce up a yellow, white, or chocolate two-layer cake mix? Here are some ideas to get you started.

Add one of these to the dry cake mix:
   ¾ teaspoon ground cinnamon
   ¾ teaspoon ground ginger
   ½ teaspoon ground allspice
   ¼ teaspoon ground nutmeg

Add one of these with the eggs:
   1 tablespoon instant coffee crystals (dissolved in the water called for in the cake-mix directions)
   1 tablespoon finely shredded orange peel
   1 teaspoon maple flavoring
   ½ teaspoon almond extract

Stir one of these into the mixed cake batter:
   1 cup coconut
   ½ cup finely chopped nuts
   ½ cup miniature semisweet chocolate pieces
   ½ cup well-drained, chopped maraschino cherries

To one-third of the white or yellow cake batter, add ½ cup chocolate-flavored syrup. Pour the plain batter into the baking pans; pour the chocolate batter on top of the plain batter. Swirl gently with a spatula.

Delicious Memories

Breakfast Bundt Cake

Our neighbors seem to have kept us in cake through the years. Neighbor and good friend Joan Prescott brought us this moist cinnamon bundt cake as a breakfast treat on Easter morning a number of years ago. It's the kind of cake you can't resist going back to again and again for just one more little sliver. We all loved it, especially our daughter, Angie. It has been her birthday cake of choice ever since.

—Lynda Haupert—

- ¼ **cup chopped nuts**
- ¼ **cup granulated sugar**
- 2 **teaspoons ground cinnamon**
- 1 **2-layer-size yellow cake mix**
- 1 **4-serving-size package instant vanilla pudding mix**
- ¾ **cup cooking oil**
- ¾ **cup water**
- 4 **eggs**
- 1 **teaspoon vanilla**
- 1 **teaspoon butter flavoring**

1 Grease a 10-inch fluted tube pan. Sprinkle nuts over the bottom of the pan. In a small bowl stir together sugar and cinnamon. Set pans and sugar mixture aside.

2 In a large mixing bowl stir together cake mix, dry pudding mix, cooking oil, and water. Beat with an electric mixer on low to medium speed about 1 minute or until well combined. Add eggs, one at a time, mixing well after each addition. Add vanilla and butter flavoring. Beat on high speed for 5 minutes.

3 Pour about one-third of the batter over nuts in pan; sprinkle with half of the cinnamon-sugar mixture. Add another one-third of the batter and sprinkle with remaining cinnamon-sugar mixture. Add remaining batter.

4 Bake in a 350° oven for 40 to 45 minutes or until a wooden toothpick inserted near the center of the cake comes out clean. Cool cake in pan on a wire rack for 15 minutes. Remove cake from pan and completely cool on the wire rack. Cover and store at room temperature for up to 3 days. Makes 12 to 16 servings.

Nutrition facts per serving: 388 calories, 3 g protein, 48 g carbohydrate, 21 g total fat (4 g saturated), 71 mg cholesterol, 348 mg sodium, 0 g fiber. Daily values: 3% vitamin A, 0% vitamin C, 8% calcium, 7% iron.

To Make Ahead

Prepare and bake cake as directed; cool completely. Place the cake on a baking sheet and freeze until firm. Once firm, place cake in a 2-gallon freezer bag and freeze for up to 3 months. Before serving, thaw at room temperature for several hours.

Pumpkin-Pear Cake

When you turn this cake upside down, a delicious caramel-pear topping appears.

- ⅔ **cup packed brown sugar**
- ¼ **cup butter or margarine, melted**
- 1 **teaspoon cornstarch**
- 1 **16-ounce can pear halves in light syrup**
- 1½ **cups all-purpose flour**
- 1½ **teaspoons pumpkin pie spice**
- 1 **teaspoon baking soda**
- ¾ **teaspoon baking powder**
- 4 **egg whites**
- 1 **cup granulated sugar**
- 1 **cup canned pumpkin**
- ½ **cup cooking oil**

1 In a small mixing bowl combine brown sugar, melted butter, and cornstarch. Drain pears, reserving 3 tablespoons of the syrup. Stir reserved syrup into brown sugar mixture.

2 Pour brown sugar mixture into a 10-inch round baking pan or a 9x9x2-inch baking pan. (If desired, cut each pear into a fan by making 3 or 4 lengthwise cuts starting ½ inch from the top of pear through the bottom.) Arrange pear halves over the syrup in the pan with the small ends to the center and rounded sides down.

3 In a medium mixing bowl combine flour, pumpkin pie spice, baking soda, and baking powder; set aside.

4 In a large mixing bowl beat the egg whites with electric mixer on medium speed until soft peaks form (tips curl). Gradually add the sugar, beating until stiff peaks form (tips stand straight). With mixer running on low speed, blend in pumpkin and oil. Fold flour mixture into pumpkin mixture just until moistened; carefully spoon over pears. Spread mixture evenly with back of spoon.

5 Bake in a 350° oven for 50 to 60 minutes or until a wooden toothpick inserted near the center of the cake comes out clean. Cool the cake in the pan on a wire rack for 5 minutes. Using a narrow metal spatula, loosen cake from sides of pan. Invert cake onto a serving plate. Serve warm. Cover any leftovers and store at room temperature for up to 3 days. Makes 10 to 12 servings.

When you arrange fruit in the bottom of a pan for an upside-down cake, remember that it will look the opposite when it's being served. Carefully spoon the batter over the fruit so the batter's flow does not rearrange it.

Nutrition facts per serving: 357 calories, 4 g protein, 56 g carbohydrate, 16 g total fat (5 g saturated), 12 mg cholesterol, 224 mg sodium, 2 g fiber. Daily values: 58% vitamin A, 2% vitamin C, 4% calcium, 11% iron.

Upside-Down Gingerbread

The crunchy nut topping, maple syrup, and crystallized ginger give this old-fashioned dessert a new twist.

3	tablespoons butter or margarine
⅓	cup packed brown sugar
⅓	cup maple syrup
1	cup coarsely chopped pecans
1½	cups all-purpose flour
½	cup granulated sugar
1	teaspoon ground cinnamon
¾	teaspoon ground ginger
½	teaspoon baking soda
½	teaspoon baking powder
¼	teaspoon ground allspice
½	cup buttermilk
¼	cup butter or margarine, softened
¼	cup maple syrup
1	egg
¼	cup chopped crystallized ginger
	Gingered Whipped Cream

1 Melt 3 tablespoons butter in a 9x1½-inch round baking pan. Stir in brown sugar and ⅓ cup maple syrup. Sprinkle with pecans. Set pan aside.

2 In a medium mixing bowl stir together flour, sugar, cinnamon, ginger, baking soda, baking powder, and allspice. Add buttermilk, ¼ cup butter, and ¼ cup maple syrup. Beat with an electric mixer on low to medium speed about 30 seconds or until combined. Then beat on high speed for 2 minutes, scraping sides of bowl occasionally. Add egg and beat for 2 minutes more. Stir in crystallized ginger.

3 Pour batter into prepared pan. Bake in a 350° oven about 35 minutes or until a wooden toothpick inserted near the center of the cake comes out clean. Cool the cake in the pan on a wire rack for 5 minutes. Loosen sides and invert the cake onto a plate. Serve warm with Gingered Whipped Cream. Makes 8 servings.

Gingered Whipped Cream: In a chilled bowl combine 1 cup whipping cream and 2 tablespoons brown sugar. Beat with chilled beaters of an electric mixer on medium speed until soft peaks form. Fold in 1 teaspoon finely chopped crystallized ginger.

Nutrition facts per serving: 419 calories, 5 g protein, 58 g carbohydrate, 20 g total fat (7 g saturated fat), 54 mg cholesterol, 232 mg sodium, 2 g fiber. Daily values: 10% vitamin A, 0% vitamin C, 5% calcium, 13% iron.

Delicious Memories

Spicy Oatmeal Cake

My Granny Eddins was famous for her great food. She had a knack for throwing a little of this and a dash of that together, which, unfortunately, meant we couldn't duplicate a wonderful dish. It's only because she copied this recipe from a newspaper that we were able to make this moist, old-fashioned cake again and again. She kept treats such as this cake on hand to fill up her grandchildren who lived nearby and dropped in frequently.
—Sandra Mosley—

2 cups boiling water
1½ cups uncooked quick or old-fashioned oats
2¼ cups all-purpose flour
1 teaspoon baking soda
½ teaspoon salt
1 teaspoon ground cinnamon
½ teaspoon ground nutmeg
¾ cup butter or margarine
1 cup granulated sugar
¾ cup packed brown sugar
1½ teaspoons vanilla
3 eggs
⅓ cup butter or margarine, melted
¾ cup packed brown sugar
⅓ cup half-and-half or light cream
1 cup chopped nuts
1⅓ cups coconut

1 Pour boiling water over oats; cover and let stand 20 minutes.

2 Grease a 13x9x2-inch baking pan. In a small mixing bowl stir together the flour, baking soda, salt, cinnamon, and nutmeg. Set the pan and flour mixture aside.

3 In a large mixing bowl beat the ¾ cup butter until fluffy. Add the sugar, ¾ cup brown sugar, vanilla, and eggs and beat until combined. Add the oat mixture and beat until well mixed. Add the flour mixture, beating on low speed just until combined.

4 Pour batter into the prepared pan. Bake in a 350° oven for 45 to 50 minutes or until a wooden toothpick inserted near the center comes out clean. Do not remove from pan.

5 For frosting, combine the ⅓ cup melted butter, ¾ cup brown sugar, the half-and-half, nuts, and coconut. Spread evenly over warm cake. Broil 3 inches from heat about 2 minutes or until bubbly and coconut is golden brown. Serve warm or cool. Cover and store at room temperature for up to 3 days. Makes 24 servings.

Nutrition facts per serving: *270 calories, 4 g protein, 34 g carbohydrate, 14 g total fat (7 g saturated fat), 50 mg cholesterol, 195 mg sodium, 1 g fiber. Daily values: 9% vitamin A, 0% vitamin C, 2% calcium, 8% iron.*

Baker's Bonus

Sizing Up

Because different cake shapes suit different occasions, you can't possibly hope to have room for all the various sizes of cake pans that might be specified in a recipe. For the cakes on pages 100-118, choose the size that suits you. Fill the baking pans no more than half full, and use any remaining batter to make cupcakes. Baking times given are approximate and may vary from cake to cake.

Pan Size	Estimated Baking Time In a 350° Oven
Two 8x1½-inch round baking pans	35 to 40 minutes
Two 9x1½-inch round baking pans	30 to 35 minutes
Two 8x8x2-inch baking pans	25 to 35 minutes
Two 9x9x2-inch baking pans	25 to 35 minutes
One 13x9x2-inch baking pan	30 to 35 minutes
One 15x10x1-inch baking pan	25 to 30 minutes
Cupcakes (half full of batter)	18 to 23 minutes

Spicy Oatmeal Cake, top, and Texas Sheet Cake (see recipe, page 117), bottom

Kid Appeal

Chocolate-Marshmallow Cake

This recipe is sure to become a family favorite. Marshmallows are sandwiched between a moist chocolate cake and candylike topping.

⅔ cup unsweetened cocoa powder
1 cup boiling water
2 cups all-purpose flour
1¾ cups granulated sugar
2 teaspoons baking powder
1 teaspoon baking soda
1 8-ounce carton dairy sour cream
¾ cup butter or margarine, softened
1½ teaspoons vanilla
3 eggs
3 cups miniature marshmallows (one 6¼-ounce package)
Crunchy Chocolate Topping

1 Grease a 13x9x2-inch baking pan; set aside.

2 In a small bowl whisk together the cocoa powder and boiling water until cocoa powder in dissolved. Cool to room temperature.

3 In a large mixing bowl stir together flour, sugar, baking powder, and baking soda. Add cooled cocoa mixture, sour cream, butter, and vanilla. Beat

with an electric mixer on low to medium speed until combined. Then beat on high speed for 2 minutes, scraping sides of bowl occasionally. Add eggs and beat for 2 minutes more.

4 Pour batter into the prepared pan. Bake in a 350° oven about 50 minutes or until a wooden toothpick inserted near the center of the cake comes out clean. Sprinkle marshmallows evenly over cake; return to oven 2 minutes more or until marshmallows are softened. Using a knife dipped in water, spread the softened marshmallows evenly over cake. Completely cool in pan on a wire rack. Frost top of cake with Crunchy Chocolate Topping. Makes 15 servings.

Crunchy Chocolate Topping: In a heavy small saucepan combine 1 cup semisweet chocolate pieces, ¾ cup peanut butter, and 2 tablespoons butter or margarine. Cook over medium-low heat, stirring constantly, until melted. Remove from heat. Stir in 1½ cups crisp rice cereal.

Nutrition facts per serving: 471 calories, 9 g protein, 59 g carbohydrate, 24 g total fat (9 g saturated fat), 77 mg cholesterol, 350 mg sodium, 1 g fiber. Daily values: 13% vitamin A, 0% vitamin C, 10% calcium, 17% iron.

Apple-Walnut Cake with Caramel Sauce

Prepare the perfect finale for a casual get-together with friends on a crisp autumn evening.

1 cup all-purpose flour
2 teaspoons baking powder
1 teaspoon ground cinnamon
½ teaspoon ground nutmeg
¼ teaspoon salt
¼ cup butter or margarine, softened
¾ cup granulated sugar
2 tablespoons milk
1 egg
2 cups finely chopped, peeled apples
½ cup chopped walnuts
Vanilla ice cream, frozen yogurt, or whipped cream (optional)
Caramel Sauce

1 Grease an 8x8x2-inch baking pan. In a small mixing bowl stir together the flour, baking powder, cinnamon, nutmeg, and salt. Set pan and flour mixture aside.

2 In a medium mixing bowl beat the butter with an electric mixer on medium to high speed about 30 seconds or until light.

3 Add sugar and milk to butter and beat until fluffy. Add egg, beating on medium speed until combined. Add flour mixture, beating on low to medium speed just until combined. Stir in apples and walnuts.

4 Spread batter into the prepared pan. Bake in a 350° oven about 40 minutes or until a wooden toothpick inserted near the center of the cake comes out clean. Completely cool cake in pan on a wire rack.

5 To serve, cut the cake into squares. If desired, place a scoop of vanilla ice cream or frozen yogurt or a dollop of whipped cream on cake. Top with warm Caramel Sauce. Cover any leftover cake and store in the refrigerator for up to 3 days. Makes 9 servings.

Caramel Sauce: In a heavy small saucepan melt ¼ cup butter or margarine. Stir in ½ cup packed brown sugar and 1 tablespoon light corn syrup. Bring mixture to a boil. Cook, stirring constantly, 1 minute or until sugar dissolves. Gradually stir in ¼ cup whipping cream; return mixture to a boil. Remove from heat. If desired, stir in 1 tablespoon rum. Serve warm. Stir before serving.

***Nutrition facts per serving:** 416 calories, 5 g protein, 52 g carbohydrate, 22 g total fat (11 g saturated fat), 80 mg cholesterol, 295 mg sodium, 1 g fiber. Daily values: 18% vitamin A, 1% vitamin C, 14% calcium, 9% iron.*

Delicious Memories

Texas Sheet Cake

I remember the first time I ever tasted this cake. A neighbor brought it to my mother on a warm spring day. Now when I need a rich dessert for a picnic or to take to church, I always think of this cake and, being a true Texan, make a big batch. I set up production assembly-line style and make two of the 15x10 cakes at the same time since it freezes so well. It is always a hit and I'm surprised at how many people are not familiar with it.
—Sandra Mosley—

1 **cup butter or margarine**
1 **cup water**
⅓ **cup unsweetened cocoa powder**
2 **cups all-purpose flour**
2 **cups granulated sugar**
1 **teaspoon baking soda**
½ **teaspoon salt**
1 **teaspoon ground cinnamon (optional)**
2 **slightly beaten eggs**
½ **cup buttermilk**
1½ **teaspoons vanilla**
Chocolate Frosting

1 Grease a 15x10x1-inch baking pan; set aside.

2 In a medium saucepan combine butter, water, and cocoa powder. Bring to a boil, stirring constantly. Remove from heat.

3 In a large mixing bowl combine flour, sugar, soda, salt, and cinnamon (if desired). Add eggs, buttermilk, and vanilla. Beat with an electric mixer on low to medium speed to combine. Add cocoa mixture and beat until blended.

4 Pour batter into prepared pan. Bake in a 375° oven 20 minutes or until cake springs back when lightly touched.

5 Immediately pour hot Chocolate Frosting over warm cake; spread evenly. Completely cool cake in pan on a wire rack. Cut into squares. Makes 60.

Chocolate Frosting: In a medium saucepan stir together ¼ cup butter or margarine, 3 tablespoons unsweetened cocoa powder, and 3 tablespoons buttermilk. Cook and stir until boiling; remove from heat. Beat in 2¼ cups sifted powdered sugar and ½ teaspoon vanilla with an electric mixer on low speed until blended. Stir in ½ cup chopped walnuts.

***Nutrition facts per serving:** 101 calories, 1 g protein, 14 g carbohydrate, 5 g total fat (2 g saturated fat), 17 mg cholesterol, 83 mg sodium, 0 g fiber. Daily values: 3% vitamin A, 0% vitamin C, 1% calcium, 2% iron.*

To Make Ahead

Prepare and bake cake as directed; cool completely. Do not frost. Place in a freezer container or bag and freeze for up to 3 months. Before serving, thaw several hours at room temperature. Frost as directed.

Baker's Bonus

Grease the Pan

To grease a cake pan without getting shortening all over your hands, use a paper towel to spread it. Grease and flour both the bottom and the sides of the pan if you want to remove the cake from the pan when it has cooled. If you want to leave the cake in the pan for serving, grease only the bottom of the pan and do not flour it.

For an 8- or 9-inch pan use 2 to 3 tablespoons shortening; for a 13x9x2- or 15x10x1-inch pan use 1½ to 2 tablespoons. Sprinkle a little flour into the pan. Tilt and tap the pan so the flour covers all the greased surfaces; tap out any excess flour.

Peanut Butter Crunch Cupcakes

Kid Appeal

2 **cups all-purpose flour**
1 **cup packed brown sugar**
1 **tablespoon baking powder**
1 **cup milk**
½ **cup butter or margarine,**
  softened
½ **cup peanut butter**
2 **eggs**
¾ **cup miniature semisweet**
  chocolate pieces
½ **cup chopped peanuts**
½ **cup coconut**

1 Line twenty-four 2½-inch muffin cups with paper bake cups. Set aside.

2 Combine the flour, brown sugar, and baking powder. Add milk, butter, and peanut butter. Beat with an electric mixer until combined. Then beat on high speed 2 minutes, scraping sides of bowl. Add eggs and beat for 2 minutes more. Stir in the chocolate pieces. Divide the batter among prepared pans.

3 For topping, in a small bowl combine peanuts and coconut. Sprinkle about 2 teaspoons topping evenly over batter in each muffin cup. Bake in a 350° oven for 20 to 25 minutes or until a wooden toothpick inserted near the center of a cupcake comes out clean. Cool cupcakes in pans on wire racks for 5 minutes. Remove cupcakes from pans and completely cool on the wire racks. Cover and store at room temperature for up to 3 days. Makes 24.

Nutrition facts per cupcake: *186 calories, 4 g protein, 21 g carbohydrate, 10 g total fat (4 g saturated fat), 29 mg cholesterol, 123 mg sodium, 1 g fiber. Daily values: 5% vitamin A, 0% vitamin C, 5% calcium, 6% iron.*

Applesauce Cupcakes

Delicious Memories

Get-togethers at Gram's house just aren't complete without her wonderful Applesauce Cupcakes. One bite of this moist, flavorful snack and I'm reminded of the family gathered in her kitchen, talking, catching up, and enjoying a meal together.
—Sarlynn Heston-Wymer—

2 **cups all-purpose flour**
2 **teaspoons baking soda**
1 **teaspoon ground cinnamon**
¼ **teaspoon salt**
1 **cup raisins**
½ **cup butter or margarine**
½ **cup shortening**
1½ **cups granulated sugar**
2 **slightly beaten eggs**
1½ **cups applesauce**
1 **teaspoon vanilla**
1 **cup chopped nuts**
  Apple-Cream Cheese Frosting

1 Line twenty-four 2½-inch muffin cups with paper bake cups. Combine the flour, baking soda, cinnamon, and salt. Set baking pans and flour mixture aside.

2 In a saucepan combine raisins and enough water to cover; heat to a boil. Remove from heat. Cover and let stand 5 minutes. Drain, reserving 2 tablespoons liquid; set aside.

3 Beat butter and shortening with an electric mixer for 30 seconds. Add sugar and beat until fluffy. Add reserved raisin liquid, eggs, applesauce, and vanilla; beat until combined. Add flour mixture; beat until combined. Stir in raisins and nuts.

4 Divide batter among prepared pans. Bake in a 350° oven 20 to 25 minutes or until cupcakes test done. Cool in pans 5 minutes. Remove from pans; completely cool. Frost with Apple-Cream Cheese Frosting. Cover and store in the refrigerator for up to 3 days. Makes 24 servings.

Apple-Cream Cheese Frosting: Beat together two 3-ounce packages cream cheese, softened, and 2 tablespoons frozen apple juice concentrate, thawed, with an electric mixer on medium speed until smooth. Gradually add about 4 cups sifted powdered sugar, beating on low speed to make the frosting easy to spread.

Nutrition facts per cupcake: *284 calories, 3 g protein, 45 g carbohydrate, 12 g total fat (4 g saturated fat), 28 mg cholesterol, 168 mg sodium, 1 g fiber. Daily values: 4% vitamin A, 4% vitamin C, 1% calcium, 5% iron.*

Peanut Butter Crunch Cupcakes, left, and Applesauce Cupcakes, right

Simply Special Cakes

One of the best parts of having a birthday used to be picking the kind of birthday cake you wanted. It didn't come in a box from the store, it came straight out of the oven at home. It didn't take a lot of fancy equipment or loads of time to create, just a steady hand, a bit of patience, and lots of imagination. (Directions begin on page 124.)

If it's flowers you like, good things come in big and small baskets. Capture the essence of a spring garden, overflowing with colors and a myriad of flowers, in a big Basket of Flowers Cake or lots of smaller Flower Basket or Flower Pot Cupcakes. Beautiful enough for a centerpiece, these cakes taste every bit as light and fresh as they look—if you can bear to eat them.

Who doesn't love the sound of an old Wurlitzer music machine grinding away as an antique carousel spins around and around and up and down. Even if you don't remember the sound, you can re-create the feel of gentler times with this incredibly delicate and irresistible Carousel Cake.

What a grrrrrrrrreat idea for a cake! This enchanting, cuddly lion will tame the wildest of kids' parties and the most ferocious of appetites. The secret to creating this king of cakes is incredibly simple—two standard cake layers and four cupcakes. You'll bring this feline friend to life when you add the finishing touches in chocolate frosting. The mane looks a bit difficult, but don't let it ruffle you—a star tip gives just the right effect.

Feel like clowning around? Up to a little monkey business? How about getting the lion's share of compliments for whipping up such terrific treats? All it takes is a few frosted cupcakes, some additional frosting in your favorite colors, and a whole lot of fun!

You know you can, you know you can, you know you can make this engaging little steam engine cake. It starts with two homemade or purchased pound cakes and, with the help of some clever cutting, winds up with a finished product that will appeal to big and small kids alike.

Lion Cake

On a foil-covered piece of cardboard arrange an 8-inch cake layer for the lion's head, a 9-inch layer for the body, and 4 cupcakes for the ears and paws. Trim cake layers and cupcakes to fit together snugly.

Frost entire lion using yellow frosting. Use chocolate frosting and a writing tip to outline the body and face; pipe the mane with a star tip. Pipe on a bow tie with green frosting and a writing tip; outline and decorate tie with orange frosting.

Steam Engine

Cut one 8x4- or 9x5-inch pound cake in half crosswise. Cut a half cake in half again diagonally. Place a whole 8x4- or 9x5-inch pound cake on foil-covered cardboard; frost with chocolate frosting.

Place the half pound cake (square) on top of the frosted whole cake so it is even with one end. Place one piece of diagonally cut half cake at the opposite end of the whole cake to represent the front of the steam engine. If desired, carve the diagonal piece into a pointed train front. (Reserve remaining cake for another use.)

Frost cake with chocolate frosting. Decorate with additional tinted frosting (green, orange, yellow, blue, and purple); use sugar cookies for large wheels, vanilla sandwich cookies for small wheels and chimney, small square cookies for window, a white candy coating disk for the engineer's face, and a white pipe cleaner for the smoke.

Basket of Flowers Cake

Place one 8- or 9-inch cake layer on a cake plate. Frost top with white frosting. Cut a second 8- or 9-inch cake layer in half crosswise. Set half aside for another use. Place cake half, cut side down, across the center of the top of the frosted layer. Use two 6-inch wooden skewers to hold the half layer upright. (Break off ends of skewers so they don't show.)

Frost sides of the half layer with white frosting. Use purchased icing roses or pipe your own flowers onto cake using a rose tip and a leaf tip. Using a basket tip, pipe stripes ¼ to ½ inch apart up sides of whole cake layer. Pipe horizontal stripes around cake, alternating stripes for a basket-weave effect. Use same tip to decorate edge of basket handle.

Use a large star tip to pipe a border around basket and basket handle. If desired, use a rose tip to pipe a bow on the basket handle and a round tip to pipe scallops on the cake plate.

Carousel Cake

Place a 8- or 9-inch cake layer on a plate; frost with white frosting. Add second layer and frost. Frost 6 sugar cookie carousel horses as desired, using round and star tips. Using a rose tip, pipe ruffles around the base of the cake. Arrange frosted cookie horses around the cake.

Use a serrated knife to cut 6 triangles (about 2x4 inches) from 3 filled toaster pastries or graham cracker squares. Arrange them on top of the cake with the longest sides down and the points toward outside edge. Use frosting to attach several pieces of round hard candy to center top.

Use a tube of decorator icing to pipe ruffles on the top edge of the toaster pastries or graham cracker triangles. If desired, add more decorations with the tinted pastel frostings (blue, pink, yellow, and purple).

Cupcakes

Flower Pot Cupcakes: Use green frosting and a grass tip to add "grass" to tops of frosted cupcakes. Insert sucker "flowers."

Flower Basket Cupcakes: Use tinted frosting (pink, green, yellow, and blue) and a star tip to pipe a basket-weave pattern (see Basket of Flowers Cake) on top of white frosted cupcakes. Add small flowers with a drop flower or star tip and leaves with a leaf tip.

Clown Cupcakes: Use tinted frosting (green, blue, yellow, and red) and a small, round tip to outline faces on white frosted cupcakes. Use a star, leaf, or rose tip to make collars. Make hats and hair with star and round tips.

Lion Cupcakes: Use chocolate frosting and a star tip to pipe a mane onto the edge of frosted cupcakes. Outline faces with a small, round tip.

Monkey Cupcakes: Use green frosting and a leaf tip to pipe leaves on frosted cupcakes. Outline faces with chocolate frosting and a round tip.

Angel Food Cake

Angel food cakes are appropriately named—they're light and high-rising.

1½ **cups egg whites (10 to 12 large)**
1½ **cups sifted powdered sugar**
 1 **cup sifted cake flour or sifted
   all-purpose flour**
1½ **teaspoons cream of tartar**
 1 **teaspoon vanilla**
 1 **cup granulated sugar**

1 In a very large mixing bowl allow egg whites to stand at room temperature for 30 minutes. Meanwhile, sift the powdered sugar and flour together 3 times. Set flour mixture aside.

2 Add cream of tartar and vanilla to the egg whites. Beat with an electric mixer on medium speed until soft peaks form (tips curl). Gradually add sugar, about 2 tablespoons at a time, beating until stiff peaks form (tips stand straight).

3 Sift about one-fourth of the flour mixture over the beaten egg whites, then gently fold in. (If bowl is too full, transfer to a larger bowl.) Repeat folding in the remaining flour mixture, using one-fourth of the flour mixture each time.

4 Gently spoon batter evenly into an ungreased 10-inch tube pan. Gently cut through the batter with a knife or narrow metal spatula. Bake on the lowest rack in a 350° oven for 40 to 45 minutes or until top springs back when lightly touched. Immediately invert cake in pan. Cool completely. Using a narrow metal spatula, loosen sides of cake from pan. Then remove the cake from the pan. Cover and store at room temperature for up to 3 days. Makes 12 servings.

Nutrition facts per serving: *161 calories, 4 g protein, 37 g carbohydrate, 0 g total fat (0 g saturated), 0 mg cholesterol, 46 mg sodium, 0 g fiber. Daily values: 0% vitamin A, 0% vitamin C, 0% calcium, 4% iron.*

Chocolate Angel Food Cake: Prepare Angel Food Cake as directed, except sift ¼ cup unsweetened cocoa powder in with the flour and powdered sugar.

To Make Ahead

Prepare and bake cake as directed; cool completely. Place the cake on a baking sheet and freeze until firm. Once firm, place cake in a 2-gallon freezer bag and freeze for up to 3 months. Before serving, thaw at room temperature for several hours.

Heavenly Whites

Lighter-than-air angel food, sponge, and chiffon cakes will hit the plate hard unless you handle the egg whites properly. These cakes primarily rely on air bubbles trapped in the beaten egg whites to reach their lofty heights, and just one speck of egg yolk or any other fat in the egg whites ruins their beating quality.

Use a glass or metal bowl that is wide enough to keep the beaters from becoming buried in the egg whites as they fluff. Make sure the bowl is clean.

Separate the egg whites from the egg yolks as soon as you take the eggs out of the refrigerator. Let them stand at room temperature for 30 minutes along with the other ingredients.

Always separate eggs one at a time into a small bowl. Transfer each egg white to the large glass or metal bowl in which the whites will be beaten. If any yolk gets mixed in with an egg white, refrigerate that white for another use. The cream of tartar is added to stabilize the egg whites and to produce a whiter cake.

Do not over- or underbeat egg whites. They should be stiff but not dry, or your cake will fall.

International Origin

Tiramisu Cake

Angel food cake replaces the traditional ladyfingers in this classic Italian dessert.

Angel Food Cake
   (see page 125)
1 **8-ounce container mascarpone cheese or one 8-ounce package cream cheese, softened**
½ **cup sifted powdered sugar**
3 **tablespoons coffee liqueur**
2 **cups whipping cream**
¼ **cup sifted powdered sugar**
2 **tablespoons coffee liqueur**
¾ **cup strong black coffee**
¼ **cup coffee liqueur**

Mocha Fudge Sauce (optional)
Unsweetened cocoa powder
   (optional)
Chocolate curls

1 Prepare the Angel Food Cake as directed.

2 For filling, combine mascarpone cheese, the ½ cup powdered sugar, and the 3 tablespoons liqueur. Beat with an electric mixer until smooth. Set aside.

3 Combine whipping cream, the ¼ cup powdered sugar, and 2 tablespoons liqueur; beat until stiff peaks form. Fold ½ cup whipped cream mixture into mascarpone mixture. Set mascarpone filling aside.

4 To assemble, cut cake horizontally into three even layers. Place first cake layer on a large serving plate. With a long-tine fork or skewers, poke holes in tops of each cake layer.

5 Combine coffee and the ¼ cup liqueur; drizzle over each cake layer. Spread half of the mascarpone filling on top of the first cake layer. Top with second cake layer, then spread with remaining mascarpone filling. Finally, top with the remaining cake layer. Frost entire cake with remaining whipped cream mixture. If desired, cover and chill for up to 2 hours.

6 To serve, if desired, drizzle Mocha Fudge Sauce over cake or sprinkle with unsweetened cocoa powder and chocolate curls. Cover any leftover cake and store in the refrigerator. Makes 16 servings.

Mocha Fudge Sauce: Heat ¼ cup fudge ice-cream topping just until warm. Stir in coffee liqueur (1 to 2 tablespoons) until easy to drizzle.

Nutrition facts per serving: *354 calories, 8 g protein, 40 g carbohydrate, 19 g total fat (11 g saturated), 59 mg cholesterol, 170 mg sodium, 0 g fiber. Daily values: 13% vitamin A, 0% vitamin C, 5% calcium, 3% iron.*

Shortcut

Substitute a purchased angel food cake for the homemade version.

To Make Ahead

Prepare and bake cake as directed; cool completely. Place the cake on a baking sheet and freeze until firm. Once firm, place cake in a 2-gallon freezer bag and freeze for up to 3 months. Before serving, thaw at room temperature for 3 hours. Cut, fill, and frost as directed.

Cake Traits

Angel food and sponge cakes, sometimes called "foam" cakes, rely on the air trapped in the beaten eggs for leavening. The main difference between the two is that angel food cakes contain no egg yolk, while sponge cakes do. Chiffon cakes are prepared similarly to angel food and sponge cakes, but they contain both whole eggs and cooking oil and, therefore, behave slightly differently.

When making a chiffon cake, the egg yolks should be added to the flour mixture after the cooking oil or they will bind with the flour and form streaks. With sponge cakes, beat the egg yolks until they're thick and the color of lemons, or an eggy bottom layer may form. This also can happen in either sponge or chiffon cakes if the egg whites are either under- or overbeaten.

So they don't fall, all three types of cakes must be cooled upside down to set their structures.

Tiramisu Cake

Cinnamon Angel Food Cake with Strawberry-Orange Compote

The perfect dessert for those individuals on low-fat, low-cholesterol diets—a cinnamon-and-orange-flavored cake topped with a colorful fruit compote.

1½ **cups egg whites (10 to 12 large)**
1½ **cups sifted powdered sugar**
1 **cup sifted cake flour or sifted all-purpose flour**
1 **teaspoon ground cinnamon**
1½ **teaspoons cream of tartar**
1 **tablespoon orange liqueur (optional)**
1 **cup granulated sugar**
1 **teaspoon finely shredded orange peel**
Cinnamon Glaze
Strawberry-Orange Compote

1 In a large mixing bowl allow egg whites to stand at room temperature for 30 minutes. Meanwhile, sift powdered sugar, flour, and cinnamon together 3 times. Set aside.

2 Add cream of tartar and liqueur (if desired) to the egg whites. Beat with an electric mixer on medium speed until soft peaks form (tips curl). Gradually add sugar, about 2 tablespoons at a time, beating until stiff peaks form (tips stand straight).

3 Sift about one-fourth of the flour mixture over the beaten egg whites, then gently fold in. (If bowl is too full, transfer to a larger bowl.) Repeat folding in the remaining flour mixture, using one-fourth of the flour mixture each time. Gently fold in orange peel.

4 Gently spoon batter evenly into an ungreased 10-inch tube pan. Gently cut through batter with a knife or narrow metal spatula. Bake on the lowest rack in a 350° oven for 40 to 45 minutes or until top springs back when lightly touched. Immediately invert cake in pan. Cool completely. Using a narrow metal spatula, loosen sides of cake from pan. Then remove cake from pan. Transfer to a serving plate and drizzle with Cinnamon Glaze. Serve cake slices with Strawberry-Orange Compote. Cover any leftover cake and store at room temperature for up to 3 days. Refrigerate any remaining compote. Serves 12.

Cinnamon Glaze: In a small bowl combine 1 cup sifted powdered sugar and ¼ teaspoon ground cinnamon. Gradually blend in enough orange liqueur, orange juice, or milk (1 to 2 tablespoons) until smooth. If necessary, add additional liquid, 1 teaspoon at a time, until glaze is easy to drizzle.

Strawberry-Orange Compote: Using a vegetable peeler, cut two 1x2-inch strips of orange peel from 1 of 3 oranges. Set strips of peel aside. Peel the 3 oranges. Section oranges over a bowl to catch the juice. Set orange sections aside. Add additional orange juice to reserved juice to equal ½ cup. In a heavy small saucepan combine orange juice, ⅓ cup honey, 3 inches

stick cinnamon, and the orange peel strips. Bring to boiling over medium heat. Simmer 10 to 12 minutes or until mixture is reduced to ⅓ cup. Discard cinnamon stick and orange peel. Stir in 2 tablespoons orange liqueur or additional orange juice. In a medium bowl combine reserved orange sections and 2 cups sliced strawberries. Pour syrup over fruit and stir.

Nutrition facts per serving: *237 calories, 4 g protein, 56 g carbohydrate, 0 g total fat (0 g saturated), 0 mg cholesterol, 47 mg sodium, 0 g fiber. Daily values: 0% vitamin A, 22% vitamin C, 1% calcium, 5% iron.*

To Make Ahead

Prepare and bake cake as directed; cool completely. Place the cake on a baking sheet and freeze until firm. Once firm, place cake in a 2-gallon freezer bag and freeze for up to 3 months. Before serving, thaw at room temperature for 3 hours. Glaze and serve as directed.

Marble Angel Food Cake

Using unsweetened cocoa powder keeps this lovely cake low in fat and cholesterol.

1½ **cups egg whites (10 to 12 large)**
1½ **cups sifted powdered sugar**
1 **cup sifted cake flour or sifted all-purpose flour**
2 **tablespoons unsweetened cocoa powder**
1½ **teaspoons cream of tartar**
1 **teaspoon vanilla**
1 **cup granulated sugar**
Chocolate Whipped Cream or fresh fruit (optional)

1 In a large mixing bowl allow egg whites to stand at room temperature for 30 minutes. Meanwhile, sift powdered sugar and flour together 3 times. Measure 1 cup of the flour mixture; sift together with the cocoa powder. Set both mixtures aside.

2 Add cream of tarter and vanilla to the egg whites. Beat with an electric mixer on medium speed until soft peaks form (tips curl). Gradually add sugar, about 2 tablespoons at a time, beating until stiff peaks form (tips stand straight). Transfer one-third of the mixture to another bowl.

3 Sift about one-fourth of the plain flour mixture over the larger portion of beaten egg whites, then gently fold in. (If bowl is too full, transfer to a larger bowl.) Repeat folding in the remaining plain flour mixture, using one-fourth of the flour mixture each time. Sift flour-cocoa mixture, one-third at a time, over smaller portion of beaten egg whites, folding in as above.

4 Gently spoon one-third of the white batter evenly into an ungreased 10-inch tube pan. Spoon half of the chocolate batter over white batter in pan. Repeat, then top with remaining white batter. Marble the batter.

5 Bake on the lowest rack in a 350° oven for 40 to 45 minutes or until top springs back when lightly touched. Immediately invert cake in pan. Cool completely. Using a narrow metal spatula, loosen sides of cake from pan. Then remove cake from pan. If desired, serve with Chocolate Whipped Cream or fresh fruit. Cover any leftover cake and store at room temperature up to 3 days. Serves 12.

Chocolate Whipped Cream: In a small saucepan combine 1 cup whipping cream and 1 ounce semisweet chocolate. Stir over low heat until chocolate is melted. Remove from heat and stir until no chocolate specks remain. Pour into a small mixing bowl; cover and chill completely. Just before serving, beat cream mixture with an electric mixer on low speed until stiff peaks form.

Nutrition facts per serving: *165 calories, 4 g protein, 37 g carbohydrate, 0 g total fat (0 g saturated), 0 mg cholesterol, 46 mg sodium, 0 g fiber. Daily values: 0% vitamin A, 0% vitamin C, 1% calcium, 5% iron.*

Using a table knife, spatula, or spoon, slowly run utensil through the batter to marble it. Using a folding motion, bring the utensil down through batter and up the other side. Go completely around the pan, using this motion, turning the pan as you fold.

To Make Ahead
Prepare and bake cake as directed; cool completely. Place the cake on a baking sheet and freeze until firm. Once firm, place cake in a 2-gallon freezer bag and freeze for up to 3 months. Before serving, thaw at room temperature for several hours. Serve as directed.

Flour Power

Angel food and sponge cakes are simple mixtures of eggs, sugar, flour, and flavorings. These cakes are easy to make if you follow their recipes closely and measure accurately.

Some recipes give you the option of using cake or all-purpose flour and, while either will work, cake flour will produce a slightly more tender crumb.

Adding the correct amount of flour is also an extremely important step. Using a rubber spatula, fold the flour mixture in just until the batter is smooth; try to keep the spatula under the surface of the batter while folding. If you add too much flour and overmix the batter when adding it, the volume will drop and your cake will be tough.

Coffee-Hazelnut Gâteau

This sensational cake bursts with the flavors of chocolate, hazelnuts, and coffee.

1½ **cups semisweet chocolate pieces, melted**
12 **whole hazelnuts (filberts)**
 1 **cup whipping cream**
 1 **teaspoon vanilla**
1½ **cups all-purpose flour**
 ¾ **cup ground hazelnuts (filberts)**
1½ **teaspoons baking powder**
 ¼ **teaspoon salt**
 3 **eggs**
 2 **teaspoons vanilla**
1½ **cups granulated sugar**
 ¾ **cup milk**
 3 **tablespoons butter or margarine**
   Coffee Buttercream

1 Dip bottoms of whole hazelnuts into some of the melted chocolate; place nuts on waxed paper to set. In a small saucepan heat cream over low heat until simmering. Stir into remaining melted chocolate until smooth and well combined. Stir in 1 teaspoon vanilla. Pour into a metal bowl; cover with plastic wrap. Refrigerate until well chilled, about 3 to 4 hours, stirring occasionally. (Do not allow chocolate mixture to set up.)

2 Grease a 15x10x1-inch jelly-roll pan and line with waxed paper. Grease and flour waxed paper. Combine flour, ground hazelnuts, baking powder, and salt; set aside.

3 In a large mixing bowl beat eggs and 2 teaspoons vanilla with an electric mixer on high speed for 4 minutes or until thick. Gradually add sugar, about 2 tablespoons at a time, beating at medium speed 5 minutes or until light. Add the dry ingredients to the egg mixture, beating at low to medium speed just until combined. In a small saucepan heat the milk and butter until butter melts; stir into batter until well combined.

4 Pour batter into prepared pan. Bake in a 350° oven about 20 minutes or until top springs back when lightly touched. Using a narrow metal spatula, immediately loosen sides of cake from pan. Invert cake onto a wire rack. Remove waxed paper; cool thoroughly. Cut cake crosswise into fourths, making 4 rectangles of approximately 10x3¾ inches each.

5 Beat the chilled chocolate mixture at medium speed about 1 to 2 minutes or until thick and light-colored (do not overbeat).

6 Place one cake rectangle on a serving plate. Spread with one-third of the chocolate mixture. Top with second cake rectangle. Repeat layers, ending with the fourth cake rectangle. Reserve ⅔ cup of the Coffee Buttercream. Frost sides and top of cake with remaining buttercream. Spoon reserved buttercream into a decorating bag fitted with a star tip. Pipe 12 rosettes lengthwise down the center of cake. Press a chocolate-dipped hazelnut into each rosette. Pipe more but-

tercream around base of cake. Cover and store in the refrigerator for up to 2 days. Let stand at room temperature for 30 to 60 minutes before serving. Makes 12 servings.

Coffee Buttercream: Dissolve 2 teaspoons instant coffee crystals in 1 tablespoon hot water. In a small saucepan combine 1 cup granulated sugar and ½ cup water. Cook over medium heat about 5 minutes or until bubbly and sugar is dissolved. Continue to boil gently until mixture reaches 240° (about 12 minutes). In the top of a double boiler, beat 4 egg yolks with an electric mixer on high speed until foamy. Continue beating egg yolks while gradually adding hot syrup in a thin stream. Place top of double boiler over boiling water. Cook while beating at high speed for 5 minutes. Transfer mixture to a large mixing bowl; beat 5 minutes more or until cool. Gradually beat in 1½ cups softened unsalted butter, about 1 tablespoon at a time, beating on medium speed until light and fluffy. (If frosting begins to soften, place bowl in ice water.) Beat in dissolved coffee crystals and 1 teaspoon vanilla.

Nutrition facts per serving: 771 calories, 8 g protein, 78 g carbohydrate, 52 g total fat (22 g saturated), 223 mg cholesterol, 157 mg sodium, 2 g fiber. Daily values: 47% vitamin A, 0% vitamin C, 10% calcium, 15% iron.

To Make Ahead

Prepare and bake cake as directed; cool completely. Cut cake crosswise into fourths, making 4 rectangles of approximately 10x3¾ inches each.

Place cake rectangles on a baking sheet and freeze until firm. Once firm, place cake in 2-gallon freezer bags; seal, label, and freeze up to 3 months. Before serving, thaw at room temperature for 3 hours. Frost as directed.

Honey-Coconut-Orange Cake

Bake a delightfully different cake that is sure to impress those who partake of it.

  6 **egg yolks**
1¼ **cups all-purpose flour**
 ⅓ **cup granulated sugar**
 ¼ **teaspoon salt**
 ½ **cup orange juice**
 ⅔ **cup granulated sugar**
  1 **tablespoon finely shredded**
     orange peel
  6 **egg whites**
  1 **teaspoon cream of tartar**
 ½ **cup honey**
     Honey-Coconut Filling
     Honey-Butter Frosting

1 In a medium mixing bowl beat egg yolks with an electric mixer on high speed about 6 minutes or until thick and the color of lemons; set aside. In a small mixing bowl stir together flour, ⅓ cup sugar, and salt. Set the flour mixture aside.

2 Add orange juice to egg yolks. Beat on low speed until combined. Gradually add ⅔ cup sugar, beating on medium speed about 5 minutes or until sugar is almost dissolved.

Gradually add about one-fourth of the flour mixture to the egg yolk mixture, beating on low to medium speed just until moistened. Repeat beating in remaining flour mixture, using one-fourth of the flour mixture each time. Stir in orange peel.

3 Thoroughly wash beaters. In a large mixing bowl beat egg whites and cream of tartar on medium speed until soft peaks form (tips curl). Gradually add honey, about 2 tablespoons at a time, beating until stiff peaks form (tips stand straight).

4 Stir about 1 cup of the egg white mixture into the egg yolk mixture. Then fold the egg yolk mixture into the remaining egg white mixture. Gently spoon batter into an ungreased 10-inch tube pan. Bake in a 325° oven about 55 minutes or until top springs back when lightly touched. Immediately invert cake in pan. Cool completely. Using a narrow metal spatula, loosen sides of cake from pan. Then remove cake from pan. Slice cake horizontally into 3 even layers.

5 Place bottom layer of cake on a serving plate. Spread with ⅔ cup of the Honey-Coconut Filling. Top with second cake layer. Spread with ⅔ cup of the Honey-Butter Frosting. Top with remaining cake layer. Spread with remaining Honey-Coconut Filling. Frost sides of cake and pipe stars around edge of cake with the remaining Honey-Butter Frosting. Cover and store at room temperature for up to 3 days. Makes 12 to 16 servings.

Honey-Coconut Filling: In a medium saucepan beat 1 egg slightly with a fork. Stir in one 5-ounce can evaporated milk (⅔ cup), ½ cup honey, and ¼ cup butter or margarine. Cook and stir over medium heat about 10 minutes or until mixture just coats a metal spoon. Remove from heat. Stir in 1⅓ cups flaked coconut (one 3-ounce can) and ½ cup toasted chopped almonds. Cool thoroughly.

Honey-Butter Frosting: In a large mixing bowl beat ½ cup butter (no substitutes) with an electric mixer on medium to high speed until light and fluffy. Gradually add 3⅓ cups sifted powdered sugar, beating well on low to medium speed until combined. Slowly beat in 3 tablespoons milk, 3 tablespoons honey, and 2 teaspoons vanilla. Gradually beat in 3⅓ cups additional sifted powdered sugar. If necessary, beat in additional milk, 1 teaspoon at a time, to make the frosting easy to spread.

Nutrition facts per serving: *638 calories, 7 g protein, 115 g carbohydrate, 19 g total fat (11 g saturated), 159 mg cholesterol, 215 mg sodium, 1 g fiber. Daily values: 28% vitamin A, 10% vitamin C, 5% calcium, 9% iron.*

To Make Ahead

Prepare and bake cake as directed; cool completely. Place cake on a baking sheet and freeze until firm. Once firm, place cake in 2-gallon freezer bags; seal, label, and freeze up to 3 months. Before serving, thaw at room temperature for 3 hours. Fill and frost as directed.

Setting Some Aside

Angel food, sponge, and chiffon cakes are best frozen unfrosted. Place them in a large freezer bag and freeze for up to 3 months.

Do not store any longer or the delicate sponge texture may deteriorate, and the cake might pick up odors from the freezer. Thaw at room temperature for several hours before serving.

Amazing Banana-Nut Roll

Shaping a jelly roll used to be a multi-step process—rolling, cooling, filling, and rerolling. Now you can bake the cake and filling together and roll just once.

- **1 8-ounce package cream cheese, softened**
- **1 3-ounce package cream cheese, softened**
- **½ cup granulated sugar**
- **1 whole egg**
- **3 tablespoons milk**
- **½ cup all-purpose flour**
- **½ teaspoon baking powder**
- **¼ teaspoon baking soda**
- **4 egg yolks**
- **½ teaspoon vanilla**
- **⅓ cup granulated sugar**

- **1 large banana, mashed (about ½ cup)**
- **½ cup finely chopped walnuts**
- **4 egg whites**
- **½ cup granulated sugar**
  Cream Cheese Frosting
  Walnut halves (optional)

1 Lightly grease a 15x10x1-inch baking pan. Line bottom and sides with waxed paper; grease paper. Set aside.

2 For filling, in a mixing bowl beat cream cheese and ½ cup sugar; with an electric mixer on medium speed until smooth. Add the whole egg and milk; beat until combined. Spread in prepared pan; chill until needed.

3 For cake, in a small mixing bowl stir together flour, baking powder, and baking soda; set aside.

4 In a medium mixing bowl beat egg yolks and vanilla with an electric mixer on high speed about 5 minutes or until mixture is thick and lemon colored. Gradually add ⅓ cup sugar, beating on medium speed about 5 minutes more or until sugar is almost dissolved. Stir in banana and nuts.

5 Thoroughly wash beaters. In a large mixing bowl beat egg whites on medium speed until soft peaks form (tips curl). Gradually add the ½ cup sugar, about 2 tablespoons at a time, beating until stiff peaks form (tips stand straight).

6 Stir about 1 cup of the egg white mixture into the yolk mixture. Fold the yolk mixture into the remaining egg white mixture. Sprinkle flour mixture evenly over egg mixture; fold in just until blended.

7 Carefully spread batter evenly over filling in pan. Bake in a 375° oven for 15 to 20 minutes or until top springs back when lightly touched. Immediately loosen sides of cake from pan. Invert cake onto a towel sprinkled with powdered sugar. Carefully peel off waxed paper. Starting with narrow end, roll up cake using towel as a guide. (Do not roll towel into cake.) Cool completely on a wire rack.

8 Spread Cream Cheese Frosting over roll and pipe a shell border along bottom edge and down the center of roll. If desired, garnish with walnuts. Cover and store in the refrigerator for up to 3 days. Makes 10 servings.

Cream Cheese Frosting: In a small mixing bowl combine one 3-ounce package cream cheese, softened, and 1 teaspoon vanilla; beat with an electric mixer on medium speed until light and fluffy. Gradually beat in 2 cups sifted powdered sugar. Beat in enough milk (1 to 2 tablespoons) to make the frosting easy to spread.

Nutrition facts per serving: *396 calories, 8 g protein, 47 g carbohydrate, 20 g total fat (10 g saturated), 151 mg cholesterol, 204 mg sodium, 1 g fiber. Daily values: 31% vitamin A, 2% vitamin C, 6% calcium, 8% iron.*

Amazing Banana-Nut Roll

Going Nuts

Nuts add an appealing crunch and unique flavor to baked goods. To store, keep unopened packages in a cool, dark place. Store opened packages in an airtight container in the refrigerator 6 months or in the freezer 2 years.

Almonds have a mild, yet rich flavor. They are available blanched or unblanched as whole, sliced, and slivered nuts.

Cashews are kidney-shape nuts with a rich, buttery flavor.

Hazelnuts (filberts) are small, round nuts wrapped in a parchmentlike deep brown skin. They have a mild, sweet flavor.

Macadamia nuts have a meat that is creamy beige, smooth, and rich in flavor.

Peanuts are available fresh or roasted for snacking and baking. For baking, it's best to use peanuts that have had their skins removed.

Pecans, often used interchangeably with walnuts, have an oily texture and delicate flavor.

Pine nuts (pignolies) are actually the seeds of a particular pine tree. The soft, pale yellow kernels, which are high in unsaturated oils, often are toasted for flavor.

Pistachio nuts are small, green kernels covered with a thin, reddish skin and encased in a brittle shell, which may be dyed red.

Walnuts have a mild flavor. With 15 varieties scattered throughout the world, the English walnut is the most popular.

Chiffon Cake

2¼ cups sifted cake flour or 2 cups
   sifted all-purpose flour
1½ cups granulated sugar
  1 tablespoon baking powder
  ¼ teaspoon salt
  ½ cup cooking oil
  7 egg yolks
  1 teaspoon vanilla
  ¾ cup water
  2 teaspoons finely shredded
    orange peel
  1 teaspoon finely shredded
    lemon peel
  7 egg whites
  ½ teaspoon cream of tartar

1 In a large mixing bowl stir together flour, sugar, baking powder, and salt. Make a well in the center of dry mixture. Then add oil, egg yolks, vanilla, and water. Beat with an electric mixer on low speed until combined. Then beat on high speed for 5 minutes or until satin smooth. Fold in orange and lemon peel. Set batter aside.

2 Thoroughly wash beaters. In a very large mixing bowl beat egg whites and cream of tartar on medium to high speed until stiff peaks form (tips stand straight). Then pour batter in a thin stream over beaten egg whites and gently fold in.

3 Pour batter into an ungreased 10-inch tube pan. Bake in a 325° oven for 65 to 70 minutes or until top springs back when lightly touched. Immediately invert cake in pan. Cool completely. Using a narrow metal spatula, loosen sides of cake from pan. Then remove cake from pan. Cover and store at room temperature for up to 3 days. Makes 16 servings.

Nutrition facts per serving: *222 calories, 4 g protein, 31 g carbohydrate, 9 g total fat (2 g saturated), 93 mg cholesterol, 129 mg sodium, 0 g fiber. Daily values: 14% vitamin A, 0% vitamin C, 6% calcium, 10% iron.*

To Make Ahead

Prepare and bake cake as directed; cool completely. Place the cake on a baking sheet and freeze until firm. Once firm, place the cake in a 2-gallon freezer bag and freeze for up to 3 months. Before serving, thaw at room temperature about 3 hours.

Praline-Pecan Roll

  1 cup pecans
  ¼ cup all-purpose flour
  5 egg yolks
  2 teaspoons vanilla
  ¾ cup granulated sugar
  5 egg whites
  ¼ teaspoon cream of tartar
    Caramel Buttercream
    Sugared pecans (optional)

1 Grease and lightly flour a 15x10x1-inch jelly-roll pan; set aside.

2 In a food processor bowl combine pecans and flour. Cover and process for 30 to 60 seconds until nuts are finely ground; set aside.

3 In a mixing bowl beat egg yolks and vanilla with an electric mixer on high speed 5 minutes or until thick and the color of lemons. Gradually add ¼ cup of the sugar, beating on medium speed about 5 minutes or until sugar is almost dissolved; set aside.

4 Thoroughly wash the beaters. In a large mixing bowl beat the egg whites and cream of tartar on medium speed until soft peaks form (tips curl). Gradually add the remaining ½ cup sugar, about 2 tablespoons at a time, beating until stiff peaks form (tips stand straight).

5 Stir about 1 cup of the egg white mixture into the yolk mixture. Then fold the egg yolk mixture into the remaining egg white mixture. Sprinkle nut mixture over egg mixture; fold in just until blended.

6 Spread batter into prepared pan. Bake in a 350° oven for 18 to 20 minutes or until top springs back when lightly touched. Immediately loosen sides of cake from pan. Invert cake onto a towel sprinkled with powdered sugar. Roll up warm cake and towel together, jelly-roll style, starting from a short side. Cool on a wire rack.

7 Gently unroll cake. Spread 1½ cups of Caramel Buttercream to within 1 inch of the edges. Roll up cake without towel, jelly-roll style, starting from one of the short sides. Frost cake with remaining Caramel Buttercream. If desired, garnish with sugared pecans. Cover and store in the refrigerator for up to 3 days. Makes 10 servings.

Caramel Buttercream: In a medium saucepan combine ⅓ cup packed brown sugar and 2 tablespoons cornstarch. Stir in 1¼ cups half-and-half or light cream. Cook and stir over medium heat until thickened and bubbly. Reduce heat, then cook and stir 2 minutes more. Gradually stir about half of the mixture into 2 slightly beaten egg yolks; return to remaining mixture in saucepan. Bring to a gentle boil. Cook and stir for 2 minutes. Remove from heat. Press plastic wrap onto surface of mixture to prevent a skin from forming. Cool to room temperature without stirring. In a medium mixing bowl beat ¾ cup softened butter, ¾ cup sifted powdered sugar, and 2 tablespoons milk with an electric mixer on medium speed until light and fluffy. Add cornstarch mixture, ¼ cup at a time, beating after each addition until smooth.

Sugared Pecans: In a small skillet combine ⅓ cup packed brown sugar, 1 tablespoon orange juice, and 2 teaspoons corn syrup. Heat over low heat about 2 minutes or until brown sugar is dissolved, stirring occasionally. Stir in 1 cup pecan halves (toasted, if desired); stir to coat well. Place ¼ cup granulated sugar in a medium mixing bowl. Add coated pecans and stir to coat with sugar. Place pecans on a baking sheet and let stand 1 hour or until dry. Store in a loosely covered container in a cool place for up to 2 weeks.

Nutrition facts per serving: *411 calories, 6 g protein, 36 g carbohydrate, 28 g total fat (12 g saturated), 197 mg cholesterol, 188 mg sodium, 1 g fiber. Daily values: 39% vitamin A, 0% vitamin C, 5% calcium, 6% iron.*

Beat the egg yolks with an electric mixer on high speed about 5 minutes or until thick and a pale lemon color. When sufficiently beaten the yolks will flow from the beaters in a thick ribbon-like stream as the beaters are lifted from the mixture.

To roll the cake it is necessary for it still to be warm. Start at a short side and loosely roll up the cake and towel together. The towel prevents the cake from sticking to itself as it cools. The powdered sugar helps keep the towel from sticking to the cake. When the cake has cooled about 5 minutes, gently unroll it and cover it with plastic wrap so it will stay moist.

Kind Cuts

All your efforts have paid off. Your baked product is a masterpiece, and you're ready to share it. Now comes the hardest part of all—cutting into it. There are ways to minimize your pain.

Cutting a cake with a fluffy icing (such as Seven-Minute Frosting), a creamy cake (such as a baked cheesecake), or a pie with a meringue is easier if, between cuts, you dip the knife in hot water, then shake it to remove excess water. Do not dry the knife completely.

For cheesecakes, a clean piece of dental floss works particularly well. Cut it several inches longer than the diameter of the cake. Holding it tight, set it on top of the cake, and press it down until it reaches the pan bottom. Release one end of the floss, and pull it through the cake (do not pull it back up).

Almond-Orange Chiffon Cake

2¼ **cups sifted cake flour or 2 cups all-purpose flour**
1½ **cups granulated sugar**
½ **cup ground almonds**
1 **tablespoon baking powder**
¼ **teaspoon salt**
½ **cup cooking oil**
7 **egg yolks**
1 **tablespoon finely shredded orange peel (set aside)**
¾ **cup orange juice**
½ **teaspoon almond extract**
7 **egg whites**
½ **teaspoon cream of tartar**
  Orange Whipped Cream Frosting
¼ **cup sliced almonds, toasted**

1 In a large mixing bowl stir together flour, sugar, ground almonds, baking powder, and salt. Make a well in the center of dry mixture. Then add cooking oil, egg yolks, orange juice, and almond extract. Beat with an electric mixer on low to medium speed until combined. Then beat on high speed for 5 minutes or until satin smooth. Fold in orange peel. Set batter aside.

2 Thoroughly wash beaters. In a very large mixing bowl beat egg whites and cream of tartar on medium speed until stiff peaks form (tips stand straight). Then pour batter in a thin stream over beaten egg whites and gently fold in.

3 Pour batter into an ungreased 10-inch tube pan, spreading evenly. Bake in a 325° oven 60 to 65 minutes or until top springs back when lightly touched. Immediately invert cake in pan. Cool completely. Loosen sides of cake from pan. Remove from pan.

4 Cut the cake into 3 layers. Place bottom layer on a serving plate. Spread with about 1 cup Orange Whipped Cream Frosting. Top with second layer and 1 cup of the frosting. Add top layer. Frost top and sides of cake with remaining frosting. Sprinkle top with toasted almonds. Cover and store in the refrigerator and use within 2 days. Makes 16 servings.

Orange Whipped Cream Frosting: In a glass measuring cup combine 3 tablespoons cold water and 1½ teaspoons unflavored gelatin. Let stand 2 minutes. In a saucepan bring about 2 inches water to boiling. Place measuring cup in saucepan of boiling water. Heat and stir 1 minute or until gelatin is dissolved. Remove from saucepan; cool slightly. In a mixing bowl beat 3 cups whipping cream, 1½ cups sifted powdered sugar, and 3 tablespoons orange liqueur (if desired), with an electric mixer on medium speed while gradually drizzling the gelatin over the cream mixture. Continue beating until stiff peaks form. Fold in 2 teaspoons finely shredded orange peel.

Nutrition facts per serving: *447 calories, 7 g protein, 44 g carbohydrate, 28 g total fat (12 g saturated), 154 mg cholesterol, 146 mg sodium, 1 g fiber. Daily values: 34% vitamin A, 11% vitamin C, 10% calcium, 11% iron.*

To Make Ahead

Prepare and bake cake as directed; cool. Place unfrosted cake on a baking sheet; freeze until firm. Once firm, place cake in a 2-gallon freezer bag and freeze for 3 months. Before serving, thaw at room temperature 3 hours. Fill and frost as directed.

Almond-Orange Chiffon Cake

Maple-Nut Chiffon Cake

An intriguing combination of flavors means both kids and adults will enjoy this cake.

2¼ cups sifted cake flour or 2 cups sifted all-purpose flour
¾ cup granulated sugar
½ cup packed brown sugar
1 tablespoon baking powder
¼ teaspoon salt
½ cup cooking oil
7 egg yolks
½ cup water
¼ cup maple-flavored syrup or real maple syrup
7 egg whites
½ teaspoon cream of tartar
1 cup finely chopped walnuts
   Golden Butter Frosting
   Walnut halves

1 In a large mixing bowl stir together flour, sugar, brown sugar, baking powder, and salt. Make a well in the center of dry mixture. Then add cooking oil, egg yolks, water, and maple syrup. Beat with an electric mixer on low to medium speed until combined. Then beat on high speed for 5 minutes or until satin smooth. Set batter aside.

2 Thoroughly wash beaters. In a very large mixing bowl beat egg whites and cream of tartar on medium speed until stiff peaks form (tips stand straight). Then pour batter in a thin stream over beaten egg whites and gently fold in. Fold in chopped walnuts.

3 Pour batter into an ungreased 10-inch tube pan. Bake in a 325° oven for 65 to 70 minutes or until the top springs back when lightly touched. Immediately invert cake in pan. Cool completely. Using a narrow metal spatula, loosen sides of cake from pan. Then remove cake from pan. Frost with Golden Butter Frosting. Garnish with walnut halves. Cover and store at room temperature for up to 3 days. Makes 16 servings.

Golden Butter Frosting: In a medium saucepan melt ½ cup butter (no substitutes) over low heat until golden brown (do not scorch). Remove from heat. Stir in 4 cups sifted powdered sugar. Stir in 1 tablespoon maple-flavored syrup or real maple syrup and 2 tablespoons milk. Place pan in ice water and beat frosting until it is easy to spread. If necessary, add additional milk 1 teaspoon at a time.

Nutrition facts per serving: 423 calories, 5 g protein, 59 g carbohydrate, 20 g total fat (6 g saturated), 109 mg cholesterol, 192 mg sodium, 1 g fiber. Daily values: 19% vitamin A, 0% vitamin C, 7% calcium, 12% iron.

To Make Ahead

Prepare and bake cake as directed; cool completely. Place the unfrosted cake on a baking sheet and freeze until firm. Once firm, place cake in a 2-gallon freezer bag and freeze for up to 3 months. Before serving, thaw at room temperature for 3 hours. Frost and garnish as directed.

Espresso Chiffon Cake

2¼ cups sifted cake flour or 2 cups sifted all-purpose flour
1½ cups granulated sugar
1 tablespoon baking powder
¼ teaspoon salt
½ cup cooking oil
7 egg yolks
¾ cup water
1 tablespoon instant espresso powder
1 teaspoon vanilla
7 egg whites
1 teaspoon cream of tartar
   Espresso-Nut Sauce

1 In a large mixing bowl stir together flour, sugar, baking powder, and salt. Make a well in the center of dry mixture. Then add cooking oil, egg yolks, water, espresso powder, and vanilla. Beat with an electric mixer on low to medium speed until combined. Then beat on high speed for 5 minutes or until satin smooth. Set batter aside.

2 Thoroughly wash beaters. In a very large mixing bowl beat egg whites and cream of tartar on medium speed until stiff peaks form (tips stand straight). Then pour batter in a thin stream over beaten egg whites and gently fold in.

3 Pour batter into an ungreased 10-inch tube pan. Bake in a 325° oven for 65 to 70 minutes or until top springs back when lightly touched. Immediately invert cake in pan. Cool completely. Using a narrow metal spatula, loosen sides of cake from pan. Then remove cake from pan. To serve, drizzle with warm Espresso-Nut Sauce. Cover any leftover cake and store at room temperature for up to 3 days. Refrigerate any remaining sauce. Makes 16 servings.

Espresso-Nut Sauce: In a heavy skillet cook 1 cup sugar over medium-high heat until sugar begins to melt, shaking skillet occasionally to heat sugar evenly. Reduce heat to low and cook until sugar is melted and golden brown (about 5 minutes more). Stir as necessary after sugar begins to melt. Remove from heat. Carefully add 1½ cups hot water. Heat and stir over medium-low heat to redissolve sugar. Mix 3 tablespoons water, 3 tablespoons cornstarch, and 1 tablespoon instant espresso powder; stir into sugar mixture. Cook and stir until thickened and bubbly; cook 2 minutes more. Remove from heat. Stir in 3 tablespoons butter or margarine and ½ cup broken walnuts.

Nutrition facts per serving: *297 calories, 5 g protein, 40 g carbohydrate, 14 g total fat (3 g saturated), 99 mg cholesterol, 153 mg sodium, 1 g fiber. Daily values: 16% vitamin A, 0% vitamin C, 6% calcium, 10% iron.*

To Make Ahead

Prepare and bake cake as directed; cool completely. Place cake on a baking sheet and freeze until firm. Once firm, place cake in a 2-gallon freezer bag and freeze up to 3 months. Before serving, thaw at room temperature about 3 hours. Serve with sauce.

Fig-Apricot-Almond Torte

1 tablespoon matzo meal
½ cup chopped dried figs
½ cup chopped dried apricots
1 cup ground almonds*
⅔ cup matzo meal
1 tablespoon shredded orange peel
½ teaspoon ground cinnamon
6 egg yolks
¾ cup granulated sugar
6 egg whites
¼ teaspoon cream of tartar
¼ teaspoon salt
¼ cup apricot preserves (optional)
Sweetened whipped cream (optional)
Sliced dried apricots (optional)

1 Grease the bottom of a 9-inch springform pan; sprinkle with the 1 tablespoon matzo meal. Set pan aside.

2 In a large food processor bowl combine figs and apricots. Process or blend until finely chopped. Add ground almonds, the ⅔ cup matzo meal, orange peel, and cinnamon. Process until combined.

3 In a large mixing bowl beat egg yolks with an electric mixer on low speed about 5 minutes or until thick and the color of lemons. Gradually add sugar, beating about 5 minutes more or until very thick. Stir in fig-apricot mixture.

4 Thoroughly wash beaters. In a large mixing bowl beat egg whites, cream of tarter, and salt on medium speed until stiff peaks form (tips stand straight). Stir about one-third of the egg whites into the fig-apricot mixture. Fold the fig-apricot mixture into remaining whites.

5 Pour batter into prepared pan; spread evenly. Bake in a 350° oven for 30 to 35 minutes or until a wooden toothpick inserted near the center of the cake comes out clean. Cool cake in pan on a wire rack for 10 minutes. Remove sides of pan; cool completely on wire rack.

6 If desired, in a small pan heat preserves until melted. Brush over cooled torte. Serve with sweetened whipped cream and garnish with sliced dried apricots. Makes 8 to 12 servings.

*Note: To make 1 cup ground almonds, place ¾ cup whole blanched almonds in a food processor bowl. Process just until finely ground.

Nutrition facts per serving: *189 calories, 6 g protein, 30 g carbohydrate, 6 g total fat (1 g saturated), 107 mg cholesterol, 33 mg sodium, 2 g fiber. Daily values: 9% vitamin A, 1% vitamin C, 4% calcium, 9% iron.*

*Notes*_____
_____
_____
_____
_____

Mocha-Pecan Torte

Mocha-Pecan Torte

- **1 cup butter (no substitutes)**
- **1⅓ cups semisweet chocolate pieces (8 ounces)**
- **6 eggs**
- **1 cup granulated sugar**
- **1½ cups pecans, toasted**
- **1 cup sifted unsweetened cocoa powder**
- **¼ cup coffee liqueur or strong coffee**
- **Mocha Glaze**
- **2 ounces white baking bar, chopped**
- **¾ cup chopped pecans, toasted**

1 Grease a 9-inch springform pan. Line the bottom of pan with parchment paper; grease paper. Dust pan and paper with flour. In a heavy, small saucepan combine butter and chocolate. Melt over low heat until smooth. Set pan and chocolate mixture aside.

2 Place eggs and sugar in a food processor bowl. Process until smooth. Add 1½ cups pecans. Process about 1 minute or until nearly smooth. Add melted chocolate mixture, cocoa powder, and liqueur; process just until combined, scraping sides as necessary.

3 Spread batter into prepared pan. Bake in a 350° oven 35 to 40 minutes or until sides are puffed and set about 2 inches in from edge of pan. Completely cool in pan on a wire rack.

4 Loosen sides of cake from pan and remove sides. Invert cake onto wire rack; remove paper. Place wire rack with cake on a baking sheet. Pour warm Mocha Glaze over cake, covering top and sides.

5 Place chopped baking bar in a glass measuring cup or custard cup. Microwave, uncovered, on 30% power (low) for 1½ to 2½ minutes or until melted, stirring every 30 seconds. Pour melted chocolate into a nonpleated plastic storage bag. Snip one corner of the bag with a sharp pair of scissors to make a small opening. Starting at the center of the cake, pipe a spiral to the outer edge. Using a toothpick, gently swirl the white lines. If necessary, refrigerate cake until glaze is partially set but still sticky (5 to 10 minutes).

6 Press ¾ cup chopped pecans onto sides of cake. Transfer cake to a serving plate. Cover; store cake in refrigerator up to 3 days. Serves 12 to 16.

Mocha Glaze: In a heavy medium saucepan melt 3 tablespoons butter or margarine and 1 tablespoon light corn syrup over low heat, stirring occasionally. Stir in 1 cup semisweet chocolate pieces until melted and smooth; remove from heat. Add an additional 3 tablespoons butter or margarine and 2 tablespoons coffee liqueur; whisk until smooth.

Nutrition facts per serving: *641 calories, 12 g protein, 55 g carbohydrate, 45 g total fat (15 g saturated), 163 mg cholesterol, 251 mg sodium, 2 g fiber. Daily values: 24% vitamin A, 0% vitamin C, 16% calcium, 22% iron.*

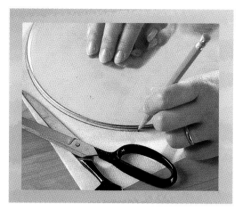

Place the pan bottom on parchment (or waxed paper, if the recipe calls for it). Draw around the pan with a pencil. Using paper scissors, cut just inside the marked line.

Torte Composition

A torte is composed of several layers of cake and filling, so its assembly is as important a process as the mixing and baking. It takes a long, serrated knife and a steady hand, although the filling can hide a multitude of sins.

Chill cake before splitting into layers. Use wooden toothpicks to mark midpoint on cake's side. Then carefully slice cake horizontally with the long, serrated knife. If the cake has a slightly domed top, slice a thin layer horizontally off the top to make it flat. This will level all the cake layers, making it easier to assemble the torte.

Coffee-Toffee-Chocolate Cake

A chocolate fancier's dream, this decadent dessert is worth the time and calories.

1 6-ounce package semisweet
   chocolate pieces (1 cup)
½ cup butter (no substitutes)
3 tablespoons crème de cacao or
   coffee liqueur
2 teaspoons instant coffee
   crystals
⅓ cup packed brown sugar
½ cup all-purpose flour
4 egg yolks
4 egg whites
¼ cup packed brown sugar
½ cup almond brickle pieces
   Chocolate-Coffee Glaze
¼ cup almond brickle pieces

1 Grease and flour the bottom of an 8-inch springform pan; set aside.

2 In a heavy medium saucepan combine chocolate pieces, butter, crème de cacao, and coffee crystals. Heat over low heat, stirring frequently, until melted and smooth. Stir in ⅓ cup brown sugar. Remove pan from heat; stir in flour. Whisk in egg yolks one at a time; cool slightly.

3 In a large mixing bowl beat egg whites on medium speed until soft peaks form (tips curl). Gradually add ¼ cup brown sugar, 1 tablespoon at a time, beating until stiff peaks form (tips stand straight). Gently fold about one-fourth of the beaten egg whites into the chocolate mixture. Repeat folding in the remaining whites by fourths. Gently fold in ½ cup almond brickle pieces.

4 Pour batter into prepared pan. Bake in a 350° oven 55 minutes or until a wooden toothpick inserted near the center of the cake comes out with only a few crumbs. Do not overbake. Cool cake in pan on a wire rack for 10 minutes (center will fall). Remove sides from pan and cool completely.

5 Remove cake from bottom of springform pan; place cake on the wire rack. Place rack with cake on a baking sheet. Spoon Chocolate-Coffee Glaze over cake. Smooth top and sides with long metal spatula. Sprinkle remaining ¼ cup almond brickle pieces around top edge of cake. Transfer cake to a serving platter. Cover any leftover cake and store in the refrigerator for up to 3 days. Makes 10 to 12 servings.

Chocolate-Coffee Glaze: In a heavy, small saucepan heat ¼ cup whipping cream with 2 tablespoons crème de cacao or coffee liqueur and 1 teaspoon instant coffee crystals over medium heat until bubbly around the edges. Remove from the heat. Add 1 cup semisweet chocolate pieces (6 ounces); let stand 1 minute. Whisk until chocolate is melted and smooth. Let stand for 15 minutes, stirring occasionally.

Nutrition facts per serving: 455 calories, 5 g protein, 50 g carbohydrate, 28 g total fat (8 g saturated fat), 123 mg cholesterol, 204 mg sodium, 0 g fiber. Daily values: 26% vitamin A, 0% vitamin C, 3% calcium, 11% iron.

Miniature Almond Cakes

1½ cups all-purpose flour
2½ teaspoons baking powder
¼ teaspoon salt
1 8-ounce package almond paste
1½ cups granulated sugar
6 eggs
1 cup butter or margarine,
   softened
1 recipe each Whipped Cream
   Frosting, Chocolate Whipped
   Cream Frosting, and
   Raspberry Whipped Cream
   Frosting (see page 151)
   Assorted toppings, such as
   raspberries, chocolate curls,
   grated chocolate, sliced
   almonds, mint leaves, and
   chocolate-dipped hazelnuts
   (optional)

1 Grease and lightly flour a 13x9x2-inch baking pan and an 8x8x2-inch baking pan. Combine flour, baking powder, and salt. Set aside.

2 Crumble almond paste into a large mixing bowl. Add the sugar and 2 of the eggs. Beat with an electric mixer* on low speed about 3 minutes or until thoroughly combined and no lumps of almond paste remain. Add the butter and beat on medium-low speed for 3 minutes. Add remaining eggs, one at a time, beating for 1 minute after each addition. Fold in the flour mixture.

3 Pour ⅔ of the batter (about 4 cups) into the prepared 13x9x2-inch baking pan and the remaining batter into the prepared 8x8x2-inch baking pan. Spread batter evenly in pans. Bake in a 350° oven for 18 to 20 minutes or until a wooden toothpick inserted near center of each cake comes out clean. Cool cakes in pans on wire racks for 10 minutes (cakes may sink slightly in center). Loosen sides and invert cakes onto wire racks; cool completely. If desired, cover and store in the refrigerator for up to 24 hours.

4 To assemble, using a 2-inch round, star, and/or diamond-shape cookie cutter with fluted or straight sides, cut about 35 cake pieces from the 2 cakes. Pipe or dollop desired frostings atop cakes. (Leave the sides of the cakes unfrosted so they are easy to pick up.) If desired, decorate with assorted toppings. Makes 35.

Note: Because of the long beating time, we recommend a full-size stand mixer instead of a hand mixer.

Nutrition facts per cake: 153 calories, 3 g protein, 16 g carbohydrates, 9 g fat (2 g saturated), 41 mg cholesterol, 113 mg sodium, 0 g fiber. Daily values: 10% vitamin A, 0% vitamin C, 2% calcium, 4% iron.

Shortcut

Use one 2-layer-size white or chocolate cake mix instead of the recipe provided. Prepare the mix according to package directions, except pour ⅔ of the batter into a greased and floured 13x9x2-inch baking pan and ⅓ of the batter into a greased and floured 8x8x2-inch baking pan. Bake in a 350° oven for 20 to 22 minutes or until a toothpick inserted near the center of each cake comes out clean. Frost and decorate as directed.

To Make Ahead

Prepare and bake cakes as directed; cool completely. Place whole cakes on baking sheets and freeze until firm. Once firm, place cakes in freezer containers and freeze up to 3 months. To serve, thaw at room temperature for several hours. Frost as directed.

Macadamia Rum Cake

Two fabulous flavors of the tropics blend for a terrific combination in this finale.

- **2 cups all-purpose flour**
- **2 teaspoons baking powder**
- **¼ teaspoon salt**
- **¾ cup butter or margarine, softened**
- **1½ cups granulated sugar**
- **3 eggs**
- **½ cup milk**
- **3 tablespoons rum**
   Creamy Rum Frosting
- **1 cup chopped macadamia nuts**

1 Grease and lightly flour two 9x1½-inch or 8x1½-inch round baking pans. Combine flour, baking powder, and salt. Set pans and flour mixture aside.

2 In a large mixing bowl beat butter with an electric mixer on medium to high speed 30 seconds or until softened. Add sugar to butter and beat until fluffy. Add eggs, one at a time, beating on medium speed after each addition until combined. Alternately add flour mixture with milk and rum, beating on low to medium speed after each addition just until combined.

3 Pour batter into prepared pans. Bake in a 350° oven 30 to 35 or until a toothpick inserted near the center of each cake comes out clean. Cool cakes in pans on wire racks 10 minutes. Remove cakes from pans and completely cool on the wire racks.

4 To assemble, place one cake layer on a serving plate. Stir ½ cup macadamia nuts into 1 cup of the Creamy Rum Frosting. Spread on cake layer. Top with second layer. Frost entire cake with remaining frosting. Sprinkle top of cake with remaining ½ cup nuts. Cover and store cake in the refrigerator for up to 3 days. Makes 12 servings.

Creamy Rum Frosting: In a medium mixing bowl beat one 8-ounce package softened cream cheese and 2 tablespoons rum with an electric mixer on medium to high speed until light and fluffy. Beat in ½ cup packed brown sugar. Whip 1 cup whipping cream until stiff peaks form. Fold into cream cheese mixture.

Nutrition facts per serving: 545 calories, 7 g protein, 50 g carbohydrate, 35 g total fat (18 g saturated), 133 mg cholesterol, 309 mg sodium, 2 g fiber. Daily values: 30% vitamin A, 0% vitamin C, 10% calcium, 12% iron.

To Make Ahead

Prepare and bake cakes as directed; cool completely. Place cakes on a baking sheet and freeze until firm. Once firm, place cakes in 2-gallon freezer bags and freeze for up to 3 months. To serve, thaw at room temperature for several hours. Frost as directed.

White Chocolate-Orange Mousse Cake

The melt-in-your-mouth frosting gives this cake its special flavor.

1   **cup all-purpose flour**
1   **teaspoon baking powder**
2   **eggs**
1   **cup granulated sugar**
½   **teaspoon vanilla**
½   **cup milk**
¼   **cup butter or margarine**
⅓   **cup orange marmalade or apricot preserves**
2   **tablespoons orange liqueur or orange juice**
     White Chocolate-Orange Mousse
     Sliced strawberries or raspberries (about 2 cups)

1 Grease and lightly flour a 9x9x2-inch baking pan. In a small mixing bowl combine flour and baking powder. Set pan and flour mixture aside.

2 In a large mixing bowl beat eggs with an electric mixer on high speed about 4 minutes or until thick and the color of lemons. Gradually add the sugar, beating on medium speed about 5 minutes or until sugar is almost dissolved. Beat in vanilla. Add flour mixture. Beat on low to medium speed just until combined.

3 In a small saucepan heat the milk and butter just until butter melts. Stir warm milk mixture into the beaten egg mixture.

4 Pour batter into prepared pan. Bake in a 350° oven 25 to 30 minutes or until top springs back when lightly touched. Cool cake in pan on a wire rack 10 minutes. Remove cake from pan and cool completely on wire rack.

5 In a bowl combine orange marmalade and orange liqueur. To assemble, cut cake in half horizontally forming 2 even layers. Place first cake layer on serving plate. Spread with marmalade mixture. Top with second cake layer. Frost top and sides with White Chocolate-Orange Mousse. Chill at least 4 hours before serving. Garnish cake with sliced strawberries. Cover and store in the refrigerator for up to 3 days. Makes 12 servings.

White Chocolate-Orange Mousse: In a 1-cup glass measuring cup combine 2 tablespoons lemon juice and 1½ teaspoons unflavored gelatin. Let stand for 5 minutes. Place measuring cup in a small saucepan of boiling water and stir until gelatin is dissolved. Set gelatin mixture aside. Discard water. In the small saucepan combine ½ cup thawed orange juice concentrate, ¼ cup granulated sugar, 6 ounces white baking bar, chopped, and the gelatin mixture. Heat and stir over low heat until chocolate is melted. Remove from heat. Whisk in ¼ cup dairy sour cream. Pour entire mixture into a large bowl. Chill until cool and very thick, about 1 hour, stirring occasionally. In a medium mixing bowl beat 1 cup whipping cream with an electric mixer on medium speed until soft peaks form. Fold into orange mixture. If necessary, chill until mousse is easy to spread (about 30 minutes).

Nutrition facts per serving: *379 calories, 5 g protein, 52 g carbohydrate, 18 g total fat (10 g saturated), 76 mg cholesterol, 110 mg sodium, 1 g fiber. Daily values: 16% vitamin A, 56% vitamin C, 8% calcium, 5% iron.*

To Make Ahead

Prepare and bake cake as directed; cool completely. Place cake on a baking sheet and freeze until firm. Once firm, place cake in a 2-gallon freezer bag and freeze up to 3 months. To serve, thaw at room temperature for several hours. Cut, fill, and frost as directed.

International Origin

Sacher Torte

Two favorite flavors—chocolate and apricot—are paired in this famous Austrian dessert.

6   **egg whites**
5   **ounces semisweet or bittersweet chocolate, chopped**
½   **cup butter or margarine**
6   **egg yolks**
1½   **teaspoons vanilla**
½   **cup granulated sugar**
¾   **cup all-purpose flour**
⅔   **cup apricot preserves**
     Chocolate Glaze
     Sweetened whipped cream (optional)

1 In a very large bowl allow egg whites to stand at room temperature 30 minutes. Grease and lightly flour a 9-inch springform pan. Set aside.

2 In a medium saucepan melt chocolate and butter; cool. Stir egg yolks and vanilla into the cooled chocolate mixture. Set mixture aside.

3 Beat egg whites with an electric mixer on medium to high speed until soft peaks form (tips curl). Gradually add the sugar, about 1 tablespoon at a time, beating about 4 minutes or until stiff peaks form (tips stand straight).

4 Fold about 1 cup of the egg white mixture into chocolate mixture. Then fold chocolate mixture into remaining egg white mixture. Sift about one-third of the flour over the egg mixture, then gently fold in. (If the bowl is too full, transfer mixture to a larger bowl.) Repeat sifting and folding in one-third of the flour mixture at a time.

5 Spread batter into prepared springform pan. Bake in a 350° oven for 35 to 40 minutes or until a wooden toothpick inserted near the center of the cake comes out clean. Completely cool cake in pan on a wire rack. Remove sides of springform pan. Brush crumbs from edges of cake. (Top crust will be slightly flaky.) Remove bottom of springform pan from cake.

6 In a small saucepan, heat preserves until melted. Then press apricot preserves through a sieve; cool slightly.

7 To assemble, cut cake horizontally into two even layers. Place the first layer on a large serving plate. Spread the preserves on top of the cake layer. Top with the second cake layer. Pour Chocolate Glaze over torte, spreading as necessary to glaze top and sides completely. Let torte stand at room temperature for at least 1 hour before serving. If desired, serve with sweetened whipped cream. Makes 12 servings.

Chocolate Glaze: In a saucepan heat 4 ounces semisweet or bittersweet chocolate, cut up, and 2 tablespoons butter or margarine over low heat just until melted, stirring occasionally; set aside. In a heavy, small saucepan bring ½ cup whipping cream and 2 teaspoons light corn syrup to a gentle boil. Reduce heat and simmer for 2 minutes. Remove from heat. Stir in chocolate mixture. Cool to room temperature before using.

Nutrition facts per serving: *356 calories, 6 g protein, 37 g carbohydrates, 23 g total fat (13 g saturated), 146 mg cholesterol, 135 mg sodium, 2 g fiber. Daily values: 29% vitamin A, 0% vitamin C, 34% calcium, 10% iron.*

To Make Ahead

Prepare and bake cake as directed; cool completely. Place cake on a baking sheet and freeze until firm. Once firm, place cake in a 2-gallon freezer bag and freeze for up to 3 months. To serve, thaw at room temperature for several hours. Cut, fill, and frost as directed.

To split the cake horizontally, first use toothpicks to mark the halfway point around the cake's side. Then, using a long sharp or serrated knife, carefully slice the cake with a sawing motion along the toothpick line. Carefully lift off the top layer with a wide spatula.

Carefully pour cooled glaze over cake and immediately spread to completely cover top and sides. Have the cake on a rack over waxed paper to catch glaze drips.

Raspberry-Lemon Torte

Raspberry-Lemon Torte

Raspberries and lemon are a flavor duo that's hard to beat. This recipe proves it.

　1　cup all-purpose flour
　2　teaspoons baking powder
　¼　teaspoon salt
　5　egg yolks
　¼　cup lemon juice
　⅔　cup granulated sugar
　1　tablespoon finely shredded
　　　lemon peel
　5　egg whites
　¼　teaspoon cream of tartar
　⅓　cup granulated sugar
　　　Lemon Curd
1½　cups raspberries
　3　recipes Whipped Cream
　　　Frosting (see page 151)
　　　Raspberries (optional)

1 Grease and flour a 15x10x1-inch jelly-roll pan. In a small mixing bowl stir together flour, baking powder, and salt. Set pan and flour mixture aside.

2 In a large mixing bowl beat egg yolks with an electric mixer on high speed about 6 minutes or until thick and the color of lemons.

3 Gradually beat lemon juice into beaten yolks. Gradually add the ⅔ cup sugar, beating on medium speed about 5 minutes or until sugar is almost dissolved. Gradually add about one-fourth of the flour mixture to the yolk mixture, beating on low to medium speed just until moistened. Repeat beating in the remaining flour mix-

ture, using one-fourth of the flour mixture at a time. Stir in lemon peel.

4 Thoroughly wash beaters. In a large mixing bowl beat egg whites and cream of tartar on medium speed until soft peaks form (tips curl). Gradually add ⅓ cup sugar, about 2 tablespoons at a time, beating until stiff peaks form (tips stand straight).

5 Stir about 1 cup of the egg white mixture into the egg yolk mixture. Fold egg yolk mixture into remaining egg white mixture. Gently spread batter into prepared pan. Bake in a 350° oven 15 to 20 minutes or until top springs back when lightly touched. Immediately loosen cake from pan; invert onto a towel sprinkled with powdered sugar. Cool completely.

6 Cut cake crosswise into thirds. Place one cake layer on a serving platter. Spread with half of the Lemon Curd. Top with half of the raspberries. Add a second cake layer and top with remaining lemon curd and raspberries. Top with remaining cake layer. Frost top and sides with Whipped Cream Frosting. If desired, garnish with additional raspberries. Cover and store in the refrigerator for up to 3 days. Makes 10 servings.

Lemon Curd: In a saucepan stir together ½ cup granulated sugar and 1 tablespoon cornstarch. Stir in 2 teaspoons finely shredded lemon peel, ½ cup lemon juice, and 2 tablespoons butter or margarine. Cook and stir over medium heat until thickened and bubbly. Slowly stir about half of the lemon mixture into 3 beaten egg

yolks. Return all of the egg yolk mixture to saucepan. Bring to a gentle boil. Cook and stir 2 minutes more. Cover surface with plastic wrap. Chill in the refrigerator until serving time.

Nutrition facts per serving: *414 calories, 6 g protein, 55 g carbohydrate, 20 g total fat (11 g saturated), 225 mg cholesterol, 197 mg sodium, 1 g fiber. Daily values: 43% vitamin A, 24% vitamin C, 10% calcium, 8% iron.*

Cakes & Cream

Cakes filled or frosted with whipped cream are best eaten right away or they'll get soggy.

Whip the cream and assemble cake no more than 2 hours before serving. Or, use Whipped Cream Frosting (see page 151) and assemble cake no more than 24 hours before serving. Store cake in the refrigerator until you're ready to use it.

Shortcut

Substitute 1 cup purchased lemon curd for the Lemon Curd recipe.

To Make Ahead

Prepare and bake cake as directed; cool completely. Cut cake as directed. Place the cake layers on a baking sheet and freeze until firm. Once firm, place layers in 2-gallon freezer bags and freeze for up to 3 months. To serve, thaw at room temperature for 2 to 3 hours. Fill and frost as directed.

International Origin

Black Forest Cherry Cake

This spectacular cake is a specialty of the Black Forest region of Germany.

1 slightly beaten egg
⅔ cup granulated sugar
½ cup milk
4 ounces unsweetened chocolate, coarsely chopped
1¾ cups all-purpose flour
1 teaspoon baking soda
½ teaspoon salt
½ cup shortening
1 cup granulated sugar
1 teaspoon vanilla
2 eggs
1 cup milk
1 recipe Chocolate Butter Frosting (see page 150)
 Tart Cherry Filling
2 recipes Whipped Cream Frosting (see page 151)

1 In a heavy medium saucepan combine the 1 slightly beaten egg, ⅔ cup sugar, ½ cup milk, and chocolate. Bring just to boiling over medium heat, stirring constantly. Remove from heat. If necessary, stir until chocolate is melted. Set aside to cool.

2 Grease and lightly flour three 9x1½-inch round baking pans. Combine flour, baking soda, and salt. Set pans and flour mixture aside.

Setting Some Aside

If the cake filling or frosting contains whipped cream, cream cheese, yogurt, or eggs, store it in the refrigerator. (If you don't have a proper cake cover, invert a large bowl over the cake.)

Freezing frosted angel food, sponge, and chiffon cakes is not recommended.

If you want to freeze a frosted cream cake be sure to choose a creamy frosting for best results. Boiled frostings and frostings made with egg whites do not freeze well. To thaw, unwrap the cake, and let it stand at room temperature for several hours.

3 In a large mixing bowl beat shortening with an electric mixer on medium to high speed about 30 seconds or until softened. Add 1 cup sugar and vanilla and beat until combined. Add the 2 eggs, one at a time, beating on medium speed after each addition until combined. Alternately add flour mixture and 1 cup milk, beating on low to medium speed after each addition just until combined. Stir in chocolate mixture.

4 Pour the batter into the prepared pans. Bake in a 350° oven for 18 to 20 minutes or until a wooden toothpick

inserted near the center of each cake comes out clean. Cool the cakes in pans on wire racks for 10 minutes. Remove cakes from pans and completely cool on the wire racks.

5 To assemble, place first cake layer on a large serving plate. Using ¾ cup of the Chocolate Butter Frosting, spread a ½-inch-wide and ¾-inch-high border around the top edge. Then spread half of the chilled Tart Cherry Filling in the center. Top with the second cake layer. Using ¾ cup Chocolate Butter Frosting, repeat spreading a border on top edge of cake and spread remaining filling in center. Finally, top with remaining cake layer. Frost sides with the remaining Chocolate Butter Frosting; frost top with the Whipped Cream Frosting. Cover and store cake in the refrigerator for up to 3 days. Makes 12 servings.

Tart Cherry Filling: Drain one 16-ounce can pitted tart red cherries (water pack), reserving ½ cup liquid. In a saucepan combine the liquid, 1 tablespoon cornstarch, and 1 tablespoon granulated sugar. Add cherries. Cook and stir until mixture is thickened and bubbly. Cook and stir for 2 minutes more. Stir in 2 tablespoons kirsch (cherry brandy); cool. Cover and chill in the refrigerator for at least 2 hours before using. (Do not stir.)

Nutrition facts per serving: *776 calories, 8 g protein, 76 g carbohydrate, 53 g total fat (23 g saturated), 252 mg cholesterol, 207 mg sodium, 0 g fiber. Daily values: 10% vitamin A, 0% vitamin C, 2% calcium, 4% iron.*

To Make Ahead

Prepare and bake cakes as directed; cool completely. Place the cakes on baking sheets and freeze until firm. Once firm, place cakes in 2-gallon freezer bags and freeze for up to 3 months. Before serving, thaw at room temperature for several hours. Fill and frost as directed.

Almond-Crusted Layer Cake

Serve this delightful almond-flavored cake with a crunchy nut topping on a special occasion.

  4 teaspoons granulated sugar
  1 cup sliced almonds
  2 cups all-purpose flour
1½ teaspoons baking powder
  ½ teaspoon baking soda
  ½ cup butter or margarine, softened
  ½ of an 8-ounce can almond paste (½ cup)
1½ cups granulated sugar
  ½ teaspoon vanilla
  4 eggs
  ½ cup milk
  Almond Butter Frosting or 1 recipe Butter Frosting (see page 150)

1 Generously grease two 9x1½-inch or 8x1½-inch round baking pans. Sprinkle bottom of each pan evenly with 2 teaspoons sugar and ½ cup sliced almonds. In a small mixing bowl stir together flour, baking powder, and baking soda. Set pans and flour mixture aside.

Going Too Far

At high altitudes angel food, sponge, and chiffon cakes can overexpand easily because so much air is beaten into the eggs.

To adapt these recipes for high-altitude baking, see the tip on page 8 on adjusting oven temperature, baking time, and the amount of sugar. You also may try beating the egg whites until soft peaks form (not until stiff as recommended in the recipe) and adding 1 or 2 tablespoons additional flour.

2 In a large mixing bowl beat butter with an electric mixer on medium to high speed about 30 seconds or until softened. Crumble the almond paste into the butter, beating until thoroughly combined and no lumps of almond paste remain.

3 Add the 1½ cups sugar and vanilla to butter mixture and beat until fluffy. Add eggs, one at a time, beating on medium speed after each addition until combined. Alternately add flour mixture and milk, beating on low to medium speed after each addition just until combined.

4 Carefully pour batter into prepared pans, being careful not to disturb the nut crust. Bake in a 350° oven for 30 to 35 minutes or until a wooden toothpick inserted near the center of each cake comes out clean. Cool cakes in pans on wire racks for 10 minutes. Remove cakes from pans and completely cool, almond side up, on the wire racks. Frost between layers and around sides with Almond Butter Frosting or Butter Frosting. Cover and store at room temperature for up to 3 days. Makes 12 servings.

  Almond Butter Frosting: In a medium mixing bowl beat ¼ cup butter with an electric mixer until softened. Crumble ½ of an 8-ounce can almond paste (½ cup); add to butter, beating until thoroughly combined and no lumps of almond paste remain. Beat in 1 cup sifted powdered sugar and 2 tablespoons milk until smooth. Slowly beat in 2 tablespoons additional milk and ½ teaspoon vanilla. Slowly beat in 3½ cups additional sifted powdered sugar.

  Nutrition facts per serving: *585 calories, 9 g protein, 90 g carbohydrate, 23 g total fat (9 g saturated), 103 mg cholesterol, 246 mg sodium, 1 g fiber. Daily values: 14% vitamin A, 0% vitamin C, 12% calcium, 15% iron.*

To Make Ahead

Prepare and bake cakes as directed; cool completely. Place cakes on a baking sheet and freeze until firm. Once firm, place cakes in 2-gallon freezer bags and freeze up to 3 months. Before serving, thaw at room temperature several hours. Frost as directed.

Butter Frosting

½ cup butter (no substitutes)
6½ cups sifted powdered sugar
⅓ cup milk
2 teaspoons vanilla
Milk

1 In a mixing bowl beat butter with an electric mixer on medium to high speed until fluffy. Gradually add 3 cups of the powdered sugar, beating well on low to medium speed. Slowly beat in the ⅓ cup milk and vanilla.

2 Gradually beat in remaining powdered sugar. If necessary, beat in additional milk to make the frosting easy to spread. Makes about 3½ cups, enough to frost the tops and sides of two or three 8- or 9-inch cake layers or one 10-inch tube cake (12 servings).

Nutrition facts per serving: 281 calories, 0 g protein, 55 g carbohydrate, 8 g total fat (5 g saturated), 21 mg cholesterol, 81 mg sodium, 0 g fiber. Daily values: 7% vitamin A, 0% vitamin C, 0% calcium, 0% iron.

Chocolate Butter Frosting: Prepare Butter Frosting as directed, except beat ¾ cup unsweetened cocoa powder into butter and reduce powdered sugar to 6 cups.

Mocha Butter Frosting: Prepare Butter Frosting as directed, except beat ¾ cup unsweetened cocoa powder into butter. Add 1 tablespoon instant coffee crystals to the ⅓ cup milk. Let stand 3 minutes; stir well.

Lemon or Orange Butter Frosting: Prepare Butter Frosting as directed, except substitute fresh lemon juice or orange juice for the milk and add ½ teaspoon finely shredded lemon peel or 1 teaspoon finely shredded orange peel with the juice.

Peanut Butter Frosting: Prepare Butter Frosting as directed, except substitute ½ cup creamy peanut butter for the butter.

To frost a cake, brush off the crumbs with a pastry brush or your fingers. Then transfer the first layer to the serving plate, placing the top side down. To keep the plate clean, tuck strips of waxed paper under the edge of the cake before frosting it. Then spread about ½ cup of the frosting or

To sift powdered sugar, place a sieve over a large bowl. Add powdered sugar until the sieve is about half full. Using a large spoon, stir and press the powdered sugar around and against the sides of the sieve until it goes through into the bowl. If desired, you also can use a sifter, but some sifter mechanisms stiffen up with the fine powdered sugar.

Place the second cake layer, top side up, on top of the frosted first layer. Spread a thin coating of frosting on the sides of the cake to seal in any crumbs. Let the cake stand a few minutes so the frosting can harden.

Add a second, thicker coating of frosting to the sides of the cake, making swirls as desired. Build up the top edge about ¼ inch above the cake. Finally, spread the remaining frosting on top of the cake, blending it at the edges and swirling as desired.

a filling on top of the cake layer. Spread creamy frosting to the edge of the layer; spread fluffy frosting only to within ¼ inch of the edge.

Fluffy White Frosting

1 cup granulated sugar
⅓ cup water
¼ teaspoon cream of tartar
2 egg whites
1 teaspoon vanilla

1 In a small saucepan combine sugar, water, and cream of tartar. Bring mixture to boiling over medium-high heat, stirring constantly until sugar dissolves.

2 In a medium mixing bowl combine egg whites and vanilla. While beating the egg white mixture with an electric mixer on high speed, very slowly add the sugar mixture. Then beat about 7 minutes or until stiff peaks form (tips stand straight). Makes about 4 cups, enough to frost the tops and sides of two or three 8- or 9-inch cake layers or one 10-inch tube cake (12 servings).

Nutrition facts per serving: 68 calories, 1 g protein, 17 g carbohydrate, 0 g total fat (0 g saturated), 0 mg cholesterol, 10 mg sodium, 0 g fiber. Daily values: 0% vitamin A, 0% vitamin C, 0% calcium, 0% iron.

Whipped Cream Frosting

When used for piping, this frosting retains its shape for up to 2 days. You also can keep it on hand in your freezer for up to one month.

2 teaspoons cold water
¼ teaspoon unflavored gelatin
½ cup whipping cream
1 tablespoon granulated sugar

1 In a 1-cup glass measuring cup combine cold water and gelatin. Let stand 2 minutes. In a small saucepan bring about 2 inches water to boiling. Place measuring cup in saucepan of boiling water. Heat and stir about 1 minute or until the gelatin is completely dissolved. Remove measuring cup from saucepan.

2 In a mixing bowl beat whipping cream and sugar with an electric mixer on medium speed while gradually drizzling the mixture with the gelatin. Continue beating until stiff peaks form. Makes 1 cup (12 servings).

Nutrition facts per serving: 38 calories, 0 g protein, 1 g carbohydrate, 4 g total fat (2 g saturated), 14 mg cholesterol, 4 mg sodium, 0 g fiber. Daily values: 4% vitamin A, 0% vitamin C, 0% calcium, 0% iron.

Chocolate Whipped Cream Frosting: Prepare Whipped Cream Frosting as directed, except increase sugar to 4 teaspoons. Mix the sugar with 1 tablespoon unsweetened cocoa powder before beating with the cream.

Raspberry Whipped Cream Frosting: Prepare Whipped Cream Frosting as directed, except beat in 2 tablespoons raspberry liqueur or seedless raspberry jam with the cream and sugar. If desired, add a few drops of red food coloring.

Powdered Sugar Icing

1 cup sifted powdered sugar
¼ teaspoon vanilla
Milk or orange juice

1 In a small mixing bowl combine powdered sugar and vanilla. Stir in 1 tablespoon milk or orange juice. Stir in additional milk or orange juice, 1 teaspoon at a time, until icing is smooth and easy to drizzle.

2 Drizzle icing over cake, bread, or cookies. Let the cake stand for 2 hours before slicing. Makes about ½ cup, enough to ice one 10-inch tube cake (12 servings).

Nutrition facts per serving: 33 calories, 0 g protein, 8 g carbohydrate, 0 g total fat (0 g saturated), 0 mg cholesterol, 1 mg sodium, 0 g fiber. Daily values: 0% vitamin A, 0% vitamin C, 0% calcium, 0% iron.

Chocolate Powdered Sugar Icing: Prepare Powdered Sugar Icing as directed, except add 2 tablespoons unsweetened cocoa powder to the powdered sugar.

Blooming Great Garnish

To eat or not to eat is often the question asked about elegant floral garnishes. To be edible, the flower must be a nontoxic variety and free of any chemicals (flowers from a florist usually are treated with chemicals and should not be used). Use only edible flowers around food whether you plan to eat them or not.

Favorite flowers to munch include the rose, viola, pansy, calendula (pot marigold), daylily, nasturtium, violet, chamomile, bachelor's button, carnation, geranium blossom (not leaf), and magnolia. If you have any doubt about whether a flower's blossom, stem, or leaf is edible, check with your local poison control center or state extension service.

Many flowers in your own garden may be edible if you and your neighbors do not use chemicals. Pick the flowers just before using, rinse, and gently pat dry.

Otherwise, a local source such as an herb garden, restaurant supplier, or produce supplier who specializes in edible flowers may be able to help. Mail-order flower and herb farms are another option.

Seven-Minute Frosting

Beating this frosting about 7 minutes makes it as fluffy and glossy as divinity.

1½ **cups granulated sugar**
⅓   **cup cold water**
2   **egg whites**
¼   **teaspoon cream of tartar or**
    2 teaspoons light corn syrup
1   **teaspoon vanilla**

1 In the top of a double boiler combine sugar, water, egg whites, and cream of tartar. Beat with an electric mixer on low speed for 30 seconds.

2 Place the upper pan over gently boiling water (upper pan should be near, but not touching water). Cook, beating constantly with the electric mixer on high speed, about 7 minutes or until stiff peaks form (tips stand straight). Remove from heat. Add vanilla.

3 Beat frosting for 2 to 3 minutes more or until the frosting is easy to spread. Makes about 5 cups, enough to frost the tops and sides of two or three 8- or 9-inch cake layers or one 10-inch tube cake (12 servings).

Nutrition facts per serving: 101 calories, 1 g protein, 25 g carbohydrate, 0 g total fat (0 g saturated), 0 mg cholesterol, 10 mg sodium, 0 g fiber. Daily values: 0% vitamin A, 0% vitamin C, 0% calcium, 0% iron.

Peppermint Seven-Minute Frosting: Prepare Seven-Minute Frosting as directed, except substitute a few drops of peppermint extract for the vanilla. Frost the cake and garnish with crushed striped, round peppermint candies.

Cream Cheese Frosting

2   **3-ounce packages cream cheese**
½   **cup butter or margarine,**
    softened
2   **teaspoons vanilla**
4½ **to 4¾ cups sifted powdered**
    sugar

1 In a large mixing bowl beat cream cheese, butter, and vanilla with an electric mixer on medium to high speed until light and fluffy.

2 Gradually add 2 cups of the powdered sugar, beating well. Gradually beat in enough of the remaining powdered sugar to make the frosting easy to spread. Store the frosted cake, covered, in the refrigerator. Makes about 3 cups, enough to frost the tops and sides of two 8- or 9-inch cake layers or one 10-inch tube cake (12 servings).

Nutrition facts per serving: 263 calories, 1 g protein, 38 g carbohydrate, 13 g total fat (8 g saturated), 36 mg cholesterol, 120 mg sodium, 0 g fiber. Daily values: 13% vitamin A, 0% vitamin C, 1% calcium, 1% iron.

Chocolate-Cream Cheese Frosting:
Prepare Cream Cheese Frosting as directed, except beat ¼ cup unsweetened cocoa powder into the cream cheese mixture. Reduce powdered sugar to 4¼ to 4½ cups.

Coconut-Pecan Frosting

    1   egg
    1   5-ounce can (⅔ cup)
        evaporated milk
    ⅔   cup granulated sugar
    ¼   cup butter or margarine
  1⅓   cups coconut
    ½   cup chopped pecans

1 In a heavy, medium saucepan slightly beat the egg with a fork. Stir in the evaporated milk and sugar. Add butter. Cook and stir over medium heat about 12 minutes or until thickened and bubbly.

2 Stir in coconut and pecans. Cool thoroughly. Spread on cake. Makes about 1¾ cups, enough to frost the tops of two 8- or 9-inch cake layers or the top of one 13x9-inch cake (12 servings).

Nutrition facts per serving: *160 calories, 2 g protein, 16 g carbohydrate, 10 g total fat (5 g saturated), 31 mg cholesterol, 58 mg sodium, 1 g fiber. Daily values: 4% vitamin A, 3% vitamin C, 3% calcium, 2% iron.*

Creamy White Frosting

Here's an icing that is just the right consistency for piping decorations.

    1   cup shortening
  1½   teaspoons vanilla
    ½   teaspoon lemon extract, orange
        extract, or almond extract
  4½   cups sifted powdered sugar
    3   to 4 tablespoons milk

1 In a large mixing bowl beat shortening, vanilla, and lemon, orange, or almond extract with an electric mixer on medium to high speed for 30 seconds.

2 Gradually add 2 cups of the powdered sugar, beating well. Slowly beat in 2 tablespoons of the milk.

3 Gradually beat in the remaining powdered sugar and enough of the remaining milk to make the frosting easy to spread. Makes about 3 cups, enough to frost the tops and sides of two 8- or 9-inch cake layers or one 10-inch tube cake (12 servings).

Nutrition facts per serving: *298 calories, 0 g protein, 38 g carbohydrate, 17 g total fat (4 g saturated), 0 mg cholesterol, 1 mg sodium, 0 g fiber. Daily values: 0% vitamin A, 0% vitamin C, 0% calcium, 0% iron.*

First Impressions

First impressions are important, and the first thing people notice about a spectacular cake, torte, or cookie is the frosting. And making a terrific frosting is not as difficult as it looks.

◆ *Let the cake cool completely before frosting (about 4 hours). After frosting the cake, let it stand at least 1 hour before slicing it.*

◆ *Always sift the powdered sugar so the frosting won't have any lumps.*

◆ *Spread the frosting with a narrow-blade, flexible spatula using light back and forth strokes. Try not to lift the spatula because it will pull the crust away from the cake.*

◆ *If the frosting becomes too thick to spread easily, stir in a few more drops of the liquid.*

◆ *Make 2 cups of frosting to frost 24 cupcakes, the tops and sides of two 8- or 9-inch cake layers, or the top of one 13x9x2-inch cake. Allow ½ cup frosting for between layers.*

Notes_____

_____

_____

_____

_____

Pecan-Strawberry Shortcake
(see recipe, page 156)

Incomparable Cakes

Some desserts are in a class by themselves, set apart by the fact that they appear more decadent and more indulgent than other mortal desserts.

❧

If ever there was a cake beyond compare, it must be an incredibly rich and silky cheesecake. Who can resist Chocolate Cheesecake or Honey-Nut Cheesecake? Ah, such temptation!

❧

A shortcake studded with pecans and topped with peak-season strawberries is basic fare, while an exotic shortcake topped with Caribbean fruits is a sophisticated twist on a cherished favorite. Each recipe is guaranteed to make sure you get your just desserts.

Pecan-Strawberry Shortcake

Choose to make either individual shortcakes or one large dessert. The large shortcake looks more spectacular but the individual desserts are easier to serve. (Pictured on page 154.)

2 cups all-purpose flour
½ cup finely ground pecans
¼ cup granulated sugar
2 teaspoons baking powder
½ cup butter or margarine
1 beaten egg
⅔ cup milk
1 tablespoon finely shredded
  orange peel
6 cups sliced fresh strawberries
¼ cup granulated sugar
1 cup whipping cream
2 tablespoons granulated sugar
½ teaspoon vanilla
  Whole strawberries (optional)

1 In a medium mixing bowl stir together flour, ground pecans, ¼ cup sugar, and the baking powder. Using a pastry blender, cut in butter until mixture resembles coarse crumbs. Make a well in center of dry mixture.

2 In a small mixing bowl combine egg, milk, and 2 teaspoons of the orange peel; add to dry mixture all at once. Using a fork, stir just until moistened.

3 Drop the dough from a tablespoon onto an ungreased baking sheet, making 8 or 10 mounds; flatten each mound with the back of a spoon until it's about ¾ inch thick.

4 Bake in a 450° oven for 7 to 8 minutes or until golden. Transfer shortcakes to a wire rack and cool about 10 minutes.

5 Meanwhile, in a bowl stir together sliced berries, the ¼ cup sugar, and remaining 1 teaspoon orange peel; let stand about 20 minutes.

6 To whip cream, in a chilled, medium, mixing bowl combine the whipping cream, the 2 tablespoons sugar, and the vanilla. Beat with chilled beaters of an electric mixer on medium speed until soft peaks form.

7 Using a sharp serrated knife, cut each shortcake in half horizontally. Carefully lift off top layers. Spoon half of the strawberries and half of the whipped cream over bottom layers. Replace shortcake tops. Top with remaining strawberries, then spoon remaining cream directly onto strawberries. If desired, top with a whole strawberry. Serve immediately. Makes 8 to 10 servings.

For a large shortcake: Grease an 8x1½-inch round baking pan; set aside. Prepare shortcake dough as directed; use a rubber spatula to spread dough in the prepared pan. Build up edges slightly so that when the cake bakes and the center rises, it will be the same level as the sides. Bake in a 450° oven for 15 to 18 minutes or until a wooden toothpick inserted near the center comes out clean (do not overbake). Cool shortcake in pan on a wire rack 10 minutes; remove from pan.

Using a long serrated knife, cut shortcake in half horizontally. Using a wide spatula, carefully lift off the top layer of shortcake. Spoon half of the strawberries and half of the whipped cream over the bottom layer. Replace shortcake top. Add remaining straw-

Breaking with Tradition

That fabulous combination of crumbly biscuit, tart strawberries, and cool, rich cream is as old as the hills and as fresh as the next pint of berries you buy. And it's what makes summer complete.

But strawberries aren't your only option. Depending on what's in season, you can use any combination of black raspberries, raspberries, blueberries, mulberries, or even peaches and nectarines to make your perfect shortcake.

berries, then spoon remaining cream directly onto strawberries. If desired, top with whole strawberries. Serve immediately.

Nutrition facts per serving: *468 calories, 6 g protein, 49 g carbohydrate, 29 g total fat (15 g saturated), 100 mg cholesterol, 238 mg sodium, 3 g fiber. Daily values: 26% vitamin A, 108% vitamin C, 13% calcium, 14% iron.*

Use some of the sugar called for in the recipe when grinding the pecans. It helps keep the nuts tossing in the blender so they do not turn to paste as easily. Blend ⅓ to ½ cup nuts and 1 tablespoon sugar at a time. Some recipes may call for a portion of flour, instead of sugar, with the nuts. This works also.

Snickerdoodle Shortcake with Caramelized Apples

Feature this dessert on a crisp autumn day when apples are at their peak but the thought of summer still lingers. Another time, skip the apples and serve the shortcakes with sweetened, fresh, sliced peaches or mixed berries.

- 2 **cups all-purpose flour**
- ¼ **cup granulated sugar**
- 2 **teaspoons baking powder**
- ½ **cup butter or margarine**
- 1 **beaten egg**
- ½ **cup milk**
- 1 **tablespoon sugar**
- 1 **teaspoon ground cinnamon**
  Caramelized Apples
  Whipped cream (optional)
  Fresh mint leaves (optional)

1 In a mixing bowl stir together flour, ¼ cup sugar, and the baking powder. Using a pastry blender, cut in butter until mixture resembles coarse crumbs. Make a well in the center.

2 In a mixing bowl combine egg and milk; add to dry mixture all at once. Using a fork, stir just until moistened.

3 In a small bowl combine the 1 tablespoon sugar with the cinnamon. Drop the dough from a tablespoon onto an ungreased baking sheet, making 12 shortcakes. Sprinkle with sugar-cinnamon mixture.

4 Bake in a 425° oven for 8 to 10 minutes or until a wooden toothpick inserted near center comes out clean. Cool on baking sheet on a wire rack for 10 minutes. Remove shortcakes from pan.

5 Using a sharp serrated knife, cut 6 of the shortcakes in half horizontally. (Wrap and freeze remaining shortcakes for another use.) Spoon the Caramelized Apples between the layers and over top. If desired, garnish with whipped cream and mint leaves. Serve immediately. Makes 6 servings.

Caramelized Apples: Peel, core, and slice 8 apples to make about 8 cups. In a large saucepan or Dutch oven melt 6 tablespoons butter until it bubbles. Add the apples, stirring to coat. Sprinkle ⅓ cup packed brown sugar and ½ teaspoon ground cinnamon over apples. Continue to cook and stir gently for 5 to 10 minutes or until apples are tender. Stir in ¼ cup calvados, apple cider, or apple juice; heat through.

Nutrition facts per serving: *375 calories, 3 g protein, 42 g carbohydrate, 20 g total fat (12 g saturated fat), 70 mg cholesterol, 269 mg sodium, 1 g fiber. Daily values: 19% vitamin A, 0% vitamin C, 8% calcium, 10% iron.*

Shortcut

The apples can be peeled and sliced up to 4 hours ahead. To help keep them from turning brown, toss them with a mixture of equal parts of lemon juice and water and store in a sealed bag in the refrigerator.

Baker's Bonus

Citrus Sampler

A bit of finely shredded citrus peel—lemon or orange—is an easy way to add a light, fresh flavor to foods in a flash.

The best part is you can shred it today and use it next month. The next time a recipe calls for shredded citrus peel, shred more than you need. Be careful to shred only the brightly colored layer of the peel, not the bitter, white pith layer beneath the peel. Place any extra in a small freezer container or bag, seal, label, and freeze. Then go ahead and juice the fruit. Freeze the juice in ice cube trays, then transfer the cubes to a freezer container or bag, seal, label, and freeze for a future use.

*Notes*_____

_____

_____

_____

_____

Cream Shortcake with Caribbean Fruits

Vary the fruit to go with the season, making good use of whatever tropical fruits are available in the produce section. Some suggestions include bananas, dates, kiwi fruit, mangoes, strawberries, oranges, and pineapple.

- **2 cups all-purpose flour**
- **¼ cup granulated sugar**
- **1 tablespoon snipped crystallized ginger**
- **2 teaspoons baking powder**
- **1 cup whipping cream**
- **3 cups desired fresh tropical fruits cut into bite-size pieces**
- **Caribbean Orange Sauce**
- **Fresh mint leaves (optional)**

1 In a medium mixing bowl stir together flour, sugar, crystallized ginger, and baking powder. Make a well in center of dry mixture, then add whipping cream all at once. Using a fork, stir just until moistened.

2 Turn dough out onto a lightly floured surface. Quickly knead dough by folding and pressing gently for 10 to 12 strokes or until the dough is nearly smooth. Pat or lightly roll to ½-thickness. Cut dough with a floured 2½-inch biscuit or cookie cutter into 8 shortcakes, dipping cutter into flour between cuts.

3 Place shortcakes 1 inch apart on an ungreased baking sheet. Bake in a 450° oven for 12 to 15 minutes or until lightly golden. Cool on baking sheet on a wire rack for 10 minutes. Remove shortcakes from pan.

4 Using a sharp serrated knife, cut each shortcake in half horizontally. Spoon the fruit between the layers and over top. Serve immediately topped with Caribbean Orange Sauce. If desired, garnish with mint leaves. Makes 8 servings.

Caribbean Orange Sauce: In a small saucepan combine 2 tablespoons granulated sugar and 1 tablespoon cornstarch. Stir in ¾ cup orange juice and 1 to 2 tablespoons rum or water. Cook and stir until thickened and bubbly. Cook and stir 2 minutes more. Remove from heat; stir in 1 teaspoon butter or margarine. Serve warm.

Nutrition facts per serving: *338 calories, 4 g protein, 54 g carbohydrate, 12 g total fat (7 g saturated fat), 42 mg cholesterol, 109 mg sodium, 3 g fiber. Daily values: 24% vitamin A, 51% vitamin C, 10% calcium, and 11% iron.*

To Make Ahead
The Caribbean Orange Sauce can be prepared ahead and refrigerated. It will thicken some. Reheat it in a small saucepan over low heat or in a microwave-safe bowl on 50% power (medium) just until warm.

Cream Shortcake with Caribbean Fruits

Nectarine-Chocolate Shortcake

A treat for the confirmed chocolate lover, this shortcake can be topped with additional chocolate in the form of whipped cream. Keep the chocolate whipped cream in mind for a simple angel food or pound cake topping.

6 cups sliced nectarines or sliced, peeled peaches
2 tablespoons granulated sugar
1¾ cups all-purpose flour
¼ cup granulated sugar
¼ cup unsweetened cocoa powder
2 teaspoons baking powder
¼ teaspoon salt
½ cup butter or margarine
1 egg
½ cup half-and-half, light cream, or milk
½ teaspoon almond extract
Chocolate Whipped Cream
Chocolate curls (optional)

1 Grease an 8x8x2-inch baking pan. Set pan aside.

2 Stir together nectarines or peaches and 2 tablespoons sugar; set aside.

3 In a medium mixing bowl stir together flour, ¼ cup sugar, cocoa powder, baking powder, and salt. Using a pastry blender, cut in butter until mixture resembles coarse crumbs. Make a well in center of dry mixture.

4 In a small mixing bowl stir together the egg, half-and-half, and almond extract; add to dry mixture all at once. Using a fork, stir just until moistened.

5 Pat dough evenly in the prepared pan. Bake in a 450° oven for 15 to 18 minutes or until a wooden toothpick inserted near center comes out clean. Cool shortcake in pan on a wire rack for 10 minutes; remove shortcake from pan. Cool completely on wire rack.

6 To serve, using a long serrated knife, cut shortcake in half horizontally. Using a wide spatula, carefully lift off the top layer of shortcake. Spoon some of the fruit and Chocolate Whipped Cream over bottom layer. Replace shortcake top. Add remaining fruit and whipped cream. If desired, garnish with chocolate curls. Makes 9 servings.

Chocolate Whipped Cream: In a chilled medium mixing bowl combine 1 cup whipping cream, 3 tablespoons powdered sugar, 2 tablespoons unsweetened cocoa powder, and ½ teaspoon vanilla. Beat with chilled beaters of an electric mixer on medium speed until soft peaks form.

Nutrition facts per serving: *388 calories, 6 g protein, 41 g carbohydrate, 23 g total fat (14 g saturated fat), 92 mg choles-*

Baked to Perfection

Contrary to popular belief, baked cheesecakes are not difficult to prepare. They are temperamental, perhaps, but certainly not tough. Follow these tips, be patient while the cheesecake is in the oven, and you should produce a perfect cheesecake on the first try.

Start with the ingredients at room temperature.

Beat the cheese and sugar thoroughly because once the batter thins, it's impossible to get lumps out.

Stir the filling gently after adding the eggs and any remaining ingredients. Vigorous beating incorporates too much air, which causes the cheesecake to puff, then fall and crack.

Test the cheesecake for doneness at the minimum baking time to avoid overbaking, which dries out the cake and causes the center to fall. Gently shake the pan rather than inserting a knife, which may start a crack in the cake. The center of the cheesecake should appear nearly set. A 1-inch portion in the center may jiggle slightly even when the cheesecake is done. (If the cheesecake contains sour cream, a slightly larger portion in the center will seem unset but will firm upon cooling.)

Set a minute timer for the exact cooling time given in the recipe. When the timer rings, follow the recipe directions for loosening the crust of the cheesecake from the sides of the pan. If you don't, the cheesecake may begin to pull away from the sides and crack.

terol, 266 mg sodium, 2 g fiber. Daily values: 30% vitamin A, 8% vitamin C, 13% calcium, 12% iron.

Strawberry-Orange and Chocolate Shortcake: Prepare the Nectarine-Chocolate Shortcake as directed, except omit the nectarines or peaches and mix 5 cups sliced fresh strawberries and 1 cup fresh orange sections with the 2 tablespoons sugar.

Cheesecake Supreme

Top this classic dessert with your favorite fruit or leave it plain. Served either way, it's hard to beat the taste.

1¾   **cups finely crushed graham crackers**
¼   **cup finely chopped walnuts**
½   **teaspoon ground cinnamon**
½   **cup butter, melted (no substitutes)**
3   **8-ounce packages cream cheese, softened**
1   **cup granulated sugar**
2   **tablespoons all-purpose flour**
1   **teaspoon vanilla**
½   **teaspoon finely shredded lemon peel (optional)**
2   **eggs**
1   **egg yolk**
¼   **cup milk**
    Fresh fruit (optional)

1 For crust, in a medium mixing bowl combine crushed crackers, walnuts, and cinnamon. Stir in melted butter. If

desired, reserve ¼ cup of the crumb mixture for topping. Press remaining crumb mixture evenly onto the bottom and about 2 inches up the sides of an 8- or 9-inch springform pan. Set pan aside.

2 For filling, in a large mixing bowl beat the cream cheese, sugar, flour, vanilla, and lemon peel (if desired) with an electric mixer on medium to high speed until combined. Add the whole eggs and egg yolk all at once. Beat on low speed just until combined. Stir in milk.

3 Pour the filling into the crust-lined springform pan. Sprinkle with reserved crumbs, if any. Place the springform pan in a shallow baking pan on the oven rack. Bake in a 375° oven for 45 to 50 minutes for an 8-inch pan (35 to 40 minutes for a 9-inch pan) or until center appears nearly set when shaken.

4 Remove springform pan from baking pan. Cool cheesecake in springform pan on a wire rack for 15 minutes. Use a small metal spatula to loosen crust from sides of pan. Cool 30 minutes more. Remove sides of the springform pan. Cool for 1 hour, then cover and chill for at least 4 hours. If desired, serve with fruit. Makes 12 to 16 servings.

Nutrition facts per serving: *429 calories, 7 g protein, 30 g carbohydrate, 32 g total fat (18 g saturated fat), 137 mg cholesterol, 329 mg sodium, 1 g fiber. Daily values: 35% vitamin A, 0% vitamin C, 5% calcium, 10% iron.*

Spread crumb mixture evenly in the springform pan, creating a thin layer on the bottom. Using a measuring cup, custard cup, or back of a spoon, firmly press crumbs along the bottom and about 2 inches up the sides.

Cool the cheesecake as directed. Then run a small metal spatula between the crust and the pan to loosen the edges of the cheesecake. Let it cool 30 minutes more before removing sides of pan entirely.

Harmonious Merge

Whenever you're combining cheesecake batter with a melted ingredient such as chocolate or butter, make sure they are close to the same temperature. If they vary greatly, lumps may form in the batter.

*Notes*_____

Peanut Butter- Chocolate Ripple Cheesecake

Appeal to all ages with this cheesecake's popular flavor combination.

**2 teaspoons butter
 (no substitutes)**
**1 cup finely ground unsalted dry
 roasted peanuts**
**2 8-ounce packages cream cheese,
 softened**
1 cup creamy peanut butter
1 cup granulated sugar
2 tablespoons all-purpose flour
1 teaspoon vanilla
2 eggs
½ cup milk
**2 ounces semisweet chocolate,
 melted and cooled**
**1 cup purchased or homemade
 chocolate frosting (optional)**

1 For crust, use the butter to grease the bottom and 1¾ inches up the sides of a 9-inch springform pan. Press ground peanuts onto the bottom and 1 ¾ inches up the sides of the pan. Set pan aside.

2 For filling, in a large mixing bowl beat cream cheese, peanut butter, sugar, flour, and vanilla with an electric mixer on medium to high speed until combined. Add eggs all at once. Beat on low speed just until combined. Stir in milk. Divide filling in half.

3 Stir melted chocolate into half of the filling. Gently pour half of the plain filling into the nut-lined spring-form pan; pour all of the chocolate filling over top. Spoon remaining plain filling over chocolate layer. Use a narrow spatula to gently swirl batters being careful not to cut into crust. Place the springform pan in a shallow baking pan on the oven rack. Bake in a 375° oven for 30 to 35 minutes or until center appears nearly set when shaken.

4 Remove springform pan from baking pan. Cool cheesecake in spring-form pan on a wire rack for 15 minutes. Use a small metal spatula to loosen crust from sides of pan. Cool 30 minutes more. Remove sides of the springform pan. Cool for 1 hour, then cover and chill for at least 4 hours. If desired, using a decorating bag fitted with a medium star tip (about ½ inch), pipe a shell border around the bottom edge of the cheese cake. Makes 12 to 16 servings.

Nutrition facts per serving: *445 calories, 13 g protein, 29 g carbohydrate, 33 g total fat (13 g saturated fat), 80 mg cholesterol, 239 mg sodium, 3 g fiber. Daily values: 19% vitamin A, 0% vitamin C, 5% calcium, 9% iron.*

*Peanut Butter-
Chocolate Ripple
Cheesecake*

Softening the Cheese

To ensure a smooth, creamy cheesecake, be sure to allow time for the cream cheese to soften before preparing the filling. To speed the softening, unwrap the cream cheese and cut each block into 10 cubes. Allow cheese cubes to stand at room temperature for 1 hour.

Chocolate Cheesecake

What could be tastier than a cheesecake made with two kinds of chocolate in a chocolate crumb crust? The two variations give you even more flavor choices.

1¾ **cups finely crushed chocolate wafers (about 35 cookies)**
⅓ **cup butter, melted (no substitutes)**
4 **ounces semisweet chocolate, chopped**
1 **ounce unsweetened chocolate or semisweet chocolate, chopped**
3 **8-ounce packages cream cheese, softened**
1¼ **cups granulated sugar**
2 **tablespoons all-purpose flour**
1 **teaspoon vanilla**
4 **eggs**
¼ **cup milk**

1 For crust, in a medium mixing bowl combine crushed wafers and melted butter. Press mixture evenly onto the bottom and 1¾ inches up the sides of a 9-inch springform pan. Set pan aside.

2 In a small heavy saucepan combine the semisweet and unsweetened chocolates; melt over low heat, stirring occasionally. Cool slightly.

3 For filling, in a large mixing bowl beat cream cheese, sugar, flour, and vanilla with an electric mixer on medium to high speed until combined. With mixer running, slowly add melted chocolate, beating until combined. Add eggs all at once. Beat on low speed just until combined. Stir in milk.

4 Pour filling into the crust-lined springform pan. Place the springform pan in a shallow baking pan on the oven rack. Bake in a 350° oven for 45 to 50 minutes or until center appears nearly set when gently shaken. (Do not overbake.)

5 Remove springform pan from baking pan. Cool cheesecake in springform pan on a wire rack for 15 minutes. Use a small metal spatula to loosen crust from sides of the pan. Cool 30 minutes more. Remove sides of the springform pan. Cool for 1 hour, then cover and chill for at least 4 hours. Makes 12 servings.

Nutrition facts per serving: *484 calories, 9 g protein, 41 g carbohydrate, 33 g total fat (19 g saturated fat), 150 mg cholesterol, 356 mg sodium, 1 g fiber. Daily values: 32% vitamin A, 0% vitamin C, 5% calcium, 12% iron.*

Chocolate Hazelnut Cheesecake: Prepare Chocolate Cheesecake as directed, except use a hazelnut crust. Omit the chocolate wafers and melted butter. Using 2 teaspoons butter, grease the bottom and 1¾ inches up the sides of a 9-inch springform pan. Press 1 cup toasted, finely ground hazelnuts or almonds onto the bottom and 1¾ inches up the sides of the pan. Cover and chill crust. For filling, prepare as directed, except substitute 3 tablespoons hazelnut liqueur for 3 tablespoons of the milk. If desired, top the chilled cheesecake with whole and/or halved small fresh strawberries.

White Chocolate Cheesecake: Prepare Chocolate Cheesecake as directed, except substitute 6 ounces white baking bar, melted, for all of the semisweet and unsweetened chocolate. (To melt white baking bars, heat and stir constantly over very low heat.)

With your mixer running, slowly add melted chocolate in a steady stream, beating just until combined. This prevents the chocolate from forming into little chips.

Raspberry Cheesecake

Finish the mixing by hand, using a spoon if the filling becomes too thick for your mixer and the motor seems to be straining.

1⅓ **cups finely crushed graham crackers**
⅓ **cup butter, melted (no substitutes)**
3 **8-ounce packages cream cheese, softened**
¾ **cup granulated sugar**
2 **tablespoons all-purpose flour**
1 **teaspoon vanilla**
2 **eggs**
1 **egg yolk**
¼ **cup raspberry liqueur or milk**
 Raspberry Sauce
 Fresh raspberries (optional)
 Fresh mint leaves (optional)

1 For crust, in a medium mixing bowl combine crushed crackers and melted butter. Press crumb mixture evenly onto the bottom and about 1 inch up the sides of an 8- or 9-inch springform pan. Set pan aside.

2 For filling, in a large mixing bowl beat cream cheese, sugar, flour, and vanilla with an electric mixer on medium to high speed until combined. Add whole eggs and egg yolk all at once. Beat on low speed just until combined. Stir in raspberry liqueur or milk.

3 Stir ¼ cup of the Raspberry Sauce into half of the filling. Gently pour half of the plain filling into the crust-lined

springform pan; pour in all of the raspberry filling. Gently pour in remaining plain filling. Use a narrow spatula to gently swirl batters being careful not to cut into crust. Place the springform pan in a shallow baking pan on the oven rack. Bake in a 375° oven for 45 to 50 minutes for an 8-inch pan (35 to 40 minutes for a 9-inch pan) or until center appears nearly set when shaken.

4 Remove springform pan from baking pan. Cool cheesecake in springform pan on a wire rack for 15 minutes. Use a small metal spatula to loosen crust from sides of pan. Cool 30 minutes more. Remove sides of the springform pan. Cool for 1 hour, then cover and chill for at least 4 hours. If desired, garnish with a few fresh raspberries and mint leaves. Serve with remaining Raspberry Sauce. Makes 12 to 16 servings.

Raspberry Sauce: Press one 10-ounce package frozen, thawed raspberries through a sieve to remove seeds. In a medium saucepan stir together ¼ cup granulated sugar and 2 teaspoons cornstarch. Stir in sieved raspberries. Cook and stir over medium heat until slightly thickened and bubbly. Reduce heat. Cook and stir for 2 minutes more. Remove from heat and cool slightly. If desired, add a few drops red food coloring.

Nutrition facts per serving: *415 calories, 7 g protein, 35 g carbohydrate, 27 g total fat (16 g saturated fat), 130 mg cholesterol, 296 mg sodium, 1 g fiber. Daily values: 33% vitamin A, 6% vitamin C, 5% calcium, 9% iron.*

Bottomless Options

If you're a purist who doesn't like to put a crust on your cheesecake or you would rather not include the additional calories, try dusting the lightly greased springform pan with some finely ground graham crackers or vanilla wafers. The crumbs will ensure the cake still comes out of the pan easily. This option works best if your cheesecake has a thick batter.

Notes

Black Forest Cheesecake

Turn this favorite cake into a cheesecake with chocolate crust, kirsch, and cherries! Then decorate the cheesecake with whipped cream rosettes, chocolate curls, and dark, sweet cherries.

1½ **cups finely crushed chocolate wafers (about 30 wafers)**
⅓ **cup butter, melted (no substitutes)**
1 **tablespoon butter (no substitutes)**
¼ **cup sliced almonds**
2 **8-ounces packages cream cheese, softened**
¾ **cup granulated sugar**
2 **tablespoons all-purpose flour**
1 **teaspoon vanilla**
½ **teaspoon almond extract**
3 **8-ounce cartons dairy sour cream**

3 **eggs**
2 **tablespoons kirsch or cherry juice**
¾ **cup dried cherries, coarsely chopped**
1 **cup whipping cream Chocolate curls (optional)**

1 For crust, in a medium mixing bowl combine crushed wafers and ⅓ cup melted butter. Press crumb mixture onto the bottom of a 9-inch springform pan. Generously grease sides of pan using the 1 tablespoon butter; press sliced almonds onto sides of pan. Set pan aside.

2 For filling, in a large mixing bowl beat cream cheese, sugar, flour, vanilla, and almond extract with an electric mixer on medium to high speed until combined. Add sour cream, eggs, and kirsch or cherry juice. Beat on low speed just until combined.

3 Pour half of the filling into the crust-lined springform pan. Layer dried cherries over the filling. Carefully pour the remaining filling over the dried cherries. Place the springform pan in a shallow baking pan on the oven rack. Bake in a 350° oven about 55 minutes or until center appears nearly set when shaken.

4 Remove springform pan from baking pan. Cool cheesecake in springform pan on a wire rack for 15 minutes. Use a small metal spatula to loosen crust from sides of pan. Cool 30 minutes more. Remove sides of the springform pan. Cool for 1 hour, then cover and chill for at least 4 hours.

5 Just before serving whip cream to soft peaks. Spoon whipped cream onto cheesecake. If desired, top with chocolate curls. Makes 12 to 16 servings.

Nutrition facts per serving: 559 calories, 9 g protein, 36 g carbohydrate, 43 g total fat (25 g saturated fat), 164 mg cholesterol, 316 mg sodium, 1 g fiber. Daily values: 50% vitamin A, 1% vitamin C, 10% calcium, 9% iron.

Baker's Bonus

Setting Some Aside

Not many people can devour an entire cheesecake at a single sitting. Fortunately there's no need to. It can be refrigerated, covered, for up to three days or frozen. To freeze, place the cheesecake in a freezer container.

If you freeze a whole cheesecake, plan to use it within 1 month of freezing. If you freeze individual pieces, use them within 2 weeks. To serve, thaw a whole cheesecake in the refrigerator for 24 hours; thaw individual pieces at room temperature for 2 hours.

Black Forest Cheesecake

Honey-Nut Cheesecake

Cover the sheets of phyllo with plastic wrap until you're ready to use them to prevent drying and cracking.

- ¾ **cup ground hazelnuts, pecans, or walnuts (3 ounces)***
- 8 **sheets frozen phyllo dough (about 17x12-inch rectangles), thawed**
- ¼ **cup butter or margarine, melted**
- 2 **tablespoons granulated sugar**
- 2 **8-ounce packages cream cheese**
- 1 **cup mascarpone or ricotta cheese (8 ounces)**
- ⅔ **cup honey**
- 2 **tablespoons all-purpose flour**
- 3 **eggs**
- ¼ **cup milk**

1 For crust, generously grease the bottom and sides of a 9-inch springform pan. Sprinkle ¼ cup of the ground nuts evenly over the bottom of the pan. Set pan aside.

2 Unfold phyllo. Cover phyllo with plastic wrap, removing phyllo sheets as needed. Brush one phyllo sheet with some of the melted butter. Top with another sheet of phyllo, overlapping to create a 17x14-inch rectangle; brush with butter. Repeat with remaining phyllo and butter to make 8 layers in a 17x14-inch rectangle.

3 Using kitchen shears, trim phyllo to a 14-inch circle, reserving trimmings. Ease the phyllo into the prepared pan, creasing as necessary and being careful not to tear dough. Trim even with top of pan, reserving trimmings.

4 Combine remaining nuts and sugar; reserve 1 tablespoon for topping. Sprinkle remaining nut mixture over phyllo in pan. Cut reserved phyllo trimmings into ½- to 1-inch pieces; place on a greased baking sheet. Bake crust and trimmings in a 425° oven until golden, allowing 4 to 6 minutes for trimmings and 6 to 8 minutes for crust. Cool slightly on a wire rack. Reduce oven temperature to 350°.

5 For filling, in a large mixing bowl beat the cream cheese, mascarpone or ricotta cheese, honey, and flour with an electric mix on low speed until smooth. Add the eggs all at once. Beat on low speed just until combined. Stir in the milk.

6 Pour filling into the phyllo crust. Bake in a 350° oven for 50 to 55 minutes or until the center appears nearly set when shaken. If necessary, to prevent overbrowning, carefully cover the crust with foil the last 20 minutes.

7 Cool cheesecake in springform pan on a wire rack for 5 to 10 minutes. Loosen sides of pan. Cool for 1 hour, then cover and chill for at least 4 hours. Store trimmings in a tightly covered container in a cool, dry place. Before serving, remove sides of the springform pan. Top cheesecake with phyllo trimmings and reserved sugar-nut mixture. Makes 12 to 16 servings.

**Note:* To grind nuts, place ½ cup at a time in a blender container or food processor bowl. Cover and blend or process until very finely chopped; be careful not to overprocess or the nuts will form a paste.

***Nutrition facts per serving:** 424 calories, 10 g protein, 28 g carbohydrate, 32 g total fat (17 g saturated fat), 130 mg cholesterol, 243 mg sodium, 1 g fiber. Daily values: 22% vitamin A, 0% vitamin C, 5% calcium, 9% iron.*

Cappuccino Cheesecake: Prepare as directed, except substitute ¾ cup orange marmalade for the honey and dissolve 1 tablespoon instant coffee crystals in the milk.

Lemon Curd Cheesecake: Prepare as directed, except substitute lemon curd for the honey.

Gently ease the phyllo layers into the springform pan, folding and making tucks as necessary to space layers evenly around the edge.

Pineapple-Vanilla Cheesecake Pie

You can make your own yogurt cheese. The cheese needs to stand awhile, so start it early.

1½ **cups finely crushed vanilla wafers (36 to 40 wafers)**
¼ **cup butter, melted (no substitutes)**
   Yogurt Cheese
1 **8-ounce container soft-style cream cheese with pineapple, softened**
¾ **cup granulated sugar**
1 **tablespoon all-purpose flour**
2 **teaspoons vanilla**
1 **teaspoon lemon juice**
2 **eggs**
   Pineapple ice-cream topping

1 For crust, in a medium mixing bowl combine crushed vanilla wafers and melted butter. Press mixture evenly onto the bottom and sides of a 9-inch pie plate to form a firm crust. Bake in a 350° oven for 4 to 5 minutes or until edge is just lightly browned. Cool on a wire rack. Set aside.

2 For filling, in a large mixing bowl beat Yogurt Cheese, pineapple cream cheese, sugar, flour, vanilla, and lemon juice with an electric mixer on medium speed until combined. Add the eggs all at once. Beat on low speed just until combined.

3 Pour filling into crust-lined pie plate. Bake in a 350° oven for 40 to 45 minutes or until cheesecake is puffed about 2 inches in from edge and shakes evenly over entire surface when jiggled. Cool on a wire rack 30 minutes. Cover and chill at least 4 hours.

4 To serve, top cheesecake with pineapple ice-cream topping. Makes 10 servings.

Nutrition facts per serving: *394 calories, 7 g protein, 58 g carbohydrate, 16 g total fat (9 g saturated fat), 89 mg cholesterol, 233 mg sodium, 0 g fiber. Daily values: 12% vitamin A, 22% vitamin C, 12% calcium, 3% iron.*

Yogurt Cheese: Spoon 32 ounces vanilla yogurt or plain fat-free yogurt that contains no gelatin into a sieve or colander lined with 100-percent-cotton cheesecloth and set over a large bowl. Let yogurt stand in refrigerator about 15 hours or overnight. Discard liquid in bowl. Use Yogurt Cheese remaining in sieve for cheesecake. If desired, wrap Yogurt Cheese in clear plastic wrap and chill. Makes about 2 cups cheese.

Cherry Cheesecake Bars

Cherry pie filling makes this delightful dessert easy to prepare.

2 **cups finely crushed chocolate wafers (about 44 wafers)**
⅓ **cup butter, melted (no substitutes)**
1 **8-ounce package cream cheese, softened**
1 **3-ounce package cream cheese, softened**
¾ **cup granulated sugar**
½ **teaspoon almond extract or vanilla**
4 **eggs**
¼ **cup milk**
1 **21-ounce can cherry pie filling**
½ **cup sliced almonds***

1 Grease a 13x9x2-inch baking pan. For crust, in mixing bowl combine crushed wafers and melted butter. Press crumb mixture evenly into the bottom of baking pan. Set pan aside.

2 For filling, in a mixing bowl beat cream cheese, sugar, and almond extract with an electric mixer on medium to high speed until combined. Add eggs all at once. Beat on low speed just until combined. Stir in milk.

3 Spread cream cheese filling evenly over crust. Bake in a 350° oven for 25 to 30 minutes or until center appears set. Cool on a wire rack.

4 For topping, in a bowl stir together pie filling and almonds. Spread over cream cheese filling. Chill thoroughly. Cut into bars. Makes 32.

***Note:** If desired, toast nuts by placing them in a shallow baking pan in a 350° oven for 5 to 10 minutes or until golden; stir once or twice.

Nutrition facts per serving: *146 calories, 3 g protein, 17 g carbohydrate, 8 g total fat (4 g saturated fat), 43 mg cholesterol, 107 mg sodium, 0 g fiber. Daily values: 7% vitamin A, 0% vitamin C, 2% calcium, 4% iron.*

Black Walnut Shortbread
(see recipe, page 198)

Honey-Nut Bars
(see recipe, page 190)

Cross-Country Cookies
(see recipe, page 173)

Homecoming Cookies

There's something incredibly comforting about homemade cookies that can make scratched knees, lonely hearts, and even stressed nerves feel better.

In this chapter we've pulled together more than 50 favorite drop cookies, bars, brownies, and cutout cookies that are guaranteed to pick up your spirits, whether you're making them for yourself or sharing them with someone else.

There are chewy oatmeal and chocolate chip cookies, sinful brownies with chunks of chocolate, delicately crisp sugar cookies and shortbreads, and lots of international best-sellers. Bet you're feeling better already!

Chewy Triple Chippers

A trio of melt-in-your mouth chips gives these chewy cookies their scrumptious flavor.

½ **cup butter or margarine**
1 **cup packed brown sugar**
½ **cup granulated sugar**
½ **teaspoon baking soda**
2 **eggs**
1 **teaspoon vanilla**
2½ **cups all-purpose flour**
1 **6-ounce package (1 cup) semisweet chocolate pieces**
1 **cup peanut butter pieces**
1 **cup butterscotch pieces**

1 In a large mixing bowl beat butter with an electric mixer on medium to high speed about 30 seconds or until softened. Add the brown sugar, sugar, and baking soda. Beat until combined. Beat in eggs and vanilla until combined. Beat in as much flour as you can with the mixer. Using a wooden spoon, stir in any remaining flour. Stir in the chocolate, peanut butter, and butterscotch pieces.

2 Drop dough from a rounded teaspoon 2 inches apart on an ungreased cookie sheet. Bake in a 375° oven for 8 to 10 minutes or until edges are lightly browned. Cool on cookie sheet for 1 minute. Remove cookies from cookie sheet and cool on a wire rack. Store in an airtight container or plastic bag at room temperature for up to 3 days. Makes about 54.

***Nutrition facts per cookie:** 105 calories, 1 g protein, 15 g carbohydrate, 5 g total fat (3 g saturated), 13 mg cholesterol, 35 mg sodium, 0 g fiber. Daily values: 1% vitamin A, 0% vitamin C, 0% calcium, 2% iron.*

Scoop up the cookie dough in a small spoon. Use the back of another spoon or a rubber scraper to push the dough off the spoon. The dough will spread while baking, so drop the dough mounds about 2 inches apart.

Drop cookies are done when the edges and bottoms are lightly browned.

Chocolate Chip Cookies: Prepare Chewy Triple Chippers as directed, except substitute one 12-ounce package (2 cups) semisweet or milk chocolate pieces for the peanut butter and butterscotch pieces.

To Make Ahead
Bake cookies as directed; cool completely. Place in a freezer container or bag and freeze for up to 1 month. Before serving, thaw for 15 minutes.

Dark Chocolate Chews

½ **cup butter or margarine**
1 **cup granulated sugar**
¾ **teaspoon baking soda**
¼ **teaspoon salt**
2 **eggs**
1 **3-ounce bar bittersweet chocolate or 3 ounces semisweet chocolate, cut up, melted, and cooled**
1¾ **cups all-purpose flour**
1 **cup miniature candy-coated semisweet chocolate pieces**

1 In a large mixing bowl beat butter with an electric mixer on medium to high speed about 30 seconds or until softened. Add the sugar, baking soda, and salt. Beat in eggs and melted chocolate until combined. Beat in as much of the flour as you can with the mixer. Stir in any remaining flour. Stir in chocolate pieces.

2 Drop dough from a rounded teaspoon 2 inches apart on an ungreased cookie sheet. Bake in a 375° oven for

10 to 12 minutes or until cookies are set. Remove cookies from cookie sheet and cool on a wire rack. Store in an airtight container or plastic bag at room temperature or in the refrigerator for 1 day. Makes about 36.

Nutrition facts per cookie: *103 calories, 1 g protein, 15 g carbohydrate, 5 g total fat (2 g saturated), 19 mg cholesterol, 71 mg sodium, 0 g fiber. Daily values: 2% vitamin A, 0% vitamin C, 0% calcium, 2% iron.*

To Make Ahead

Bake the cookies as directed; cool completely. Place in a freezer container or bag and freeze for up to 1 month. Before serving, thaw for 15 minutes.

Cross-Country Cookies

All the essentials of a handy trail mix are packed in these appealing cookies. (Pictured on page 170.)

½ **cup butter or margarine**
½ **cup peanut butter**
¾ **cup granulated sugar**
¾ **cup packed brown sugar**
 1 **teaspoon baking powder**
¼ **teaspoon baking soda**
 2 **eggs**
 1 **teaspoon vanilla**
1½ **cups all-purpose flour**
1¾ **cups rolled oats**
 1 **cup candy-coated chocolate pieces**
½ **cup peanuts**
½ **cup raisins**
¼ **cup wheat germ**

1 In large mixing bowl beat butter and peanut butter with an electric mixer on medium to high speed about 30 seconds or until combined. Add the sugar, brown sugar, baking powder, and baking soda. Beat until combined. Beat in eggs and vanilla until combined. Beat in as much of the flour as you can with the mixer. Using a wooden spoon, stir in any remaining flour. Stir in the rolled oats, chocolate pieces, peanuts, raisins, and wheat germ.

2 Drop dough from a rounded teaspoon 2 inches apart on an ungreased cookie sheet. Bake in a 375° oven about 9 minutes or until edges are lightly browned. Cool on cookie sheet for 1 minute. Remove cookies from cookie sheet and cool on a wire rack. Store in an airtight container or plastic bag at room temperature for up to 3 days. Makes about 60.

Nutrition facts per cookie: *92 calories, 2 g protein, 12 g carbohydrate, 4 g total fat (1 g saturated), 11 mg cholesterol, 40 mg sodium, 1 g fiber. Daily values: 1% vitamin A, 0% vitamin C, 1% calcium, 2% iron.*

Cross-Country Megacookies: Prepare Cross-Country Cookies as directed, except drop dough in ¼-cup mounds 4 inches apart on an ungreased cookie sheet and flatten slightly. Bake in a 375° oven for 10 to 12 minutes or until edges are lightly browned. Makes 25.

To Make Ahead

Bake the cookies as directed; cool completely. Place in a freezer container or bag and freeze for up to 1 month. Before serving, thaw for 15 minutes.

Drop What You're Doing

Chocolate chip cookies and oatmeal cookies are just two of the many kinds of drop cookies you know well. These days there are so many types of cookies available at the supermarket that you may think it's not worth making them yourself. But when you do, you'll taste the difference. Besides, to show you that it is as easy to make drop cookies as it is to buy them, here's all you need to know.

◆ *Stir in the last bit of flour by hand if your electric mixer begins to strain and feel warm.*

◆ *Refrigerate the dough until it feels cool to the touch.*

◆ *Use a light coating of shortening when recipes call for greased cookie sheets. If you use too much, the cookies may spread too far. When recipes specify ungreased cookie sheets, use regular or nonstick sheets.*

◆ *Drop cookie dough using spoons from your everyday flatware set, not measuring spoons, to get the right number of cookies from each batch. Make sure the dough mounds are rounded and are approximately the same size so that they will cook evenly.*

◆ *Allow the cookie sheets to cool between batches so that the dough won't spread too much.*

◆ *Bake on only one oven rack at a time for even browning.*

Notes

Kid Appeal

Three-In-One Oatmeal Cookies

Ten-minute freezer dough is today's best-kept secret for fresh, homemade cookies. Prepare cookie dough as directed, except instead of baking, wrap each portion in freezer wrap; seal, label, and freeze for up to 3 months. Thaw the frozen dough in the refrigerator overnight before adding your favorite flavor and baking as directed stacks of spicy raisin, nutty brickle, or old-fashioned gumdrop delights.

1½	**cups butter or margarine**
2	**cups packed brown sugar**
1	**cup granulated sugar**
2	**eggs**
¼	**cup milk**
2	**teaspoons baking powder**
2	**teaspoons vanilla**
½	**teaspoon baking soda**
3	**cups all-purpose flour**
2	**cups rolled oats**

1 In an extra-large mixing bowl beat butter with an electric mixer on medium to high speed for 30 seconds. Add the brown sugar, sugar, eggs, milk, baking powder, vanilla, and baking soda. Beat until combined. Beat in as much flour as you can with the mixer. Using a wooden spoon, stir in remaining flour. Then stir in the oats.

2 Divide dough into 3 portions. Choose one of the following cookie variations for each portion of dough.

3 Drop dough onto an ungreased cookie sheet. (For large cookies, drop into scant ¼-cup mounds 4 inches apart; for small cookies, drop from a rounded teaspoon 2 inches apart.) Bake in a 375° oven until edges are golden but centers are soft, allowing 13 to 15 minutes for large cookies and 9 to 11 minutes for small cookies. Cool on the cookie sheet for 1 minute. Remove cookies from cookie sheet and cool on a wire rack. Store in an airtight container or plastic bag at room temperature for up to 3 days. Makes about 11 large cookies or 32 small cookies.

Nutrition facts per large Spicy Raisin Round cookie: *249 calories, 3 g protein, 41 g carbohydrate, 9 g total fat (2 g saturated), 13 mg cholesterol, 145 mg sodium, 1 g fiber. Daily values: 14% vitamin A, 1% vitamin C, 5% calcium, 10% iron.*

Spicy Raisin Rounds: Stir in 1 cup raisins or currants, 1 teaspoon ground cinnamon, and ¼ teaspoon ground cloves. Continue as directed.

Nutty Brickle Chippers: Stir in 1 cup of chopped chocolate-covered English toffee or semisweet chocolate pieces and ½ cup chopped walnuts or hazelnuts. Continue as directed.

Candy Cookies: Stir in 1 cup snipped or chopped gumdrops or candy-coated milk chocolate pieces. Continue as directed.

To Make Ahead

Bake cookies as directed; cool completely. Place in a freezer container or bag and freeze for up to 1 month. Before serving, thaw for 15 minutes.

Three-In-One Oatmeal Cookies

Big Fat Deal

The firmness of your cookie dough will vary depending on whether you use butter or margarine. If you use margarine, it will depend on what type of margarine it is. To ensure the best cookies every time, use only butter or use margarine that contains at least 60% vegetable oil. Do not use the "extra light" spreads that contain only about 40% oil.

Orange Snowdrops

½ **cup shortening**
½ **cup butter (no substitutes)**
1 **cup sifted powdered sugar**
½ **teaspoon baking soda**
1 **egg**
½ **of a 6-ounce can (⅓ cup) frozen orange juice concentrate, thawed**
1 **teaspoon vanilla**
2 **cups all-purpose flour**
  Orange Frosting

1 In large mixing bowl beat shortening and butter with an electric mixer on medium to high speed about 30 seconds or until softened. Add the powdered sugar and baking soda. Beat until combined. Beat in the egg, orange juice concentrate, and vanilla

until combined. Beat in as much of the flour as you can with the mixer. Using a wooden spoon, stir in any remaining flour.

2 Drop dough from a rounded teaspoon 2 inches apart on an ungreased cookie sheet. Bake in a 375° oven about 8 minutes or until edges are lightly browned. Cool on cookie sheet for 1 minute. Remove cookies from cookie sheet and cool on a wire rack.

3 Frost cookies with Orange Frosting. Store in a single layer in an airtight container up to 1 day. Makes about 36.

Orange Frosting: In a small mixing bowl stir together ½ of a 6-ounce can (⅓ cup) frozen orange juice concentrate, thawed, and 3 cups sifted powdered sugar until smooth.

Nutrition facts per cookie: 125 calories, 1 g protein, 18 g carbohydrate, 6 g total fat (2 g saturated), 13 mg cholesterol, 45 mg sodium, 0 g fiber. Daily values: 2% vitamin A, 13% vitamin C, 0% calcium, 2% iron.

To Make Ahead
Bake cookies as directed; cool completely. Do not frost. Place unfrosted cookies in a freezer container or bag and freeze for up to 1 month. Before serving, thaw for 15 minutes. Frost with Orange Frosting.

Sour Cream- Apricot Cookies

Make a lighter cookie by using nonfat sour cream and low-sugar preserves.

1 **cup butter or margarine**
1½ **cups granulated sugar**
1 **teaspoon baking soda**
¼ **teaspoon salt**
2 **eggs**
1 **8-ounce carton dairy sour cream**
½ **cup apricot preserves**
3¼ **cups all-purpose flour**
  Apricot preserves, melted (optional)

1 In a large mixing bowl beat butter with an electric mixer on medium to high speed about 30 seconds or until softened. Add the sugar, baking soda, and salt. Beat until combined. Beat in eggs, sour cream, and apricot preserves until combined. Beat in as much of the flour as you can with the mixer. Using a wooden spoon, stir in any remaining flour.

2 Drop dough from a rounded teaspoon 2 inches apart on an ungreased cookie sheet. Bake in a 350° oven for 8 to 10 minutes or until edges are lightly browned. Cool on cookie sheet for 1 minute. Remove cookies from cookie sheet and cool on a wire rack. Store in layers separated by waxed paper in an airtight container in the refrigerator for up to 3 days. Just before serving, if desired, brush with melted apricot preserves. To melt preserves, heat them in a saucepan over low heat, stirring constantly. Makes about 60.

Nutrition facts per cookie: *87 calories, 1 g protein, 12 g carbohydrate, 4 g total fat (2 g saturated), 17 mg cholesterol, 65 mg sodium, 0 g fiber. Daily values: 4% vitamin A, 0% vitamin C, 0% calcium, 2% iron.*

To Make Ahead

Bake the cookies as directed; cool completely. Do not brush with melted preserves. Place in layers separated by waxed paper in a freezer container and freeze for up to 1 month. Before serving, thaw for 15 minutes. If desired, brush with melted preserves.

Delicious Memories

Double Whammy Oatmeal Chews

I celebrated many treat days at school with these old-fashioned, chewy oatmeal cookies. My favorite part is the combination of chocolate and butterscotch chips.
—Jennifer Darling—

1 **cup butter or margarine**
1 **cup granulated sugar**
1 **cup packed brown sugar**
2 **eggs**
1 **teaspoon vanilla**
1½ **cups all-purpose flour**

1 **teaspoon baking soda**
½ **teaspoon salt**
3 **cups rolled oats**
1 **6-ounce package (1 cup) semisweet chocolate pieces**
1 **cup butterscotch pieces**

1 In a large mixing bowl, beat butter with an electric mixer on medium to high speed about 30 seconds or until softened. Add sugar and brown sugar. Beat until combined. Beat in the eggs and vanilla. Beat in flour, baking soda, and salt. Stir in the oats. Stir in the chocolate and butterscotch pieces.

2 Drop dough from a rounded teaspoon 2 inches apart on an ungreased cookie sheet. Bake in a 375° oven for 8 to 10 minutes or until golden. Cool on the cookie sheet for 1 minute. Remove cookies from cookie sheet and cool on a wire rack. Store in an airtight container or plastic bag at room temperature for up to 3 days. Makes about 60.

Nutrition facts per cookie: *107 calories, 1 g protein, 15 g carbohydrate, 5 g total fat (3 g saturated), 15 mg cholesterol, 76 mg sodium, 0 g fiber. Daily values: 3% vitamin A, 0% vitamin C, 0% calcium, 3% iron.*

Any-Way-You-Want-'Em Oatmeal Chews: Prepare Double Whammy Oatmeal Chews as directed, except substitute your favorite combination of candy-coated milk chocolate pieces, raisins, dried chopped fruit, chopped nuts, or peanut butter-flavored (or other flavored) pieces for the 1 cup semisweet chocolate pieces and 1 cup butterscotch pieces.

Baker's Bonus

Setting Some Aside

Storing baked cookies properly is essential if you want them to keep that just-baked freshness.

Short-term: *Cool cookies completely, and, if possible, leave them unfrosted so they won't stick together. In an airtight container, arrange the cookies in single layers separated by sheets of waxed paper. Do not mix soft and crisp cookies in the same container because the crisp cookies will soften. Store cookies at room temperature for up to 3 days. If the cookies are frosted with a cream cheese or yogurt icing, you'll need to refrigerate them.*

Long-term: *Baked cookies packaged in freezer bags, freezer containers, or foil can be kept for up to 1 month. Before serving, thaw the frozen cookies in the container for about 15 minutes. If the cookies are to be frosted, glazed, or sprinkled with sugar, wait until they have thawed to decorate them.*

To Make Ahead

Bake the cookies as directed; cool completely. Place in a freezer container or bag and freeze for up to 1 month. Before serving, thaw for 15 minutes.

White Chocolate-Raspberry Cookies

White Chocolate-Raspberry Cookies

Make any special occasion even nicer when you serve these cookies topped with a favorite jam. Cherry, apricot, or strawberry jam tastes every bit as good surrounded by white chocolate as the raspberry suggested here.

8 ounces white baking bar
½ cup butter (no substitutes)
1 cup granulated sugar
1 teaspoon baking soda
¼ teaspoon salt
2 eggs
2¾ cups all-purpose flour
½ cup seedless raspberry jam
3 ounces white baking bar
½ teaspoon shortening

1 Grease a cookie sheet; set aside. Chop 4 ounces of the white baking bar; set aside. In a heavy small saucepan, melt 4 ounces of the white baking bar over low heat while stirring constantly; cool.

2 In a large mixing bowl beat butter with an electric mixer on medium to high speed about 30 seconds or until softened. Add the sugar, baking soda, and salt. Beat until combined. Beat in eggs and melted white baking bar until combined. Beat in as much of the flour as you can with the mixer. Using a wooden spoon, stir in any remaining flour. Stir in the 4 ounces of chopped white baking bar.

3 Drop dough from a rounded teaspoon 2 inches apart on the prepared cookie sheet. Bake in a 375° oven for 7 to 9 minutes or until cookies are lightly browned around edges. Cool on cookie sheet for 1 minute. Remove cookies from cookie sheet and cool on a wire rack. Store in an airtight container or plastic bag at room temperature for up to 3 days.

4 Just before serving, melt the raspberry jam in a small saucepan over low heat. Spoon about ½ teaspoon of jam onto the top of each cookie. In a heavy small saucepan combine the 3 ounces white baking bar and shortening. Melt over low heat, stirring constantly. Drizzle each cookie with some of the melted mixture. If necessary, refrigerate cookies about 15 minutes to firm chocolate. Makes about 48.

Nutrition facts per cookie: *104 calories, 1 g protein, 16 g carbohydrate, 4 g total fat (2 g saturated), 14 mg cholesterol, 66 mg sodium, 0 g fiber. Daily values: 2% vitamin A, 0% vitamin C, 1% calcium, 2% iron.*

To Make Ahead

Bake the cookies as directed; cool completely. Do not decorate. Place in a freezer container or bag and freeze for up to 1 month. Before serving, thaw for 15 minutes. Decorate as directed.

Healthy Alternatives

It may be tempting to reduce or make substitutions for the sugar and fat in a cookie recipe, but any change in ingredient proportions also changes the cookies.

Besides adding flavor, sugar and fat make cookies crisp and tender. Reducing sugar and fat makes cookies more cakelike. Substituting an artificial sweetener or a lower-fat product will not produce a good cookie.

There are some things you can do to make the cookies healthier, however.

Higher fiber: *Substitute rolled oats or whole wheat flour for one-fourth of the all-purpose flour. Add fruits such as raisins or dried cherries, cranberries, or mixed fruit bits.*

Lower cholesterol: *Use a refrigerated or frozen egg product instead of a whole egg, or use two egg whites in place of one whole egg.*

Lower calories: *Reduce the amount of nuts, and sprinkle them atop bar cookies where they show rather than stirring them into the batter.*

Substitute mini, semisweet chocolate pieces for the regular-size pieces, and use just half as many. You still will get chocolate in every bite.

Being Exact

Ever wonder why the number of cookies you finish with is never the amount the recipe says you should have? There's an easy way to get the exact yield from a cookie recipe, as long as you don't sample too much of the dough or eat cookies before you count them.

Pat the dough into a square. Cut the dough square into the number of pieces the recipe should yield. If you want 48 cookies, cut the dough into six equal strips one way and eight equal strips the other way. Then shape the resulting pieces into 48 balls and bake them.

Cashew Cookies

Your blender or food processor can make quick work of grinding the cashews, but just as quickly can turn them into cashew butter. Add about ¼ cup of the flour with the cashews and pulse the blender or processor on and off for evenly ground nuts.

- ½ **cup butter or margarine**
- 1 **cup packed brown sugar**
- 1 **teaspoon baking powder**
- ¼ **teaspoon baking soda**
- 1 **egg**
- 1 **teaspoon finely shredded lemon peel**
- 2 **tablespoons lemon juice**
- 1 **teaspoon vanilla**
- 1¾ **cups all-purpose flour**
- 1 **cup cashews, ground**
- ½ **cup chopped cashews**

1 In a medium mixing bowl beat butter with an electric mixer on medium or high speed about 30 seconds or until softened. Add the brown sugar, baking powder, and baking soda. Beat until combined. Beat in egg, lemon peel, lemon juice, and vanilla. Using a wooden spoon, stir in the flour. Stir in the ground and chopped cashews.

2 Drop dough from a rounded teaspoon 2 inches apart on an ungreased cookie sheet. Bake in a 350° oven for 10 to 12 minutes or until edges are lightly browned. Cool on cookie sheet for 1 minute. Remove cookies from cookie sheet and cool on a wire rack. Store in an airtight container or plastic bag at room temperature for up to 3 days. Makes about 48.

Nutrition facts per cookie: 71 calories, 1 g protein, 8 g carbohydrate, 4 g total fat (2 g saturated), 10 mg cholesterol, 61 mg sodium, 0 g fiber. Daily values: 1% vitamin A, 0% vitamin C, 1% calcium, 3% iron.

To Make Ahead

Bake cookies as directed; cool completely. Place in a freezer container or bag and freeze for up to 1 month. Before serving, thaw for 15 minutes.

Praline Cookies

If you like a crisp florentine or that old Southern favorite, praline candies, you'll be hooked on these cookies.

- ⅓ **cup butter (no substitutes)**
- ⅓ **cup milk**
- ¼ **cup packed brown sugar**
- 1½ **cups finely chopped pecans, toasted**
- ¼ **cup all-purpose flour**
- 2 **1.55-ounce bars milk chocolate**

1 Grease and flour a cookie sheet; set aside. (Repeat greasing and flouring cookie sheet for each batch.)

2 In a heavy medium saucepan combine the butter, milk, and brown sugar. Bring mixture to a full rolling boil, stirring occasionally. Remove from heat. Stir in pecans. Then stir in flour.

3 Drop batter from a level tablespoon at least 3 inches apart on the prepared cookie sheet. Then, using a wet knife, spread the batter into 3-inch circles. Bake in a 350° oven about 8 minutes or until the edges are slightly browned. Cool on the cookie sheet for 1 minute. Transfer cookies from the cookie sheet to a piece of waxed paper.

4 Break each chocolate bar into 12 pieces. Place a piece of chocolate on each hot cookie. Let stand about 1 minute or until melted. Use a knife to spread chocolate over cookies. Let cool completely. If necessary, chill the cookies about 15 minutes to set chocolate. Store in layers separated by waxed paper in an airtight container for up to 1 day. Makes about 24.

Nutrition facts per cookie: *99 calories, 1 g protein, 6 g carbohydrate, 8 g total fat (3 g saturated), 7 mg cholesterol, 32 mg sodium, 0 g fiber. Daily values: 2% vitamin A, 0% vitamin C, 1% calcium, 1% iron.*

To Make Ahead

Bake the cookies as directed; cool completely. Place in layers separated by waxed paper in a freezer container and freeze for up to 1 month. Before serving, thaw for 15 minutes.

Kid Appeal

Malted Milk Cookies

Remember the taste of a creamy chocolate malt on a sizzling summer day? Enjoy that wonderful flavor any time of year with a chocolaty cookie you'll want to dunk into a glass of cold milk.

- 1 **cup butter or margarine**
- ¾ **cup granulated sugar**
- ¾ **cup packed brown sugar**
- 1 **teaspoon baking soda**
- 2 **eggs**
- 1 **teaspoon vanilla**
- 2 **ounces unsweetened chocolate, melted and cooled**

- 2¼ **cups all-purpose flour**
- ½ **cup instant malted milk powder**
- 1 **cup chopped malted milk balls**

1 In a large mixing bowl beat butter with an electric mixer on medium to high speed about 30 seconds or until softened. Add the sugar, brown sugar, and baking soda. Beat until combined. Beat in eggs, vanilla, and melted chocolate until combined. Beat in as much of the flour as you can with the mixer. Using a wooden spoon, stir in any remaining flour and the malted milk powder. Stir in malted milk balls.

2 Drop dough from a rounded teaspoon 2½ inches apart on an ungreased cookie sheet. Bake in a 375° oven about 10 minutes or until edges are firm. Cool on cookie sheet for 1 minute. Remove cookies from cookie sheet and cool on a wire rack. Store in an airtight container or plastic bag at room temperature for up to 3 days. Makes about 36.

Nutrition facts per cookie: *138 calories, 2 g protein, 18 g carbohydrate, 7 g total fat (4 g saturated), 26 mg cholesterol, 112 mg sodium, 0 g fiber. Daily values: 5% vitamin A, 0% vitamin C, 1% calcium, 4% iron.*

To Make Ahead

Bake the cookies as directed; cool completely. Place in a freezer container or bag and freeze for up to 1 month. Before serving, thaw for 15 minutes.

Baker's Bonus

Soften 'em Up

To restore soft cookies that have hardened, place an apple wedge on a piece of waxed paper in the container with the cookies. Seal the container tightly and leave for 1 day. Remove the apple and continue to store the cookies tightly sealed.

*Notes*_____
_____
_____
_____
_____
_____
_____
_____
_____
_____
_____
_____

Date-Granola Cookies

Be sure to use a plain granola, such as a honey-oatmeal. A granola with bits of fruit or nuts will change the texture of these cookies.

½ **cup butter or margarine**
⅓ **cup granulated sugar**
⅓ **cup packed brown sugar**
½ **teaspoon baking soda**
1 **egg**
1 **teaspoon vanilla**
1¼ **cups all-purpose flour**
1½ **cups granola**
½ **cup chopped pitted dates**

1 In a large mixing bowl beat butter with an electric mixer on medium to high speed about 30 seconds or until softened. Add the sugar, brown sugar, and baking soda. Beat until combined. Beat in egg and vanilla until combined. Beat in as much of the flour as you can with the mixer. Using a wooden spoon, stir in any remaining flour. Stir in the granola and dates.

2 Drop dough from a rounded teaspoon 2 inches apart on an ungreased cookie sheet. Bake in a 375° oven for 8 to 10 minutes or until golden. Cool on cookie sheet for 1 minute. Remove cookies from cookie sheet and cool on a wire rack. Store in an airtight container or plastic bag at room temperature for up to 3 days. Makes about 28.

Nutrition facts per cookie: 103 calories, 1 g protein, 15 g carbohydrate, 5 g total fat (3 g saturated), 16 mg cholesterol, 71 mg sodium, 1 g fiber. Daily values: 3% vitamin A, 0% vitamin C, 0% calcium, 3% iron.

To Make Ahead

Bake the cookies as directed; cool completely. Place in a freezer container or bag and freeze for up to 1 month. Before serving, thaw for 15 minutes.

Applesauce-Ginger Drops

Crystallized ginger—small pieces of gingerroot coated in sugar—can be found in the spice section of your supermarket. It lends an exotic spicy-sweet flavor to these soft, cakelike cookies.

½ **cup shortening**
½ **cup butter or margarine**
1 **cup packed brown sugar**
1 **tablespoon finely chopped crystallized ginger or**
  ¼ **teaspoon ground ginger**
1½ **teaspoons baking powder**
½ **teaspoon baking soda**
½ **teaspoon ground cinnamon**
¼ **teaspoon salt**
2 **eggs**
1 **cup unsweetened applesauce**
2½ **cups all-purpose flour**
½ **cup raisins**

1 In large mixing bowl beat the shortening and butter with an electric mixer on medium to high speed about 30 seconds or until softened. Add the brown sugar, ginger, baking powder, baking soda, cinnamon, and salt. Beat until combined. Beat in eggs and applesauce. Beat in as much of the flour as you can with the mixer. Using a wooden spoon, stir in any remaining flour. Stir in the raisins.

2 Drop dough from a rounded teaspoon 2 inches apart on an ungreased cookie sheet. Bake in a 375° oven for 10 to 12 minutes or until edges are lightly browned. Cool on cookie sheet for 1 minute. Remove cookies from cookie sheet and cool on a wire rack. Place in an airtight container and store at room temperature or in the refrigerator for up to 3 days. Makes about 54.

Nutrition facts per cookie: 73 calories, 1 g protein, 9 g carbohydrate, 4 g total fat (2 g saturated fat), 12 mg cholesterol, 52 mg sodium, 0 g fiber. Daily values: 1% vitamin A, 0% vitamin C, 1% calcium, 2% iron.

To Make Ahead

Bake the cookies as directed; cool completely. Place in a freezer container or bag and freeze for up to 1 month. Before serving, thaw for 15 minutes.

Mocha Macaroons

Based on traditional macaroons, but sporting an irresistible coffee-chocolate flavor, these cookies are perfect as a coffee-break snack or teatime accompaniment.

2   ounces semisweet chocolate
2   egg whites
½   teaspoon vanilla
⅔   cup granulated sugar
2   teaspoons instant coffee
   crystals
1   cup coconut
½   cup chopped almonds
1   teaspoon shortening

1 Grease a cookie sheet. Grate ½ ounce of the chocolate. Set the cookie sheet and chocolate aside.

2 In a large mixing bowl beat egg whites and vanilla with an electric mixer on medium to high speed until soft peaks form (tips curl). Combine sugar and coffee crystals. Gradually add to the egg whites, beating until stiff peaks form (tips stand straight). Fold in the coconut, almonds, and grated chocolate.

3 Drop dough from a rounded teaspoon 2 inches apart on prepared cookie sheet. Bake in a 325° oven about 20 minutes or until set and lightly browned on the edges. Cool on cookie sheet for 1 minute. Remove cookies from cookie sheet and cool on a wire rack.

4 In a small saucepan over low heat melt the remaining 1½ ounces of chocolate and the shortening. Drizzle over cookies. Let chocolate set. Store in an airtight container at room temperature for up to 3 days. Makes about 30.

Nutrition facts per cookie: *63 calories, 1 g protein, 8 g carbohydrate, 3 g total fat (1 g saturated), 14 mg cholesterol, 7 mg sodium, 0 g fiber. Daily values: 0% vitamin A, 0% vitamin C, 0% calcium, 1% iron.*

To Make Ahead
Bake the cookies as directed; cool completely. Place in a freezer container or bag and freeze for up to 1 month. Before serving, thaw for 15 minutes.

Baker's Bonus

The Easiest Cookie, Bar None

Just stir and bake—that's all you have to do to get chewy fudge brownies and peanut butter bars, cookie dough bars, and tangy citrus bars.

The tough part is holding out to eat them until they've cooled enough to be cut. And that's important because bar cookies should be thoroughly cooled.

To cut the bars evenly, use a ruler to measure and a wooden toothpick to mark the lines. It's easiest to serve bar cookies if you remove a corner piece first.

If you feel like dressing them up a bit, lay some waxed paper strips across the top of the unfrosted bars in a pattern, then sprinkle with a mixture of powdered sugar and a spice from the recipe. Grated chocolate, chopped nuts, or chopped dried fruit also works well, particularly on frosted bars.

Notes

*Carrot-Pumpkin Bars
with Orange Icing*

Carrot-Pumpkin Bars with Orange Icing

Need a quick cake instead of bars? Simply substitute a 13x9x2-inch baking pan and bake for 28 to 33 minutes or until cake tests done.

2 cups all-purpose flour
2 teaspoons baking powder
1 teaspoon finely shredded orange peel
½ teaspoon baking soda
¼ teaspoon salt
3 eggs, beaten
1½ cups packed brown sugar
1 cup canned pumpkin
⅔ cup cooking oil
¼ cup milk
1 teaspoon vanilla
1 cup finely shredded carrots
1 cup chopped walnuts
Orange Icing
Walnut halves (optional)

1 Grease a 15x10x1-inch baking pan; set aside.

2 In a large mixing bowl stir together the flour, baking powder, orange peel, baking soda, and salt. Set the flour mixture aside.

3 In a medium bowl combine eggs and brown sugar. Stir in pumpkin, oil, milk, and vanilla. Then stir in carrots and walnuts.

4 Add egg mixture to flour mixture, stirring with a wooden spoon until combined. Spread batter into the prepared pan. Bake in a 350° oven for 20 to 25 minutes or until a wooden toothpick inserted near the center comes out clean. Cool in pan on a wire rack. Spread with Orange Icing and cut into triangles or bars. If desired, garnish each with a walnut half. Store in an airtight container in the refrigerator for up to 3 days. Makes 36.

Orange Icing: In a mixing bowl combine 1½ cups sifted powdered sugar and enough orange liqueur or orange juice (1 to 2 tablespoons) to make an icing that is easy to drizzle.

Nutrition facts per bar: *137 calories, 2 g protein, 18 g carbohydrate, 7 g total fat (1 g saturated), 18 mg cholesterol, 63 mg sodium, 1 g fiber. Daily values: 24% vitamin A, 1% vitamin C, 3% calcium, 4% iron.*

To Make Ahead

Bake bars as directed; cool completely. Do not drizzle with icing. Place cut bars in a freezer container and freeze for up to 1 month. Before serving, thaw for 15 minutes. Prepare Orange Icing and drizzle as directed.

Thinking Outside The Square

There's more than one way to cut bars and brownies, and shapes are a whole lot more fun to eat.

Make triangles by cutting cookie bars or brownies into 2- or 2½-inch squares. Then, cut each of the squares in half diagonally. For diamonds, first cut straight lines 1 or 1½ inches apart down the length of the pan. Then cut diagonal lines 1 to 1½ inches apart across the pan, forming a diamond pattern.

Notes

Fudge Dream Bars

Friday was always baking day at our house. I remember waiting impatiently for the last school bell to ring, then running down the sidewalk to our cozy home. Mom would be waiting on the front step and she'd have all the ingredients ready on the counter. It was time to bake.

I just found out recently that the traditional name for these creamy, tender brownies is Fudge Dream Bars—we always called them "gooey brownies."
—Shelli McConnell—

    1   cup butter or margarine
    ⅓   cup unsweetened cocoa powder
    4   eggs
    2   cups granulated sugar
    1½ cups all-purpose flour
    1   teaspoon vanilla
    ¼   teaspoon salt
    8   ounces miniature
           marshmallows (scant 5 cups)
        Creamy Chocolate Frosting

1 Grease a 13x9x2-inch baking pan; set aside.

2 In a medium saucepan melt together the butter and cocoa powder over low heat. In a large mixing bowl, using an electric mixer on medium speed, beat the eggs until well mixed. Add the sugar, flour, and butter-chocolate mixture to the eggs; beat well. Add vanilla and salt and beat well.

3 Pour batter into prepared pan. Bake in a 350° oven for 30 to 35 minutes or until a wooden toothpick inserted near the center comes out clean. Sprinkle with marshmallows and return to oven for 2 to 3 minutes to melt marshmallows. Remove from oven and cool in the pan on a wire rack. Spread with Creamy Chocolate Frosting and cut into bars. Store in an airtight container at room temperature for up to 3 days. Makes 36.

Creamy Chocolate Frosting: In a medium saucepan melt ¼ cup butter or margarine and ⅓ cup unsweetened cocoa powder over low heat. Remove from heat. Gradually beat in 2 cups sifted powdered sugar with an electric mixer on low speed. Beat in 2 tablespoons milk. Gradually beat in another 2 cups sifted powdered sugar and enough milk to make the frosting easy to spread.

Nutrition facts per bar: *200 calories, 2 g protein, 33 g carbohydrate, 7 g total fat (4 g saturated), 41 mg cholesterol, 90 mg sodium, 0 g fiber. Daily values: 6% vitamin A, 0% vitamin C, 2% calcium, 4% iron.*

Apricot-Nut Bars

Tangy apricot and sweet orange pair up for this delectable nut-topped fruit bar. (Pictured on page 192.)

    1   cup all-purpose flour
        Dash salt
    ¼   cup butter or margarine
    ½   cup snipped dried apricots
    ¾   cup packed brown sugar
    2   eggs
    1   cup chopped walnuts
    ½   cup coconut
    1   teaspoon vanilla
    2   tablespoons all-purpose flour
    2   tablespoons butter or
           margarine
    2   teaspoons finely shredded
           orange peel
    1¼ cups sifted powdered sugar
    1   to 2 tablespoons orange juice
    ½   cup chopped walnuts

1 Lightly grease an 11x7x1½-inch baking pan; set aside.

2 For crust, in a medium mixing bowl combine the 1 cup flour and salt. With a pastry blender, cut in the ¼ cup butter until mixture is crumbly; press into the bottom of the prepared pan. Bake in a 375° oven for 12 minutes.

3 Meanwhile, in a small saucepan combine the apricots and enough water to cover them. Bring mixture to boiling; reduce heat. Simmer, covered, for 10 minutes. Drain and set aside.

4 In a large mixing bowl stir together brown sugar and eggs until combined. Stir in the drained apricots, the 1 cup walnuts, coconut, and vanilla. Add the 2 tablespoons flour; stir until combined. Carefully spread apricot mixture evenly over baked crust. Bake in a 375° oven for 15 minutes. Cool in the pan on a wire rack.

5 For frosting, in a medium mixing bowl, beat the 2 tablespoons butter and the orange peel with an electric mixer on medium to high speed until combined. At low speed, gradually beat in the powdered sugar. Add orange juice, a little at a time, until the frosting is easy to spread. Spread frosting over cooled bars in pan. Sprinkle with the ½ cup walnuts. Cut into bars. Store in an airtight container at room temperature up to 3 days. Makes 32.

Nutrition facts per bar: 121 calories, 2 g protein, 15 g carbohydrate, 6 g total fat (1 g saturated), 13 mg cholesterol, 36 mg sodium, 1 g fiber. Daily values: 4% vitamin A, 0% vitamin C, 1% calcium, 4% iron.

To Make Ahead

Prepare bars as directed, except line the pan with foil, extending foil over the edges of the pan. Grease the foil instead of the pan. Continue as directed; bake and cool completely. Do not frost. Using the edges of the foil, lift the uncut bars out of the pan and place in a freezer container and freeze for up to 1 month. Before serving, thaw for 1 hour. Prepare frosting, frost, and cut as directed.

Kid Appeal

Peanut Butter And Jelly Bars

It's the great American flavor combination packed into easy-to-eat treats that are perfect for lunch boxes and after-school snacks. Let your kids select a favorite jelly (you can use more than one flavor) and set them to work pressing the crust mixture into the pan.

1⅓ **cups all-purpose flour**
1⅓ **cups quick-cooking rolled oats**
¾ **cup packed brown sugar**
½ **cup granulated sugar**
1 **teaspoon baking powder**
½ **teaspoon baking soda**
½ **cup butter (no substitutes)**
½ **cup peanut butter**
1 **cup chopped peanuts**
1 **egg, beaten**
1 **10-ounce jar (1 cup) grape jelly or your favorite jelly**

1 For crumb mixture, in a large mixing bowl stir together the flour, rolled oats, brown sugar, sugar, baking powder, and baking soda. With a pastry blender, cut in the butter and peanut butter until mixture resembles fine crumbs. Stir in ½ cup of the chopped peanuts.

2 For topping, reserve 1 cup of the crumb mixture; set aside.

3 For crust, stir the egg into the remaining crumb mixture. Press mixture into the bottom of an ungreased 13x9x2-inch baking pan. Bake in a 350° oven for 15 minutes. Carefully spoon the jelly evenly over the partially baked crust. Sprinkle with topping and remaining chopped peanuts.

4 Bake in the 350° oven for 15 to 18 minutes more or until lightly browned around the edges. Cool in the pan on a wire rack. Cut into bars. Store in an airtight container in the refrigerator for up to 3 days. Makes 36.

Nutrition facts per bar: 143 calories, 3 g protein, 19 g carbohydrate, 7 g total fat (2 g saturated), 13 mg cholesterol, 75 mg sodium, 1 g fiber. Daily values: 2% vitamin A, 0% vitamin C, 1% calcium, 4% iron.

Notes

Fudge Brownies

Choose from five fabulous versions of these dense, rich chocolate brownies.

½ **cup butter or margarine**
2 **ounces unsweetened chocolate**
1 **cup granulated sugar**
2 **eggs**
1 **teaspoon vanilla**
⅔ **cup all-purpose flour**
    Chocolate Glaze (optional)
    Powdered sugar (optional)

1 Grease a 9x9x2-inch baking pan and set aside.

2 In a medium saucepan melt butter and chocolate over low heat. Stir in sugar, eggs, and vanilla. Using a wooden spoon, beat lightly by hand just until combined. Stir in flour.

3 Spread batter in prepared pan. Bake in a 350° oven for 20 minutes. Cool on a wire rack. If desired, spread Chocolate Glaze over the cooled brownies. Cut into bars. If desired, sprinkle with powdered sugar. Store in an airtight container at room temperature for up to 3 days. Makes 16.

Chocolate Glaze: In a saucepan cook and stir 3 tablespoons butter or margarine, 2 tablespoons unsweetened cocoa powder, and 2 tablespoons milk until mixture comes to a boil. Remove from heat. Stir in 1½ cups sifted powdered sugar and ½ teaspoon vanilla until smooth.

Nutrition facts per brownie: *143 calories, 2 g protein, 17 g carbohydrate, 8 g total fat (2 g saturated), 27 mg cholesterol, 75 mg sodium, 0 g fiber. Daily values: 6% vitamin A, 0% vitamin C, 0% calcium, 3% iron.*

Caramel-Nut Brownies: Prepare Fudge Brownies as directed, except stir ½ cup chopped pecans into the batter before spreading in the prepared pan. Sprinkle batter with ½ cup miniature semisweet chocolate pieces. Bake as directed. In a small saucepan combine one 6¼-ounce package vanilla caramels and 2 tablespoons milk. Cook and stir over medium-low heat until smooth. Drizzle the caramel atop brownies. Cool completely. Cut into bars.

Peanut Butter Brownies: Prepare Fudge Brownies as directed. For frosting, in a medium mixing bowl beat ¼ cup peanut butter until fluffy. Gradually add 1 cup sifted powdered sugar, beating well. Beat in ¼ cup milk and 1 teaspoon vanilla. Gradually beat in about ½ cup additional sifted powdered sugar until the frosting is easy to spread. Spread frosting atop brownies and sprinkle with ¼ cup finely chopped dry-roasted peanuts. Cool completely. Cut into bars.

Chocolate Chunk Brownies: Prepare Fudge Brownies as directed, except stir one 2.2-ounce bar milk chocolate, coarsely chopped, and one 2.2-ounce vanilla-flavored bar with almonds (Alpine bar), coarsely chopped, into the batter.

Crème de Menthe Brownies: Prepare Fudge Brownies as directed, except omit vanilla and stir ¼ teaspoon mint extract into batter. Bake as directed. For frosting, in a medium mixing bowl beat ¼ cup butter or margarine until fluffy. Gradually add 1 cup sifted powdered sugar. Beat in 2 tablespoons crème de menthe. Gradually beat in about ½ cup sifted powdered sugar until the frosting is easy to spread. Spread atop brownies. In a small, heavy saucepan melt 1 ounce semisweet chocolate over low heat. Drizzle atop brownies. Let chocolate set, then cut into bars.

To Make Ahead

Prepare any of the brownie variations as directed, except line the pan with foil, extending foil over the edges of the pan. Grease the foil instead of the pan. Continue as directed; bake and cool completely. Do not frost. Using the edges of foil, lift the uncut brownies out of the pan and place in a freezer container or bag and freeze up to 1 month. Before serving, thaw for 1 hour. Frost and cut as directed.

Fudge Brownies

Honey-Nut Bars

Honey has long been prized not only for its ability as a sweetener but also for the softness and chewiness it imparts to baked goods. In addition, the moistness honey adds to baked products improves the amount of time they can be stored. (Pictured on page 170.)

½ **cup butter or margarine**
¼ **cup shortening**
1 **cup honey**
1 **teaspoon baking powder**
¼ **teaspoon salt**
3 **eggs**
1 **teaspoon vanilla**
1½ **cups all-purpose flour**
1 **cup coconut**
1 **cup chopped walnuts**
  Powdered sugar

1 Grease a 13x9x2-inch baking pan; set aside.

2 In a large mixing bowl beat butter and shortening with an electric mixer on medium to high speed about 30 seconds or until softened. Add honey, baking powder, and salt. Beat until combined. Beat in eggs and vanilla until combined. Beat in as much of the flour as you can with the mixer. Using a wooden spoon, stir in any remaining flour. Stir in the coconut and walnuts.

3 Spread batter in prepared pan. Bake in a 350° oven for 25 to 30 minutes or until a wooden toothpick inserted near the center comes out clean. Cool in the pan on a wire rack. Sprinkle with powdered sugar. Cut into bars. Store in an airtight container in the refrigerator for up to 3 days. Makes 24.

Nutrition facts per bar: 179 calories, 2 g protein, 20 g carbohydrate, 11 g total fat (4 g saturated), 37 mg cholesterol, 86 mg sodium, 1 g fiber. Daily values: 4% vitamin A, 0% vitamin C, 2% calcium, 4% iron.

To Make Ahead

Bake bars as directed; cool completely. Do not sprinkle with powdered sugar. Place cut bars in a freezer container and freeze for up to 1 month. Before serving, thaw for 15 minutes. Sprinkle with sifted powdered sugar.

Karen's Dream Bars

Whenever any of my Mom's schoolmates came to visit, they always asked for Karen's Dream Bars. Mom taught me how to make these bars when I was in elementary school. It's an easy recipe and a great way to get your own kids started baking.
—Lisa Mannes—

1 **cup all-purpose flour**
½ **cup packed brown sugar**
½ **cup butter (no substitutes)**
1½ **teaspoons all-purpose flour**
½ **teaspoon baking powder**
¼ **teaspoon salt**
1 **cup packed brown sugar**
2 **eggs**
1 **teaspoon vanilla**
1 **cup coconut**
1 **cup chopped pecans**

1 In a medium mixing bowl stir together the 1 cup all-purpose flour and the ½ cup brown sugar. With a pastry blender, cut in the butter until mixture is crumbly. Pat into an ungreased 13x9x2-inch baking pan. Bake in a 350° oven for 15 minutes.

2 Meanwhile, in a small bowl stir together the 1½ teaspoons all-purpose flour, the baking powder, and salt. Set dry ingredients aside.

3 In a large mixing bowl beat the 1 cup brown sugar, eggs, and vanilla with an electric mixer on medium speed until well combined. Add the dry ingredients and mix well. Fold in the coconut and pecans. Carefully spread onto hot baked crust and bake in the 350° oven about 20 minutes or until golden. Cool in the pan on a wire rack. Cut into bars. Store in an airtight container at room temperature for up to 3 days. Makes 36.

Nutrition facts per bar: *96 calories, 1 g protein, 11 g carbohydrate, 6 g total fat (2 g saturated), 19 mg cholesterol, 52 mg sodium, 0 g fiber. Daily values: 2% vitamin A, 0% vitamin C, 1% calcium, 3% iron.*

To Make Ahead

Bake bars as directed; cool completely. Place cut bars in a freezer container and freeze for up to 1 month. Before serving, thaw for 15 minutes.

Raspberry Citrus Bars

Whether you prefer raspberry or blueberry, the berry flavor is enhanced by the tang of orange and lemon.

  1 **cup butter (no substitutes)**
  ¾ **cup sifted powdered sugar**
  2 **cups all-purpose flour**
  4 **eggs**
1½ **cups granulated sugar**
  ⅓ **cup lemon juice**
  2 **tablespoons finely shredded orange peel**
  ¼ **cup all-purpose flour**
  1 **teaspoon baking powder**
1½ **cups fresh raspberries and/or blueberries**
     Powdered sugar

1 Grease a 13x9x2-inch baking pan; set aside.

2 For the crust, in a medium mixing bowl beat butter with an electric mixer on medium to high speed for 30 seconds or until softened. Add the 3/4 cup powdered sugar. Beat until combined. Beat in the 2 cups flour until combined.

3 Press crust mixture onto bottom of prepared pan. Bake in a 350° oven about 20 minutes or until golden.

4 Meanwhile, for filling, in a large mixing bowl combine eggs, sugar, lemon juice, orange peel, the ¼ cup flour, and baking powder. Beat for 2 minutes with an electric mixer on medium speed until combined. Sprinkle berries over baked crust. Pour filling over berries, arranging berries evenly with a spoon.

Size Counts

It is important to use the proper size pan for baking bar cookies and brownies.

If you don't have a 15x10x1-inch pan, use two 9x9x2-inch pans; if you don't have a 13x9x2-inch pan, use two 8x8x2-inch pans. Use the same oven temperature but check for doneness 5 minutes before the minimum baking time given in the recipe is reached.

5 Bake in the 350° oven for 30 to 35 minutes or until light brown and filling is set. Cool in the pan on a wire rack. Cut into bars and/or triangles. Just before serving, sprinkle with powdered sugar. Store in an airtight container in the refrigerator for up to 2 days. Makes 30.

Nutrition facts per bar: *149 calories, 2 g protein, 21 g carbohydrate, 7 g total fat (4 g saturated), 45 mg cholesterol, 83 mg sodium, 1 g fiber. Daily values: 7% vitamin A, 5% vitamin C, 1 % calcium, 3% iron.*

To Make Ahead

Bake the bars as directed; cool completely. Place cut bars in a freezer container or bag and freeze for up to 1 month. Thaw, covered, in the refrigerator for 24 hours or until no longer frozen.

Apple Pie Squares, top, and Apricot-Nut Bars (see recipe, page 186), bottom

Delicious Memories

Apple Pie Squares

I've always had a sweet tooth and I always enjoy a dessert to finalize a meal. As I was growing up, one of the many desserts Mom made that I particularly enjoyed was Apple Pie Squares topped with a sweet powdered sugar frosting. Mmmm, I can smell the apples baking even now!
—*Margie Schenkelberg*—

2½ **cups all-purpose flour**
  1 **teaspoon salt**
  1 **cup shortening**
  1 **egg yolk, beaten**
      Milk
  1 **cup crushed dry cereal**
      (such as cornflakes)
10 **apples, peeled, cored, and sliced**
  ¾ **cup granulated sugar**
  1 **teaspoon ground cinnamon**
  ½ **teaspoon vanilla**
      Powdered sugar (optional)
  1 **recipe Powdered Sugar Icing**
      (see page 151) (optional)

1 In medium mixing bowl stir together flour and salt. With a pastry blender, cut in shortening until pieces are the size of small peas. Combine egg yolk and enough milk to equal ⅓ cup; sprinkle 1 tablespoon at a time over flour mixture, tossing until evenly moistened.

2 On a lightly floured surface roll half the dough into a rectangle the size to fit in the bottom of a 15x10x1-inch pan. Place dough in the ungreased pan. Spread crushed cereal over dough in pan. In a large mixing bowl combine apples, sugar, cinnamon, and vanilla; spread atop crushed cereal. Roll out remaining dough, and place it on top of filling. Seal edges. Prick the top layer of dough.

3 Bake in a 375° oven about 1 hour or until golden. Cool in pan on a wire rack. Sprinkle with sifted powdered sugar or frost with Powdered Sugar Icing. Cut into squares. Store in an airtight container in the refrigerator for up to 3 days. Makes 24.

Nutrition facts per square: *186 calories, 2 g protein, 25 g carbohydrate, 9 g total fat (2 g saturated), 9 mg cholesterol, 114 mg sodium, 1 g fiber. Daily values: 4% vitamin A, 5% vitamin C, 0% calcium, 5% iron.*

Shortcut

Prepare Apple Pie Squares as directed, except substitute two 21-ounce cans apple pie filling for the apples, sugar, cinnamon, and vanilla mixture. Bake in the 375° oven for 35 to 40 minutes or until golden.

To Make Ahead

Prepare the squares as directed, except line the 15x10x1-inch pan with foil, extending foil over the edges of pan. Continue as directed; bake and cool completely. Do not sprinkle with powdered sugar or frost. Using the edges of foil, lift the uncut bars out of the pan. Cut rectangle in half crosswise. Place each portion in a freezer container and freeze for up to 1 month. Before serving, thaw for 1 hour. Top as directed and cut into squares.

Notes

Orange-Ginger Cutouts

If you don't plan on using these cookies within a day or so, freeze them to keep them crispy.

½ **cup butter (no substitutes)**
½ **cup packed brown sugar**
 1 **teaspoon ground ginger**
 1 **teaspoon finely shredded orange peel**
½ **teaspoon baking soda**
½ **cup molasses**
2½ **cups all-purpose flour**
    Orange Icing

1 In a large mixing bowl beat butter with an electric mixer on medium to high speed for 30 seconds or until softened. Add the brown sugar, ginger, orange peel, and baking soda. Beat until combined. Beat in molasses until combined. Beat in as much flour as you can with the mixer. Using a wooden spoon, stir in any remaining flour. Divide dough into 2 or 3 portions.

2 On a lightly floured surface, roll each portion of dough to ⅛-inch thickness. Using 2- to 2½-inch cookie cutters dipped in flour, cut into desired shapes. Place 1 inch apart on an ungreased cookie sheet. Bake in a 375° oven for 6 to 7 minutes or until edges are firm. Cool on cookie sheet for 1 minute. Then remove cookies from cookie sheet and cool on a wire rack. Drizzle Orange Icing over cookies. Place cookies in layers separated by waxed paper in an airtight container

and store at room temperature up to 2 days. Makes about 54.

Orange Icing: In a small mixing bowl combine 1 cup sifted powdered sugar, ½ teaspoon finely shredded orange peel, and enough orange juice (3 to 4 teaspoons) to make an icing that is easy to drizzle.

Nutrition facts per cookie: *55 calories, 1 g protein, 10 g carbohydrate, 2 g total fat (1 g saturated), 5 mg cholesterol, 30 mg sodium, 0 g fiber. Daily values: 1% vitamin A, 0% vitamin C, 0% calcium, 2% iron.*

To Make Ahead

Bake cookies as directed; cool completely. Do not drizzle with Orange Icing. Place cookies in layers separated by waxed paper in a freezer container or bag and freeze for up to 1 month. Before serving, thaw for 15 minutes. Drizzle with Orange Icing.

Dip the cutting edge of a cookie cutter into flour every few cuts to prevent the dough from sticking to it.

Delicious Memories

Rolled Cocoa Cookies

Every time we visited Grandma she would pull out tins of homemade cookies from the freezer. She had a constant supply. It wasn't a trip to Grandma's without one (or two, or three) of her cookies. She passed these precious recipes on to me, and they really do bring back delicious memories. Now it's up to me to carry on the tradition—except I'm the one who eats most of the cookies out of my freezer!
—*Colleen Weeden*—

 4 **cups all-purpose flour**
 1 **cup unsweetened cocoa powder**
 4 **teaspoons baking powder**
½ **teaspoon salt**
 2 **cups granulated sugar**
½ **cup shortening**
 2 **eggs**
½ **cup milk**
 1 **recipe Butter Frosting or Cream Cheese Frosting (see pages 150 and 152) (optional)**

1 In a medium mixing bowl stir together the flour, cocoa powder, baking powder, and salt; set aside.

2 In a large mixing bowl beat sugar and shortening together with an electric mixer until combined. Beat in eggs and milk. Gradually beat or stir dry ingredients into beaten mixture. Cover and chill dough until easy to handle.

3 On a lightly floured surface, roll dough to ⅛-inch thickness. Using 2½- to 3-inch cookie cutters dipped in flour, cut dough into desired shapes. Place cookies 1 inch apart on a lightly greased baking sheet. Bake in a 375° oven for 8 to 10 minutes or until firm. Remove cookies from cookie sheet and cool on a wire rack. If desired, decorate with Cream Cheese or Butter Frosting. Place cookies in layers separated by sheets of waxed paper in an airtight container or plastic bag and store overnight at room temperature. Makes about 60.

Nutrition facts per cookie: *78 calories, 1 g protein, 13 g carbohydrate, 2 g total fat (1 g saturated), 7 mg cholesterol, 45 mg sodium, 0 g fiber. Daily values: 0% vitamin A, 0% vitamin C, 3% calcium, 4% iron.*

To Make Ahead

Bake cookies as directed; cool completely. Do not frost. Place in a freezer container or bag and freeze up to 1 month. Before serving, thaw for 15 minutes. Decorate cookies as desired.

Pineapple Cookies

  1 **cup butter (no substitutes)**
  1 **3-ounce package cream cheese**
  ¾ **cup granulated sugar**
  1 **teaspoon baking powder**
  1 **egg**
  ¼ **cup pineapple preserves or**
      apricot-pineapple preserves
3½ **cups all-purpose flour**
     Powdered sugar (optional)

1 In a large mixing bowl beat butter and cream cheese with an electric mixer on medium to high speed for 30 seconds or until softened. Add sugar and baking powder. Beat until combined. Beat in the egg and preserves until combined. Beat in as much of the flour as you can with the mixer. Using a wooden spoon, stir in any remaining flour. Divide dough in half.

2 On a lightly floured surface, roll each portion of dough to ⅛-inch thickness. Using 2- to 2½-inch cookie cutters dipped in flour, cut into desired shapes. Place 1 inch apart on an ungreased cookie sheet. Bake in a 375° oven for 7 to 8 minutes or until edges are firm and cookies are lightly browned. Cool on cookie sheet for 1 minute. Then remove cookies from cookie sheet and cool on a wire rack. If desired, sprinkle with powdered sugar. Place in an airtight container or plastic bag and store at room temperature for up to 3 days. Makes about 80.

Nutrition facts per cookie: *53 calories, 1 g protein, 6 g carbohydrate, 3 g total fat (2 g saturated), 10 mg cholesterol, 32 mg sodium, 0 g fiber. Daily values: 2% vitamin A, 0% vitamin C, 0% calcium, 1% iron.*

To Make Ahead

Bake cookies as directed; cool completely. Place in a freezer container or bag and freeze for up to 1 month. Before serving, thaw for 15 minutes.

On the Surface

Use as little flour as possible when rolling out cookie dough or pastry because additional flour can toughen baked goods.

The easiest way to work is to sprinkle a small amount of flour onto a clean countertop, and smooth it into an even, thin layer. Add flour, as necessary, to keep the dough from sticking. Another option is to rollout the dough between two pieces of waxed paper. Although the size of the rolled dough is limited by the width of the paper, this technique works well for cookies, biscuits, and piecrust.

If you plan to do a lot of baking, it may be worth investing in a pastry cloth and a pastry stocking for your rolling pin to make cleanup a lot quicker. These are available from mail-order catalogs and at specialty shops, hardware stores, and grocery stores.

Notes

Kid Appeal

Sour Cream Cutouts

Kids love to decorate cookies almost as much as they love to eat them, so why not have a cookie decorating party? Decorate the cookies after they have completely cooled. Prepare Decorator Frosting and Confectioners' Icing; divide each into bowls and tint with some favorite colors. Spread cookies with the frosting and allow it to dry slightly. Continue decorating by piping additional frosting or icing. Top with decorative candies or sprinkles before the frosting or icing sets.

½ **cup butter (no substitutes)**
⅓ **cup shortening**
 1 **cup granulated sugar**
⅓ **cup dairy sour cream**
 1 **egg**
 1 **teaspoon vanilla**
 1 **teaspoon finely shredded
      lemon peel (optional)**
¾ **teaspoon baking powder**
½ **teaspoon ground mace**
¼ **teaspoon baking soda**
      Dash salt
2½ **cups all-purpose flour**
      Decorator Frosting (optional)
      Confectioner's Icing (optional)
      **Decorative candies or sprinkles
      (optional)**

1 In a large mixing bowl beat the butter and shortening with an electric mixer on medium to high speed about 30 seconds or until softened. Add the sugar, sour cream, egg, vanilla, lemon peel, baking powder, mace, baking soda, and salt. Beat until thoroughly combined. Beat in as much of the flour as you can with the mixer. Using a wooden spoon, stir in any remaining flour. Divide dough in half. Cover and chill dough for 1 to 2 hours or until easy to handle.

2 On a well-floured pastry cloth, roll each half of dough (keep remaining portion chilled) to ⅛- to ¼-inch thickness. Using 2- to 3-inch cookie cutters dipped in flour, cut dough into desired shapes. Use a wide spatula to place cookies 1 inch apart on an ungreased cookie sheet.

3 Bake in a 375° oven for 7 to 8 minutes or until edges are firm and bottoms are very light brown. Remove cookies from cookie sheet and cool on a wire rack. If desired, decorate with Decorator Frosting, Confectioner's Icing, and assorted decorative candies. Let frosting dry. Place cookies by layers separated by waxed paper in an airtight container and store at room temperature up to 3 days. Makes about 48.

Decorator Frosting: In a large mixing bowl beat ⅔ cup butter or margarine with an electric mixer on medium speed for 30 seconds or until softened. Gradually add 4 cups sifted powdered sugar, beating well. Beat in 2 tablespoons milk, lemon juice or orange juice, and 1 teaspoon vanilla. Frosting will be thick but easy to pipe.

Confectioners' Icing: In a medium mixing bowl stir together 3 cups sifted powdered sugar and 1 tablespoon lemon juice or orange juice or other flavorings, such as 1½ teaspoons vanilla, 1 teaspoon maple flavoring, or ½ teaspoon peppermint extract. Add enough milk to make an icing that is easy to spread or drizzle.

Nutrition facts per undecorated cookie: 71 calories, 1 g protein, 9 g carbohydrate, 4 g total fat (2 g saturated), 10 mg cholesterol, 36 mg sodium, 0 g fiber. Daily values: 2% vitamin A, 0% vitamin C, 0% calcium, 2% iron.

Anise Cutouts: Prepare Sour Cream Cutouts as directed, except substitute ½ teaspoon anise extract for the ground mace and omit the lemon peel. Decorate as directed.

To Make Ahead

Bake cookies as directed; cool completely. Do not frost. Place in layers separated by waxed paper in a freezer container or bag and freeze up to 1 month. Before serving, thaw for 15 minutes. Decorate as desired.

Sour Cream Cutouts

Black Walnut Shortbread

These crisp shortbreads really show-case the stronger flavored, more aromatic black walnuts. If black walnuts aren't available, use the milder English walnuts. (Pictured on page 170.)

1 **cup butter (no substitutes), softened**
1 **cup granulated sugar**
1½ **cups chopped black walnuts or English walnuts, toasted**
2 **cups all-purpose flour**
½ **teaspoon baking powder**
¼ **teaspoon salt**
1 **6-ounce package (1 cup) semisweet chocolate pieces**
2 **tablespoons shortening**

1 Beat butter with an electric mixer on medium to high speed 30 seconds or until softened. Add ¾ cup of the sugar. Beat on medium speed until light and fluffy. Stir in 1 cup of the walnuts; set aside.

2 Combine flour, baking powder, and salt. Stir flour mixture into butter mixture. Mix thoroughly to form a dough.

3 On a lightly floured surface, roll dough to ½-inch thickness. Combine remaining sugar and remaining walnuts; sprinkle evenly atop dough. Roll dough to ¼-inch thickness. Using a 2-inch cookie cutter dipped in flour, cut into desired shapes. Place cookies 1 inch apart on an ungreased cookie sheet. Bake in a 375° oven for 8 to 10 minutes or until edges just begin to brown. Remove from cookie sheet and cool on a wire rack.

4 Melt chocolate pieces and shortening over low heat, stirring occasionally. Drizzle chocolate over cookies. Let chocolate set. Place cookies in an airtight container and store at room temperature up to 3 days. Makes 36 to 48.

Nutrition facts per cookie: *121 calories, 2 g protein, 11 g carbohydrate, 8 g total fat (3 g saturated), 14 mg cholesterol, 72 mg sodium, 0 g fiber. Daily values: 4% vitamin A, 0% vitamin C, 0% calcium, 3% iron.*

To Make Ahead

Bake cookies as directed; cool completely. Do not drizzle with chocolate. Place cookies in a freezer container or bag and freeze up to 1 month. Before serving, thaw for 15 minutes. Drizzle with chocolate.

Use a spoon to drizzle chocolate on the cookies. To eliminate big drips on your cookies, once you fill the spoon with melted chocolate, hold it briefly over the middle of the saucepan, then carry it over the edge and drizzle the chocolate on the cookies in desired patterns.

For cookies decorated with thin chocolate lines, fill a pastry bag fitted with a small round tip (or, as shown above, a small, clear plastic bag with one corner snipped off) with the melted chocolate. Pipe straight or wavy lines in desired patterns.

Double Fudge Pockets

Sprinkle the tops of these cookies with powdered sugar or drizzle them with an icing to make them more festive.

1 **cup butter (no substitutes)**
1 **cup granulated sugar**
1 **teaspoon baking powder**
1 **egg**
1 **egg yolk**
1 **teaspoon vanilla**
2½ **cups all-purpose flour**
½ **cup unsweetened cocoa powder**
Fudge Filling

1 Beat butter with an electric mixer on medium to high speed 30 seconds or until softened. Add sugar and baking powder. Beat until combined. Beat in whole egg, egg yolk, and vanilla until well combined. Using a wooden spoon, stir in flour and cocoa powder. Divide dough in half. Cover and chill dough 1 hour or until easy to handle.

2 On a lightly floured surface, roll each portion of dough to ⅛-inch thickness. Using a 2½-inch cookie cutter dipped in flour, cut dough into rounds. Place half of the rounds 1 inch apart on an ungreased cookie sheet. Spoon a rounded teaspoon of Fudge Filling into the center of each round. Place another round over top of filling. Press edges together to seal. Bake in a 350° oven 10 to 12 minutes or until edges are firm. Cool on cookie sheet 1 minute. Remove from cookie sheet and cool on a wire rack. Place in an airtight container and chill for up to 2 days. Makes about 30.

Fudge Filling: In a heavy small saucepan melt 4 ounces semisweet chocolate over low heat, stirring constantly. Remove from heat. Stir in ½ cup dairy sour cream and ¼ cup finely chopped walnuts. Mixture will stiffen as it cools.

Nutrition facts per cookie: 157 calories, 2 g protein, 18 g carbohydrate, 9 g total fat (4 g saturated), 32 mg cholesterol, 79 mg sodium, 0 g fiber. Daily values: 7% vitamin A, 0% vitamin C, 3% calcium, 5% iron.

Ravioli Cookies

Just like their pasta namesake, tender Ravioli Cookies have a surprise inside.

⅔ **cup butter (no substitutes)**
½ **cup granulated sugar**
1 **teaspoon baking powder**
½ **teaspoon finely shredded orange peel**
1 **egg**
1 **teaspoon vanilla**
2 **cups all-purpose flour**
¼ **cup raspberry or strawberry preserves**
 Powdered sugar

1 In a mixing bowl beat the butter with an electric mixer on medium to high speed 30 seconds or until softened. Add sugar, baking powder, and orange peel. Beat until combined. Beat in egg and vanilla. Beat in as much of the flour as you can with the mixer. Stir in any remaining flour. Divide dough in half. Cover and chill dough about 3 hours or until easy to handle.

2 Grease a cookie sheet; set aside. On a lightly floured surface, roll each portion of the dough into a 12x8-inch rectangle. Using a fluted pastry wheel, cut each half into twenty-four 2-inch squares. Place squares 1 inch apart on the prepared cookie sheet. Spoon a level ½ teaspoon jam onto center of each square. Top each with a second square of dough. Press edges together

to seal. Bake cookies in a 375° oven 9 to 11 minutes or until lightly browned. Remove cookies from cookie sheet and cool on a wire rack. Sprinkle with powdered sugar. Place in an airtight container or bag and store at room temperature up to 2 days. Makes 24.

Nutrition facts per cookie: 112 calories, 1 g protein, 15 g carbohydrate, 5 g total fat (3 g saturated), 23 mg cholesterol, 64 mg sodium, 0 g fiber. Daily values: 6% vitamin A, 0% vitamin C, 0% calcium, 3% iron.

To Make Ahead

Bake cookies as directed; cool completely. Do not sprinkle with powdered sugar. Place in a freezer container or bag and freeze for up to 1 month. Before serving, thaw for 15 minutes. Sprinkle with powdered sugar.

To prevent the jam from oozing out of the cookies, seal the cut edges by pressing them together with the tines of a fork. If necessary, dip the tines in flour to prevent sticking.

Mantecados

Lebkuchen

International Origin

Mantecados

- 1 **cup butter (no substitutes)**
- 1 **cup granulated sugar**
- 2 **cups all-purpose flour**
- ½ **cup blanched almonds, very finely ground**
- 1 **tablespoon finely shredded lemon peel**
- 1 **egg**
- 1 **teaspoon water**
- 10 **ounces chocolate-flavored candy coating, melted**

1 Beat butter with an electric mixer on medium to high speed 30 seconds or until softened. Gradually add sugar, beating until mixture is thick. Gradually add flour, beating on low speed until well combined. Stir in almonds and lemon peel. Divide dough in thirds. Cover; chill 1 hour.

2 On a lightly floured surface, roll each portion of dough to ⅛- to ¼-inch thickness. Using 2-inch cookie cutters dipped in flour, cut dough into desired shapes. Place cookies 1 inch apart on an ungreased cookie sheet.

3 Mix egg and water; brush on tops of cookies. Bake in a 350° oven 8 to 10 minutes or until lightly golden. Cool on cookie sheets 2 minutes. Remove cookies and cool on wire racks. Dip each cookie into melted candy coating. Let coating set. Place cookies in layers separated by waxed paper in an airtight container and store at room temperature up to 3 days. Makes about 60.

Nutrition facts per cookie: 85 calories, 1 g protein, 9 g carbohydrate, 5 g total fat (3 g saturated), 12 mg cholesterol, 36 mg sodium, 0 g fiber. Daily values: 3% vitamin A, 0% vitamin C, 1% calcium, 1% iron.

To Make Ahead

Bake cookies as directed; cool completely. Do not dip in candy coating. Place in layers separated by waxed paper in a freezer container or bag and freeze for up to 1 month. Before serving, thaw for 15 minutes. Dip in candy coating as directed.

International Origin

Lebkuchen

- 1 **egg**
- ¾ **cup packed brown sugar**
- ½ **cup honey**
- ½ **cup dark molasses**
- 1 **teaspoon ground cinnamon**
- ½ **teaspoon baking soda**
- ½ **teaspoon ground cloves**
- ½ **teaspoon ground ginger**
- ¼ **teaspoon ground cardamom**
- 3 **cups all-purpose flour**
- ½ **cup chopped almonds**
- ½ **cup finely chopped mixed candied fruit and peels**
- **Lemon Glaze**
- **Additional chopped mixed candied fruit and peels**

1 Beat the egg with an electric mixer on high speed 1 minute. Add brown sugar, honey, molasses, cinnamon, soda, cloves, ginger, and cardamom; beat until light and fluffy.

2 Beat in as much of the flour as you can. Stir in any remaining flour. Stir in almonds and fruit and peels. Divide dough in half. Cover and chill dough 3 hours or until easy to handle.

3 Lightly grease a cookie sheet; set aside. On a lightly floured surface, roll each portion of dough into a 12x8-inch rectangle. Cut each rectangle into 2-inch squares. Place squares 1 inch apart on the prepared cookie sheet. Bake cookies in a 350° oven 8 to 10 minutes or until lightly browned around edges. Cool cookies on cookie sheet 1 minute. Remove cookies and cool on wire racks. Brush warm cookies with Lemon Glaze. If desired, garnish with additional candied fruits and peels. Allow glaze to dry. Place in an airtight container and store at room temperature overnight or up to 7 days to soften. Makes 48.

Lemon Glaze: Combine 1½ cups sifted powdered sugar; 1 tablespoon butter or margarine, melted; and 1 tablespoon lemon juice. Add enough water (about 3 to 4 teaspoons) to make a glaze that is easy to drizzle.

Nutrition facts per cookie: 100 calories, 1 g protein, 22 g carbohydrate, 1 g total fat (0 g saturated), 5 mg cholesterol, 21 mg sodium, 0 g fiber. Daily values: 0% vitamin A, 0% vitamin C, 2% calcium, 6% iron.

Sesame Cookies

Believe it or not, it's sesame seed that gives these cookies their unique, nutty flavor. Toasting the sesame seed will give the cookies even more flavor. To toast it, spread the sesame seed in a thin layer in a shallow baking pan. Bake in a 350° oven for 5 to 10 minutes or until light golden brown, stirring once or twice.

½ **cup butter (no substitutes)**
1 **cup packed brown sugar**
¼ **teaspoon baking soda**
1 **egg**
½ **teaspoon vanilla**
¼ **cup toasted sesame seed**
1¼ **cups all-purpose flour**
2 **tablespoons granulated sugar**

1 In a large mixing bowl beat butter with an electric mixer on medium to high speed 30 seconds or until softened. Add the brown sugar and baking soda. Beat until combined. Beat in the egg and vanilla until combined. Beat in the sesame seed and as much of the flour as you can with the mixer. Stir in any remaining flour. Cover; chill 1 hour or until easy to handle.

2 Shape dough into 1-inch balls. Roll balls in the sugar. Place 2 inches apart on an ungreased cookie sheet. Bake in a 375° oven for 8 to 10 minutes or until edges are lightly browned. Cool on cookie sheet for 1 minute. Remove cookies from cookie sheet and cool on a wire rack. Place in an airtight container and store at room temperature for up to 3 days. Makes about 36.

Nutrition facts per cookie: 66 calories, 1 g protein, 9 g carbohydrate, 3 g total fat (2 g saturated), 13 mg cholesterol, 38 mg sodium, 0 g fiber. Daily values: 2% vitamin A, 0% vitamin C, 0% calcium, 2% iron.

To Make Ahead

Bake cookies as directed; cool completely. Place in a freezer container or bag and freeze for up to 1 month. Before serving, thaw for 15 minutes.

Delicious Memories

Spicy Molasses Cookies

When my wife, Tracy, was pregnant with our son, she invented these cookies for her diet plan that was rich in nutrients. She wanted the iron from the molasses and a snack that wasn't filling. I enjoyed them because I love frosted cookies and the flavor of allspice. Tracy actually had only two cookies in the first batch because our 6-year-old daughter and I ate them as quickly as they were baked.
—Graham Benson—

⅓ **cup butter or margarine**
⅔ **cup packed brown sugar**
1 **egg**
½ **cup molasses**
2 **cups all-purpose flour**
1 **tablespoon ground allspice**
1 **teaspoon baking soda**
1 **teaspoon ground nutmeg**
Vanilla Almond Frosting

1 Grease a cookie sheet; set aside. In a large mixing bowl beat butter with an electric mixer on medium to high speed about 30 seconds or until softened. Add brown sugar. Beat until combined. Beat in the egg and molasses until combined.

2 Stir together flour, allspice, baking soda, and nutmeg. Beat as much of the flour mixture into the molasses mixture as you can with the mixer. Stir in any remaining flour mixture. Cover; chill 1 hour or until easy to handle.

3 Shape dough into 1-inch balls. Place 2 inches apart on prepared cookie sheet. Bake in a 350° oven for 10 to 12 minutes or until edges are firm. Cool on cookie sheet for 1 minute. Remove cookies from cookie sheet and cool on a wire rack. Frost with Vanilla Almond Frosting; let set. Place in layers separated by waxed paper in an airtight container and store at room temperature up to 3 days. Makes about 48.

Vanilla Almond Frosting: In a medium mixing bowl beat ¼ cup butter or margarine with an electric mixer on medium to high speed until softened. Beat in 2 cups sifted powdered sugar, 1 teaspoon vanilla, ¼ to ½ teaspoon almond extract, and enough milk (1 to 2 tablespoons) to make the frosting easy to spread.

Nutrition facts per cookie: 73 calories, 1 g protein, 13 g carbohydrate, 2 g total fat (1 g saturated), 10 mg cholesterol, 52 mg sodium, 0 g fiber. Daily values: 2% vitamin A, 0% vitamin C, 0% calcium, 3% iron.

Nutrition facts per cookie: 212 calories, 3 g protein, 27 g carbohydrate, 11 g total fat (4 g saturated), 18 mg cholesterol, 131 mg sodium, 1 g fiber. Daily values: 2% vitamin A, 0% vitamin C, 2% calcium, 4% iron.

To Make Ahead

Bake cookies as directed; cool completely. Do not frost. Place in layers separated by waxed paper in a freezer container or bag and freeze for up to 1 month. Before serving, thaw for 15 minutes. Frost with Vanilla Almond Frosting.

Kid Appeal

Candy Bar Cookies on a Stick

What kid can resist the fun of a cookie and a piece of candy wrapped into one terrific treat on a stick! Let your kids insert the sticks into the candy bar pieces and shape the dough around the candy.

1 **cup peanut butter**
½ **cup butter or margarine**
½ **cup shortening**
1½ **cups granulated sugar**
½ **cup packed brown sugar**
1½ **teaspoons baking soda**
2 **eggs**
1 **teaspoon vanilla**
2¼ **cups all-purpose flour**
40 **wooden sticks**
40 **miniature-size
      (about 1-inch square)
      chocolate-coated caramel-
      topped nougat candy bars
      (with or without peanuts) or
      20 fun-size candy bars
      (about 2x1-inch rectangles),
      halved crosswise**

Small multicolored decorative candies, chopped nuts, and/or colored sugar (optional)
Melted chocolate or 1 recipe Powdered Sugar Icing (see page 151) (optional)

1 In a large mixing bowl beat peanut butter, butter, and shortening with an electric mixer on medium to high speed about 30 seconds or until softened. Add sugar, brown sugar, and baking soda. Beat until combined. Beat in eggs and vanilla until combined. Beat in as much of the flour as you can with the mixer. Using a wooden spoon, stir in any remaining flour.

2 Insert a wooden stick into each candy bar piece. For each cookie, form about 2 tablespoons of dough into a ball and shape it around a piece of candy bar, making sure the candy is completely covered. If desired, roll ball in decorative candies, nuts, or colored sugar, gently pushing candies or nuts into dough.

3 Place cookies 2½ inches apart on an ungreased cookie sheet. Bake in a 325° oven for 15 to 20 minutes or until golden and set. Cool on cookie sheet for 5 minutes. Remove cookies from cookie sheet and cool completely on a wire rack. If desired, drizzle or frost the cookies with melted chocolate or icing. Place in an airtight container and store at room temperature for up to 3 days. Makes about 40.

Insert a wooden stick into one end of a candy piece. Take about 2 tablespoons of cookie dough and form it into a ball around the candy and the base of the stick.

Taking Shape

Some shaped cookie recipes require special tools, such as cookie stamps or cookie molds. Because the consistency of the dough was developed with a particular tool in mind, be sure to use the tool called for in the recipe. If you're using a cookie stamp or mold, follow the directions that came with it. That's the best way to ensure good results every time.

Peanut Butter-Apple Cookies

Here's a new taste combination for you with the same all-around appeal as peanut butter and jelly.

½ **cup peanut butter**
¼ **cup shortening**
¼ **cup butter (no substitutes)**
½ **cup granulated sugar**
½ **cup packed brown sugar**
½ **teaspoon baking powder**
½ **teaspoon baking soda**
1 **egg**
1 **teaspoon vanilla**
1½ **cups all-purpose flour**
½ **cup shredded peeled apple**
¾ **cup finely chopped peanuts**

1 In a large mixing bowl beat the peanut butter, shortening, and butter with an electric mixer on medium to high speed about 30 seconds or until mixture is combined.

2 Add the sugar, brown sugar, baking powder, and baking soda. Beat until combined. Beat in egg and vanilla until combined. Beat in as much of the flour as you can with the mixer. Using a wooden spoon, stir in any remaining flour. Stir in apple.

3 Shape the dough into 1-inch balls. Roll balls in chopped peanuts. Place 2 inches apart on an ungreased cookie sheet. Using the bottom of a glass, slightly flatten balls to ½-inch thickness. Bake in a 375° oven for 10 to 12 minutes or until bottoms are lightly browned. Cool on cookie sheet for 1 minute. Remove cookies from cookie sheet and cool on a wire rack. Place cookies in an airtight container and store at room temperature for up to 2 days. Makes about 48.

Nutrition facts per cookie: *78 calories, 2 g protein, 8 g carbohydrate, 5 g total fat (1 saturated), 7 mg cholesterol, 41 mg sodium, 0 g fiber. Daily values: 1% vitamin A, 0% vitamin C, 0% calcium, 2% iron.*

To Make Ahead
Bake cookies as directed; cool completely. Place in a freezer container or bag and freeze for up to 1 month. Before serving, thaw for 15 minutes.

Delicious Memories

Cracked Sugar Cookies

On the corner of Grandma's Hoosier cupboard stood a cake safe with a battered metal lid, a red wooden handle, and something delicious always inside—usually a chocolate cream pie, an angel food cake, or these buttery, melt-in-your-mouth sugar cookies. Grandma always said, "Don't try to hurry the cookies by turning up the temperature; slow baking is the trick."
—Shelli McConnell—

½ **cup butter (no substitutes)**
½ **cup shortening**
2 **cups granulated sugar**
½ **teaspoon vanilla**
3 **egg yolks**
2 **cups all-purpose flour**
1 **teaspoon baking soda**
1 **teaspoon cream of tartar**
⅛ **teaspoon salt**

1 In a large mixing bowl beat the butter and shortening with an electric mixer on medium to high speed about 30 seconds or until softened. Add sugar and vanilla. Beat until combined. Beat in the egg yolks.

2 In a small mixing bowl stir together the flour, baking soda, cream of tartar, and salt. Beat in as much of the flour mixture as you can with the mixer. Using a wooden spoon, stir in any remaining flour mixture.

3 Shape dough into uniform small balls (about 1 inch). Place 2 inches apart on an ungreased cookie sheet. Bake in a 300° oven about 20 minutes or until tops are cracked and sides are set (do not let edges brown). Remove cookies from cookie sheet and cool on a wire rack. Place in an airtight container and store at room temperature for up to 3 days. Makes about 48.

Nutrition facts per cookie: *89 calories, 1 g protein, 12 g carbohydrate, 4 g total fat (2 g saturated), 18 mg cholesterol, 52 mg sodium, 0 g fiber. Daily values: 3% vitamin A, 0% vitamin C, 0% calcium, 1% iron.*

To Make Ahead
Bake cookies as directed; cool completely. Place in a freezer container or bag and freeze for up to 1 month. Before serving, thaw for 15 minutes.

Peanut Butter-Apple Cookies, left, and Cracked Sugar Cookies, right

Lemon-Poppy Seed Cookies

The secret to flattening these delicate, old-fashioned cookies is to dip the bottom of a glass into sugar. That keeps the dough from sticking to the glass.

1 cup butter (no substitutes)
1 cup granulated sugar
1 egg
1 teaspoon vanilla
2 teaspoons poppy seed
1 teaspoon finely shredded
    lemon peel
2 cups all-purpose flour
    Granulated sugar
    Powdered sugar (optional)

1 In a large mixing bowl beat the butter with an electric mixer on medium to high speed about 30 seconds or until softened. Add 1 cup sugar. Beat until combined. Add egg and vanilla. Beat until combined. Beat in poppy seed, lemon peel, and as much flour as you can with the mixer. Using a wooden spoon, stir in any remaining flour. Cover and chill dough for 1 to 2 hours or until easy to handle.

2 Shape dough into 1-inch balls. Place 2 inches apart on an ungreased cookie sheet. Using the bottom of a glass dipped in additional sugar, slightly flatten balls to ½-inch thickness. Bake in a 375° oven for 8 to 10 minutes or until edges are firm and bottoms are lightly browned. Cool on cookie sheet for 1 minute. Remove cookies from cookie sheet and cool on a wire rack. If desired, sprinkle cookies

with powdered sugar. Place cookies in layers separated by waxed paper in an airtight container and store at room temperature for up to 3 days. Makes about 50.

Nutrition facts per cookie: *67 calories, 1 g protein, 8 g carbohydrate, 4 g total fat (2 g saturated), 14 mg cholesterol, 39 mg sodium, 0 g fiber. Daily values: 3% vitamin A, 0% vitamin C, 0% calcium, 1% iron.*

To Make Ahead

Bake cookies as directed; cool completely. Place in layers separated by waxed paper in a freezer container or bag and freeze for up to 1 month. Before serving, thaw for 15 minutes.

Choco-Orange Shortbread

Bits of chocolate imbedded in crisp, orange-accented shortbread is a dynamite combination. Nibble at your own risk!
(Pictured on page 209.)

1½ cups all-purpose flour
½ cup sifted powdered sugar
⅔ cup butter (no substitutes)
½ to 1 teaspoon finely shredded
    orange peel
¾ cup miniature semisweet
    chocolate pieces

1 In a medium mixing bowl stir together the flour and powdered sugar. Using a pastry blender, cut in the butter and orange peel until the mixture resembles fine crumbs and starts to cling. Stir in chocolate pieces. Form the mixture into ball and knead until smooth.

2 Shape dough into 1-inch balls. Place 2 inches apart on an ungreased cookie sheet. Using the bottom of a glass, slightly flatten balls to ½-inch thickness. Bake in a 350° oven for 10 to 12 minutes or until the bottoms just start to brown. Cool on cookie sheet for 1 minute. Remove cookies from cookie sheet and cool on a wire rack. Place in an airtight container and store at room temperature for up to 3 days. Makes about 24.

Nutrition facts per cookie: *104 calories, 1 g protein, 11 g carbohydrate, 7 g total fat (3 g saturated), 14 mg cholesterol, 52 mg sodium, 0 g fiber. Daily values: 4% vitamin A, 0% vitamin C, 0% calcium, 3% iron.*

To Make Ahead

Bake cookies as directed; cool completely. Place in a freezer container or bag and freeze up to 1 month. Before serving, thaw for 15 minutes.

Butter-Pecan Balls

The sophisticated flavor of these short-bread-type cookies is due in part to a secret ingredient—instant pudding.

¾ cup butter (no substitutes)
¼ cup granulated sugar
1 4-serving-size package instant
    butter pecan pudding mix
¼ teaspoon salt
1 egg
1 teaspoon vanilla
1½ cups all-purpose flour
¼ cup chopped pecans
    Powdered sugar (optional)

1 In a large mixing bowl beat the butter with an electric mixer on medium to high speed about 30 seconds or until softened. Add the sugar, pudding mix, and salt. Beat until combined. Beat in egg and vanilla until combined. Beat in as much of the flour as you can with the mixer. Using a wooden spoon, stir in any remaining flour. Stir in pecans.

2 Shape dough into 1-inch balls. Place 2 inches apart on an ungreased cookie sheet. Bake in a 325° oven about 20 minutes or until edges are firm and bottoms are lightly browned. Cool on cookie sheet for 1 minute. Remove cookies from cookie sheet and, if desired, gently roll in powdered sugar. Cool on a wire rack. Place in an airtight container and store at room temperature for up to 3 days. Makes about 36.

Nutrition facts per cookie: *76 calories, 1 g protein, 8 g carbohydrate, 5 g total fat (3 g saturated), 16 mg cholesterol, 100 mg sodium, 0 g fiber. Daily values: 3% vitamin A, 0% vitamin C, 0% calcium, 1% iron.*

Chocolate-Pecan Balls: Prepare the Butter-Pecan Balls as directed, except substitute one 4-serving-size package instant chocolate fudge pudding mix for the butter pecan pudding mix.

To Make Ahead
Bake cookies as directed; cool completely. Place in a freezer container or bag and freeze for up to 1 month. Before serving, thaw for 15 minutes.

Chocolate-Cinnamon Crisscrosses

In Mexico and South America chocolate and cinnamon are a favorite flavor combination. One bite and you'll see why.

½ **cup butter or margarine**
1 **cup granulated sugar**
2 **teaspoons baking powder**
1 **teaspoon ground cinnamon**
4 **ounces semisweet chocolate, melted and cooled**
2 **eggs**
1 **teaspoon vanilla**
2¼ **cups all-purpose flour**
  Granulated sugar

1 In a large mixing bowl beat the butter with an electric mixer on medium to high speed about 30 seconds or until softened. Add the 1 cup sugar, baking powder, and cinnamon and beat until combined. Beat in the melted chocolate, eggs, and vanilla. Beat in as much of the flour as you can with the mixer. Using a wooden spoon, stir in any remaining flour. Cover and chill the dough for 1 to 2 hours or until easy to handle.

2 Shape dough into 1-inch balls. Place 2 inches apart on an ungreased cookie sheet. Using the tines of a fork dipped in additional sugar, flatten balls to about ½-inch thickness by pressing the fork in 2 directions to form crisscross marks. Bake in a 375° oven for 8 to 10 minutes or until edges are set.

Cool on cookie sheet for 1 minute. Remove cookies from cookie sheet and cool on a wire rack. Place in an airtight container and store at room temperature for up to 3 days. Makes about 48.

Nutrition facts per cookie: *68 calories, 1 g protein, 10 g carbohydrate, 3 g total fat (1 g saturated), 14 mg cholesterol, 37 mg sodium, 0 g fiber. Daily values: 2% vitamin A, 0% vitamin C, 1% calcium, 2% iron.*

To Make Ahead
Bake cookies as directed; cool completely. Place in a freezer container or bag and freeze for up to 1 month. Before serving, thaw for 15 minutes.

Flatten the dough balls to about ½ inch thick by pressing them with the tines of a fork. Make the crisscross pattern by pressing twice at right angles to each other. Dip the tines in sugar to prevent sticking and add sparkle to the cookies.

International Origin

Chocolate-Almond Pretzels

Austrians call these cookies Schokolade Mandel Bretzels. In any language, they taste terrific.

    3   ounces unsweetened chocolate
 1½   cups all-purpose flour
    ¾   cup ground almonds
    ¾   cup butter (no substitutes)
    ½   cup granulated sugar
    1   egg
         Confectionary pearl sugar, colored sugar, or multicolored decorative candies

1 In a heavy small saucepan melt the chocolate over low heat, stirring often. Remove from heat; cool.

2 Meanwhile, combine the flour and almonds. In a large mixing bowl beat butter with an electric mixer on medium to high speed about 30 seconds or until softened. Add sugar and beat until fluffy. Add egg and cooled chocolate; beat well. Gradually add flour mixture, beating until combined. Divide dough in half. Cover and chill for 30 minutes or until easy to handle.

3 Pinch off about 1 tablespoon of dough. On a lightly floured surface, roll into a rope about ¼ inch thick and 8 inches long. Cross one end over the other to form a circle, leaving 1-inch ends free. Lift ends across to opposite edge of circle to make the pretzel. Press to seal. Carefully invert pretzel into decorative sugar or candies; place sugar side up on an ungreased cookie sheet. Repeat with remaining dough. Bake in a 375° oven for 6 to 8 minutes or until firm. Remove pretzels from cookie sheet and cool on a wire rack. Place in an airtight container and store at room temperature for up to 3 days. Makes 40.

Nutrition facts per cookie: 83 calories, 1 g protein, 8 g carbohydrate, 6 g total fat (3 g saturated), 15 mg cholesterol, 37 mg sodium, 0 g fiber. Daily values: 3% vitamin A, 0% vitamin C, 0% calcium, 3% iron.

To Make Ahead

Bake cookies as directed; cool completely. Place in a freezer container and freeze up to 1 month. Before serving, thaw for 15 minutes.

Nutty Crescents

Use your imagination and create a variety of shapes—balls, ropes, or whatever springs to mind—from this dough.

    1   cup butter (no substitutes)
    ⅓   cup packed brown sugar
    1   tablespoon crème de cacao or milk
    1   teaspoon vanilla
 2¼   cups all-purpose flour
    1   cup finely chopped pecans
         Chocolate Drizzle

1 In a large mixing bowl beat butter with an electric mixer on medium to high speed about 30 seconds or until softened. Add the sugar, crème de cacao, and vanilla. Beat until combined. Stir in the flour and pecans.

2 Roll rounded teaspoons of dough into 2-inch ropes; shape into crescents. Place 2 inches apart on an ungreased cookie sheet. Bake in a 375° oven 8 to 10 minutes or until edges are firm and bottoms are lightly browned. Cool on cookie sheet 1 minute. Remove cookies and cool on a wire rack. Drizzle with Chocolate Drizzle; let dry. Place in an airtight container and store at room temperature up to 3 days. Makes about 48.

Chocolate Drizzle: In a small saucepan combine ¼ cup semisweet chocolate pieces and 2 teaspoons shortening. Melt over low heat, stirring constantly. Stir in ¾ cup sifted powdered sugar and 1 to 2 tablespoons crème de cacao or milk to make an icing that is easy to drizzle.

Nutrition facts per cookie: 87 calories, 1 g protein, 8 g carbohydrate, 6 g total fat (3 g saturated), 10 mg cholesterol, 39 mg sodium, 0 g fiber. Daily values: 3% vitamin A, 0% vitamin C, 0% calcium, 2% iron.

To Make Ahead

Bake cookies as directed; cool completely. Do not drizzle. Place cookies in layers separated by waxed paper in a freezer container or bag and freeze for up to 1 month. Before serving, thaw for 15 minutes. Drizzle with Chocolate Drizzle.

Chocolate-Almond Pretzels, top, Choco-Orange Shortbread (see recipe, page 206), lower left, and Nutty Crescents, lower right

Hidden Treasure Nuggets

If you select a variety of centers so that every cookie contains a different candy treasure, each cookie will be just as exciting as the last.

¾ **cup butter or margarine**
½ **cup granulated sugar**
¼ **teaspoon baking powder**
 1 **egg yolk**
½ **teaspoon vanilla**
¼ **teaspoon almond extract**
    (optional)
1¾ **cups all-purpose flour**
    Small candies
    (small gumdrops, jelly beans,
    candy-coated milk chocolate
    pieces, and candy-coated
    chocolate and peanut butter
    pieces)
    Brightly colored sugar or small
    multicolored decorative
    candies

1 Grease a cookie sheet; set aside. Beat butter in a large mixing bowl with an electric mixer on medium to high speed about 30 seconds or until softened. Add the sugar and baking powder and beat until combined. Beat in egg yolk, vanilla, and, if desired, almond extract, until combined. Beat in as much of the flour as you can with the mixer. Using a wooden spoon, stir in any remaining flour. Do not chill the dough.

2 For each cookie, shape a rounded teaspoon of dough around a small piece of candy. Roll in colored sugar or decorative candies. Place cookies 2 inches apart on prepared cookie sheet. Bake in a 375° oven 8 to 10 minutes or until edges are firm but not brown. Remove cookies from cookie sheet and cool on a wire rack. Place in an airtight container and store at room temperature up to 3 days. Makes about 30.

Nutrition facts per cookie: 99 calories, 1 g protein, 13 g carbohydrate, 5 g total fat (3 g saturated), 19 mg cholesterol, 52 mg sodium, 0 g fiber. Daily values: 5% vitamin A, 0% vitamin C, 0% calcium, 2% iron.

International Origin

Richmond Maids of Honor

 1 **cup all-purpose flour**
¼ **teaspoon salt**
 6 **tablespoons butter**
    (no substitutes)
 3 **to 4 tablespoons cold water**
4½ **teaspoons raspberry jam**
½ **cup granulated sugar**
 3 **tablespoons butter or**
    margarine, softened
 1 **egg**
⅔ **cup ground almonds**
⅔ **teaspoon almond extract**

1 Combine flour and salt. Using a pastry blender, cut in the 6 tablespoons butter until pieces are size of small peas. Sprinkle water, 1 tablespoon at a time, over mixture until all is moistened, tossing gently with fork. Form dough into a ball.

2 On a lightly floured surface, roll dough to ⅛-inch thickness. Using a 2 ¾-inch cookie cutter, cut dough into 18 circles. Fit each circle into an ungreased 1¾-inch muffin cup. Place ¼ teaspoon jam in each dough cup.

3 Beat together sugar and the 3 tablespoons butter with an electric mixer on medium speed. Beat in egg. Stir in almonds and almond extract. Spoon about 1 tablespoon of almond mixture atop jam in each shell. Bake in a 375° oven about 25 minutes or until golden. Cool in muffin cups for 5 minutes. Remove cookies from muffin cups; cool on a wire rack. Makes 18.

Nutrition facts per cookie: 132 calories, 2 g protein, 13 g carbohydrate, 9 g total fat (4 g saturated), 27 mg cholesterol, 92 mg sodium, 1 g fiber. Daily values: 5% vitamin A, 0% vitamin C, 1% calcium, 3% iron.

Chocolate-Coconut Tarts

½ **cup butter (no substitutes)**
 1 **3-ounce package cream cheese,**
    softened
 1 **cup all-purpose flour**
 2 **beaten eggs**
½ **cup packed brown sugar**
⅓ **cup toasted coconut**
 2 **tablespoons milk**
⅓ **cup semisweet chocolate pieces,**
    melted and cooled

1 For crust, in a small mixing bowl beat the butter and cream cheese with an electric mixer on medium to high speed about 30 seconds or until softened. Using a wooden spoon, stir in the flour. Cover and chill dough about 1 hour or until easy to handle.

2 Form the chilled dough into a ball. Divide the ball into 24 equal portions. Roll each portion into a ball. Place each ball in an ungreased 1¾-inch muffin cup. Press the dough evenly against the bottoms and up the sides of the cups. Cover and set aside.

3 For filling, in a small mixing bowl stir together the eggs, brown sugar, coconut, and milk. Stir in melted chocolate. Fill each dough-lined muffin cup with about 1 tablespoon filling. Bake in a 375° oven for 15 to 18 minutes or until filling is set and crust is lightly browned. Cool slightly in pans. Remove tarts from pan and cool on wire racks. Place tarts in layers separated by waxed paper in an airtight container and store at room temperature or in the refrigerator for up to 3 days. Makes 24.

Nutrition facts per tart: *101 calories, 2 g protein, 9 g carbohydrate, 7 g total fat (3 g saturated), 32 mg cholesterol, 59 mg sodium, 0 g fiber. Daily values: 5% vitamin A, 0% vitamin C, 1% calcium, 3% iron.*

To Make Ahead

Bake tarts as directed; cool completely. Place tarts in layers separated by waxed paper in a freezer container or bag and freeze for up to 1 month. Before serving, thaw for 15 minutes.

Cinnamon Snaps

½ **cup packed brown sugar**
⅓ **cup butter (no substitutes), softened**
¼ **cup light corn syrup**
¾ **cup all-purpose flour**
½ **teaspoon ground cinnamon**
 Choco-Cinnamon Cream Filling (optional)

1 Line a cookie sheet with foil. Grease foil and set baking sheet aside.

2 In a medium mixing bowl beat together brown sugar, butter, and corn syrup. Stir in flour and cinnamon.

3 Drop batter from a slightly rounded teaspoon 3 inches apart on the prepared cookie sheet. (Bake only 4 or 5 cookies at a time.) Bake in a 350° oven 5 to 6 minutes or until cookies are bubbly and a deep golden brown. Cool cookies on cookie sheet about 2 minutes or until set. Quickly remove cookies, one at a time, and roll around a metal cone (for cone shapes) or the greased handle of a wooden spoon (for cigar shapes); cool. (If cookies harden before shaping, return to oven 1 minute or until softened and repeat shaping process.) Place in an airtight container and store at room temperature up to 1 day.

4 If filling, prepare it just before serving. Spoon filling into a decorating bag fitted with a large star tip. Pipe Choco-Cinnamon Cream Filling into each cookie. Makes about 36.

Choco-Cinnamon Cream Filling: Combine 2 cups whipping cream, ¼ cup sifted powdered sugar, 2 tablespoons unsweetened cocoa powder, and ½ teaspoon ground cinnamon. Beat with an electric mixer on medium speed until stiff peaks form.

Nutrition facts per unfilled cookie: *39 calories, 0 g protein, 6 g carbohydrate, 2 g total fat (1 g saturated), 5 mg cholesterol, 20 mg sodium, 0 g fiber. Daily values: 1% vitamin A, 0% vitamin C, 0% calcium, 1% iron.*

To Make Ahead

Bake and shape cookies as directed; do not fill. Place cookies in a freezer container or bag and freeze for up to 1 month. Before serving, thaw for 15 minutes. If desired, fill with Choco-Cinnamon Cream Filling.

Quickly roll each warm cookie around a metal cone. As they cool, they crisp up and hold their shape. If you don't have a metal cone, shape a cone out of pliable cardboard and cover it with foil, or roll cookies around the greased handle of a large wooden spoon.

Brownie Biscotti

Honey-Sesame Biscotti

International Origin

Brownie Biscotti

A chocoholic's version of this crispy Italian favorite, it's perfect for dunking in hot coffee, hot tea, or hot chocolate.

⅓ **cup butter (no substitutes)**
⅔ **cup granulated sugar**
2 **teaspoons baking powder**
2 **eggs**
1 **teaspoon vanilla**
⅓ **cup unsweetened cocoa powder**
1¾ **cups all-purpose flour**
½ **cup miniature semisweet chocolate pieces**
¼ **cup finely chopped walnuts**
1 **beaten egg yolk**
1 **tablespoon milk or water**

1 In a large mixing bowl beat butter with an electric mixer on medium to high speed 30 seconds or until softened. Add sugar and baking powder. Beat until combined. Beat in eggs and vanilla until combined. Beat in cocoa powder and as much flour as you can with the mixer. Stir in any remaining flour. Stir in chocolate pieces and walnuts. Divide dough in half.

2 Lightly grease a cookie sheet. Shape each portion into a 9x2x1-inch loaf. Place the loaves about 4 inches apart on prepared cookie sheet. In a small bowl stir together the egg yolk and milk. Brush mixture over loaves. Bake in a 375° oven for 25 minutes. Cool on the cookie sheet for 30 minutes.

3 Cut each loaf diagonally into ½-inch-thick slices. Lay slices, cut side down, on cookie sheet. Bake in a 325° oven 15 minutes. Turn slices over. Bake 10 to 15 minutes more or until dry and crisp. Remove from cookie sheet and cool on a wire rack. Store in an airtight container at room temperature for up to 3 days. Makes about 30.
Nutrition facts per cookie: *91 calories, 2 g protein, 12 g carbohydrate, 4 g total fat (1 g saturated), 27 mg cholesterol, 50 mg sodium, 0 g fiber. Daily values: 3% vitamin A, 0% vitamin C, 3% calcium, 4% iron.*

To Make Ahead
Bake the cookies as directed; cool completely. Place in a freezer container and freeze for up to 1 month. Before serving, thaw for 15 minutes.

International Origin

Honey-Sesame Biscotti

⅓ **cup butter (no substitutes)**
½ **cup sugar**
2 **teaspoons baking powder**
⅛ **teaspoon salt**
2 **eggs**
¼ **cup honey**
2¾ **cups all-purpose flour**
⅓ **cup toasted sesame seed**
¼ **cup sesame seed**

1 Beat butter with an electric mixer on medium to high speed 30 seconds. Add sugar, baking powder, and salt. Beat until combined. Beat in eggs and honey. Beat in as much flour as you can with the mixer. Stir in ⅓ cup toasted sesame seed and any remaining flour. Divide dough in half.

2 Lightly grease a cookie sheet. With floured hands, shape each portion into a 12-inch-long loaf. Roll loaves in remaining sesame seed. Place loaves about 4 inches apart on the prepared cookie sheet. Flatten slightly to 2 inches wide. Bake in a 375° oven for 15 to 20 minutes or until lightly browned. Cool on cookie sheet 1 hour.

3 Cut each loaf diagonally into ½-inch slices. Lay slices, cut side down, on the cookie sheet. Bake in a 325° oven 10 minutes. Turn slices over. Bake 8 to 10 minutes more or until dry and crisp. Remove from cookie sheet and cool on a wire rack. Makes about 40.
Nutrition facts per cookie: *73 calories, 2 g protein, 10 g carbohydrate, 3 g total fat (1 g saturated), 15 mg cholesterol, 38 mg sodium, 0 g fiber. Daily values: 1% vitamin A, 0% vitamin C, 1% calcium, 3% iron.*

After biscotti loaves have cooled from the first baking, use a serrated knife to cut them diagonally into thick slices.

Chilling Thoughts

The softness of your cookie dough is determined by the type of butter or margarine you use. You can speed the chilling of the dough by freezing it for about one-third of the specified refrigeration time. However, do not freeze dough made entirely with butter; it gets too firm.

Don't forget to keep half of the dough chilled while you slice and bake the other half.

Key Lime Wafers

Key limes, grown in the Florida Keys, are packed with special flavor, but any lime will work. If you do use key limes, use the lesser amount of grated peel. After grating the peel, roll limes on the countertop before juicing to increase the amount of juice released.

 1   **cup butter (no substitutes)**
 1   **3-ounce package cream cheese, softened**
 1   **cup granulated sugar**
 2   **to 4 teaspoons grated lime peel**
 ¼   **teaspoon salt**
 1   **egg yolk**
 1   **tablespoon lime juice**
 2½ **cups all-purpose flour**
     Lime Icing

1 In a large mixing bowl beat butter and cream cheese with an electric mixer on medium to high speed for 30 seconds or until softened. Add the sugar, lime peel, and salt. Beat until combined. Beat in egg yolk and lime juice until combined. Beat in as much flour as you can with the mixer. Using a wooden spoon, stir in any remaining flour. If necessary, chill dough for 1 hour or until easy to handle.

2 Shape the dough into two 10-inch-long rolls. Wrap the rolls in waxed paper or clear plastic wrap, then chill for 4 to 48 hours.

3 Cut dough into ⅛-inch-thick slices. Place 1 inch apart on an ungreased cookie sheet. Bake in a 375° oven about 8 minutes or until edges are lightly browned. Cool on cookie sheet for 1 minute. Remove cookies from cookie sheet and cool on a wire rack. Drizzle with Lime Icing; let set. Place in an airtight container and store at room temperature for up to 3 days. Makes about 108.

Lime Icing: Combine 1½ cups sifted powdered sugar and enough lime juice (3 to 4 teaspoons) to make an icing that is easy to drizzle. If desired, tint with green food coloring.

Nutrition facts per cookie: 40 calories, 0 g protein, 5 g carbohydrate, 2 g total fat (1 g saturated), 7 mg cholesterol, 25 mg sodium, 0 g fiber. Daily values: 2% vitamin A, 0% vitamin C, 0% calcium, 0% iron.

To Make Ahead
Bake the cookies as directed; cool completely. Do not drizzle with Lime Icing. Place cookies in a freezer container or bag and freeze for up to 1 month. Before serving, thaw for 15 minutes. Prepare Lime Icing and drizzle over cookies.

Cheesecake Cookies

A double dose of rich cream cheese, one in the dough and one for the topping, ought to cure your cravings.

 ¾   **cup butter (no substitutes)**
 1   **3-ounce package cream cheese, softened**
 ½   **cup granulated sugar**
 1   **teaspoon vanilla**
 1½ **cups all-purpose flour**
 1   **8-ounce container soft-style cream cheese with strawberries**

1 In a mixing bowl beat butter and plain cream cheese with an electric mixer on medium to high speed for 30 seconds or until softened. Add the sugar and vanilla. Beat until combined. Using a wooden spoon, stir in flour until combined.

2 Shape the dough into two 6-inch-long rolls. Wrap the rolls in waxed paper or clear plastic wrap, then chill for 4 to 48 hours.

3 Cut dough into ¼-inch-thick slices. Place 2 inches apart on an ungreased cookie sheet. Bake in a 375° oven for 8 to 10 minutes or until edges are lightly browned. Cool on cookie sheet for 1 minute. Remove cookies from cookie sheet and cool on a wire rack. Before serving, frost cookies with strawberry cream cheese. Place cookies in layers separated by waxed paper in an airtight container or plastic bag and store at room temperature for up to 3 days. Makes about 48.

Nutrition facts per cookie: *68 calories, 1 g protein, 6 g carbohydrate, 5 g total fat (3 g saturated), 14 mg cholesterol, 44 mg sodium, 0 g fiber. Daily values: 3% vitamin A, 0% vitamin C, 0% calcium, 1% iron.*

To Make Ahead

Bake cookies as directed; cool completely. Do not spread with strawberry cream cheese. Place in layers separated by waxed paper in a freezer container or bag and freeze up to 1 month.

Place the wrapped rolls in narrow glasses before chilling. This will help them retain their round shape rather than developing a flat side from resting on the refrigerator shelf.

Before serving, thaw for 15 minutes. Spread with strawberry cream cheese.

Butterscotch Bites

You'll want to munch these bite-size cookies by the handfuls. They will keep well in an airtight container or plastic bag at room temperature— if they last that long!

1	**cup butter (no substitutes)**
1	**cup packed brown sugar**
½	**cup butterscotch-flavored pieces, melted and cooled**
1	**teaspoon vanilla**
2½	**cups all-purpose flour**

1 In a large mixing bowl beat butter with an electric mixer on medium to high speed for 30 seconds or until softened. Add the brown sugar, melted butterscotch pieces, and vanilla. Beat until combined. Beat in as much flour as you can with the mixer. Using a wooden spoon, stir in any remaining flour. Divide dough into four portions.

2 Shape each portion into a 9-inch-long roll. Wrap the rolls in waxed paper or clear plastic wrap, then chill for 4 to 48 hours.

3 Cut dough into ¼-inch-thick slices. Place slices 1 inch apart on an ungreased cookie sheet. Bake in a 350° oven for 8 to 10 minutes or until edges are set. Cool on cookie sheet for 1 minute. Remove cookies from cookie sheet and cool on a wire rack. Place in an airtight container and store at room

Tender Touch

If you need to do quite a bit of rerolling cutout cookie dough, use a mixture of equal parts all-purpose flour and powdered sugar to dust the surface. The cookies won't be as tough as those made with dough rerolled on a surface dusted only with flour.

temperature for up to 3 days. Makes about 110.

Nutrition facts per cookie: *34 calories, 0 g protein, 4 g carbohydrate, 2 g total fat (1 g saturated), 4 mg cholesterol, 18 mg sodium, 0 g fiber. Daily values: 1% vitamin A, 0% vitamin C, 0% calcium, 1% iron.*

To Make Ahead

Bake cookies as directed; cool completely. Place in a freezer container or bag and freeze up to 1 month. Before serving, thaw for 15 minutes.

Notes
_____

_____

_____

_____

_____

_____

Around in Circles

To keep the cookie dough in a perfect cylinder while it's chilling, slide the roll of dough into a tall drinking glass. Then rotate the roll as you slice it to avoid flattening one side.

Blueberry Pinwheels

You can store these fruit-filled rolls in the freezer for anytime use. Simply slice the frozen dough, then bake as directed.

½ **cup butter (no substitutes)**
1 **cup granulated sugar**
½ **teaspoon baking powder**
1 **egg**
3 **tablespoons milk**
1 **teaspoon vanilla**
2¾ **cups all-purpose flour**
1 **cup blueberry pie filling**
    (about ½ of a 21-ounce can)
½ **cup ground hazelnuts (filberts)**
    or almonds
    Powdered sugar
    (optional)

1 In a large mixing bowl beat butter with an electric mixer on medium to high speed for 30 seconds or until soft-ened. Add the sugar and baking pow-der. Beat until combined. Beat in the egg, milk, and vanilla until combined. Beat in as much of the flour as you can with the mixer. Using a wooden spoon, stir in any remaining flour.

2 Divide dough in half. Roll each half between waxed paper into a 12x8-inch rectangle. Remove top sheets of waxed paper. Combine pie filling and ground nuts; spread half the filling over each dough rectangle to within ½ inch of edges. From a long side, roll up each half jelly-roll style, removing waxed paper as you roll. Press edges to seal. Wrap each filled roll in waxed paper or clear plastic wrap, then chill for 4 to 48 hours.

3 Line a baking sheet with foil. Grease the foil and set baking sheet aside. Cut dough into ¼-inch-thick slices. Place slices 2 inches apart on prepared bak-ing sheets. Bake in a 375° oven for 10 to 12 minutes or until edges are firm and bottoms are lightly browned. Cool on baking sheet for 1 minute. Remove cookies from baking sheet and cool on a wire rack. Before serving, if desired, sprinkle lightly with powdered sugar. Place cookies in layers separated by waxed paper in an airtight container and store at room temperature for up to 3 days. Makes about 60.

Nutrition facts per cookie: *59 calories, 1 g protein, 9 g carbohydrate, 2 g total fat (1 g saturated), 8 mg cholesterol, 21 mg sodium, 0 g fiber. Daily values: 1% vitamin A, 0% vitamin C, 0% calcium, 2% iron.*

To Make Ahead

Bake cookies as directed; cool com-pletely. Do not sprinkle with pow-dered sugar. Place cookies in layers separated by wax paper in a freezer container and freeze up to 1 month. Before serving, thaw for 15 minutes. Sprinkle with powdered sugar.

Coconut-Pecan Chocolate Slices

Sweet chocolate cookies wrapped in a coconut-pecan coating bake up crisp and light and stay that way in an airtight container or plastic bag at room temperature for up to 3 days.

½ **cup butter (no substitutes)**
½ **cup shortening**
½ **cup granulated sugar**
½ **cup packed brown sugar**
½ **teaspoon baking powder**
¼ **teaspoon baking soda**
¼ **teaspoon salt**
1 **egg**
1 **4-ounce package sweet baking**
    chocolate, melted and cooled
2½ **cups all-purpose flour**
½ **cup coconut**
½ **cup finely chopped pecans**

1 In a large mixing bowl beat the but-ter and shortening with an electric mixer on medium to high speed for 30 seconds or until softened. Add the sugar, brown sugar, baking powder, baking soda, and salt. Beat until combined. Beat in the egg and melted chocolate until combined. Beat in as much of the flour as you can with the mixer. Using a wooden spoon, stir in any remaining flour.

2 Shape dough into two 8-inch-long rolls. In a small mixing bowl stir together coconut and pecans. Roll dough rolls in coconut-pecan mixture. Wrap in waxed paper or clear plastic wrap, then chill for 4 to 48 hours.

3 Cut dough into ¼-inch-thick slices. Place 2 inches apart on an ungreased cookie sheet. Bake in a 375° oven for 8 to 10 minutes or until edges are firm. Cool on cookie sheet for 1 minute. Remove cookies from cookie sheet and cool on a wire rack. Place in an airtight

Place the coconut-pecan mixture on waxed paper or a small tray. Roll the shaped rolls in the mixture to coat evenly. Press mixture lightly into dough, if necessary.

container and store at room temperature for up to 3 days. Makes about 60.

Nutrition facts per cookie: *78 calories, 1 g protein, 8 g carbohydrate, 5 g total fat (2 g saturated), 8 mg cholesterol, 34 mg sodium, 0 g fiber. Daily values: 1% vitamin A, 0% vitamin C, 0% calcium, 2% iron.*

To Make Ahead

Bake cookies as directed; cool completely. Place in a freezer container or bag and freeze up to 1 month. Before serving, thaw for 15 minutes.

Sugar and Spice Slices

Sugar, spice, and everything nice goes into these simple, homespun cookies. You can make your own pumpkin pie spice by combining ¾ teaspoon ground cinnamon, ¼ teaspoon ground nutmeg, ⅛ teaspoon ground ginger, and ⅛ teaspoon allspice.

   ½ **cup butter (no substitutes)**
   ½ **cup shortening**
   1 **cup packed brown sugar**
   1 **teaspoon pumpkin pie spice**
   ½ **teaspoon baking soda**
   ¼ **teaspoon salt**
   1 **egg**
   1 **teaspoon vanilla**
   ½ **cup toasted wheat germ**
   2 **cups all-purpose flour**

1 In a large mixing bowl beat butter and shortening with an electric mixer on medium to high speed for 30 seconds or until softened. Add the brown sugar, pumpkin pie spice, baking soda, and salt. Beat until combined. Beat in the egg and vanilla until combined. Beat in the wheat germ and as much of the flour as you can with the mixer. Using a wooden spoon, stir in any remaining flour.

2 Shape the dough into two 7-inch-long rolls. Wrap the rolls in waxed paper or clear plastic wrap, then chill for 4 to 48 hours.

3 Cut dough into ¼-inch-thick slices. Place 2 inches apart on an ungreased cookie sheet. Bake in a 375° oven for 8 to 10 minutes or until edges are firm and bottoms are lightly browned. Cool on cookie sheet for 1 minute. Remove cookies from cookie sheet and cool on a wire rack. Place in an airtight container and store at room temperature for up to 3 days. Makes about 48.

Nutrition facts per cookie: *73 calories, 1 g protein, 8 g carbohydrate, 4 g total fat (2 g saturated), 10 mg cholesterol, 46 mg sodium, 0 g fiber. Daily values: 1% vitamin A, 0% vitamin C, 0% calcium, 2% iron.*

To Make Ahead

Bake the cookies as directed; cool completely. Place in a freezer container or bag and freeze for up to 1 month. Before serving, thaw for 15 minutes.

Butterflies

Peppermint
Swirls

Basic
Spirals

Quilt Cookies

Nutty
Chocolate Slices

Ready When You Are

Slice and bake cookies are perfect for today's hectic households. You can have fresh, wholesome cookies ready in short order . Mix the basic dough, then color and shape it to suit the occasion. Rolls of dough will keep in the refrigerator for up to 1 week or in the freezer for up to 6 months. There's no need to thaw it—just slice and bake. There's no mess, hardly any dirty dishes, and lots of happy faces!

Chocolate-Dipped Chocolate Slices

Quilt Cookies

Sandwich Spirals

Chocolate Slices

Basic Slice Dough

- **1 cup butter (no substitutes)**
- **1½ cups granulated sugar**
- **1½ teaspoons baking powder**
- **½ teaspoon salt**
- **1 egg**
- **1 teaspoon vanilla**
- **2½ cups all-purpose flour**

In a large mixing bowl beat butter with an electric mixer on medium to high speed about 30 seconds or until softened. Add the sugar, baking powder, and salt. Beat until combined. Beat in the egg and vanilla. Beat in as much of the flour as you can with the mixer. Using a wooden spoon, stir in any remaining flour.

Basic Spirals: Divide dough in half. Tint each portion of the dough with contrasting paste food coloring. Knead coloring into dough until well mixed.

If necessary, wrap dough in waxed paper or clear plastic wrap and chill for 1 hour or until easy to handle.

On a lightly floured surface, roll out each color of dough into a 12x8-inch rectangle (¼ to ⅛ inch thick). Place one rectangle on top of the other. Press down gently with your hands to seal. Tightly roll up, jelly-roll style, starting from one of the long sides. Wrap in waxed paper or clear plastic wrap. Refrigerate 2 to 4 hours or until firm.

Using a sharp knife, cut each roll into ¼-inch-thick slices. Place slices 1 inch apart on an ungreased cookie sheet. Bake in a 375° oven for 8 to 10 minutes or until edges are firm and light brown. Cool on cookie sheet for 1 minute. Then remove cookies from cookie sheet and cool on a wire rack.

If desired, glaze with Powdered Sugar Icing (see page 151), dip in or drizzle with melted chocolate, and/or sprinkle with nuts or colored sugars. Or, if desired, sandwich 2 cookies together using Butter Frosting (see page 150) or purchased frosting. Store in layers separated by waxed paper in an airtight container or plastic bag at room temperature up to 3 days or freeze up to 1 month. Makes about 48.

Butterflies: Prepare Basic Spirals as directed. After cutting the ¼-inch-slices, cut the slices in half. Press rounded sides of half-slices together for a butterfly shape. Bake, cool, decorate, and store as directed for Basic Spirals. Makes about 48.

Peppermint Swirls: Prepare Basic Slice Dough as directed, except add ½ teaspoon peppermint extract with the vanilla. Divide dough into 3 equal portions. Tint one portion with red paste food coloring and one with green. Leave the third portion plain.

Roll each portion of dough into a

12-inch rope. Gather the ropes together and twist to swirl colors like a candy cane. Press ropes together and gently roll on a smooth surface to make a smooth, uniform, 12-inch log. Wrap in waxed paper or clear plastic wrap and chill for 2 to 4 hours or until firm.

Using a sharp knife, cut log into ¼-inch-thick slices. Bake, cool, decorate, and store as directed for Basic Spirals. Makes about 48.

***Nutrition facts per serving (for Basic Spirals, Butterflies, and Peppermint Swirls):** 81 calories, 4 g total fat (2 g saturated), 15 mg cholesterol, 63 mg sodium, 11 g carbohydrate, 0 g fiber, 1 g protein. Daily values: 3% vitamin A, 0% vitamin C, 1% calcium 2% iron.*

Chocolate Slices: Prepare Basic Slice Dough as directed. Remove one-third of the dough and, if desired, tint it with a paste coloring; set aside.

Stir 2 ounces melted, cooled, unsweetened chocolate into the remaining ⅔ of the dough. Divide chocolate dough in half. (You now have 3 equal portions of dough.)

On a lightly floured surface or between 2 sheets of waxed paper, roll one of the chocolate portions into a 7x6-inch rectangle. Roll plain dough into a 7x6-inch rectangle. Place plain rectangle on top of chocolate rectangle; press down gently. Roll remaining chocolate dough into a 7x6-inch rectangle. Place on top of plain rectangle; press down gently.

Using a sharp knife, cut stack lengthwise into three 7x2-inch pieces. Wrap each piece in waxed paper or clear plastic wrap. Chill for 2 to 4 hours or until firm.

Using a sharp knife, cut piece crosswise into ¼-inch-thick slices. Bake, cool, decorate, and store as directed for Basic Spirals. Makes about 80.

Quilt Cookies: Prepare Basic Slice Dough as directed. Divide dough in half. Tint each half with desired paste food coloring. On a lightly-floured surface, roll one color of dough into a 6x8-inch rectangle. Cut rectangle lengthwise into three 2x8-inch strips. Repeat with remaining color of dough. Stack 3 strips of dough together, alternating colors. (You will have 2 square logs, each with 3 layers.) Press layers together gently to seal. Wrap logs in waxed paper or clear plastic wrap. Chill for 2 hours or until firm.

Using a sharp knife, cut each log lengthwise into 3 thin strips. Trim edges to straighten as necessary. (Each strip will have 3 layers of alternating color.) Lay thin strips on their sides. Stack three strips together, alternating colors, for a checkerboard effect. Wrap the 2 logs in waxed paper or clear plastic wrap and chill for 2 to 4 hours or until firm.

Using a sharp knife, cut logs into ¼-inch-thick slices. Bake, cool, decorate, and store as directed for Basic Spirals. Makes about 60.

Almond-Glazed Cherry Pie
(see recipe, page 232)

A Piece of The Pie

Everybody will want pieces of the pies you can make from the recipes in this chapter.

With all the information we've included on making pastries, preparing fillings, and working with meringues, there's nothing you can't do.

Your choices are not limited to an array of enticing fruit, custard, and cream pies. In addition, there's all you need to know to make light cream puffs and puff pastry cream horns.

If that still isn't enough, there are Danish pastries and strudel to fulfill your desire for the ultimate in utterly sophisticated pastries.

Better get your piece of the pie before there isn't one left!

Pastry for Single-Crust Pie

1¼ cups all-purpose flour
¼ teaspoon salt
⅓ cup shortening
4 to 5 tablespoons cold water

1 In a medium mixing bowl stir together flour and salt. Using a pastry blender, cut in shortening until pieces are the size of small peas.

2 Sprinkle 1 tablespoon of the water over part of mixture, then gently toss with a fork. Push moistened dough to side of the bowl. Repeat, using 1 tablespoon of water at a time, until all is moistened. Form dough into a ball.

Loosely wrap the pastry around a rolling pin to transfer it to the pie plate. Carefully lift the rolling pin, then unroll the pastry in the center of the plate. Or, if desired, fold the pastry in quarters, carefully lift and center it in pie plate, and unfold.

3 On a lightly floured surface, use your hands to slightly flatten dough. Roll dough from center to edges, forming a 12-inch circle. Transfer pastry, to a 9-inch pie plate; ease into pie plate, being careful not to stretch it.

4 Trim pastry to ½ inch beyond edge of pie plate. Fold under extra pastry. Flute edges. Do not prick shell. Bake as directed in recipes.

Baked Pastry Shell: Prepare Pastry for Single-Crust Pie as directed. Using a fork, prick the bottom and sides of pastry. Line the pastry-lined pie plate with a double thickness of foil. Bake in a 450° oven for 8 minutes. Remove foil. Bake for 5 to 6 minutes more or until golden. Cool on a wire rack.

Coconut Pastry: Prepare Pastry for Single-Crust Pie as directed, except add ¼ cup finely chopped toasted coconut into the flour mixture before adding water.

Chocolate Pastry: Prepare Pastry for Single-Crust Pie as directed, except stir 2 tablespoons granulated sugar and 2 tablespoons unsweetened cocoa powder into the flour mixture.

Nut Pastry: Prepare Pastry for Single-Crust Pie as directed, except stir ¼ cup finely chopped peanuts, pecans, walnuts, or shelled pistachio nuts into the flour mixture.

Spicy Pastry: Prepare Pastry for Single-Crust Pie as directed, except stir 1 teaspoon ground cinnamon, ground nutmeg or pumpkin pie spice into the flour mixture.

Whole Wheat Pastry: Prepare Pastry for Single-Crust Pie as directed, except substitute ½ cup whole wheat flour for ½ cup of all-purpose flour.

To Make Ahead
Prepare any of the variations up to the point of forming dough into a ball. Flatten dough between layers of waxed paper or fit it into a pie plate. Place in a freezer container or bag and freeze for up to 2 months. To use, let rolled-out pastry thaw at room temperature about 30 minutes before fitting into a pie plate. Use others as you would an unfrozen shell.

Pastry for Double-Crust Pie

Use either a double crust or lattice top as recipes specify. Substituting one for the other doesn't always work. Some fillings need to be covered to cook properly; others need the extra venting provided by a lattice.

2 cups all-purpose flour
½ teaspoon salt
⅔ cup shortening
6 to 7 tablespoons cold water

1 In a bowl combine flour and salt. Using a pastry blender, cut in shortening until pieces are size of small peas.

2 Sprinkle 1 tablespoon of the water over part of mixture; gently toss with a fork. Push to side of bowl. Repeat, using 1 tablespoon of water at a time, until all is moistened. Divide dough in half. Form each half into a ball.

3 On a lightly floured surface, slightly flatten one ball of dough. Roll dough from center to edges, forming a 12-inch circle. Transfer pastry to a 9-inch pie plate. Carefully ease pastry into pie plate. Add filling as directed in recipes. Trim bottom pastry even with rim of pie plate.

4 For top crust, repeat rolling remaining dough. Cut slits in top crust; place on filling. Trim pastry to ½ inch beyond edge of plate. Fold top crust under bottom pastry. Seal; flute edge (see photos, pages 228 and 237). Bake as directed in recipes.

Note: For Coconut, Chocolate, Nut, Spicy, or Whole Wheat Pastry for Double-Crust Pie, use the directions for these flavor variations following the Pastry for Single-Crust Pie, except use 1½ times the amount of the varied ingredients.

Pastry for Lattice-Top Pie: Prepare Pastry for Double-Crust Pie as directed, except after rolling out top crust, cut it into ½- to ¾-inch-wide strips. Transfer desired filling to pastry-lined pie plate. Trim bottom pastry to ½-inch beyond edge of plate. Start lattice with the two longest strips crosswise to each other in the center of the filling. Add strips on each side of the center strips about ½ inch apart. Fold every other strip back as necessary to make a woven top. Repeat until there are 5 to 7 strips in each direction (see photo, page 237). Press ends of strips into edge of bottom crust. Fold bottom pastry over ends of strips; seal and flute edge. Bake as directed in recipes.

Apple Pie

Try Golden Delicious, Rome, or Jonathan apples; if they lack tartness, add the optional lemon juice.

 1 **recipe Pastry for Double-Crust Pie (see page 224)**
 ⅔ **to ¾ cup granulated sugar**
 2 **tablespoons all-purpose flour**
 1 **teaspoon ground cinnamon**
 ⅛ **teaspoon ground cardamom (optional)**
 6 **cups thinly sliced, peeled, cooking apples (about 2¼ pounds)**
 1 **tablespoon lemon juice (optional)**

1 Prepare and roll out Pastry for Double-Crust Pie as directed. Line a 9-inch pie plate with half of the pastry.

2 For filling, in a large mixing bowl stir together sugar, flour, cinnamon, and cardamom (if desired). Add apple slices and lemon juice (if desired); gently toss until coated. Transfer apple mixture to the pastry-lined pie plate. Trim bottom pastry to the edge of pie plate. Cut slits in the top crust for steam to escape. Place top crust on filling. Seal and flute edge.

3 To prevent overbrowning, cover edge of pie with foil. Bake in a 375° oven for 25 minutes. Remove foil. Bake for 25 to 30 minutes more or until the top is golden. Cool on a wire rack before serving. Cover and refrigerate any leftovers and use within 2 days. Makes 8 servings.

Nutrition facts per serving: *372 calories, 3 g protein, 52 g carbohydrate, 18 g total fat (4 g saturated), 0 mg cholesterol, 135 mg sodium, 1 g fiber. Daily values: 0% vitamin A, 0% vitamin C, 1% calcium, 11% iron.*

Pear Pie: Prepare Apple Pie as directed, except substitute sliced fresh pears for apples and increase flour to 3 tablespoons.

To Make Ahead
Prepare and fill pastry as directed, except do not cut slits in top crust. Cover unbaked pie with inverted 10-inch paper plate. Seal in freezer bag, label, and freeze up to 4 months. To bake frozen pie, remove from bag, remove paper plate, and cut slits in top crust. Add foil to edges and bake at 450° for 15 minutes. Reduce oven temperature to 375° and bake 15 minutes more. Remove foil and bake about 30 minutes more or until top is golden.

Cran-Apple Crunch Pie

Cran-Apple Crunch Pie

When using frozen cranberries, let them stand 15 to 30 minutes to partially thaw.

- **1 recipe Pastry for Single-Crust Pie (see page 224)**
- ⅓ **cup granulated sugar**
- ⅓ **cup packed brown sugar**
- ¼ **cup all-purpose flour**
- ½ **teaspoon ground cinnamon**
- **3 cups thinly sliced, peeled, cooking apples (about 1 pound)**
- **2 cups cranberries**
- ⅓ **cup packed brown sugar**
- ¼ **cup quick-cooking rolled oats**
- ¼ **cup all-purpose flour**
- ¼ **cup butter (no substitutes)**
- ¼ **cup chopped pecans or walnuts**

1 Prepare and roll out Pastry for Single-Crust Pie as directed. Line a 9-inch pie plate with pastry. Trim and flute edge of pastry. Do not prick shell.

2 For filling, in large mixing bowl stir together sugar, ⅓ cup brown sugar, ¼ cup flour, and cinnamon. Add apple slices and cranberries, then gently toss until coated. Transfer fruit mixture to unbaked pastry shell.

3 For topping, in medium mixing bowl combine ⅓ cup brown sugar, rolled oats, and ¼ cup flour. With a pastry blender or two forks, cut in butter until crumbly. Stir in pecans. Sprinkle crumb mixture over fruit.

4 To prevent overbrowning, cover edge of pie with foil. Bake in a 375° oven for 25 minutes. Remove foil. Bake for 25 to 30 minutes more or until top is golden. Cool pie on a wire rack before serving. Cover and refrigerate any leftovers. Makes 8 servings.

Nutrition facts per serving: *372 calories, 3 g protein, 54 g carbohydrate, 17 g total fat (6 g saturated), 15 mg cholesterol, 130 mg sodium, 3 g fiber. Daily values: 5% vitamin A, 9% vitamin C, 2% calcium, 11% iron.*

Cranberry-Pear Crunch Pie: Prepare Cran-Apple Crunch Pie as directed, except substitute sliced fresh pears for apples and increase the flour in fruit filling to ⅓ cup.

Sour Cream Plum Pie

- **1 recipe Pastry for Single-Crust Pie (see page 224)**
- **2 eggs, beaten**
- ¾ **cup granulated sugar**
- ½ **cup dairy sour cream**
- **1 tablespoon all-purpose flour**
- **3 cups sliced, pitted plums**
- ½ **cup all-purpose flour**
- ½ **cup granulated sugar**
- **2 tablespoons butter (no substitutes)**
- ½ **cup coconut**

1 Prepare and roll out pastry as directed. Line a 9-inch pie plate with the pastry. Trim and flute edge of pastry. Do not prick shell. Set aside.

2 For filling, combine eggs, ¾ cup sugar, sour cream, and 1 tablespoon flour. Place plums in unbaked pastry shell. Top with sour cream mixture.

3 To prevent overbrowning, cover edge of pie with foil. Bake in a 375° oven for 15 minutes.

4 Meanwhile, combine ½ cup flour and ½ cup sugar. Cut in butter until crumbly. Stir in coconut. Remove foil from pie. Sprinkle crumb mixture on top of pie. Bake 25 to 30 minutes more or until pie appears nearly set in center when gently shaken. Cool and refrigerate within 2 hours; add cover for longer storage. Makes 8 servings.

Nutrition facts per serving: *437 calories, 6 g protein, 68 g carbohydrate, 17 g total fat (7 g saturated), 67 mg cholesterol, 119 mg sodium, 2 g fiber. Daily values: 10% vitamin A, 17% vitamin C, 2% calcium, 10% iron.*

Big Fat Deal

It does make a difference whether you use butter or margarine when making a piecrust. To ensure best results, use only butter or shortening. If you use margarine, your piecrust will be unacceptably tough and not flaky or crisp.

Autumn Blush Pie

If desired, use 1¾ cups snipped, dried mixed fruits instead of the cranberries or cherries and apricots.

1 recipe Whole Wheat or plain Pastry for Double-Crust Pie (see page 224)
½ cup orange juice
1 cup dried cranberries or dried cherries
¾ cup snipped dried apricots
¾ cup granulated sugar
2 tablespoons all-purpose flour
1 tablespoon finely shredded orange peel
3 cups thinly sliced, peeled, cooking apples or pears (about 1 pound)

1 Prepare and roll out Pastry for Double-Crust Pie as directed. Line a 9-inch pie plate with half of the pastry.

2 For filling, in small saucepan heat orange juice to boiling. Add cranberries or cherries and apricots. Remove from heat and let stand 10 minutes or until fruit is softened; do not drain. In a large mixing bowl stir together sugar, flour, and orange peel. Add apples and the undrained fruit, then gently mix until coated. Transfer fruit mixture to the pastry-lined pie plate. Trim pastry to edge of pie plate. Cut slits in the top crust for steam to escape. Place top crust on filling. Seal and flute edge.

3 To prevent overbrowning, cover edge of pie with foil. Bake in a 375° oven for 25 minutes. Remove foil. Bake

for 25 to 30 minutes more or until top is golden. Cool pie on a wire rack before serving. Cover and refrigerate any leftovers and use within 2 days. Makes 8 servings.

Nutrition facts per serving: *442 calories, 4 g protein, 70 g carbohydrate, 18 g total fat (4 g saturated), 0 mg cholesterol, 138 mg sodium, 5 g fiber. Daily values: 9% vitamin A, 18% vitamin C, 1% calcium, 14% iron.*

Shortcut

Prepare pie as directed above, except use one 15-ounce package folded, refrigerated, unbaked piecrust (2 crusts) for the pastry. Let stand at room temperature according to package directions before fitting bottom crust into pie plate.

A good seal between the top and bottom crusts will prevent juices from boiling out of the pie. After trimming the top crust to about ½ inch beyond edge of the plate, lift the edge of the bottom crust away from the plate and fold the excess top crust under it to form a seal.

Scalloped edge: Make a large scallop by placing your thumb flat against outside edge of pastry and pressing dough around your thumb with thumb and index finger of your other hand on inside edge of pastry. Repeat around crust at 1- to 2-inch intervals. For a rickrack edge, hold your thumb on its side and make intervals closer together.

To prevent the edge from getting too brown, cover it with foil during the first half of baking. To make a foil frame, fold a 12-inch square of foil into quarters. Tear or cut out the center portion, creating an opening about 7 inches across. Unfold and loosely mold the foil rim over the edge of the pie.

To Make Ahead

Prepare and fill pastry as directed, except do not cut slits in top crust. Cover unbaked pie with inverted 10-inch paper plate. Seal in freezer bag, label, and freeze up to 4 months. To bake frozen pie, remove from bag, remove paper plate, and cut slits in top crust. Add foil to edge and bake at 450° for 15 minutes. Reduce oven temperature to 375° and bake 15 minutes more. Remove foil and bake about 30 minutes more.

French Berry-Apple Pie

½ **cup granulated sugar**
3 **tablespoons all-purpose flour**
¼ **teaspoon ground cinnamon**
3 **cups thinly sliced, peeled, cooking apples (about 1 pound)**
2 **cups fresh or frozen unsweetened blueberries or raspberries**
1 **tablespoon lemon juice**
1 **recipe Pastry for Single-Crust Pie (see page 224)**
1 **recipe Crumb Topping (at right)**

1 For filling, in a large bowl combine sugar, flour, and cinnamon. Add fruit and lemon juice, then gently toss until coated. (If using frozen berries, let mixture stand 15 to 30 minutes or until partially thawed but still icy.)

2 Prepare and roll out Pastry for Single-Crust Pie as directed. Line a 9-inch pie plate with pastry. Trim and flute edge of pastry. Do not prick shell. Transfer fruit mixture to unbaked pastry shell. Sprinkle Crumb Topping over fruit.

3 To prevent overbrowning, cover edge of pie with foil. Bake in a 375° oven 25 minutes (50 minutes if using frozen berries). Remove foil. Bake 25 to 30 minutes more or until golden. Cool pie on a wire rack before serving. Cover and refrigerate any leftovers and use within 2 days. Makes 8 servings.

Nutrition facts per serving: 380 calories, 4 g protein, 60 g carbohydrate, 15 g total fat (6 g saturated), 15 mg cholesterol, 131 mg sodium, 3 g fiber. Daily values: 5% vitamin A, 13% vitamin C, 1% calcium, 12% iron.

Crumb Topping

½ **cup rolled oats**
½ **cup all-purpose flour**
½ **cup packed brown sugar**
¼ **teaspoon ground nutmeg or cinnamon**
¼ **cup butter (no substitutes)**
¼ **cup chopped walnuts or pecans (optional)**

1 In a medium mixing bowl combine rolled oats, flour, brown sugar, and nutmeg. Using a pastry blender or two forks, cut in butter until crumbly. If desired, stir in walnuts.

2 Spoon topping over pie filling and bake as directed in recipes.

Baker's Bonus

Foolproof Pastry

Make sure your pastry turns out perfectly every time. Read these tips and you'll be ready to roll.

◆ *Measure ingredients accurately. Too much flour makes pastry tough, too much shortening makes it crumbly, and too much water makes it tough and soggy.*

◆ *Stir together flour and salt. Cut in the shortening until the mixture resembles small peas.*

◆ *Add water gradually to the flour mixture, and toss it together just until evenly moistened.*

◆ *Use a prepared surface for rolling out dough to avoid sticking. Use as little flour as possible to avoid toughening pastry, and roll to an even thickness.*

◆ *Don't stretch the pastry when transferring it to the pie plate. Use a glass pie plate or dull metal pie pan so the pastry browns evenly.*

◆ *If pastry is for a double-crust pie, trim edge of bottom pastry after you add filling so it doesn't pull pastry down into pie plate. If pastry is to be prebaked without filling, lightly press pastry into pan so that there are no air pockets under crust; prick it with a fork to prevent it from puffing up.*

◆ *Patch any cracks with a pastry scrap before adding the filling.*

◆ *Check that the oven temperature is accurate. If it is too low, the bottom crust will be soggy.*

◆ *After baking, cool the pie on a wire rack. Allowing air to circulate under the pie keeps the crust from becoming soggy.*

Triple Berry Pie

Triple the flavor with three kinds of berries.

⅔ **cup granulated sugar**
⅓ **cup all-purpose flour**
2 **cups sliced fresh or frozen unsweetened strawberries**
2 **cups fresh or frozen unsweetened blueberries**
1 **cup fresh or frozen unsweetened raspberries**
1 **tablespoon lemon juice**
1 **recipe Pastry for Double-Crust Pie (see page 224)**

1 For filling, in a large mixing bowl stir together sugar and flour. Add berries and lemon juice, then gently toss until coated. (If using frozen fruit, let the mixture stand for 15 to 30 minutes or until fruit is partially thawed but still icy.)

2 Prepare and roll out Pastry for a Double-Crust pie as directed. Line a 9-inch pie plate with half of the pastry. Transfer berry mixture to the pastry-lined pie plate. Trim bottom pastry to edge of pie plate. Cut slits in the top crust for steam to escape. Place top crust on filling. Seal and flute edge.

3 To prevent overbrowning, cover edge of pie with foil. Bake in 375° oven for 25 minutes (50 minutes if using frozen fruit). Remove foil. Bake 25 to 30 minutes more or until golden. Cool pie on a wire rack. Cover and refrigerate any leftovers. Makes 8 servings.

Nutrition facts per serving: 377 calories, 4 g protein, 52 g carbohydrate, 18 g total fat (4 g saturated), 0 mg cholesterol, 137 mg sodium, 3 g fiber. Daily values: 0% vitamin A, 50% vitamin C, 1% calcium, 12% iron.

To Make Ahead

If fresh berries are available, prepare and fill pastry as directed, except do not cut slits in top crust. Cover unbaked pie with inverted 10-inch paper plate. Seal in freezer bag, label, and freeze up to 4 months. To bake frozen pie, remove from bag, remove paper plate, and cut slits in top crust. Add foil to edge and bake at 450° for 15 minutes. Reduce oven temperature to 375°; bake 15 minutes. Remove foil; bake 30 minutes more or until golden.

Banana Streusel Pie

1 **recipe Pastry for Single-Crust Pie (see page 224)**
4 **cups sliced ripe bananas**
½ **cup unsweetened pineapple juice**
1½ **teaspoons finely shredded lemon peel**
2 **tablespoons lemon juice**
¼ **cup granulated sugar**
½ **teaspoon ground cinnamon**
1 **teaspoon cornstarch**
½ **cup all-purpose flour**
½ **cup packed brown sugar**
⅓ **cup chopped macadamia nuts or almonds**
1 **teaspoon ground cinnamon**
¼ **cup butter (no substitutes)**

1 Prepare and roll out Pastry for Single-Crust Pie as directed. Line a 9-inch pie plate with pastry. Trim and flute edge. Do not prick shell. Line pastry with a double thickness of foil. Bake in a 450° oven for 8 minutes. Remove the foil. Bake for 4 to 6 minutes more or until pastry is set and dry. Remove from oven. Reduce oven temperature to 375°.

2 In a medium bowl gently toss together bananas, pineapple juice, and lemon juice. Drain, reserving juices. Add lemon peel, granulated sugar, and the ½ teaspoon cinnamon to the bananas; gently toss. Transfer fruit mixture to warm pastry shell.

3 In a saucepan combine reserved juices and cornstarch. Cook and stir over medium heat until thickened and bubbly. Pour over banana mixture.

4 For streusel, combine flour, brown sugar, macadamia nuts, and the 1 teaspoon cinnamon. Cut in butter until mixture resembles coarse crumbs. Sprinkle over banana mixture.

5 Cover edge of pie with foil. Bake in a 375° oven 40 minutes or until topping is golden and edges are bubbly. Cool on a wire rack. Cover and refrigerate any leftovers. Makes 8 servings.

Nutrition facts per serving: 410 calories, 4 g protein, 60 g carbohydrate, 19 g total fat (6 g saturated), 15 mg cholesterol, 132 mg sodium, 2 g fiber. Daily values: 5% vitamin A, 17% vitamin C, 2% calcium, 13% iron.

Banana Streusel Pie

*Triple
Berry Pie*

Peach Melba Pie

Crystallized ginger adds extra flavor to this peach-raspberry classic.

⅓ **cup granulated sugar**
⅓ **cup all-purpose flour**
1 **tablespoon finely chopped crystallized ginger or**
 ¼ **teaspoon ground ginger**
3 **cups thinly sliced, peeled peaches or frozen unsweetened peach slices**
1 **10-ounce package frozen sweetened raspberries, thawed but not drained**
1 **recipe Pastry for Double-Crust Pie (see page 224)**
 Vanilla ice cream (optional)

1 For filling, in large mixing bowl stir together sugar, flour, and ginger. Add peaches and raspberries with their syrup, then gently toss until coated. (If using frozen peaches, let mixture stand 15 to 30 minutes or until peaches are partially thawed but still icy.)

2 Prepare and roll out Pastry for Double-Crust Pie as directed. Line a 9-inch pie plate with half of the pastry.

3 Transfer fruit mixture to the pastry-lined pie plate. Trim bottom pastry to edge of pie plate. Cut slits in the top crust. Place top crust on filling. Seal and flute edge. Place pie plate on baking sheet to catch any spills.

4 To prevent overbrowning, cover edge of pie with foil. Bake in a 375° oven for 25 minutes (50 minutes if using frozen fruit). Remove foil. Bake for 25 to 30 minutes more or until top is golden. Cool pie on a wire rack. If desired, serve warm with ice cream. Cover and refrigerate any leftovers. Makes 8 servings.

Nutrition facts per serving: *373 calories, 4 g protein, 51 g carbohydrate, 18 g total fat (4 g saturated), 0 mg cholesterol, 135 mg sodium, 3 g fiber. Daily values: 3% vitamin A, 16% vitamin C, 1% calcium, 12% iron.*

Peach Melba Streusel Pie: Prepare Peach Melba Pie as directed, except use Pastry for Single-Crust Pie (see page 224). Top fruit mixture with Crumb Topping (see page 229). Bake as directed.

Almond-Glazed Cherry Pie

For a traditional cherry pie, omit the Almond Glaze and before baking, lightly brush the top crust with milk and sprinkle with granulated sugar. (Pictured on page 222.)

1 **to 1¼ cups granulated sugar**
⅓ **cup all-purpose flour**
5 **cups fresh stemmed cherries, pitted, or 20 ounces frozen, unsweetened, pitted, tart red cherries**
¼ **teaspoon almond extract**
1 **recipe Pastry for Lattice-Top Pie (see page 224)**
 Almond Glaze
 Vanilla ice cream (optional)

1 In a large bowl combine sugar and flour. Add cherries and almond extract; gently toss until coated. (If using frozen cherries, let mixture stand 15 to 30 minutes or until cherries are partially thawed but still icy.)

2 Prepare and roll out Pastry for Lattice-Top Pie as directed, except after rolling out top crust, cut eight 1-inch strips. Cut leaf shapes from remaining pastry. Line a 9-inch pie plate with half of the pastry. Stir cherry mixture and transfer to pastry-lined pie plate. Trim bottom pastry to edge of pie plate. Using 4 of the 1-inch pastry strips, form a square close to edge. Repeat with 4 more strips, forming a smaller square. Place the pastry leaves in corners of squares atop pie. Fold bottom pastry over ends of strips; seal and flute edge.

3 Cover edge of pie with foil. Bake in a 375° oven 25 minutes for fresh cherries (50 minutes for frozen cherries). Remove foil. Bake 25 to 35 minutes or until golden. Pour Almond Glaze over hot pie. Cool on a wire rack. If desired, serve with ice cream. Serves 8.

Almond Glaze: In a saucepan combine 3 tablespoons brown sugar and 2 tablespoons half-and-half or light cream. Cook and stir over low heat until sugar melts (mixture may appear slightly curdled). Stir in ¼ cup chopped toasted almonds.

Nutrition facts per serving: *458 calories, 5 g protein, 67 g carbohydrate, 20 g total fat (5 g saturated), 1 mg cholesterol, 140 mg sodium, 2 g fiber. Daily values: 12% vitamin A, 16% vitamin C, 3% calcium, 14% iron.*

To Make Ahead

Prepare and fill pastry as directed. Cover unbaked pie with inverted 10-inch paper plate. Seal in a freezer bag, label, and freeze up to 4 months. To bake frozen pie, remove from bag and remove paper plate. Add foil to edge and bake at 450° for 15 minutes. Reduce oven temperature to 375° and bake 15 minutes more. Remove foil and bake about 30 minutes more or until the top is golden. Add the glaze as directed.

Peach Crunch Pie

½ **to ⅔ cup granulated sugar**
3 **tablespoons all-purpose flour**
¼ **teaspoon ground cinnamon**
¼ **teaspoon ground nutmeg**
6 **cups thinly sliced, peeled peaches or frozen unsweetened peach slices**
1 **recipe Pastry for Double-Crust Pie (see page 224)**
¼ **cup packed brown sugar**
2 **tablespoons butter (no substitutes)**
1 **tablespoon water**
1 **teaspoon cornstarch**
½ **cup chopped pecans**

1 For filling, in large mixing bowl stir together sugar, flour, cinnamon, and nutmeg. Add peaches, then gently toss until coated. (If using frozen fruit, let mixture stand 15 to 30 minutes or until partially thawed but still icy.)

2 Prepare and roll out Pastry for Double-Crust Pie as directed. Line a 9-inch pie plate with half of the pastry.

3 Transfer peach mixture to the pastry-lined pie plate. Trim bottom pastry to edge of pie plate. Cut slits in the top crust. Place top crust on filling. Seal and flute edge.

4 To prevent overbrowning, cover edge of pie with foil. Bake in a 375° oven for 25 minutes (50 minutes if using frozen fruit). Remove foil. Bake 25 to 30 minutes more or until golden.

5 Meanwhile, for pecan topping, in small saucepan combine brown sugar, butter, water, and cornstarch until mixed. Cook and stir over medium heat until mixture boils. Stir in pecans. Spread warm pecan mixture over hot crust. Bake for 5 minutes more. Cool pie on a wire rack. Cover and refrigerate any leftovers. Makes 8 servings.

Nutrition facts per serving: *466 calories, 5 g protein, 59 g carbohydrate, 25 g total fat (6 g saturated), 8 mg cholesterol, 166 mg sodium, 3 g fiber. Daily values: 9% vitamin A, 14% vitamin C, 1% calcium, 12% iron.*

Peach-Pear Crunch Pie: Prepare Peach Crunch Pie as directed, except substitute 3 cups sliced pears for 3 cups of the peaches.

Peach Pie: Prepare the Peach Crunch Pie as directed, except omit the pecan topping.

To Make Ahead

Prepare and fill pastry as directed, except do not cut slits in top crust. Cover unbaked pie with inverted 10-inch paper plate. Seal in freezer bag, label, and freeze up to 4 months. To bake frozen pie, remove from bag, remove paper plate, and cut slits in top crust. Add foil to edge and bake at 450° for 15 minutes. Reduce oven temperature to 375° and bake 15 minutes more. Remove foil and bake about 25 minutes more or until golden. Prepare pecan topping and spread over pie. Bake 5 minutes more.

Pick a Plate

You need to use standard glass or dull metal pie plates if you want your pie as nicely browned on the bottom as it is on the top. Shiny metal pie pans—which do work just fine for crumb-crust pies—can cause the bottom pastry crust to turn out soggy.

Check the size of ceramic or pottery pie plates; they may not be standard. (A standard-size plate holds about 3¾ cups liquid.) You may need to adjust the amount of filling and the baking time.

Disposable foil pie pans usually are smaller than standard pie plates, although foil deep-dish pie pans are closer to the norm.

Fresh Pineapple Pie

Fresh Pineapple Pie

1 recipe Pastry for Double-Crust
    Pie (see page 224)
⅔ cup granulated sugar
¼ cup all-purpose flour
4 cups peeled, cored, cubed,
    fresh pineapple
    (about 1½ medium
    pineapples)
½ cup snipped dried apricots
⅓ cup chopped macadamia nuts
    or almonds
2 tablespoons rum or
    ½ teaspoon rum flavoring
    plus 2 tablespoons water
1 teaspoon granulated sugar
⅛ teaspoon ground cinnamon
1 tablespoon milk

1 Prepare and roll out Pastry for Double-Crust Pie as directed. Line a 9-inch pie plate with half of the pastry.

2 For filling, combine ⅔ cup sugar and the flour. Add pineapple, apricots, nuts, and rum, then gently toss until coated. Transfer fruit mixture to the pastry-lined pie plate. Trim bottom pastry to edge of pie plate. Cut slits in the top crust. Place top crust on filling. Seal and flute edge.

3 Combine 1 teaspoon sugar and the cinnamon. Brush top crust with milk. Sprinkle with sugar-cinnamon.

4 Cover edge of pie with foil. Bake in a 375° oven 25 minutes. Remove foil. Bake 20 to 25 minutes more or until golden. Cool pie on a wire rack. Cover and refrigerate any leftovers. Makes 8 servings.

Nutrition facts per serving: *446 calories, 4 g protein, 58 g carbohydrate, 22 g total fat (5 g saturated), 0 mg cholesterol, 151 mg sodium, 2 g fiber. Daily values: 9% vitamin A, 21% vitamin C, 1% calcium, 15% iron.*

Creamy Rhubarb Pie

4 cups fresh or frozen
    unsweetened sliced rhubarb
1 recipe Pastry for Single-Crust
    Pie (see page 224)
2 eggs, beaten
1 8-ounce carton vanilla yogurt
1 cup granulated sugar
3 tablespoons all-purpose flour
¼ teaspoon ground nutmeg or
    cinnamon
⅓ cup all-purpose flour
⅓ cup packed brown sugar
2 tablespoons butter
    (no substitutes)
¼ cup chopped pecans

1 Thaw rhubarb, if frozen, but do not drain.

2 Prepare and roll out Pastry for Single-Crust Pie as directed. Line a 9-inch pie plate with pastry. Trim and flute edge of pastry. Do not prick shell.

3 For filling, combine eggs, yogurt, sugar, 3 tablespoons flour, and nutmeg. Add rhubarb (and juice, if thawed), then gently toss until coated.

Transfer to pastry shell. Combine ⅓ cup flour and brown sugar. Cut in butter until crumbly. Stir in pecans. Sprinkle crumb mixture on top of pie.

4 Cover edge of pie with foil. Bake in a 375° oven 25 minutes. Remove foil. Bake 25 to 30 minutes more or until pie appears nearly set in center when gently shaken. Cool on a wire rack. Refrigerate within 2 hours; cover for longer storage. Makes 8 servings.

Nutrition facts per serving: *398 calories, 6 g protein, 60 g carbohydrate, 16 g total fat (5 g saturated), 62 mg cholesterol, 134 mg sodium, 2 g fiber. Daily values: 6% vitamin A, 8% vitamin C, 9% calcium, 11% iron.*

Freezing Point

Get a head start on your next pastry project. Prepare your pastry as directed, but do not roll it out. Instead, flatten it into a patty; place in a freezer bag and freeze up to 2 months. When you're ready to use it, thaw it overnight in refrigerator.

You also can roll pastry out and fit it into a pie plate or tart pans. Place pastry in a freezer bag and freeze as above. Frozen pastry shells can be baked without thawing, but you may need to add 5 or 10 minutes to the baking time.

Juicy Fruits

Fruit pies are in season all year since you can use fresh or frozen, unsweetened fruit to make one. Take advantage of packaged frozen fruit that comes already peeled, sliced, or pitted. Or, freeze your own fruit when it's in season.

The easiest way is freeze fresh fruit is to dry-pack prepared fruit in a freezer container, adding no sugar or liquid. This method works best with berries (allow 1½ to 2½ pounds per quart) that need be only washed and dried prior to freezing.

No matter if you're using fresh or frozen fruit, follow this chart to make your own fruit fillings for a 9-inch double-crust fruit pie. First prepare Pastry for Double-Crust Pie (see page 224). Then stir together the sugar and flour in a large mixing bowl. If desired, stir in ½ teaspoon finely shredded lemon peel, ¼ to ½ teaspoon ground cinnamon, ¼ teaspoon ground allspice or ginger, or ⅛ teaspoon ground nutmeg. Then add the fruit and toss until coated. (If using frozen fruit, let the mixture stand for 15 to 30 minutes or until fruit is partially thawed but still icy.) Transfer fruit to pastry in pie plate and continue as directed in pastry recipe. Cover edge of pie with foil. Bake in a 375° oven for 25 minutes for fresh fruit (50 minutes for frozen). Remove the foil. Bake for 25 to 30 minutes more or until the top is golden and the fruit is tender.

Fresh or Frozen Fruit	Amount of Fruit	Granulated Sugar	All-Purpose Flour
Apples; peeled, cored and thinly sliced	6 cups	½ to ¾ cup	1 tablespoon
Apricots; pitted and sliced	4 cups	1¼ cups	⅓ cup
Blackberries	4 cups	¾ to 1 cup	¼ cup
Blueberries	4 cups	½ to ¾ cup	3 tablespoons
Cherries, tart red; pitted	4 cups	1 to 1¼ cups	¼ cup
Gooseberries; stemmed	4 cups	1 cup	¼ cup
Nectarines; pitted and thinly sliced	6 cups	½ to ¾ cup	3 tablespoons
Peaches; peeled, pitted, and thinly sliced	6 cups	⅓ to ½ cup	¼ cup
Pears; peeled, cored, and thinly sliced	6 cups	⅓ to ½ cup	¼ cup
Raspberries	5 cups	½ to ¾ cup	3 tablespoons
Rhubarb; cut into 1-inch pieces	4 cups	1 cup	¼ cup

Ruby Raspberry Pie

1 **recipe Pastry for Lattice-Top Pie (see page 225)**
¾ **to 1 cup granulated sugar**
⅓ **cup all-purpose flour**
3 **cups fresh or frozen unsweetened sliced rhubarb**
3 **cups fresh raspberries or one 12-ounce package frozen loose-pack lightly sweetened raspberries, thawed**
1 **teaspoon almond extract**

1 For filling, combine sugar and flour. Add fruit and almond extract; gently toss until coated. (If using frozen fruit, let mixture stand 15 to 30 minutes or until partially thawed but still icy.)

2 Prepare and roll out Pastry for Latice-Top Pie as directed. Line a 9-inch pie plate with half of the pastry. Transfer fruit mixture to the pastry-lined pie plate. Trim bottom pastry to ½ inch beyond edge of pie plate. Top with a lattice crust. Seal and flute edge.

3 Cover edge of pie with foil. Bake in a 375° oven for 25 minutes. Remove foil. Bake 25 to 30 minutes more or until golden. Cool on a wire rack. Cover and refrigerate any leftovers. Makes 8 servings.

Nutrition facts per serving: 380 calories, 4 g protein, 52 g carbohydrate, 18 g total fat (4 g saturated fat), 0 mg cholesterol, 136 mg sodium, 4 g fiber. Daily values: 1% vitamin A, 25% vitamin C, 4% calcium, 12% iron.

To Make Ahead

If fresh rhubarb and raspberries are available, prepare and fill pastry as directed. Cover unbaked pie with inverted 10-inch paper plate. Place in freezer bag and freeze up to 4 months. To bake frozen pie, remove from bag and remove paper plate. Add foil to edge and bake at 450° for 15 minutes. Reduce oven temperature to 375° and bake 15 minutes more. Remove foil and bake about 30 minutes more.

Using a pastry cutter or knife, cut the top pastry into ¹/₂- to ³/₄-inch-wide strips. Start lattice with the two longest strips crosswise to each other in the center of the filling. Add strips on each side of the center strips about ¹/₂ inch apart. Fold every other strip back as necessary to make a woven top. Repeat until there are 5 to 7 strips in each direction.

Raisin-Nectarine Pie

1 **recipe Pastry for Double-Crust Pie (see page 224)**
²/₃ **cup packed brown sugar**

¹/₄ **cup all-purpose flour**
3 **cups thinly sliced nectarines or peeled peaches (about 1 pound)**
1 **cup raisins**
¹/₄ **teaspoon maple flavoring**
2 **teaspoons granulated sugar Pecan or vanilla ice cream (optional)**

1 Prepare and roll out Pastry for Double-Crust Pie as directed. Line a 9-inch pie plate with half of the pastry.

2 For filling, combine brown sugar and flour. Add nectarines, raisins, and maple flavoring, then gently toss until coated. Transfer fruit mixture to the pastry-lined pie plate. Trim bottom pastry to edge of pie plate. Cut slits in the top crust for steam to escape. Place top crust on filling. Seal and flute edge. Sprinkle top of pie with sugar.

3 Cover edge of pie with foil. Bake in a 375° oven 25 minutes. Remove foil. Bake 25 to 30 minutes more or until golden. Cool on a wire rack. If desired, serve warm with ice cream. Cover; refrigerate any leftovers. Serves 8.
   Nutrition facts per serving: *408 calories, 4 g protein, 60 g carbohydrate, 18 g total fat (4 g saturated), 0 mg cholesterol, 141 mg sodium, 2 g fiber. Daily values: 3% vitamin A, 5% vitamin C, 2% calcium, 15% iron.*

To Make Ahead

Prepare and fill pastry as directed, except do not cut slits in top crust. Cover unbaked pie with inverted 10-inch paper plate. Place in a freezer bag and freeze up to 4 months. To bake frozen pie, remove from bag, remove paper plate, and cut slits in top crust. Add foil to edge and bake at 450° for 15 minutes. Reduce oven temperature to 375° and bake 15 minutes more. Remove foil and bake 30 minutes more or until golden.

Rope-shaped edge: Crimp around the pie's edge by pinching it diagonally. When pinching, push forward on a slant with your index finger bent and pull back slightly with your thumb.

For a glossy crust use a soft basting brush to apply an even coating of milk, water, or cream. For extra crunch, also sprinkle with sugar or a mixture of sugar and cinnamon or nutmeg.

Turning a Crust

The mysterious thing about homemade pies is that they look more difficult to make than they really are. And so they should! Keep the mystery alive by adding some new twists to the traditional crimped pie shell and by infusing perpetually plain pastries with flavor. Pair pinwheels, leaves, ropes, and braids with spices, chocolate, nuts, cheese, and coconut to create pie sensations that will have guests begging for the recipes. (Pastry recipes are on page 224.)

Combining crumb topping and traditional pastry in a French Berry-Apple Pie (see page 229) makes for great textures and taste. Prepare pie as directed, except prepare Pastry for Double-Crust Pie. After adding the crumb topping, roll top crust to ⅛ inch thickness, and cut it into leaf shapes. Brush edge of crust with water. Arrange leaves around edge and partially over topping, moistening pastry where leaves overlap. Bake as directed.

For Autumn Blush Tarts, prepare two quantities of Autumn Blush Pie filling (see page 228). Use four 3- to 4-inch tart pans. Roll pastry circles 4 inches larger than pans; fold up over filling. Bake in a 375° oven 35 minutes or till fruit is tender.

Put a spin on a lattice top by twisting whole wheat pastry strips into a breezy pinwheel. To top this Raisin-Nectarine Pie (see page 237), prepare Whole Wheat Pastry for Double-Crust Pie. After rolling out the top crust, cut it into ½-inch-wide strips. Twist strips and form a pinwheel atop pie.

Great-Grandma Kleespie would have approved of giving her Butterscotch Pie (see page 244) a chocolate crust with an updated edge. Prepare Chocolate Pastry for a Single-Crust Pie. After filling pastry, snip the edge on a diagonal, making cuts about ½ inch deep and at ½ inch intervals.

Double the flavor in your next pumpkin pie—bake it in a spiced crust and top it with a spicy stencil. Prepare Almond-Crunch Pumpkin Pie (see page 243) and Spice Pastry for a Double-Crust Pie as directed. Braid extra pastry for edge.

Chocolate and pistachio flavors definitely go together, especially when it's a Milk-Chocolate Cream Pie (see page 246) in a pistachio-nut crust. Prepare pie as directed, except use Nut Pastry for a Single-Crust Pie.

Pear Dumplings (see page 257) become tropical when wrapped in a coconut pastry. Prepare Coconut Pastry for a Double-Crust Pie. Roll two-thirds of the pastry into a 14-inch square; cover pears as directed in recipe. Roll remaining pastry to 1/8 inch thickness; cut into leaf shapes. Moisten and place atop pears.

Lattice-topped pies look spectacular. Use two flavors of pastry to make sure yours taste spectacular, too. Peach Melba Pie (see page 232) goes well with plain and chocolate pastry.

Custard's Best Stand

The best custard pies are smooth and velvety. They may look difficult, but they are easy as pie.

When you have mixed the filling, put the prepared pastry shell on the oven rack, then add the custard filling. This eliminates the chance you might spill between the counter and oven.

A custard pie is done if the liquid area in the center of the pie is smaller than a quarter when you gently shake the pie. (The filling continues to set after you remove the pie from the oven.) Or, insert a knife near the pie's center. If the knife comes out clean, the pie is done. The knife test may cause the filling to crack, however, so the first test is preferable.

After the pie cools, cover and refrigerate it until serving time. Cover and chill any leftovers, too.

Notes

Pecan Pie

Shelled pecans will keep in an airtight container in the refrigerator up to 1 year and in the freezer at least 2 years. Bring to room temperature before using them in this pie.

1 **recipe Pastry for Single-Crust Pie (see page 224)**
3 **eggs, beaten**
1 **cup corn syrup**
½ **cup granulated sugar**
2 **tablespoons butter or margarine, melted**
1 **tablespoon finely shredded orange peel (optional)**
1¼ **cups pecan halves**

1 Prepare and roll out Pastry for Single-Crust Pie as directed. Line a 9-inch pie plate with pastry. Trim and flute edge of pastry. Do not prick shell.

2 For filling, in a medium bowl stir together the eggs, corn syrup, sugar, butter, and orange peel (if desired). Mix well. Stir in pecan halves.

3 Place the pastry shell on the oven rack. Carefully pour the filling into the pastry shell. To prevent overbrowning, cover edge of pie with foil. Bake in a 350° oven for 25 minutes. Remove foil. Bake 20 to 25 minutes more or until a knife inserted near center comes out clean. Cool on a wire rack before serving. Refrigerate within 2 hours; cover for longer storage. Makes 8 servings.

Nutrition facts per serving: 482 calories, 6 g protein, 63 g carbohydrate, 25 g total fat (5 g saturated), 88 mg cholesterol, 148 mg sodium, 2 g fiber. Daily values: 6% vitamin A, 2% vitamin C, 2% calcium, 11% iron.

Choco-Peanut Butter Pie

1 **recipe Pastry for Single-Crust Pie (see page 224)**
½ **cup semisweet chocolate pieces**
3 **eggs**
1 **cup light corn syrup**
½ **cup granulated sugar**
⅓ **cup chunky-style peanut butter**
½ **teaspoon vanilla**
Whipped cream (optional)
Semisweet chocolate pieces (optional)
Chopped peanuts (optional)

1 Prepare and roll out Pastry for Single-Crust Pie as directed. Line a 9-inch pie plate with pastry. Trim and flute edge of pastry. Do not prick shell. Sprinkle evenly with chocolate pieces.

2 For filling, stir together eggs, syrup, sugar, peanut butter, and vanilla. Pour over chocolate pieces in pastry shell.

3 To prevent overbrowning, cover edge of pie with foil. Bake in a 375° oven for 20 minutes. Remove foil. Bake for 15 to 20 minutes more or until a knife inserted near the center comes out clean.

4 Cool on a wire rack before serving. Refrigerate within 2 hours; add cover for longer storage. If desired, garnish with whipped topping, chocolate pieces, and peanuts. Makes 8 servings.

Nutrition facts per serving: *449 calories, 7 g protein, 67 g carbohydrate, 18 g total fat (4 g saturated), 80 mg cholesterol, 178 mg sodium, 1 g fiber. Daily values: 3% vitamin A, 0% vitamin C, 4% calcium, 21% iron.*

Almond-Crunch Pumpkin Pie

Instead of measuring individual spices you can use 1½ teaspoons pumpkin pie spice in the pumpkin layer that covers the rich praline bottom.
(Pictured on page 240.)

1 **recipe Pastry for Single-Crust Pie (see page 224)**
¼ **cup finely chopped almonds or pecans**
¼ **cup packed brown sugar**
2 **tablespoons butter (no substitutes), softened**
1 **teaspoon finely shredded orange peel**
2 **eggs, beaten**
1 **16-ounce can (1¾ cups) pumpkin**
¾ **cup packed brown sugar**
1 **tablespoon all-purpose flour**
1 **teaspoon ground cinnamon**
½ **teaspoon ground nutmeg**
¼ **teaspoon ground ginger**
1 **12-ounce can (1½ cups) evaporated milk or 1½ cups half-and-half or light cream**
Whipped cream (optional)

1 Prepare and roll out Pastry for Single-Crust Pie as directed. Line a 9-inch pie plate with pastry. Trim and flute edge of pastry. Do not prick shell. Line pastry with a double thickness of foil. Bake pastry shell in a 450° oven for 8 minutes. Remove foil.

2 For praline layer, in a small mixing bowl stir together almonds, ¼ cup brown sugar, butter, and orange peel. Spoon mixture into the hot, partially baked pastry shell, spreading it over the bottom as butter melts. Bake for 5 to 6 minutes more or until shell is set and dry and praline is bubbly.

3 For filling, combine eggs, pumpkin, ¾ cup brown sugar, flour, cinnamon, nutmeg, and ginger. Gradually stir in the evaporated milk. Mix well.

4 Reduce oven temperature to 375°. Place partially baked pastry shell on the oven rack. Pour pumpkin filling into the pastry shell. To prevent over-browning, cover edge of pie with foil. Bake 25 minutes. Remove foil. Bake 20 to 25 minutes more or until a knife inserted near center comes out clean.

5 Cool on a wire rack before serving. Refrigerate within 2 hours; add cover for longer storage. If desired, serve with whipped cream. Serves 8.

Nutrition facts per serving: *373 calories, 8 g protein, 47 g carbohydrate, 19 g total fat (7 g saturated), 73 mg cholesterol, 167 mg sodium, 2 g fiber. Daily values: 133% vitamin A, 6% vitamin C, 13% calcium, 17% iron.*

Cutout edge: Roll the pastry for single-crust pie or for a top crust slightly larger than usual. Trim as directed and fold under edge of pastry to make it smooth. Roll pastry scraps very thin. Use a canapé cutter or a knife to cut the scraps into desired shapes. Brush the pastry edge with water. Arrange the cutouts on the edge and press lightly to secure.

To test for doneness, insert a knife about ½ inch deep near the center of the baked pie. The knife should come out clean with no soft custardlike mixture clinging to it.

Butterscotch Pie

This was my Grandpa's favorite pie as a boy growing up in Zearing, Iowa. And once I tasted it, it went to the top of my list.
—Lisa Mannes—

**1 recipe Baked Pastry Shell
     (see page 224)
1 cup packed brown sugar
¼ cup cornstarch
3 egg yolks
¼ teaspoon salt
2 cups hot milk
1 teaspoon butter
     (no substitutes)
½ teaspoon maple flavoring
1 recipe Meringue for Pie
     (see page 246)**

1 Prepare and bake pastry shell as directed; set aside.

2 For filling, in a small mixing bowl stir together the brown sugar and cornstarch. Set aside.

3 In the top of a double broiler stir together the egg yolks and salt. Gradually stir in the milk until smooth. Stir in the brown sugar mixture. Cook and stir over, not touching, boiling water until thick and smooth (6 to 10 minutes). Add butter and stir until melted. Remove from heat. Add maple flavoring.

4 Prepare Meringue for Pie as directed. Pour hot filling into baked pastry shell. Evenly spread meringue over filling, carefully sealing to edge of pastry to prevent shrinkage. Bake in a 350° oven for 15 minutes. Cool pie on a wire rack for 1 hour. Chill for 4 hours before serving; add cover for longer storage. Makes 8 servings.

Nutrition facts per serving: 361 calories, 6 g protein, 57 g carbohydrate, 12 g total fat (4 g saturated), 86 mg cholesterol, 204 mg sodium, 1 g fiber. Daily values: 16% vitamin A, 0% vitamin C, 9% calcium, 10% iron.

Caramel-Chocolate Pecan Pie

Creamy cheesecake tops the rich, chocolate-caramel layer.

**1 recipe Pastry for Single-Crust
     Pie (see page 224)
1 cup pecan pieces
1 6-ounce package semisweet
     chocolate pieces (1 cup)
½ cup caramel ice-cream topping
1 8-ounce package cream cheese,
     softened
1 8-ounce carton dairy sour
     cream
½ cup granulated sugar
1 teaspoon vanilla
3 eggs
   Whipped cream (optional)
   Unsweetened cocoa powder
     (optional)
   Pecan halves (optional)**

1 Prepare and roll out Pastry for Single-Crust Pie as directed. Line a 9-inch pie plate with pastry. Trim and flute edge of pastry. Do not prick shell.

2 For chocolate-caramel layer, sprinkle pecans and chocolate pieces evenly in unbaked pastry shell; drizzle with caramel topping. Set aside.

3 For cheesecake layer, in a medium mixing bowl beat cream cheese, sour cream, sugar, and vanilla with an electric mixer on low until smooth. Add eggs, beating just until combined.

4 Pour cheesecake layer over chocolate-caramel layer in pastry shell. To prevent overbrowning, cover edge with foil. Bake in a 350° oven 20 minutes. Remove foil; bake 20 to 25 minutes more or until center appears set.

5 Cool pie on a wire rack 2 hours. Chill for 1 hour before serving; add cover for longer storage. If desired, pipe or dollop with whipped cream, sprinkle with cocoa powder, and add pecan halves. Refrigerate any leftovers. Makes 8 to 10 servings.

Nutrition facts per serving: 621 calories, 10 g protein, 59 g carbohydrate, 42 g total fat (14 g saturated), 124 mg cholesterol, 263 mg sodium, 1 g fiber. Daily values: 23% vitamin A, 0% vitamin C, 7% calcium, 15% iron.

Butterscotch Pie, top, and Caramel-Chocolate Pecan Pie, bottom

Sticky Job

There's no doubt that storing a meringue-topped cream pie is a sticky matter. First, let it cool for 1 hour, then refrigerate. Chill it for 3 to 6 hours before serving. (There's no need to cover the pie unless you're going to store it longer.)

If you need to cover a meringue-topped pie, insert wooden toothpicks halfway between the centers and edges of the pie and loosely drape them with clear plastic wrap. Be sure to dip your knife into water before cutting the pie into pieces.

Vanilla Cream Pie

If you prefer whipped cream covered pies, omit the meringue and cover and chill the filled pie shell, then top it with whipped cream before serving.

- 1 **recipe Baked Pastry Shell (see page 224)**
- ¾ **cup granulated sugar**
- ¼ **cup cornstarch or ½ cup all-purpose flour**
- 3 **cups milk**
- 4 **beaten egg yolks**
- 1 **tablespoon butter or margarine**
- 1½ **teaspoons vanilla**
- 1 **recipe Four-Egg-White Meringue (see page 247)**

1 Prepare and bake pastry shell as directed; set aside.

2 For filling, in a medium saucepan combine sugar and cornstarch. Gradually stir in milk. Cook and stir over medium heat until thickened and bubbly. Reduce heat; cook and stir 2 minutes more. Remove from heat.

3 Gradually stir about 1 cup hot filling into beaten egg yolks. Return egg yolk mixture to filling in saucepan. Bring to a gentle boil. Cook and stir 2 minutes more; remove from heat. Stir in butter and vanilla. Set filling aside.

4 Prepare Four-Egg-White Meringue as directed. Pour hot filling into baked pastry shell. Evenly spread meringue over hot filling, carefully sealing to edge of pastry. Bake in a 325° oven 25 minutes. Cool on a wire rack 1 hour. Chill 3 to 6 hours before serving; add cover for longer storage. Serves 8.

Nutrition facts per serving: *378 calories, 8 g protein, 54 g carbohydrate, 14 g total fat (5 g saturated), 117 mg cholesterol, 159 mg sodium, 1 g fiber. Daily values: 23% vitamin A, 1% vitamin C, 10% calcium, 8% iron.*

Banana Cream Pie: Prepare Vanilla Cream Pie as directed, except before adding filling, arrange 3 medium bananas, sliced (about 2¼ cups), over the bottom of the Baked Pastry Shell.

Milk-Chocolate Cream Pie: Prepare Vanilla Cream Pie as directed, except stir in 3 ounces semisweet chocolate, chopped, with the milk.

Shortcut

Prepare pie as directed, except use half of a 15-ounce package folded, refrigerated, unbaked piecrust (1 crust) for pastry. Let stand at room temperature according to package directions before fitting into pie plate. Bake as directed.

Using a spatula or the back of a spoon, spread the meringue over hot filling. Carefully push meringue to the edge of the crust to help prevent shrinkage.

Meringue For Pie

- 3 **egg whites**
- ½ **teaspoon vanilla**
- ¼ **teaspoon cream of tartar**
- 6 **tablespoons granulated sugar**

1 In a large mixing bowl let egg whites stand at room temperature for 30 minutes.

2 Add vanilla and cream of tartar to egg whites. Beat with an electric mixer on medium to high speed 1 minute or until soft peaks form (tips curl).

3 Gradually add sugar, 1 tablespoon at a time, beating on high speed about 4 minutes more or until stiff, glossy peaks form (tips stand straight) and sugar is completely dissolved.

4 Immediately spread meringue over hot pie filling, carefully sealing it to edge of pastry shell to prevent shrinkage. Bake as directed in recipes.

Four-Egg-White Meringue: Prepare Meringue for Pie as directed above, except use 4 egg whites, 1 teaspoon vanilla, ½ teaspoon cream of tartar, and ½ cup granulated sugar. Increase beating time while adding sugar to about 5 minutes. (Baking time will be longer and oven temperature lower because of larger volume.)

Double-Coconut Cream Pie

1 **recipe Baked Pastry Shell (see page 224)**
⅓ **cup granulated sugar**
¼ **cup cornstarch**
¼ **teaspoon salt**
2 **cups milk**
1 **8-ounce can cream of coconut (¾ cup)**
3 **beaten egg yolks**
2 **tablespoons butter or margarine**

1 **cup coconut**
2 **teaspoons vanilla**
1 **recipe Meringue for Pie (at left)**
2 **tablespoons coconut**

1 Prepare and bake pastry shell as directed; set aside.

2 For filling, in a medium saucepan combine sugar, cornstarch, and salt. Stir in milk and cream of coconut. Cook and stir over medium heat until thickened and bubbly. Reduce heat. Cook and stir 2 minutes more.

3 Gradually stir about 1 cup hot milk mixture into beaten egg yolks, stirring constantly. Return egg yolk mixture to filling in saucepan. Cook and stir until bubbly. Cook and stir 2 minutes more; remove from heat. Stir in butter until melted. Stir in 1 cup coconut and vanilla.

4 Prepare Meringue for Pie as directed. Pour hot filling into baked pastry shell. Evenly spread meringue over hot filling, carefully sealing it to edge of pastry. Sprinkle with the 2 tablespoons coconut. Bake in a 350° oven for 15 minutes. Cool on a wire rack for 1 hour. Chill for 3 to 6 hours before serving; add cover for longer storage. Makes 8 servings.

Nutrition facts per serving: *565 calories, 7 g protein, 50 g carbohydrate, 38 g total fat (13 g saturated), 92 mg cholesterol, 229 mg sodium, 1 g fiber. Daily values: 18% vitamin A, 0% vitamin C, 7% calcium, 10% iron.*

Crowning Glory

A perfectly golden, tender meringue is a noble topping for any cream pie. Its regal appearance is as impressive as it is delicious.

To make sure your meringue is the crown jewel of your pie, follow these suggestions.

Let egg whites stand at room temperature for 30 minutes, and use a clean bowl.

Begin to add the sugar gradually as soon as soft peaks form (tips bend over slightly).

After adding all the sugar, continue beating the egg whites until stiff peaks form, the sugar is completely dissolved, and they feel completely smooth between your fingers. If you underbeat the whites the meringue may shrink when it bakes.

Spread the meringue over the filling while the filling is still hot, sealing it well by pushing it into the edge of the fluted pastry.

Be sure the oven temperature is correct; if it is too low, the meringue may bead or weep (the release of small droplets of sugar syrup from the baked meringue). To be thoroughly cooked, a four-egg-white meringue has to be baked for a longer time at a lower temperature than a three-egg-white meringue, so follow the times and temperatures carefully.

Get Your Hands on It

Choosing a rolling pin is no different than choosing the right pen. It must fit your grip.

An all-purpose wooden rolling pin suits most needs, from rolling out pie pastry to cookie dough. You also might want to consider other types, such as a marble rolling pin (which can be chilled for use with temperamental pastries), a hollow rolling pin, or a tapered French rolling pin, for specialty baking needs.

Rich Tart Pastry

Egg yolk and butter make this richer than ordinary piecrust.

½ **cup cold butter**
      (no substitutes)
1¼ **cups all-purpose flour**
1 **beaten egg yolk**
2 **to 3 tablespoons ice water**

1 In a medium mixing bowl use a pastry blender to cut butter into flour until pieces are the size of small peas.

2 In a small mixing bowl combine the egg yolk and 1 tablespoon of the ice water. Gradually stir egg yolk mixture into flour mixture. Add remaining water, 1 tablespoon at a time, until all of the dough is moistened.

3 Using your fingers, gently knead the dough just until a ball forms. If necessary, cover dough with plastic wrap and chill for 30 to 60 minutes or until dough is easy to handle. Makes enough for one 9- to 12-inch tart.

Black-Bottom Raspberry Tart

Raspberries top a sumptuous vanilla and chocolate cream filling. Try it with strawberries, too.

1 **recipe Rich Tart Pastry**
      (at left)
½ **cup granulated sugar**
2 **tablespoons cornstarch**
1½ **cups milk**
1 **beaten egg yolk**
1 **teaspoon vanilla**
1 **ounce semisweet chocolate,**
      finely chopped
2 **cups fresh raspberries**

1 Spray nonstick coating onto 9- or 10-inch tart pan with removable bottom. Prepare Rich Tart Pastry as directed. Roll pastry between 2 sheets of waxed paper into a circle 2 inches larger than tart pan. Remove top paper. Carefully invert pastry into prepared tart pan. Remove remaining waxed paper while easing pastry into pan. Press pastry into fluted sides of tart pan and trim edges. Prick pastry. Line pastry in tart pan with double thickness of foil. Bake in a 375° oven for 10 minutes. Remove foil and bake for 5 to 10 minutes more or until pastry is golden. Completely cool pastry shell in pan on a wire rack.

2 For vanilla filling, in a heavy medium saucepan stir together sugar and cornstarch. Gradually stir in milk. Cook and stir over medium heat until thickened and bubbly. Reduce heat. Cook and stir for 2 minutes more. Remove from heat. Stir about 1 cup of the hot mixture into the beaten egg yolk. Return egg yolk mixture to the filling in the saucepan. Bring to a gentle boil. Cook and stir 2 minutes more. Remove from heat. Stir in vanilla.

3 For chocolate filling, combine ¾ cup of the hot vanilla filling with the chocolate, stirring until melted.

4 To assemble, spread chocolate filling over bottom of cooled pastry shell. Cover surface of both chocolate and vanilla fillings with clear plastic wrap. Chill up to 24 hours. Carefully spread the cooled vanilla filling over the chocolate filling in pastry shell. Up to 1 hour before serving, arrange raspberries on filling.

5 To serve, remove sides of the tart pan. Cover and refrigerate any leftovers. Makes 10 servings.

Nutrition facts per serving: *234 calories, 4 g protein, 29 g carbohydrate, 12 g total fat (7 g saturated), 70 mg cholesterol, 113 mg sodium, 2 g fiber. Daily values: 17% vitamin A, 10% vitamin C, 5% calcium, 7% iron.*

To Make Ahead

Prepare as directed, except do not add fruit. Cover and chill up to 24 hours. Up to 1 hour before serving, add fruit.

Almond Tarts With Strawberry Topping

- 1 **recipe Pastry for Single-Crust Pie (see page 224)**
- ¼ **cup finely chopped almonds**
- 1 **8-ounce can almond paste**
- ⅓ **cup granulated sugar**
- 2 **tablespoons butter or margarine, softened**
- 2 **eggs**
- 1 **cup sliced fresh strawberries**
- 3 **tablespoons currant jelly**

1 Spray nonstick coating onto four 4- or 4½-inch tart pans with removable bottoms. Prepare Pastry for Single-Crust Pie as directed, except stir almonds into the flour mixture. Divide pastry into 4 equal portions. Using your fingers, press 1 portion onto the bottom and up the sides of each tart pan; set aside.

2 For filling, in a medium mixing bowl beat together almond paste, sugar, and butter with an electric mixer until combined. Beat in eggs, one at a time.

3 Spread one-fourth of the almond mixture (a scant ½ cup) into each tart shell. Bake in a 375° oven about 20 minutes or until golden. Cool on a wire rack.

4 Arrange strawberry slices on tarts. In a saucepan heat and stir jelly until melted. Cool 5 minutes. Spoon jelly over strawberries.

5 Loosen and remove sides of pans. Serve immediately or let stand up to 1 hour. Cut each tart in half. Serves 8.

Nutrition facts per serving: *384 calories, 8 g protein, 41 g carbohydrate, 22 g total fat (5 g saturated), 61 mg cholesterol, 116 mg sodium, 1 g fiber. Daily values: 5% vitamin A, 8% vitamin C, 7% calcium, 14% iron.*

Almond Tarts with Nectarine Topping: Prepare Almond Tarts with Strawberry Topping as directed, except substitute sliced, pitted nectarines for strawberries and apple jelly for currant jelly.

To make one 9- or 10-inch tart: Spray nonstick coating onto a 9- or 10-inch tart pan with removable bottom. Prepare pastry as directed, except on a lightly floured surface roll all of the pastry into a circle 2 inches larger than pan. Transfer pastry to pan. Press into fluted sides; trim edges. Line pastry with a double thickness of foil. Bake in a 450° oven 8 minutes. Remove foil; bake 5 minutes. Reduce oven temperature to 375°. Spread shell with almond mixture; bake 20 minutes or until golden. Cool, then continue as directed using 2 cups sliced fruit and 6 tablespoons jelly.

Baker's Bonus

Edging Your Bets

The edge that you put on your piecrust serves two purposes: to look good and to keep the pie filling sealed in. Making it look good is as easy as a few pinches, presses, tucks, and twists.

Rope-shape edge: Trim and fold under the edge of the pastry for a single-crust, double-crust, or lattice-top pie. Then crimp around the edge of the pastry by pinching it. When pinching, push forward on a slant with a bent finger and pull back with your thumb (see photo, page 237).

Flower-petal edge: Trim and turn under the edge of the pastry for a single- or double-crust pie. Make a large scallop by placing your thumb flat against the inside pastry edge and pressing the dough around it with your other hand's thumb and index finger. Then lightly press the tines of a fork in the center of each scallop.

Cutout edge: Line the pie plate with pastry, and trim pastry to the edge of the pie plate. Roll pastry scraps until they are thin. Use a knife or canapé cutter to cut the pastry scraps into desired shapes. Brush the edge of the pastry shell with water. Arrange the pastry cutouts on the edge of the pastry shell, and press lightly to secure (see photo, page 243).

Twisted edge: Line the pie plate with pastry, and trim pastry to the edge of the plate. Brush the edge of the pastry shell with water. Loosely twist two ½-inch-wide strips of pastry dough around the edge of the pastry shell. As a strip runs out, seal another strip to it by pressing the ends together. Secure the twist by lightly pressing the bottom strip against the edge of the pastry shell.

Fresh Blueberry Tart

Fresh Blueberry Tart

Juicy fresh blueberries top a luscious cream cheese filling.

Lemon and Poppy Seed Pastry
1 **8-ounce package cream cheese, softened**
½ **cup marshmallow creme**
½ **teaspoon finely shredded lemon peel**
3 **cups fresh blueberries**
¼ **cup grape jelly**
   Lemon peel curls (optional)

1 Grease a 10- to 11-inch tart pan with removable bottom (use vegetable shortening, not nonstick spray coating). Prepare Pastry for Lemon and Poppy Seed Pastry as directed. On a lightly floured surface, use your hands to slightly flatten pastry ball. Roll dough from center to edges, forming a circle 2 inches larger than tart pan. Ease pastry into pan. Press pastry into fluted sides of tart pan and trim edges. Prick pastry. Line pastry in tart pan with a double thickness of foil.

2 Bake in a 375° oven for 10 minutes. Remove foil and bake for 5 to 10 minutes more or until pastry is golden. Completely cool pastry shell in pan on a wire rack.

3 For filling, in a medium mixing bowl beat cream cheese with an electric mixer on medium speed until light. Fold in marshmallow creme and lemon peel. Spread filling in the cooled pastry shell. Arrange blueberries on filling. In a small saucepan heat and stir jelly over medium heat until jelly is melted. Brush jelly over berries. Chill for 1 hour or until jelly is set.

4 To serve, loosen and remove sides of the tart pan. If desired, garnish with lemon peel curls. Cover and refrigerate any leftovers. Makes 10 servings.

Lemon and Poppy Seed Pastry: In a medium mixing bowl stir together 1¼ cups all-purpose flour and ¼ cup granulated sugar. Using a pastry blender, cut in ½ cup cold butter (no substitutes), until pieces are the size of small peas. In a small mixing bowl combine 2 beaten egg yolks, 1 tablespoon lemon juice, and 2 teaspoons poppy seed. Gradually stir egg yolk mixture into the flour mixture. Dough will not be completely moistened. Using your fingers, gently knead the dough just until a ball forms. If necessary, cover dough with plastic wrap and chill for 30 to 60 minutes or until dough is easy to handle. Makes enough dough for one 9- to 12-inch tart.

Nutrition facts per serving: *307 calories, 4 g protein, 32 g carbohydrate, 19 g total fat (11 g saturated), 92 mg cholesterol, 169 mg sodium, 2 g fiber. Daily values: 25% vitamin A, 11% vitamin C, 3% calcium, 8% iron.*

To prevent pastry from shrinking during baking, prick it with a fork and line it with a double thickness of foil during first half of baking. To make lining, shape a double layer of foil in pan before rolling out crust. Remove foil, shape pastry, then ease foil into pastry.

The Done Thing

Any juicy pie, such as a fruit pie, needs to bubble in the center to be properly cooked. If it doesn't, the thickener (usually flour, cornstarch, or tapioca) won't be clear. Using a clear pie plate makes it easy to check as you can carefully lift it to look at the bottom crust. The crust should not look doughy in the center.

To see if the pie is done, make a small hole in the top crust and spoon out some of the juice. If the juice is clear, the pie is done. If the juice is cloudy, return the pie to the oven to finish cooking.

Sweet Tart Pastry

1¼ cups all-purpose flour
¼ cup granulated sugar
½ cup cold butter (no substitutes)
2 beaten egg yolks
1 tablespoon water

1 In a medium mixing bowl stir together flour and sugar. Using a pastry blender, cut in butter until pieces are the size of small peas.

2 In a small mixing bowl stir together egg yolks and water. Gradually stir egg yolk mixture into flour mixture.

3 Using your fingers, gently knead the dough just until a ball forms. If necessary, cover with plastic wrap and chill for 30 to 60 minutes or until dough is easy to handle. Makes enough for one 9- to 12-inch tart.

Nutty Sweet Tart Pastry: Prepare Sweet Tart Pastry as directed, except stir ½ cup ground toasted almonds, hazelnuts (filberts), pecans, or walnuts into the flour mixture. If dough appears dry after adding yolk mixture, add 1 to 2 teaspoons additional water until all of the dough is moistened. Continue as directed.

Fruit 'n' Nut Tarts

Walnuts, pistachios, macadamia nuts, or cashews also can be used in this delightful dessert.

1 recipe Sweet Tart Pastry (at left)
1 egg, beaten
⅓ cup corn syrup
2 tablespoons granulated sugar
1 tablespoon butter or margarine, melted
1 tablespoon orange juice
¼ cup pecan halves
¼ cup whole unblanched almonds
¼ cup whole hazelnuts (filberts)
¼ cup chopped dried apricots or dried cranberries

1 Spray nonstick coating onto four 4- or 4½-inch tart pans with removable bottoms. Prepare Sweet Tart Pastry as directed. Divide pastry into 4 equal portions. Using your fingers, press 1 portion onto the bottom and up the sides of each tart pan; set aside.

2 For filling, in a bowl combine egg, corn syrup, sugar, butter, and orange juice. Mix well. Stir in pecans, almonds, hazelnuts, and apricots.

3 Spoon one-fourth of mixture into each tart shell. Bake in 350° oven for 30 to 35 minutes or until golden. If necessary, cover with foil the last 10 minutes to prevent overbrowning. Cool on a wire rack.

4 To serve, carefully loosen and remove sides of tart pans. Cut each tart in half. Cover and refrigerate any leftovers and use within 2 days. Makes 8 servings.

Nutrition facts per serving: 358 calories, 5 g protein, 38 g carbohydrate, 22 g total fat (9 g saturated), 114 mg cholesterol, 151 mg sodium, 2 g fiber. Daily values: 24% vitamin A, 1% vitamin C, 3% calcium, 14% iron.

Choco-Toffee Torte

Instead of coffee liqueur, you can use ½ teaspoon instant coffee granules dissolved in 1 tablespoon hot water plus ½ teaspoon vanilla.

1 recipe Pastry for Double-Crust Pie (see page 224)
⅔ cup granulated sugar
2 tablespoons all-purpose flour
1 teaspoon cornstarch
1 cup milk
1 egg, slightly beaten
2 ounces semisweet chocolate, melted and cooled
2 tablespoons butter or margarine
1 teaspoon vanilla
1 cup whipping cream
2 tablespoons powdered sugar
2 tablespoons coffee liqueur
½ cup chocolate-covered toffee pieces (3 ounces)

1 Prepare pastry for Double-Crust Pie as directed, except divide dough into thirds. Form each third into a ball. Roll as directed, except form 9-inch circles. Place pastry circles on ungreased baking sheets. Using the tines of a fork, generously prick pastry circles.

2 Bake in a 450° oven for 10 to 12 minutes or until golden. Remove the pastry circles from baking sheets and cool on a wire rack.

3 For filling, in a heavy saucepan stir together sugar, flour, and cornstarch. Gradually stir in milk. Cook and stir over medium heat until thickened and bubbly. Reduce heat. Cook and stir 2 minutes more. Remove from heat. Gradually stir about 1 cup of the hot filling into beaten egg. Return egg mixture to filling in saucepan. Bring to a gentle boil. Cook and stir 2 minutes more. Remove from heat. Stir in chocolate, butter, and vanilla. Cover surface with plastic wrap. Chill 2 hours or until firm.

4 In a mixing bowl beat whipping cream, powdered sugar, and liqueur using electric mixer at medium to high speed, until stiff peaks form.

5 To assemble, place one cooled pastry circle on a flat serving plate. Spread one-third of the chocolate filling over pastry to within ½ inch of the edge. Spread one-third of whipped cream over chocolate. Sprinkle with one-third of toffee pieces. Repeat two more times with remaining pastry, chocolate filling, whipped cream, and toffee pieces. Cover and chill the torte for 3 to 4 hours before serving. Cover and refrigerate any leftovers. Serves 12.

Nutrition facts per serving: 394 calories, 4 g protein, 38 g carbohydrate, 25 g total fat (10 g saturated), 54 mg cholesterol, 161 mg sodium, 1 g fiber. Daily values: 13% vitamin A, 0% vitamin C, 4% calcium, 8% iron.

Country Nectarine-Berry Tart

There's no fancy fluting or special pan needed for this tart—a simple pleat around the edge helps hold the filling in.

½ **cup granulated sugar**
1 **tablespoon all-purpose flour**
½ **teaspoon ground cinnamon**
¼ **teaspoon ground nutmeg**
4 **medium nectarines, pitted and thinly sliced (4 cups)**
1 **teaspoon lemon juice**
1 **recipe Pastry for Single-Crust Pie (see page 224)**
1 **cup red raspberries, blueberries, or blackberries**
¼ **cup crushed vanilla wafers (5 or 6 vanilla wafers)**
1 **tablespoon chopped macadamia nuts or almonds**
2 **teaspoons butter (no substitutes), melted**
Milk
Vanilla ice cream (optional)

1 In a large mixing bowl stir together the sugar, flour, cinnamon, and nutmeg. Add nectarines and lemon juice; gently toss until nectarines are coated.

2 Prepare Pastry for Single-Crust Pie as directed, except roll dough into 13-inch circle. Transfer dough to an ungreased, 12-inch pizza pan or a 15x10x1-inch baking pan. Trim pastry to edge of pizza pan or to a 12-inch circle. Stir raspberries, blueberries, or blackberries into nectarine mixture.

Mound the fruit mixture in the center of the pastry, leaving about a 2-inch border. Fold the border up over the fruit mixture.

3 In a small mixing bowl stir together the crushed vanilla wafers, chopped macadamia nuts, and butter. Sprinkle crumb mixture atop the fruit. Lightly brush the pastry with milk. To prevent overbrowning, cover the crumb topping with foil.

4 Bake in a 375° oven for 25 minutes. Remove foil. Bake for 15 to 20 minutes more or until the crust is golden. Cool in the pan on a wire rack. Serve warm or cool, with ice cream, if desired. Cover and refrigerate any leftovers and use within 2 days. Makes 8 servings.

Nutrition facts per serving: 263 calories, 3 g protein, 39 g carbohydrate, 11 g total fat (3 g saturated), 4 mg cholesterol, 84 mg sodium, 2 g fiber. Daily values: 6% vitamin A, 13% vitamin C, 1% calcium, 7% iron.

Carefully fold the extra pastry about 2 inches over the fruit, making pleats as necessary to enclose the edge.

Chocolate-Hazelnut Cookie Torte

Chocolate-Hazelnut Cookie Torte

2 **cups shelled whole hazelnuts (filberts) or almonds**
⅔ **cup granulated sugar**
1 **cup all-purpose flour**
¾ **cup butter, cut in pieces**
½ **teaspoon salt**
1 **egg yolk**
 Granulated sugar
 Chocolate Mousse
1 **cup whipping cream**
1 **tablespoon granulated sugar**
1 **teaspoon vanilla**
2 **cups sliced strawberries**
2 **to 3 ounces semisweet chocolate, chopped**
1 **teaspoon shortening**
 Whole strawberries (optional)

1 Place nuts in a shallow baking pan in a single layer. Toast in a 350° oven for 8 minutes, stirring once; cool.

2 Place toasted nuts and the ⅔ cup sugar in a food processor bowl. Cover; process until nuts are finely ground (do not overprocess). Add flour, butter, and salt. Process until combined. Add egg yolk. Process until thoroughly combined. Divide dough into four equal balls. Cover and chill two balls.

3 Grease and lightly flour two baking sheets; place each on a towel to prevent slipping while rolling dough. On each baking sheet, draw an 8-inch circle with your finger using an 8-inch cake pan as a guide. On one of the prepared baking sheets, roll one portion of the dough to fit the circle, trimming edges of dough with a knife to make an even circle. Repeat with another portion of dough on the second baking sheet. Score one dough round into 8 to 12 wedges, keeping circle intact. Sprinkle both rounds with sugar.

4 Bake in a 375° oven 10 to 12 minutes or until edges are browned. Cool on baking sheets 5 minutes. Cut scored cookie into wedges. Carefully transfer whole cookie and wedges to a wire rack; cool completely. Allow baking sheets to cool. Grease and flour baking sheets again. Repeat shaping and baking remaining dough portions, except do not score either portion.

5 Meanwhile, prepare the Chocolate Mousse. Chill until ready to use. In a chilled mixing bowl beat the whipping cream, the 1 tablespoon sugar, and vanilla with an electric mixer on medium speed just until stiff peaks form. Spoon whipped cream into a pastry bag fitted with a large star tip.

6 To assemble torte, place a whole cookie on a flat serving plate. Spread with half of the Chocolate Mousse and top with half of the sliced strawberries. Place another cookie atop. Repeat with remaining Chocolate Mousse and sliced strawberries. Top with remaining whole cookie. Pipe large dollops of whipped cream atop torte. Cover and chill about 2 hours to soften the cookies. Chill remaining whipped cream.

7 For top garnish, in a heavy small saucepan over low heat, heat chocolate (use the 3 ounces if also dipping berries) and shortening, stirring constantly until it is partially melted. Remove from heat; stir until smooth. Dip one long side of each cookie wedge into melted chocolate. Place on waxed paper until chocolate is set. If desired, dip whole strawberries in remaining melted chocolate.

8 To serve, arrange chocolate-dipped cookie wedges atop whipped cream, placing the chocolate edges up and tilting slightly in a pinwheel pattern. Pipe a large star of whipped cream in the center where the cookie wedges meet. If desired, garnish with chocolate-dipped or plain strawberries. Using a serrated knife, cut into wedges. Serve immediately. Makes 12 servings.

Chocolate Mousse: In a chilled mixing bowl combine ¼ cup granulated sugar and 3 tablespoons unsweetened cocoa powder. Add 1½ cups whipping cream. Beat on medium speed until stiff peaks form. Cover and chill up to 2 hours.

Nutrition facts per serving: *539 calories, 6 g protein, 34 g carbohydrate, 44 g total fat (21 g saturated), 116 mg cholesterol, 225 mg sodium, 3 g fiber. Daily values: 35% vitamin A, 24% vitamin C, 7% calcium, 10% iron.*

To Make Ahead

Bake large cookies and wedges as directed. Place in layers separated by waxed paper in an airtight container and store at room temperature for up to 2 days. Or, place in a freezer container and freeze up to 1 month. Before using, thaw cookies 15 minutes.

Raspberries and Cream Torte

For a smoother filling, sieve the raspberries.

1 recipe Pastry for Double-Crust
   Pie (see page 224)
½ cup finely chopped almonds
¼ cup granulated sugar
2 tablespoons cornstarch
1 10-ounce package frozen
   raspberries, thawed
⅓ cup butter or margarine,
   softened
½ cup almond paste, crumbled
   (about ½ of an 8-ounce can)
1½ cups sifted powdered sugar
   Whipped cream (optional)
   Fresh raspberries (optional)

1 Prepare Pastry for Double-Crust Pie as directed, except add chopped almonds after cutting in shortening. Divide dough into fourths and roll each portion into an 8-inch circle. Place pastry circles on ungreased baking sheets. Using the tines of a fork, generously prick the pastry. Bake in a 450° oven about 8 minutes or until golden. Remove the pastries from baking sheet and cool on a wire rack.

2 For raspberry filling, in a heavy saucepan stir together sugar and cornstarch. Gradually stir in raspberries. Cook and stir over medium heat until thickened and bubbly. Reduce heat.

Cook and stir for 2 minutes more. Cover the surface with clear plastic wrap and cool without stirring.

3 For almond butter cream, in a medium mixing bowl beat butter and almond paste with an electric mixer on medium speed until light and creamy. Beat in powdered sugar until combined. If necessary to make fluffy, add 1 to 2 teaspoons water.

4 To assemble, spread one-fourth of the almond butter cream over each pastry circle to within ½ inch of the edge. Spread one-fourth of the raspberry filling over each butter-cream layer. Carefully stack pastry layers on a flat serving plate. Chill the torte for 3 to 4 hours before serving. If desired, top with whipped cream and fresh raspberries. Cover and refrigerate any leftovers. Makes 10 servings.

Nutrition facts per serving: 451 calories, 5 g protein, 52 g carbohydrate, 26 g total fat (8 g saturated), 16 mg cholesterol, 171 mg sodium, 2 g fiber. Daily values: 5% vitamin A, 7% vitamin C, 4% calcium, 12% iron.

Peach Dumplings

Dates and nuts hide inside cinnamon-pastry-wrapped peaches.

1 recipe Spicy Pastry for Single-
   Crust Pie (see page 224)
2 medium peaches, peeled,
   halved, and pitted
¼ cup chopped dates

2 tablespoons chopped walnuts
2 tablespoons brown sugar
¾ cup apricot nectar
2 tablespoons granulated sugar
1 tablespoon cornstarch
1 tablespoon brandy or rum
   (optional)

1 Lightly grease a 2-quart square baking dish; set aside. Prepare and roll out Spicy Pastry as directed, except flatten the pastry to a square. Roll pastry from center to edges into a 14-inch square. Cut into four 7-inch squares.

2 Place one peach half, cut side up, on the center of each pastry square. Top each peach half with 1 tablespoon of the dates, ½ tablespoon walnuts, and ½ tablespoon brown sugar.

3 Moisten edges of pastry with water. Fold corners to the center on top of the fruit, pinching edges together to seal. Place in the prepared baking dish. Brush dumplings with 1 teaspoon of the apricot nectar. Bake in a 400° oven for 30 to 35 minutes or until golden. Cool slightly on a wire rack.

4 Meanwhile, for sauce, in a medium saucepan stir together sugar and cornstarch. Stir in remaining nectar. Cook and stir over medium heat until slightly thickened and bubbly. Reduce heat. Cook and stir for 2 minutes more. Remove from heat. Stir in brandy.

5 To serve, spoon warm sauce over warm dumplings. Makes 4 servings.

Nutrition facts per dumpling: *435 calories, 5 g protein, 62 g carbohydrate, 20 g total fat (5 g saturated), 0 mg cholesterol, 138 mg sodium, 3 g fiber. Daily values: 8% vitamin A, 31% vitamin C, 2% calcium, 15% iron.*

Apple Dumplings: Prepare Peach Dumplings as directed, except substitute apple halves for peach halves and use apple juice instead of apricot nectar in sauce.

Pear Dumplings With Raspberry Sauce

Other forms of chocolate that you can use inside the pears include chocolate fudge ice-cream topping, semisweet chocolate pieces, or vanilla-flavored pieces. (Pictured on page 241.)

1 recipe Pastry for Single-Crust Pie (see page 224)
4 medium pears
2 tablespoons milk chocolate pieces
   Milk
   Granulated sugar
1 10-ounce package frozen raspberries, thawed
¼ cup granulated sugar
2 teaspoons cornstarch

1 Lightly grease a 2-quart square baking dish; set aside. Prepare and roll out Pastry for Single-Crust Pie as directed, except flatten the pastry to a square.

Roll the pastry from center to edges into a 14-inch square. Cut the pastry into four 7-inch squares.

2 Peel pears. Cut off about ½ inch from each blossom end so pears stand upright. Use an apple corer to core pears, but do not cut all the way to the bottom of pear. Place a pear on each pastry square. Spoon about ½ tablespoon chocolate pieces into each pear.

3 Moisten edges of pastry with water. Fold corners to the center on top of each pear, pinching edges together to seal. Place in the prepared baking dish. Brush pastry with milk and sprinkle with sugar. Bake in a 375° oven about 40 minutes or until pears are tender and pastry is golden brown.

4 Meanwhile, for raspberry sauce, press undrained raspberries through a sieve to remove seeds. In a medium saucepan stir together sugar and cornstarch. Stir in sieved raspberries. Cook and stir over medium heat until slightly thickened and bubbly. Reduce heat. Cook and stir for 2 minutes more. Remove from heat and cool slightly.

5 To serve, transfer dumplings to a serving plate. Spoon warm raspberry sauce over warm or cooled dumplings. Makes 4 servings.

Nutrition facts per dumpling: *557 calories, 5 g protein, 92 g carbohydrate, 21 g total fat (6 g saturated), 0 mg cholesterol, 144 mg sodium, 9 g fiber. Daily values: 1% vitamin A, 30% vitamin C, 4% calcium, 17% iron.*

Baker's Bonus

Setting Some Aside

Fruit dumplings and pies must be treated carefully to preserve their fresh flavor and crisp texture. They can stand at room temperature for up to 24 hours, but cover and refrigerate them if you want to keep them longer.

To freeze unbaked dumplings and fruit pies, treat any light-color fruit with an ascorbic acid color keeper. Assemble the pie as directed in a metal or freezer-to-oven pie plate. Place it in a freezer bag, then seal, label, and freeze for up to 4 months. To bake a frozen pie, unwrap it and cover the edges with foil. Bake in a 450° oven for 50 minutes. Remove the foil and bake 15 minutes more or until crust is golden.

To freeze baked dumplings and fruit pies, cool the dumpling or pie completely. Place the baked good in a freezer bag, then seal, label, and freeze up to 8 months. To use, thaw the dumpling or pie, covered, at room temperature. If desired, reheat it by baking it, covered, in a 325° oven until warm.

Do not freeze cream, custard, or pecan pies.

Cream Puff Pastry

The rough top of this pastry reminded early French cooks of cabbage or "chou."

½ **cup butter or margarine**
1 **cup water**
¼ **teaspoon salt**
1 **cup all-purpose flour**
4 **eggs**

1 In a medium saucepan combine butter, water, and salt. Bring mixture to boiling, stirring until butter melts.

2 Add flour all at once, stirring vigorously. Cook and stir until the mixture forms a ball that doesn't separate. Remove from heat and cool for 10 minutes.

3 Add eggs to butter mixture, one at a time, beating with a wooden spoon after each addition for 1 to 2 minutes or until smooth. Use as directed in recipes.

Chocolate Cream Puff Pastry: Prepare Cream Puff Pastry as directed, except in a small bowl combine the flour, 3 tablespoons unsweetened cocoa powder, and 2 tablespoons granulated sugar. Add flour mixture all at once to boiling mixture, stirring vigorously. Continue as directed.

Raspberry Puff Ring

A double-cream filling plus fresh berries make this a dessert to remember.

1 **recipe Cream Puff Pastry (at left)**
1 **8-ounce package cream cheese, softened**
1 **cup granulated sugar**
1 **teaspoon vanilla**
1 **teaspoon finely shredded orange peel**
1 **tablespoon cold water**
¾ **teaspoon unflavored gelatin**
1½ **cups whipping cream**
2 **cups fresh raspberries, strawberries, or blueberries**
2 **tablespoons orange liqueur or honey**
  Powdered sugar (optional)

1 Grease a baking sheet; set aside.

2 Prepare Cream Puff Pastry as directed. Drop dough by rounded tablespoons into an 8-inch ring on the prepared baking sheet. (For easier serving, spoon 15 mounds.) Bake in a 400° oven for 30 to 35 minutes or until golden and puffy. Carefully slide ring from the baking sheet onto a wire rack; cool completely.

3 For filling, in a large mixing bowl beat cream cheese, sugar, and vanilla with an electric mixer on medium speed until creamy. Stir in orange peel; set aside. Wash beaters.

4 In a 1-cup glass measuring cup or custard cup, combine cold water and gelatin. Let stand 2 minutes. Place measuring cup in a saucepan of boiling water. Cook and stir about 1 minute or until the gelatin is completely dissolved.

5 Place whipping cream in a clean mixing bowl. Use clean beaters to beat with an electric mixer on medium speed while gradually adding the gelatin. Continue beating until soft peaks form. Fold whipped cream mixture into cream cheese mixture. Cover and chill until ready to use.

6 In a serving bowl, combine berries and orange liqueur. Cover and chill up to 4 hours.

7 To assemble, cut off top third of ring. Use a fork to remove any soft

Grease a baking sheet. Using a pan lid as a guide, mark an 8-inch circle in the grease. With a tablespoon, drop the cream puff dough onto the greased baking sheet inside the marked circle. Use another spoon or spatula to push the dough off of the spoon.

dough from inside. Place bottom on flat serving plate. Spoon filling into ring, spreading evenly. Replace top of ring. If desired, cover and chill for up to 2 hours. Just before serving, set bowl of berries in center of ring. If desired, sprinkle ring with powdered sugar. Cut into sections to serve. Makes 15 servings.

Nutrition facts per serving: *305 calories, 4 g protein, 23 g carbohydrate, 22 g total fat (13 g saturated), 123 mg cholesterol, 169 mg sodium, 1 g fiber. Daily values: 25% vitamin A, 7% vitamin C, 3% calcium, 5% iron.*

To Make Ahead

Prepare, bake, and cool cream puff ring as directed. Do not fill. Place in a freezer container or wrap and freeze up to 2 months. Before serving, thaw 15 minutes. Prepare filling and fruit; cover and refrigerate up to 4 hours. Fill and serve with fruit as directed.

International Origin

Double Chocolate Cream Puffs

Want more chocolate? Combine 1 tablespoon powdered sugar and ¼ teaspoon unsweetened cocoa powder; sift over filled puffs. For a chocolate-mint flavor, substitute 2 tablespoons white crème de menthe for the vanilla.

1 **recipe Chocolate Cream Puff Pastry (at left)**
⅔ **cup granulated sugar**
⅓ **cup all-purpose flour**
⅛ **teaspoon salt**
1½ **cups milk**
1 **ounce unsweetened chocolate, chopped**
2 **slightly beaten egg yolks**
⅓ **cup butter (no substitutes), softened**
1 **teaspoon vanilla**
  Powdered sugar

1 Grease a baking sheet; set aside.

2 Prepare Chocolate Cream Puff Pastry as directed. Drop batter by heaping tablespoons into 12 mounds 3 inches apart on the prepared baking sheet. For evenly shaped puffs, if possible, avoid going back to add more batter to mounds. Bake in a 400° oven about 30 minutes or until firm and bottoms are browned. Remove puffs from the baking sheet, and cool on a wire rack.

3 Meanwhile, for chocolate filling, in a heavy medium saucepan stir together sugar, flour, and salt. Gradually stir in milk. Add chopped chocolate. Cook and stir over medium heat until thickened and bubbly. Reduce heat. Cook and stir for 2 minutes more. Remove from heat. Gradually stir about 1 cup of the hot filling into the beaten egg yolks. Return egg yolk mixture to filling in the saucepan. Bring to a gentle boil. Cook and stir 2 minutes more. Remove from heat. Cover surface with clear plastic wrap. Refrigerate about 2 hours or until cold.

4 In a medium mixing bowl beat butter until creamy. Continue beating and gradually add chilled filling, beating until light and creamy. Beat in vanilla.

5 To assemble, cut off the top fourth of each puff. Use a fork to remove any soft dough from inside. Spoon a scant ¼ cup chocolate filling into each puff. Replace tops of the puffs. If desired, chill for up to 2 hours. Before serving, sift powdered sugar over the tops. Makes 12 servings.

Nutrition facts per cream puff: *279 calories, 6 g protein, 27 g carbohydrate, 17 g total fat (10 g saturated), 143 mg cholesterol, 234 mg sodium, 1 g fiber. Daily values: 22% vitamin A, 0% vitamin C, 6% calcium, 8% iron.*

Chocolate-Filled Cream Puffs: Prepare Double Chocolate Cream Puffs as directed, except substitute Cream Puff Pastry for the Chocolate Cream Puff Pastry. Continue as directed.

Shortcut

Instead of homemade filling, use your favorite flavor pudding from a can or prepared from a box to fill the puffs.

To Make Ahead

Prepare, bake, and cool puffs as directed. Do not fill. Place puffs in a freezer container and freeze for up to 2 months. Before serving, thaw for 15 minutes. Fill as directed.

*Strawberry-Filled
Almond Puffs*

Strawberry-Filled Almond Puffs

To serve six, freeze half of the almond paste-flavor puffs for a later use and make half as much filling.

1 recipe Cream Puff Pastry (see page 258)
½ cup almond paste (about half of an 8-ounce can)
1 cup whipping cream
2 tablespoons powdered sugar
2 tablespoons amaretto or ¼ teaspoon almond extract
½ cup dairy sour cream
3 cups strawberries, sliced Powdered sugar

1 Grease a baking sheet; set aside.

2 Prepare Cream Puff Pastry as directed, except heat almond paste with butter and water. Drop dough by heaping tablespoon into 12 mounds 3 inches apart on the prepared baking sheet. For evenly shaped puffs, if possible, avoid going back to add more batter to mounds. Bake in a 400° oven for 25 to 30 minutes or until golden and firm. Remove puffs from the baking sheet, and cool on a wire rack.

3 For whipped cream filling, in a medium mixing bowl combine whipping cream, powdered sugar, and amaretto. Beat just until stiff peaks form. Fold in sour cream. Cover and refrigerate.

4 To assemble, cut off the top fourth of each puff. Use a fork to remove any soft dough from inside. Spoon a heaping tablespoon of whipped cream filling into each puff. Top with about ¼ cup strawberries. Replace tops of the puffs. If desired, cover and chill for up to 2 hours. Before serving, sift powdered sugar over the tops. Makes 12 servings.

Nutrition facts per cream puff: *285 calories, 5 g protein, 18 g carbohydrate, 21 g total fat (11 g saturated), 123 mg cholesterol, 158 mg sodium, 1 g fiber. Daily values: 21% vitamin A, 35% vitamin C, 5% calcium, 7% iron.*

Peach-Filled Almond Puffs: Prepare Strawberry-Filled Almond Puffs as directed, except substitute sliced, fresh peaches for strawberries.

Shortcut

Instead of the homemade filling, use vanilla or chocolate pudding from a can or prepared from a box to fill the puffs. Top with berries.

To Make Ahead

Prepare, bake, and cool cream puffs as directed. Do not fill. Place in a freezer container and freeze for up to 2 months. Before serving, thaw for 15 minutes. Fill as directed.

Dough How

Perfect chou pastry dough produces puffy, crisp, and tender cream puffs and éclairs. To make sure yours doesn't fall short of expectations, keep these tips in mind.

✦ *Measure the water carefully.*

✦ *Add the flour as soon as the butter or margarine is melted and the water boils, so the water does not boil away.*

✦ *Set a minute timer so the pastry dough cools exactly 10 minutes. Then beat in the first egg.*

✦ *Drop the dough into mounds onto the baking sheet (avoid adding more dough to the mounds if you want evenly shaped puffs). For éclairs, if you don't have a decorating bag, use two spoons to drop and shape the dough.*

✦ *Make sure the pastry is golden brown, firm, and dry before removing it from the oven.*

✦ *Use a fork to remove any soft dough inside the cream puff or éclair shells before filling them.*

✦ *So the bottoms don't get soggy, fill the shells just before serving or fill and chill shells for up to 2 hours.*

Sophisticated Chou

Chou (pronounced "shoe") pastry has a myriad of uses. The baked pastry can be a sophisticated shell for both savory and sweet fillings and can hold everything from appetizers to desserts. Try petite pâté bites, main-dish salads, ice cream, pudding, flavored whipped cream, or whatever you fancy.

So your cream puffs or éclairs will puff fully during baking—and for easier stirring—be sure to add the eggs to the dough one at a time. Remember that all the recipes in this book were tested using large eggs; using eggs of another size could throw off the balance of ingredients.

Quick Puff Pastry

Whenever you're cutting puff pastry, use a sharp knife and cut straight down through the dough. If you pull the knife or cut the dough at an angle, the edges will puff unevenly during baking.

> 4 **cups all-purpose flour**
> 1 **teaspoon salt**
> 2 **cups cold butter (1 pound) (no substitutes)**
> 1¼ **cups ice water**

1 In a large mixing bowl combine flour and salt. Cut cold butter into ½-inch-thick slices (not cubes). Add butter slices to the flour mixture, then toss until the butter slices are coated with the flour mixture and are separated. Pour ice water over the mixture. Using a spoon, quickly mix. (The butter will remain in large pieces and flour will not be completely moistened.)

2 On a lightly floured pastry cloth, knead dough 10 times by pressing and pushing it together to form a rough-looking ball, lifting pastry cloth if necessary to press dough. Shape dough into a rectangle (dough will have dry-looking areas). Make corners as square as possible. Slightly flatten dough.

3 On a well-floured pastry cloth, roll dough into a 15x12-inch rectangle. Fold crosswise into thirds to form a 12x5-inch rectangle. Give dough a quarter turn, then fold crosswise into thirds to form a 5x4-inch rectangle of 9 layers. Repeat the rolling, folding, turning, and folding process once-more, forming a 5x4-inch rectangle. Wrap dough with plastic wrap; refrigerate 20 minutes. Repeat rolling and folding process 2 more times. Refrigerate dough 20 minutes more.

4 With a sharp knife, cut dough crosswise in half. Then use as directed in recipes. Makes 2 portions.

To Make Ahead

Prepare dough as directed. Wrap each portion of dough in plastic wrap and refrigerate up to 3 days. Or, overwrap with heavy foil and freeze up to 3 months. Before using, thaw dough, covered, in the refrigerator 24 hours.

Queen of Hearts Pastries

Use a cardboard heart pattern and a sharp knife if you don't have a 2-inch, heart-shape cookie cutter.

> 1 **portion Quick Puff Pastry (at left) or one 17¼-ounce package (2 sheets) frozen puff pastry, thawed**
> ⅓ **cup peach or apricot all-fruit spread or preserves**
> 1 **teaspoon finely shredded lemon peel**
> 1 **cup peeled and finely chopped peaches (about 2)**
> 1 **cup blueberries**
> 1 **8-ounce package cream cheese, softened**
> ¼ **cup packed brown sugar**
> 1 **teaspoon vanilla Powdered sugar**

1 On a lightly floured surface, roll the portion of dough into a 10x18-inch rectangle. Or, if using frozen pastry, unfold pastry sheets. Using a 2-inch, heart-shape cookie cutter dipped in flour, cut pastry into about 45 hearts (do not reroll scraps).

2 Place pastry hearts on an ungreased baking sheet. Bake in a 375° oven about 18 minutes (10 to 12 minutes for purchased pastry) or until puffed and golden. Cool on a wire rack.

3 For fruit filling, melt together fruit spread and lemon peel. Heat and stir until melted; cool. In a large mixing bowl combine peaches and blueberries. Add spread or preserves mixture and gently toss to combine; set aside.

4 For cheese filling, beat cream cheese, brown sugar, and vanilla with an electric mixer on medium-high speed until fluffy.

5 To assemble pastries, using a serrated knife, cut pastry hearts in half horizontally. Spread each of the bottom halves with about 1 teaspoon cheese filling. Top each with a spoonful of fruit filling and a pastry top. If desired, cover and chill for up to 4 hours. Sprinkle with powdered sugar and serve immediately. Makes about 45.

Nutrition facts per pastry: 80 calories, 1 g protein, 8 g carbohydrate, 5 g total fat (1 g saturated), 6 mg cholesterol, 57 mg sodium, 0 g fiber. Daily values: 2% vitamin A, 1% vitamin C, 0% calcium, 0% iron.

To Make Ahead

Prepare, bake, and cool pastry hearts as directed. Place in an airtight container and store at room temperature for up to 12 hours. Assemble as directed with cheese and fruit fillings.

Chocolate-Hazelnut Pretzel Puffs

¾ **cup semisweet chocolate pieces**
¾ **cup finely chopped hazelnuts (filberts)**
1 **portion Quick Puff Pastry (at left) or one 17¼-ounce package (2 sheets) frozen puff pastry, thawed**
1 **egg, slightly beaten**
1 **tablespoon water**
2 **tablespoons granulated sugar (optional)**
¼ **teaspoon ground cinnamon (optional)**

1 For filling, in a heavy small saucepan heat and stir chocolate over low heat until melted. Stir in hazelnuts; set aside.

2 On a lightly floured surface, roll the portion of dough into an 18x12-inch rectangle. Or, if using purchased pastry, unfold and roll each sheet into a 12x9-inch rectangle. Cut pastry into twelve 9x2-inch strips.

3 Carefully spread 2 teaspoons filling down center of each strip. Moisten one side of each strip with a little water. Pinch edges together to seal in filling. Place seam side down on an ungreased baking sheet. To form a pretzel-like shape, cross 1 end over to form a circle, overlapping about 2 inches from each end. Take an end of dough in each hand and twist once at the point where dough overlaps.

4 With fork mix together egg and water. Brush mixture over pastries. If desired, combine sugar and cinnamon. Sprinkle over pastries. Bake in a 375° oven for 20 to 25 minutes or until golden. Remove from baking sheet and cool on a wire rack. Makes 12.

Nutrition facts per pastry: 327 calories, 4 g protein, 25 g carbohydrate, 25 g total fat (10 g saturated), 59 mg cholesterol, 320 mg sodium, 1 g fiber. Daily values: 15% vitamin A, 0% vitamin C, 2% calcium, 10% iron.

If desired, instead of spreading the filling, place it in a plastic bag, snip off one end of the bag, and pipe the filling down the center of the strips.

Rosy Peach-a-Boos

Rosy Peach-a-Boos

Chopped apples work as well as peaches for the filling.

1 **portion Quick Puff Pastry (see page 262) or one 17¼-ounce package (2 sheets) frozen puff pastry, thawed**
1 **beaten egg**
1 **tablespoon water**
1 **tablespoon granulated sugar**
⅛ **teaspoon ground cinnamon**
2 **tablespoons seedless raspberry jam**
1 **tablespoon butter or margarine**
1 **large peach, peeled and finely chopped**
3 **tablespoons granulated sugar**
1 **tablespoon all-purpose flour**
Dash ground nutmeg

1 On a lightly floured surface, roll the portion of dough into a 19x13-inch rectangle. Then trim to an 18x12-inch rectangle. Or, if using purchased pastry, unfold and trim each sheet into a 12x9-inch rectangle. Cut pastry into twenty-four 3-inch squares. Place half of the squares on an ungreased baking sheet. Using a 1½-inch, circle-shape cookie cutter, cut out center of remaining 12 squares.

2 Stir together beaten egg and water. Brush some of the mixture over squares on baking sheet. Top with squares with holes in center. Place round cutouts on baking sheet next to stacked squares. Brush stacked squares as well as round cutouts with remaining egg-water mixture. Stir together 1 tablespoon sugar and cinnamon. Sprinkle over squares and rounds. Refrigerate while preparing filling.

3 For filling, melt together jam and butter. Stir in peaches, 3 tablespoons sugar, and the flour. Cook and stir until slightly thickened and bubbly. Stir in nutmeg. Cool 15 minutes.

4 Spoon warm filling into center holes of pastry squares. Place a round cutout lightly on top of filling. Bake in a 400° oven 18 to 20 minutes or until golden. Remove from baking sheet and cool on a wire rack. Makes 12.

Nutrition facts per pastry: *240 calories, 3 g protein, 22 g carbohydrate, 16 g total fat (10 g saturated), 59 mg cholesterol, 207 mg sodium, 1 g fiber. Daily values: 15% vitamin A, 1% vitamin C, 0% calcium, 6% iron.*

Baker's Bonus

Setting Some Aside

Most of the puff pastry recipes in this chapter call for half of a recipe (one portion) of Quick Puff Pastry. To store the other portion until needed, wrap the dough in plastic wrap, and refrigerate it for up to 3 days. To freeze, wrap the dough in heavy foil or place in a freezer bag; seal well, label, and freeze for up to 3 months. Thaw the dough, covered, in the refrigerator for 24 hours.

Notes

International Origin

Raspberry Danish

You need just 30 minutes and four ingredients to create these pastry miniatures for your dessert or breakfast tray.

½ **of 1 portion Quick Puff Pastry (see page 262) or ½ of a 17¼-ounce package (1 sheet) frozen puff pastry, thawed**
⅓ **cup seedless raspberry preserves**
Pressurized whipped dessert topping
Chopped pistachio nuts or almonds

1 On a lightly floured surface, roll the half portion of dough into a 12x9-inch rectangle. Or, if using purchased pastry, unfold pastry sheet and trim into a 12x9-inch rectangle. Cut the pastry into twelve 9x1-inch strips. Loosely coil each strip into a circle or spiral. Moisten the outside end of each strip with a little water and secure it to the coil to prevent it from unwrapping during baking.

2 Place pastries on an ungreased baking sheet. Bake in a 400° oven for 15 to 18 minutes (12 to 15 minutes for purchased pastry) or until golden. Cool on a wire rack.

3 Before serving, in a small saucepan heat preserves until melted, stirring often; drizzle over pastries. Let preserves cool slightly, then top with whipped topping and sprinkle with chopped nuts. Serve immediately or place in an airtight container and chill up to 24 hours. Makes 12.

Nutrition facts per danish: 149 calories, 1 g protein, 15 g carbohydrate, 9 g total fat (1 g saturated), 6 mg cholesterol, 87 mg sodium, 0 g fiber. Daily values: 2% vitamin A, 0% vitamin C, 0% calcium, 1% iron.

Almond Crunch Pastries

Transform these quick, yet impressive cookies into an extra-special dessert by filling them with whipped cream. Use a fork to separate each pastry rectangle horizontally into two layers. Spoon sweetened whipped cream between layers. Garnish with a little whipped cream and toasted, sliced almonds.

½ **of 1 portion Quick Puff Pastry (see page 262) or ½ of a 17¼-ounce package (1 sheet) frozen puff pastry, thawed**
½ **teaspoon almond extract**
2 **tablespoons butter or margarine, melted**
¼ **cup granulated sugar**
½ **cup chopped almonds**

1 On lightly floured surface, roll the half portion of dough into a 12x9-inch rectangle. Or, if using purchased pastry, unfold pastry sheet; trim into a 12x9-inch rectangle. Cut into eighteen 3x2-inch rectangles. Place 1 inch apart on an ungreased baking sheet.

2 Stir almond extract into melted butter; brush over pastries. Sprinkle with sugar and top with almonds.

3 Bake in a 375° oven 18 minutes (12 to 15 minutes for purchased pastry) or until golden. Remove from baking sheet; cool on a wire rack. Makes 18.

Nutrition facts per pastry: 98 calories, 1 g protein, 8 g carbohydrate, 7 g total fat (1 g saturated), 3 mg cholesterol, 64 mg sodium, 0 g fiber. Daily values: 1% vitamin A, 0% vitamin C, 0% calcium, 0% iron.

Minted Cream-Filled Horns

For Mocha Cream-Filled Horns, substitute coffee liqueur for the green crème de menthe.

1 **portion Quick Puff Pastry (see page 262) or one 17¼-ounce package (2 sheets) frozen puff pastry, thawed**
1 **slightly beaten egg white**
1 **tablespoon water**
1 **tablespoon granulated sugar**
1 **cup whipping cream**
2 **tablespoons powdered sugar**
1 **tablespoon green crème de menthe or few drops mint extract and 1 drop green food coloring**
1 **tablespoon grated semisweet chocolate**

1 On a lightly floured surface, roll the portion of dough into a 16x12-inch rectangle. Using a sharp knife, cut pastry lengthwise into twelve 16x1-inch strips. Or, if using purchased pastry, unfold and trim each sheet into a 12x8-inch rectangle. Cut each sheet into twelve 8x1-inch strips. Make a 16x1-inch strip by overlapping the ends of two strips of purchased pastry and pressing them together. Repeat with remaining short strips for a total of 12 long strips.

2 Wrap each strip of dough around a well-greased cream horn mold* or ¾-inch-wide cannoli tube. Overlap layers slightly and press gently. Place 1 inch apart on an ungreased baking sheet. Beat together egg white and water. Brush over pastry. Sprinkle with sugar.

3 Bake in a 425° oven for 15 to 20 minutes (12 to 15 minutes for purchased pastry) or until golden. Transfer from baking sheet to a wire rack. While still warm, slightly twist the molds and remove from pastry horns. Cool completely.

4 For filling, in a medium mixing bowl combine whipping cream, powdered sugar, and crème de menthe. Beat with an electric mixer on low speed just until stiff peaks form. Fold in grated chocolate.

5 To assemble, spoon the whipped cream into a decorating bag fitted with a large star tip; pipe the whipped cream into each horn. If desired, chill up to 1 hour. Makes 12.

Note: If cream horn molds are not available, cut heavy-duty foil into 6-inch squares. Roll up each to make a tube about ¾-inch in diameter. Use a little shortening along edge to hold in place. Spray with nonstick coating before wrapping with dough. Insert a wooden spoon handle into the foil roll when wrapping it with dough to assist in pressing the dough layers together.

Nutrition facts per pastry: 289 calories, 3 g protein, 18 g carbohydrate, 23 g total fat (14 g saturated), 68 mg cholesterol, 256 mg sodium, 1 g fiber. Daily values: 22% vitamin A, 0% vitamin C, 1% calcium, 6% iron.

Strawberry-Banana Tarts

Dip the banana slices in orange juice to prevent them from turning dark. (Pictured on page 269.)

- 8 **18x12-inch sheets frozen phyllo dough, thawed**
- ¼ **cup butter (no substitutes), melted**
- 1 **tablespoon granulated sugar**
- ¼ **teaspoon ground cinnamon**
- 1 **cup whipping cream**
- 2 **tablespoons powdered sugar**
- 1 **teaspoon finely shredded orange peel**
- ½ **teaspoon vanilla**
- ⅓ **cup dairy sour cream**
- 2 **cups sliced fresh strawberries**
- 1 **cup sliced banana**

1 Grease six 6-ounce custard cups; set aside. Unfold phyllo dough. Remove 1 sheet, keeping rest covered with plastic wrap and a damp towel. Place the 1 sheet of phyllo on a waxed-paper-lined cutting board. Brush with some of the ¼ cup melted butter. Top with a second sheet of phyllo, then brush with more butter. Repeat layering with the remaining phyllo and butter.

2 Cut stack crosswise into six 3-inch-wide strips. Cut lengthwise into thirds, forming eighteen 4x3-inch rectangles. Press three rectangles into each custard cup with shorter edges overlapping in bottoms of cups. Place cups in a 15x10x1-inch baking pan. Combine sugar and cinnamon. Sprinkle over phyllo. Bake in a 350° oven 15 to 18 minutes or until golden. Cool in cups.

3 For filling, in medium mixing bowl combine whipping cream, powdered sugar, orange peel, and vanilla. Beat with an electric mixer on low speed just until stiff peaks form. Fold in sour cream. Set aside ¾ cup of mixture.

4 To assemble, carefully lift baked phyllo shells from custard cups and place on a serving plate. Spoon about ¼ cup filling into each shell. Top with strawberry and banana slices. Spoon or pipe a rounded tablespoon of the remaining filling on top of each tart. Makes 6.

Nutrition facts per tart: 376 calories, 4 g protein, 32 g carbohydrate, 27 g total fat (16 g saturated), 80 mg cholesterol, 223 mg sodium, 2 g fiber. Daily values: 28% vitamin A, 54% vitamin C, 4% calcium, 8% iron.

Setting Some Aside

Strudels do not store well so should be eaten the same day they are made.

Most phyllo pastries, however, can be stored. Their filling determines whether or not they must be refrigerated. Phyllo pastry recipes with cream cheese or pudding fillings, for instance, need to be stored tightly covered in the refrigerator.

Phyllo cookies, such as baklava, may be stored in an airtight container at room temperature for up to 3 days. For longer storage, place them in an airtight container or freezer bag, then seal, label, and freeze for up to 3 months. Thaw phyllo cookies, covered, at room temperature.

Notes

_____

_____

_____

_____

_____

_____

_____

Lemon Cups

- 8 **18x12-inch sheets frozen phyllo dough, thawed**
- ¼ **cup butter (no substitutes), melted**
- ⅓ **cup granulated sugar**
- 2 **teaspoons cornstarch**
- 2 **teaspoons finely shredded lemon peel**
- ¼ **cup lemon juice**
- 2 **tablespoons butter (no substitutes)**
- 1 **egg, slightly beaten**
- 1 **cup whipping cream**
- 2 **tablespoons powdered sugar**
- ½ **teaspoon vanilla**
  Kiwi fruit slices (optional)

1 Grease six 6-ounce custard cups; set aside. Unfold phyllo dough. Remove 1 sheet, keeping remaining phyllo covered with plastic wrap or waxed paper and a damp towel. Place the 1 sheet of phyllo on a waxed-paper-lined cutting board. Brush phyllo with some of the ¼ cup melted butter. Top with a second sheet of phyllo, then brush with more butter. Repeat layering with remaining phyllo and butter.

2 Using a sharp knife, cut the stack crosswise into six 3-inch-wide strips. Then cut lengthwise into thirds, forming eighteen 4x3-inch rectangles. Press three rectangles into each prepared custard cup with shorter edges overlapping in the bottoms of the cups. Place cups in a 15x10x1-inch baking pan. Bake in a 350° oven for 15 to 18 minutes or until golden. Cool in custard cups on a wire rack.

3 Meanwhile, prepare lemon curd. In a heavy saucepan stir together sugar, cornstarch, and lemon peel. Gradually stir in lemon juice. Add 2 tablespoons butter. Cook and stir over medium heat until thickened and bubbly. Reduce heat. Cook and stir for 2 minutes more. Remove from heat. Gradually stir half the mixture into beaten egg. Return entire egg mixture to saucepan; heat just until it begins to boil. Cook and stir for 2 minutes more. Remove from heat. Cover surface with plastic wrap; chill. Just before using, gently stir.

4 For filling, in a medium mixing bowl combine whipping cream, powdered sugar, and vanilla. Beat with an electric mixer on low speed just until stiff peaks form. Fold about a fourth of the whipped cream into chilled lemon curd; fold in remaining whipped cream.

5 To assemble, carefully lift the baked phyllo shells from custard cups and place on a serving plate. Spoon or pipe filling equally among the baked phyllo shells. If desired, garnish with kiwi fruit. Makes 6.

Nutrition facts per serving: *384 calories, 4 g protein, 30 g carbohydrate, 28 g total fat (17 g saturated), 121 mg cholesterol, 264 mg sodium, 0 g fiber. Daily values: 29% vitamin A, 9% vitamin C, 3% calcium, 6% iron.*

Shortcut

Use ⅔ cup purchased lemon curd in place of the homemade lemon filling.

Lemon Cups, left, and Strawberry-Banana Tarts (see recipe, page 267), right

International Origin

Baklava

Package individual pieces in colorful plastic wrap to give as gifts or sell at fund-raisers.

- **4 cups walnuts, finely chopped (1 pound)**
- **½ cup granulated sugar**
- **1 teaspoon ground cinnamon**
- **1¼ cups butter (no substitutes), melted**
- **1 16-ounce package frozen phyllo dough, thawed**
- **1½ cups granulated sugar**
- **1 cup water**
- **¼ cup honey**
- **½ teaspoon finely shredded lemon peel**
- **2 tablespoons lemon juice**
- **2 inches stick cinnamon**

1 For filling, in a large mixing bowl combine walnuts, the ½ cup sugar, and cinnamon. Set filling aside.

2 Brush the bottom of a 15x10x1-inch baking pan with some of the melted butter. Unfold phyllo dough. Remove about one-fourth of the phyllo sheets, keeping the rest covered with plastic wrap or waxed paper and a damp towel. Layer phyllo sheets in prepared pan, generously brushing each sheet with melted butter and allowing phyllo to extend up the sides of the pan. Sprinkle about 1½ cups of

the filling on top of the phyllo in the pan. Repeat layering phyllo and filling 2 more times. Layer remaining phyllo sheets in the pan, brushing each sheet with butter. Drizzle any remaining butter over the top layer.

3 Trim edges of phyllo to fit pan. Using a sharp knife, cut through all layers to make triangle- or diamond-shape pieces. Bake in a 325° oven for 45 to 50 minutes or until golden. Slightly cool in pan on a wire rack.

4 Meanwhile, for syrup, in a medium saucepan stir together the 1½ cups sugar, water, honey, lemon peel, lemon juice, and stick cinnamon. Bring mixture to boiling. Reduce heat. Simmer, uncovered, for 20 minutes. Remove the stick cinnamon.

5 Pour the syrup over the warm baklava in the pan. Cool completely. Place in an airtight container and store at room temperature for up to 3 days. Makes about 60 pieces.

Nutrition facts per serving: *130 calories, 2 g protein, 13 g carbohydrate, 9 g total fat (3 g saturated), 10 mg cholesterol, 76 mg sodium, 00 g fiber. Daily values: 3% vitamin A, 00% vitamin C, 00% calcium, 3% iron.*

To Make Ahead

Prepare and bake as directed. Add syrup and cool completely. Place in a freezer container or bag and freeze for up to 1 month. Before serving, thaw for 30 minutes.

Cream Cheese Strudel Sticks

- **1 egg yolk, slightly beaten**
- **1 3-ounce package cream cheese, softened**
- **3 tablespoons granulated sugar**
- **¼ cup light raisins, mixed dried fruit bits, or dried cranberries**
- **¼ cup chopped hazelnuts, almonds, or pecans**
- **½ teaspoon vanilla**
- **6 18x12-inch sheets frozen phyllo dough, thawed**
- **⅓ cup butter (no substitutes), melted**
- **1 egg white**
- **1 tablespoon water**
- **1 tablespoon granulated sugar**

1 Grease a baking sheet. For filling, in medium mixing bowl beat together egg yolk, cream cheese, and 3 tablespoons sugar until combined. Stir in raisins, nuts, and vanilla. Set baking sheet and filling aside.

2 Unfold phyllo dough. Remove 1 sheet, keeping remaining phyllo dough covered with plastic wrap or waxed paper and damp towel. Place the 1 sheet on a lightly floured surface and brush with some of the melted butter. Place another phyllo sheet on top, brushing again with butter.

3 Cut sheets lengthwise into three 4x18-inch strips. On each strip, spread 1 tablespoon of filling in a 1-inch-wide band 3 inches in from short end and to within ½ inch of sides. Fold the

3-inch section over filling. Fold in sides. Roll each strip up jelly-roll style. Seal seam. Place seam side down on prepared baking sheet. Repeat with remaining sheets and filling, making 3 rolls from each set of phyllo sheets.

4 Beat together egg white and water; brush over phyllo rolls. Sprinkle with remaining sugar.

5 Bake in a 350° oven about 20 minutes or until golden. Remove from baking sheet and cool on a wire rack. Within 2 hours, place in airtight container and store in the refrigerator for up to 3 days. Makes 9 servings.

Nutrition facts per serving: *195 calories, 3 g protein, 17 g carbohydrate, 52 mg cholesterol, 13 g total fat (7 g saturated), 166 mg sodium, 0 g fiber. Daily values: 13% vitamin A, 0% vitamin C, 1% calcium, 5% iron.*

International Origin

Apple Strudel

Use a tablecloth or sheet under the phyllo dough to make it easier to roll into strudel.

3 cups finely chopped, peeled tart apples
¼ cup granulated sugar
⅓ cup raisins or snipped dried apricots
¼ cup chopped walnuts or pecans
½ teaspoon ground cinnamon

12 18x12-inch sheets frozen phyllo dough, thawed
½ cup butter (no substitutes), melted
1 slightly beaten egg white
1 tablespoon water
Powdered sugar

1 Lightly grease a 15x10x1-inch baking pan; set aside. For filling, in a large mixing bowl combine apples, sugar, raisins, walnuts, and cinnamon. Set baking pan and filling aside.

2 Cover a large surface (at least 4x3 feet) with a floured cloth. Unfold phyllo dough. Remove 6 sheets, keeping the rest covered with plastic wrap or waxed paper and a damp towel. Arrange the 6 sheets of phyllo on the floured cloth, overlapping as necessary to form a rectangle about 40x20-inches. Brush each sheet of phyllo with butter; seal the seams. Top with 6 more sheets of phyllo dough, brushing each sheet with butter and overlapping as necessary (but do not overlap in the same places where the bottom layer overlaps). Trim to form a 40x20-inch rectangle. Brush with remaining melted butter.

3 Beginning 4 inches from one of the 20-inch sides of dough, spoon the filling across the dough in a 4-inch-wide band. Using the cloth beneath the dough as a guide, gently lift the 4-inch section of dough and lay it over the filling. Slowly and evenly lift the cloth and tightly roll up the dough and filling, jelly-roll style. Fold the ends under to seal.

4 Carefully transfer the strudel roll to the prepared baking pan. Curve the ends to form a half ring (crescent). With a fork, stir together egg white and water; brush over top of strudel. Bake in a 350° oven for 35 to 40 minutes or until golden. Carefully remove from pan, and cool on a wire rack. Just before serving, sift powdered sugar over strudel. Makes 12 to 16 servings.

Nutrition facts per serving: *187 calories, 2 g protein, 22 g carbohydrate, 10 g total fat (5 g saturated), 20 mg cholesterol, 175 mg sodium, 1 g fiber. Daily values: 7% vitamin A, 0% vitamin C, 0% calcium, 5% iron.*

Cranberry-Apple Strudel: Prepare Apple Strudel as directed, except reduce apples to 2 cups and add 1 cup chopped cranberries. Increase granulated sugar to ⅔ cup.

To Make Ahead
Prepare strudel for baking. Cover and refrigerate up to 6 hours. About 1½ hours before serving, bake as directed.

Use the cloth under the pastry to lift and roll the pastry over the filling and then to roll up the dough.

Raspberry-Blackberry Cobbler
(see recipe, page 278)

The Best Of the Rest

When it comes to down-home baked desserts, many close-to-the-heart favorites spring to mind.

❧

Remember cobblers topped with rich "cobbled" biscuit dough, crisps crowned with spicy oatmeal crumble, betties topped with crisp bread cubes, and moist bread-and-butter puddings studded with raisins? Could you ever forget creamy baked puddings, velvety custards, or ethereal chocolate soufflés?

❧

Fortunately, you don't have to. All those fundamentally satisfying desserts are right here in this chapter. Now you can add a bit of comfort to your next meal.

Strawberry-Pear Cobbler

You'll add just the right amount of sweetness to this cobbler when you scoop on your choice of strawberry or vanilla ice cream.

½ **cup all-purpose flour**
2 **tablespoons granulated sugar**
1 **teaspoon baking powder**
½ **teaspoon finely shredded orange peel**
1 **tablespoon butter or margarine**
¼ **cup granulated sugar**
2 **tablespoons cornstarch**
½ **cup water**
2 **cups fresh or frozen strawberries**
1 **large pear, peeled, cored, and thinly sliced**
¼ **cup buttermilk**
   Strawberry or vanilla ice cream

1 For biscuit topping, in a small mixing bowl stir together flour, 2 tablespoons sugar, baking powder, and orange peel. Using a pastry blender, cut in butter until mixture resembles coarse crumbs. Make a well in the center of the dry mixture, then set dry mixture aside.

2 For filling, in a medium saucepan stir together ¼ cup sugar and cornstarch; stir in water. Halve any large strawberries. Add berries and pear slices to saucepan. Cook and stir over medium heat until thickened and bubbly. Reduce heat and keep filling hot.

Add buttermilk all at once to the dry biscuit topping. Using a fork, stir just until moistened.

3 Transfer the hot filling to an ungreased 1-quart glass casserole. Immediately spoon biscuit topping into 6 mounds on top of the hot filling. Bake in a 400° oven for 20 to 25 minutes or until a wooden toothpick inserted into the center of a dumpling comes out clean. Serve warm with ice cream. Makes 6 servings.

Nutrition facts per serving: 279 calories, 4 g protein, 46 g carbohydrate, 10 g total fat (6 g saturated fat), 34 mg cholesterol, 128 mg sodium, 3 g fiber. Daily values: 9% vitamin A, 56% vitamin C, 10% calcium, 5% iron.

Peanutty Fruit Cobbler

It's important to spoon the topping onto hot filling so that the dumplings cook evenly.

¾ **cup all-purpose flour**
2 **tablespoons granulated sugar**
1 **teaspoon baking powder**
⅛ **teaspoon salt**
3 **tablespoons butter or margarine**
1 **16-ounce can peach slices or 17-ounce can unpeeled apricot halves**
1 **8½-ounce can pear slices or halves**

¼ **cup packed brown sugar**
1 **tablespoon cornstarch**
¼ **cup orange juice**
¼ **cup butter or margarine**
1 **tablespoon peanut butter**
¼ **cup chopped peanuts**
¼ **cup raisins**
¼ **cup milk**
3 **tablespoons chopped peanuts**

1 For biscuit topping, in a small mixing bowl stir together the flour, granulated sugar, baking powder, and salt. Using a pastry blender, cut in the 3 tablespoons butter until mixture resembles coarse crumbs. Make a well in the center of the dry mixture, then set dry mixture aside.

2 For filling, drain canned fruits, reserving syrup. Cut up fruit and set aside. In medium saucepan stir together brown sugar and cornstarch. Stir in the reserved syrup and orange juice. Cook and stir over medium heat until thickened and bubbly. Stir in the ¼ cup butter and the peanut butter until smooth. Stir in chopped fruit, ¼ cup peanuts, and raisins; reduce heat and keep mixture hot.

3 Add milk all at once to the dry biscuit topping. Using a fork, stir just until moistened.

4 Transfer the hot filling to an ungreased 2-quart square glass baking dish. Immediately spoon biscuit topping into 6 mounds on top of the hot filling. Sprinkle with the 3 tablespoons peanuts. Bake in a 400° oven for 20 to

25 minutes or until a wooden tooth-pick inserted into the center of a dumpling comes out clean. Serve warm. Makes 6 servings.

Nutrition facts per serving: 409 calories, 6 g protein, 55 g carbohydrate, 20 g total fat (9 g saturated fat), 37 mg cholesterol, 270 mg sodium, 2 g fiber. Daily values: 15% vitamin A, 10% vitamin C, 8% calcium, 11% iron.

Peach-Pecan Cobbler

A new twist on an old favorite, this cobbler contains oatmeal and chopped pecans for extra texture and flavor. Sprinkle on the cinnamon-sugar to enhance the appearance.

  1 **cup all-purpose flour**
  ¼ **cup rolled oats**
  ¼ **cup packed brown sugar**
  1 **teaspoon baking powder**
  ½ **teaspoon ground nutmeg**
  3 **tablespoons butter or margarine**
  ⅓ **cup chopped pecans**
  ⅓ **cup granulated sugar**
  1 **tablespoon cornstarch**
  ¼ **cup water**
  ¼ **teaspoon almond extract**
  4 **cups sliced, peeled peaches or sliced nectarines or frozen unsweetened peach slices**
  1 **egg**
  ¼ **cup milk**

  1 **tablespoon granulated sugar**
  ¼ **teaspoon ground cinnamon**
      Peach ice cream or whipped cream (optional)

1 For biscuit topping, in a medium mixing bowl stir together flour, rolled oats, brown sugar, baking powder, and nutmeg. Using a pastry blender, cut in butter until mixture resembles coarse crumbs; add pecans. Make a well in the center of the dry mixture, then set dry mixture aside.

2 For filling, in a medium saucepan stir together granulated sugar and cornstarch. Stir in water and almond extract; add fruit. Cook and stir over medium heat until slightly thickened and bubbly. Reduce heat and keep mixture hot.

3 In a small mixing bowl use a fork to beat together egg and milk; add all at once to the dry biscuit topping. Using the fork, stir just until moistened.

4 Transfer the hot filling to an un-greased 2-quart square glass baking dish. Immediately spoon biscuit topping into 8 mounds on top of the hot filling. Stir together the 1 tablespoon sugar and the cinnamon. Sprinkle over topping. Bake in a 400° oven for 20 to 25 minutes or until a wooden tooth-pick inserted into the center of a dumpling comes out clean. If desired, serve warm with peach ice cream or whipped cream. Makes 8 servings.

Nutrition facts per serving: 248 calories, 4 g protein, 41 g carbohydrate, 9 g total fat (3 g saturated fat), 39 mg cholesterol, 104 mg sodium, 2 g fiber. Daily values: 10% vitamin A, 9% vitamin C, 6% calcium, 8% iron.

Cobbled Together

It's not hard to see how cobblers were matched with their moniker—the "cobbled" biscuit topping is responsible for much of this dish's appeal. A distant relation to the deep-dish pie, cobblers have the same bubbly fruit filling.

Always use the size dish specified in the recipe. The cobbler will bubble up during baking and the dish needs to be deep enough to allow for this. If you don't want to risk the filling bubbling over, place a baking sheet beneath the dish to catch any spills.

Make sure the fruit filling is hot when you put the biscuit topping on. Otherwise the bottom of the topping won't cook properly. If necessary, keep the filling warm over low heat while mixing the topping. Check the doneness of the cobbler by inserting a wooden toothpick into the center of one or two mounds of topping (don't stick it in too far or you'll hit the gooey filling). It's done when the toothpick comes out clean.

Ginger-Plum Cobbler

Add the desired amount of brown sugar according to the tartness of the plums and your sweet tooth.

- **1 cup all-purpose flour**
- **2 tablespoons granulated sugar**
- **1 teaspoon baking powder**
- **⅛ teaspoon salt**
- **2 tablespoons butter or margarine**
- **½ to ¾ cup packed brown sugar**
- **4 teaspoons cornstarch**
- **½ teaspoon ground ginger or 1 teaspoon grated fresh gingerroot**
- **¼ cup water**
- **1 tablespoon lemon juice**
- **2 pounds plums or apricots, pitted and quartered (5 cups)**
- **1 tablespoon butter or margarine**
- **1 egg**
- **¼ cup milk**
  Vanilla ice cream (optional)

1 For biscuit topping, in a medium mixing bowl stir together flour, granulated sugar, baking powder, and salt. Using a pastry blender, cut in 2 tablespoons butter until mixture resembles coarse crumbs. Make a well in the center of the dry mixture, then set dry mixture aside.

2 For filling, in a large saucepan stir together brown sugar, cornstarch, and ginger. Stir in water and lemon juice. Stir in plums. Cook and stir over medium heat until slightly thickened and bubbly. Stir in 1 tablespoon butter. Reduce heat and keep mixture hot.

3 In a small mixing bowl use a fork to beat together egg and milk; add all at once to the dry biscuit topping. Using the fork, stir just until moistened.

4 Transfer the hot filling to an ungreased 2-quart square glass baking dish. Immediately spoon the biscuit topping into 6 mounds on top of the hot filling. Bake in a 400° oven for 20 to 25 minutes or until a wooden toothpick inserted into the center of a dumpling comes out clean. If desired, serve cobbler warm with ice cream. Makes 6 servings.

Nutrition facts per serving: *300 calories, 5 g protein, 56 g carbohydrate, 8 g total fat (4 g saturated fat), 52 mg cholesterol, 184 mg sodium, 4 g fiber. Daily values: 12% vitamin A, 26% vitamin C, 8% calcium, 10% iron.*

Shortcut

Stir together the dry ingredients for the biscuit topping early in the day or the night before. Cover and refrigerate. Just before baking, prepare fruit and measure liquid ingredients. Finish topping and bake as directed.

Blackberry-Nectarine Crisp: Prepare Blueberry-Peach Crisp as directed above, except substitute 2 cups fresh blackberries or frozen unsweetened blackberries for the blueberries and 2 cups sliced nectarines for the peaches.

Blueberry-Peach Crisp

Make this summer-fresh treat year-round with the frozen-fruit options.

- **3 cups sliced, peeled peaches or frozen unsweetened peach slices**
- **2 cups fresh blueberries or frozen unsweetened blueberries**
- **¼ cup granulated sugar**
- **⅓ cup rolled oats**
- **⅓ cup all-purpose flour**
- **¼ cup packed brown sugar**
- **½ teaspoon ground coriander**
- **3 tablespoons butter (no substitutes)**
  Vanilla ice cream (optional)

1 Thaw fruit, if frozen. Do not drain. Transfer fruit to an ungreased 2-quart square glass baking dish. Stir in granulated sugar. Set fruit aside.

2 For topping, in a medium mixing bowl stir together oats, flour, brown sugar, and coriander. Using a pastry blender, cut in butter until mixture resembles coarse crumbs.

3 Sprinkle topping over fruit. Bake in a 375° oven 30 to 40 minutes or until topping is golden. If desired, serve warm with ice cream. Serves 6.

Nutrition facts per serving: *225 calories, 3 g protein, 43 g carbohydrate, 6 g total fat (4 g saturated fat), 15 mg cholesterol, 64 mg sodium, 4 g fiber. Daily values: 11% vitamin A, 22% vitamin C, 1% calcium, 6% iron.*

Blueberry-Peach Crisp, top, and Ginger-Plum Cobbler, bottom

Warm and Crispy

Betties and crisps have different toppings than cobblers but all of the desserts feature a bubbly fruit filling.

Betties are topped with soft bread cubes. It's easiest to cut the cubes if the bread is frozen. Whether the bread is frozen or not, use a serrated knife and a gentle sawing motion to cut the bread into the ½-inch cubes.

Crisps are topped with a crunchy oatmeal mixture. This topping stores well, so try mixing a double batch next time you bake a crisp. Put the extra topping in a freezer bag, and seal, label, and freeze it for up to 1 month.

Like other baked fruit desserts, betties and crisps taste their best when eaten warm, but not hot. To serve, let them cool about 30 minutes after you take them out of the oven. If you like, top them with ice cream, whipped cream, or even just a bit of light cream or milk.

Raspberry-Blackberry Cobbler

Sprinkle this cobbler with a little powdered sugar and top it with a mint leaf for a spectacular dessert.
(Pictured on page 272.)

½ **cup all-purpose flour**
¾ **teaspoon baking powder**
⅛ **teaspoon salt**
2 **tablespoons butter or margarine**
½ **cup granulated sugar**
2 **tablespoons cornstarch**
¼ **teaspoon ground nutmeg**
⅓ **cup water**
2 **cups fresh raspberries or frozen lightly sweetened red raspberries**
2 **cups fresh blackberries or frozen unsweetened blackberries**

1 **egg**
1 **tablespoon honey**
1 **tablespoon milk**

1 For biscuit topping, in a small mixing bowl stir together flour, baking powder, and salt. Using a pastry blender, cut in butter until mixture resembles coarse crumbs. Make a well in the center of the dry mixture, then set dry mixture aside.

2 For filling, in a medium saucepan stir together sugar, cornstarch, and nutmeg. Add water. Cook and stir over medium heat until slightly thickened and bubbly. Add fresh or frozen fruit. Cook and gently stir until boiling. Reduce heat and keep mixture hot.

3 In a small mixing bowl use a fork to beat together the egg, honey, and milk; add all at once to the dry mixture. Using the fork, stir just until moistened.

4 Transfer hot filling to an ungreased 2-quart square glass baking dish. Immediately spoon biscuit topping into 6 mounds on top of the hot filling. Bake in a 400° oven for 20 to 25 minutes or until a wooden toothpick inserted into the center of a dumpling comes out clean. Serve warm. Makes 6 servings.

Nutrition facts per serving: 213 calories, 3 g protein, 41 g carbohydrate, 5 g total fat (3 g saturated fat), 46 mg cholesterol, 141 mg sodium, 5 g fiber. Daily values: 6% vitamin A, 33% vitamin C, 6% calcium, 7% iron.

Apricot-Plum Crisp

Choose plums in your favorite variety for this fruit crisp and team them with fresh apricots.

½ **cup rolled oats**
½ **cup packed brown sugar**
¼ **cup all-purpose flour**
¼ **teaspoon ground mace or ground nutmeg**
¼ **cup butter (no substitutes)**
¾ **pound apricots, pitted and quartered (2 cups)**
¾ **pound plums, pitted and quartered (2 cups)**
2 **tablespoons granulated sugar**
Vanilla ice cream (optional)

1 For topping, in a medium mixing bowl stir together oats, brown sugar, flour, and mace or nutmeg. Using a pastry blender, cut in butter until mixture resembles coarse crumbs. Set topping aside.

2 In a large mixing bowl combine apricots, plums, and granulated sugar, tossing gently until combined. Transfer fruit mixture to an ungreased 2-quart square glass baking dish.

3 Sprinkle topping over the fruit. Bake in a 375° oven for 30 to 35 minutes or until fruit is tender and topping is golden. If desired, serve warm with ice cream. Makes 6 servings.

Nutrition facts per serving: *263 calories, 3 g protein, 46 g carbohydrate, 9 g total fat (5 g saturated fat), 20 mg cholesterol, 83 mg sodium, 2 g fiber. Daily values: 24% vitamin A, 24% vitamin C, 2% calcium, 8% iron.*

Raspberry-Pear Crisp

Had a busy day? Here's a special dessert that goes together with little fuss.

1 12-ounce package frozen lightly sweetened red raspberries
½ cup granulated sugar
2 tablespoons cornstarch
2 medium pears, peeled, cored, and thinly sliced (2 cups)
2 cups granola
Vanilla ice cream (optional)

1 Thaw and drain the raspberries, reserving juice.

2 For filling, in a medium saucepan stir together sugar and cornstarch; stir in raspberry juices. Cook and stir over medium heat until thickened and bubbly. Remove from heat; stir in raspberries and pears.

3 Transfer filling to an ungreased 9-inch glass pie plate. Sprinkle granola over the fruit. Bake in a 375° oven for 20 to 25 minutes or until pears are tender and topping is golden. If desired, serve warm with ice cream. Serves 6.

Nutrition facts per serving: *303 calories, 5 g protein, 59 g carbohydrate, 7 g total fat (4 g saturated fat), 0 mg cholesterol, 78 mg sodium, 6 g fiber. Daily values: 1% vitamin A, 27% vitamin C, 3% calcium, 11% iron.*

Tropical Crisp

Tropical fruits have become so popular that some now are available peeled, seeded, sliced, and canned in sugar syrup. If you decide to use canned instead of fresh fruit, be sure to drain it first.

½ cup rolled oats
¼ cup all-purpose flour
¼ cup packed brown sugar
¼ teaspoon ground nutmeg
2 tablespoons butter (no substitutes)
¼ cup coconut
4 cups desired fruit, such as fresh orange sections, papaya slices, mango slices, and pineapple chunks
⅓ cup orange juice or pineapple juice
2 tablespoons granulated sugar
Vanilla ice cream (optional)

1 For topping, in a bowl stir together oats, flour, brown sugar, and nutmeg. Cut in butter until mixture resembles coarse crumbs. Stir in coconut.

Cream on Call

Beating whipping cream can be a nerve-wracking experience, but there are options if you really dislike doing it.

There are aerosol cream products sold in cans that can be kept in your refrigerator for several weeks. The cream is pressurized, and all you have to do is point and shoot. Use it as a topping and not as a substitute for whipped cream in fillings.

You also can freeze leftover whipped cream. Spoon extra whipped cream into mounds on a waxed-paper-lined baking sheet. Freeze until firm, then transfer mounds to a freezer container and freeze for up to 1 month.

To use the frozen whipped cream, remove the number of mounds you need, let them stand at room temperature for 5 minutes, and, presto, top your dessert.

2 Transfer desired fruit to an ungreased 2-quart square glass baking dish. Drizzle with orange juice; sprinkle with granulated sugar. Sprinkle topping over fruit. Bake in a 375° oven for 30 to 35 minutes or until topping is golden. If desired, serve warm with vanilla ice cream. Makes 9 servings.

Nutrition facts per serving: *133 calories, 2 g protein, 25 g carbohydrate, 4 g total fat (2 g saturated fat), 7 mg cholesterol, 29 mg sodium, 2 g fiber. Daily values: 15% vitamin A, 56% vitamin C, 2% calcium, 4% iron.*

Strawberry-Rhubarb Betty

Apple Crumble

Apple Crumble

Complement the tartness of apples with the rich flavor of the brown sugar-butter mixture.

- 6 **cups apples, peeled, cored, and sliced**
- ¼ **cup packed brown sugar**
- 3 **tablespoons butter (no substitutes)**
- 1 **tablespoon water**
- ½ **teaspoon pumpkin pie spice**
- ½ **cup all-purpose flour**
- ¼ **cup packed brown sugar**
- ½ **teaspoon pumpkin pie spice**
- 3 **tablespoons butter (no substitutes)**
- ¼ **cup chopped pecans**
- 1 **pint vanilla ice cream**

1 Place apples in an ungreased 2-quart square glass baking dish.

2 In a small saucepan combine ¼ cup brown sugar, 3 tablespoons butter, the water, and ½ teaspoon pumpkin pie spice. Cook and stir over medium-high heat until boiling. Continue to boil, without stirring, for 1 minute. Pour over apples. Set aside.

3 For topping, in a mixing bowl stir together flour, ¼ cup brown sugar, and ½ teaspoon pumpkin pie spice. Using a pastry blender, cut in 3 tablespoons butter until mixture resembles coarse crumbs. Stir in pecans.

4 Sprinkle topping over the apples. Bake in a 375° oven for 45 to 50 minutes or until apples are tender and topping is golden. Serve warm with ice cream. Makes 6 servings.

Nutrition facts per serving: 355 calories, 3 g protein, 45 g carbohydrate, 20 g total fat (10 g saturated fat), 50 mg cholesterol, 157 mg sodium, 1 g fiber. Daily values: 16% vitamin A, 0% vitamin C, 6% calcium, 7% iron.

Strawberry-Rhubarb Betty

Add the maximum amount of sugar if the strawberries or rhubarb are particularly tart. For a flavor variation, substitute cinnamon bread for the white bread.

- 3 **cups sliced fresh or frozen unsweetened strawberries**
- 2 **cups thinly sliced fresh or frozen unsweetened rhubarb**
- ¾ **to 1 cup granulated sugar**
- 2 **tablespoons all-purpose flour**
- ¼ **teaspoon salt**
- 4 **cups soft bread cubes (about 5 slices)**
- ¼ **cup butter (no substitutes), melted**

1 Thaw strawberries and rhubarb, if frozen. Do not drain. For filling, in a large mixing bowl stir together sugar, flour, and salt. Add strawberries, rhubarb, and their juice, then gently toss until coated.

2 For topping, place the bread cubes in a medium mixing bowl. Drizzle with the melted butter, then toss until mixed. Transfer half the buttered bread cubes to an ungreased 1½-quart round glass casserole. Pour the fruit mixture over the bread cubes. Sprinkle the remaining bread topping over the fruit filling.

3 Bake in a 375° oven for 25 to 30 minutes or until fruit is tender and topping is golden. Serve warm. Makes 6 servings.

Nutrition facts per serving: 256 calories, 3 g protein, 44 g carbohydrate, 9 g total fat (5 g saturated fat), 20 mg cholesterol, 272 mg sodium, 3 g fiber. Daily values: 7% vitamin A, 75% vitamin C, 6% calcium, 7% iron.

Setting Some Aside

If you are so lucky as to have some cobbler, betty, crisp, bread pudding, or baked fruit left over, you can keep it for up to 2 days. Transfer the leftovers to a smaller casserole or ovenproof dish, cover, and chill. If you want to reheat a cobbler, baked fruit, betty, or crisp, cover it with the casserole lid or foil and bake in a 350° oven until warm in the center.

Cranberry-Pear Cinnamon Betty

If you'd rather prepare individual servings, assemble the dessert in six 10-ounce casseroles. Bake for 25 to 30 minutes or until pears are tender and topping is golden.

⅔ cup packed brown sugar
1 tablespoon all-purpose flour
½ teaspoon ground cinnamon
¼ teaspoon salt
3 pears, peeled, cored, and thinly sliced (3 cups)
2 cups cranberries
4 cups cinnamon-raisin or cinnamon bread cubes (about 5 slices)*
3 tablespoons butter (no substitutes), melted
2 teaspoons coarse sugar

1 For filling, in a large mixing bowl stir together brown sugar, flour, cinnamon, and salt. Add sliced pears and cranberries and gently toss until coated. Transfer half of the fruit filling to an ungreased 2-quart square baking dish.

2 For topping, place bread cubes in a medium mixing bowl. Drizzle with melted butter; toss until mixed. Sprinkle half of the bread cubes over the fruit filling. Repeat fruit and bread cube layers. Sprinkle with coarse sugar. Bake in a 375° oven for 35 to 40 minutes or until pears are tender and topping is golden. Serve warm. Makes 6 servings.

Allow bread slices to set out for a few hours so they become firmer but not dry. Or, freeze the bread until slices are firm. Using a serrated knife, cut the bread into strips about ½ inch wide. Turn and cut again to cut the strips into cubes.

*Note: Look for unfrosted cinnamon bread. However, if you can't find cinnamon or cinnamon-raisin bread, replace it with 4 cups whole wheat bread cubes or 2 cups whole wheat and 2 cups white bread cubes.

***Nutrition facts per serving:** 277 calories, 3 g protein, 53 g carbohydrate, 7 g total fat (4 g saturated fat), 15 mg cholesterol, 306 mg sodium, 4 g fiber. Daily values: 5% vitamin A, 13% vitamin C, 5% calcium, 11% iron.*

Apple-Apricot Betty

Another time, try your favorite flavor of preserves in place of the apricot called for here. Raspberry or cherry also go well with apples.

¼ cup granulated sugar
1 tablespoon all-purpose flour
¼ teaspoon salt
5 medium apples, peeled, cored, and sliced (5 cups)
¾ cup apricot preserves
4 cups soft bread cubes (about 5 slices)
2 tablespoons butter (no substitutes), melted
    Whipped cream or vanilla ice cream (optional)

1 For filling, in a mixing bowl combine sugar, flour, and salt. Add apples and apricot preserves and gently toss until coated. Add 2 cups of the bread cubes and toss until mixed. Transfer fruit-bread mixture to an ungreased 2-quart square glass baking dish.

2 For topping, place remaining bread cubes in a medium mixing bowl. Drizzle with melted butter; toss until mixed. Sprinkle the bread mixture over the fruit-bread mixture. Bake in a 375° oven for 25 to 30 minutes or until apples are tender and topping is golden. Serve warm. If desired, top with whipped cream or ice cream. Makes 6 servings.

***Nutrition facts per serving:** 270 calories, 2 g protein, 57 g carbohydrate, 5 g total fat (3 g saturated fat), 10 mg cholesterol, 236 mg sodium, 2 g fiber. Daily values: 3% vitamin A, 1% vitamin C, 3% calcium, 7% iron.*

Baked Stuffed Pears

Stuff fresh pears with marzipan and dried fruit for a surprise filling, then bake them. Good pear choices for baking include Bartlett and Bosc varieties.

- **1 lemon**
- **2 cups white grape juice**
- **2 tablespoons butter or margarine**
- **4 medium pears**
- **4 teaspoons marzipan or almond paste**
- **4 pitted prunes or 8 dried apricot halves**
- **¼ cup apricot preserves**
  Lemon balm leaves (optional)

1 Remove just the yellow part of the peel from the lemon; set aside. Squeeze the juice from ½ of the lemon; set juice aside. In a medium saucepan stir together the white grape juice, butter, and lemon peel. Bring to boiling.

2 Meanwhile, wash pears and pat dry. Using an apple corer, core the pears from the bottom, leaving the stems attached. Peel pears. Rub the pears with the reserved lemon juice to prevent them from turning brown.

3 Divide marzipan into 4 equal portions and roll each portion into the shape of an almond. Stuff marzipan inside prunes or between apricot halves. Place a stuffed prune or apricot inside the base of each pear. Place pears on sides in an ungreased 2-quart square glass baking dish. Pour hot grape juice mixture over pears.

4 Bake, uncovered, in a 350° oven 45 minutes or until pears are tender, basting and turning them every 15 minutes. Transfer pears to dessert bowls.

5 For sauce, return liquid to saucepan. Boil liquid about 8 minutes or until it's reduced to 1 cup. Discard lemon peel. Stir in preserves and continue cooking and stirring 5 to 8 minutes more or until sauce is slightly thickened. Spoon sauce over pears. Serve warm or chilled. If desired, garnish with lemon balm leaves. Serves 4.

Nutrition facts per pear: 341 calories, 2 g protein, 72 g carbohydrate, 8 g total fat (4 g saturated fat), 15 mg cholesterol, 66 mg sodium, 6 g fiber. Daily values: 7% vita-min A, 20% vitamin C, 4% calcium, 9% iron.

To remove the core but leave the stem intact, use a fruit corer or a sharp narrow-blade knife and start from the bottom end. With the pear resting firmly in your hand or on a cutting surface, press the corer into the center of the bottom of the pear. Aim straight through the pear toward the stem. Turn the corer around and use an in-and-out cutting motion to remove the core but not the stem.

Fill It Up

Coring whole fruit is a lot easier if you invest in a long, cylindrical apple corer. Then it takes just a couple of twists of the corer to easily remove the core and seeds from an apple or pear, freeing you up to concentrate on the filling.

Experiment with different fillings for baked fruit. Try granola, chocolate chips, coconut, nuts, cinnamon and sugar, or a combination of any of these. Follow the baking times given in the recipe.

To see if the fruit is done, poke it with a fork. If the fork goes in and comes out easily, the fruit is done. If your apples or pears are larger or smaller than those specified in the recipe, the baking time may need to be adjusted accordingly.

Baked Bananas and Berries

When baking bananas, choose those that are not too ripe. They should be firm with a touch of green on the tips. Also, avoid overbaking so that they'll retain their shape and won't become mushy.

4 bananas
1 12-ounce carton cranberry-strawberry, cranberry-orange, or cranberry-raspberry crushed fruit
⅓ cup honey
3 tablespoons butter or margarine
½ teaspoon ground cinnamon
⅓ cup broken pecans
    Vanilla ice cream

1 Peel and slice bananas, making about 3 cups. Place bananas in an ungreased 2-quart rectangular or square baking dish.

2 In a medium saucepan stir together crushed fruit, honey, butter, and cinnamon. Bring to boiling. Pour hot mixture over bananas. Sprinkle with pecans.

3 Bake, uncovered, in a 350° oven for 10 minutes or until bananas are hot. Serve the baked bananas and berries over vanilla ice cream. Serves 6.

Nutrition facts per serving: 450 calories, 4 g protein, 73 g carbohydrate, 17 g total fat (8 g saturated fat), 44 mg cholesterol, 123 mg sodium, 2 g fiber. Daily values: 13% vitamin A, 12% vitamin C, 8% calcium, and 3% iron.

Classic Rice Pudding

3 egg yolks
1½ cups milk, half-and-half, or light cream
1½ cups cooked rice
⅓ cup granulated sugar
⅓ cup raisins, chopped dried fruit, or chopped candied fruit (optional)
1 tablespoon butter or margarine, melted
1 tablespoon finely shredded orange peel
1 teaspoon vanilla
⅛ teaspoon salt
    Cherry-Rhubarb Sauce

1 Place an ungreased 1 quart casserole in an 8x8x2-inch baking pan. Set baking pan aside.

2 In a large mixing bowl use a rotary beater or wire whisk to lightly beat egg yolks just until mixed. Then stir in milk or cream, cooked rice, sugar, raisins (if desired), melted butter, orange peel, vanilla, and salt.

3 Place baking pan with casserole on oven rack. Pour egg mixture into casserole. Then pour boiling or hottest tap water into pan around casserole.

4 Bake in a 325° oven for 40 to 45 minutes or until a knife inserted near the center comes out clean. Remove casserole from water in pan. Cool on a wire rack. Serve warm or cover and chill for at least 4 hours. Serve with Cherry-Rhubarb Sauce. Serves 6.

Cherry-Rhubarb Sauce: In a medium saucepan stir together ½ cup granulated sugar and ¼ cup orange juice. Bring to boiling. Thoroughly drain one 16-ounce can pitted tart red cherries (water pack). Add drained cherries and 1 cup rhubarb cut into ¼-inch slices to sugar mixture. Return to boiling. Reduce heat. Cover and simmer 10 minutes or until rhubarb is tender. In a small bowl combine 1 tablespoon cornstarch and 1 tablespoon water. Stir into fruit mixture. Cook and stir until thickened and bubbly; cook and stir for 2 minutes more. If desired, stir in 4 to 5 drops red food coloring.

Nutrition facts per serving: 278 calories, 5 g protein, 52 g carbohydrate, 6 g total fat (3 g saturated fat), 116 mg cholesterol, 104 mg sodium, 1 g fiber. Daily values: 27% vitamin A, 17% vitamin C, 9% calcium, and 12% iron.

Pour boiling or the hottest tap water possible into the square baking pan around the pudding-filled casserole dish. The water in the baking pan should be 1 inch deep. This water bath helps distribute the heat evenly so the pudding's edges don't overcook while the center is getting done.

Delicious Memories

Chocolate Sundae Pudding Cake

Chocolate was a hands-down family favorite when I was growing up. My father didn't consider dessert complete without ice cream, so his serving of the pudding cake always included a generous scoop of vanilla—sort of a deluxe hot fudge sundae.
—Betty Rice—

- 1 **cup all-purpose flour**
- ⅔ **cup granulated sugar**
- 2 **tablespoons unsweetened cocoa powder**
- 2 **teaspoons baking powder**
- ¼ **teaspoon salt**
- ½ **cup milk**
- ½ **cup chopped nuts**
- 2 **tablespoons butter or margarine, melted**
- 1 **teaspoon vanilla**
- ½ **cup packed brown sugar**
- ¼ **cup granulated sugar**
- 3 **tablespoons unsweetened cocoa powder**
- 1 **teaspoon vanilla**
- ⅛ **teaspoon salt**
- 1 **cup boiling water**

1 Grease a 1½-quart glass casserole. Set casserole aside.

2 In a large mixing bowl stir together the flour, ⅔ cup granulated sugar, 2 tablespoons cocoa powder, baking powder, and ¼ teaspoon salt.

3 In a small mixing bowl stir together the milk, nuts, melted butter, and 1 teaspoon vanilla. Add to the dry ingredients and stir to combine. Pour into the casserole.

4 In another bowl stir together the brown sugar, ¼ cup granulated sugar, 3 tablespoons cocoa powder, 1 teaspoon vanilla, and ⅛ teaspoon salt. Sprinkle the mixture evenly over the batter. Pour the boiling water over batter; do not stir.

5 Bake in 350° oven about 45 minutes or until a wooden toothpick inserted into the cake portion comes out clean. Makes 4 to 6 servings.

Nutrition facts per serving: *563 calories, 8 g protein, 98 g carbohydrate, 17 g total fat (5 g saturated fat), 18 mg cholesterol, 464 mg sodium, 1 g fiber. Daily values: 7% vitamin A, 1% vitamin C, 26% calcium, and 22% iron.*

Chocolate-Cinnamon Custard

- 1½ **cups milk**
- ⅓ **cup granulated sugar**
- 2 **ounces semisweet chocolate, coarsely chopped**
- 1 **teaspoon vanilla**
- ½ **teaspoon ground cinnamon**
- 3 **eggs**

1 Place 4 ungreased 6-ounce custard cups or one 1-quart soufflé dish in an 8x8x2- or 9x9x2-inch baking pan. Set baking pan aside.

2 In a heavy medium saucepan combine milk, sugar, and chocolate. Cook and stir over medium heat until the mixture is bubbly and the chocolate is melted. Remove saucepan from the heat. (If flecks of chocolate remain, beat the hot mixture with a rotary beater or a wire whisk until smooth.) Stir in vanilla and cinnamon.

3 In a large bowl use a rotary beater to lightly beat eggs just until mixed. Gradually stir in chocolate mixture.

4 Place baking pan with custard cups or soufflé dish on oven rack. Pour egg mixture into cups or dish. Pour boiling or hottest tap water about 1 inch deep into pan around the cups or dish.

5 Bake in a 325° oven for 30 to 35 minutes (40 to 50 minutes for soufflé dish) or until a knife inserted near the center comes out clean. Remove container(s) from water in pan. Cool on a wire rack, then chill for at least 1 hour or for up to 8 hours. If desired, unmold individual custards. Serve warm or chilled. Makes 4 servings.

Nutrition facts per serving: *238 calories, 9 g protein, 31 g carbohydrate, 10 g total fat (5 g saturated fat), 167 mg cholesterol, 94 mg sodium, 1 g fiber. Daily values: 12% vitamin A, 1% vitamin C, 11% calcium, 8% iron.*

Baked Custard: Prepare Chocolate-Cinnamon Custard as directed above, except omit the chocolate and the cinnamon. If desired, sprinkle ground cinnamon or nutmeg over the top of the filled mold(s) before baking.

Crème Brûlée

International Origin

Crème Brûlée

*Caramelize the sugar topping in
a skillet and spoon it atop the creamy
custard for this version of a classic.*

**2 cups half-and-half or light
cream**
5 egg yolks
⅓ cup granulated sugar
1 teaspoon vanilla
¼ teaspoon salt
⅓ cup granulated sugar

1 Place four 4-inch quiche dishes or oval or round tart pans without removable bottoms in a 13x9x2-inch baking pan. Set the baking pan aside.

2 In a small, heavy saucepan heat half-and-half or light cream over medium-low heat just until bubbly. Remove from heat; set aside.

3 In a medium mixing bowl use a rotary beater or wire whisk to lightly beat egg yolks just until mixed. Then beat in the ⅓ cup sugar, vanilla, and salt just until combined. Slowly whisk or stir hot cream into egg mixture.

4 Place baking pan with the dishes on the oven rack. Pour the egg mixture evenly into the 4 dishes. Then pour boiling or hottest tap water into the pan around the dishes until it's about halfway up the sides.

5 Bake in 325° oven for 18 to 24 minutes or until a knife inserted near the center of each dish comes out clean. Remove dishes from the water in pan. Cool on a wire rack, then cover and chill for at least 1 hour or for up to 8 hours.

6 Before serving, let custards stand at room temperature for 20 minutes.

7 Meanwhile, place remaining ⅓ cup sugar in a large, heavy skillet. Heat skillet over medium-high heat until sugar begins to melt, shaking skillet occasionally so sugar will heat evenly. Do not stir. Once sugar starts to melt, reduce heat to low; cook until sugar is completely melted and golden (3 to 5 minutes more), stirring as needed.

8 Spoon melted sugar quickly over custards in a lacy pattern or in a solid piece. If melted sugar starts to harden in pan, return pan to heat, stirring until sugar melts again. If it starts to form clumps, carefully stir in 1 to 2 teaspoons water. Serve immediately. Makes 4 servings.

Nutrition facts per serving: *364 calories, 7 g protein, 39 g carbohydrate, 20 g total fat (11 g saturated fat), 311 mg cholesterol, 192 mg sodium, 0 g fiber. Daily values: 56% vitamin A, 1% vitamin C, 13% calcium, 5% iron.*

Amaretto Crème Brûlée: Prepare Crème Brûlée as directed above, except substitute 2 tablespoons amaretto for the vanilla.

Custard Conundrums

One of the secrets to a smooth custard is simply how you beat the eggs. Beat them just until the egg yolks and whites are blended. If you beat them until foamy, the surface of the custard will have bubbles.

Another secret is the hot water bath. While it may seem a bit of a hassle, the hot water bath is vitally important. It evens out the heat so the custard cooks all the way through without the edges getting overdone.

Test the custard to see if it's done by inserting a clean knife ½ inch into the custard about 1 inch from the center. If the knife comes out clean, the custard is done. If any clings to the knife, bake the custard a few more minutes, then test it again.

Once the custard tests done, immediately remove it from the oven and the hot water bath, being careful not to drip the hot water on yourself. If you leave the custard sitting in the hot water bath, it will continue to cook.

Dried Up

When you're making bread pudding remember that various breads absorb the pudding mixture differently, so don't substitute one type of bread for another.

If you don't have dry bread, you can oven-dry fresh bread. Spread the ½-inch (torn or cut) bread cubes in a single layer in a baking pan, and bake them in a 300° oven about 15 minutes or until the cubes are dry, stirring several times. To air-dry, spread the cubes in a single layer in a shallow baking pan and cover with a towel. Let them stand at room temperature for 8 to 12 hours or until the cubes are dry.

Peach-Sauced Bread Pudding

This unusual bread pudding contains cheese. Top it off with a flavorful fruit sauce made with frozen peaches or frozen sweet cherries.

- **4 eggs**
- **2 cups milk**
- **⅓ cup granulated sugar**
- **1 teaspoon ground cinnamon**

- **3 cups dry French bread cubes (about 4 slices)***
- **½ cup currants or raisins**
- **½ cup shredded cheddar cheese (2 ounces)**
- **¼ cup pine nuts or chopped pecans**
  Peach Sauce

1 In a large mixing bowl use a rotary beater to beat together eggs, milk, sugar, and cinnamon. Set the egg mixture aside.

2 In an ungreased 2-quart square glass baking dish toss together bread cubes, currants, and cheese. Pour egg mixture evenly over the bread mixture. Sprinkle nuts over the top.

3 Bake in a 325° oven for 40 to 45 minutes or until knife inserted near the center comes out clean. Serve the pudding warm with Peach Sauce. Makes 9 servings.

*Note: To make dry bread cubes for bread puddings, cut bread into ½-inch cubes. Spread cubes in a single layer in a shallow baking pan. Bake in a 300° oven for 10 to 15 minutes or until dry, stirring twice during baking. Or, let bread cubes stand, covered, at room temperature for 8 to 12 hours.

Peach Sauce: In a medium saucepan combine ¼ cup granulated sugar, 2 tablespoons cornstarch, and ¼ teaspoon ground cinnamon; stir in 1 teaspoon finely shredded orange peel, ½ cup orange juice, and ¼ cup water.

Partially thaw and chop one 16-ounce package frozen unsweetened peach slices; stir into mixture in saucepan. Cook and stir until thickened and bubbly. Cook and stir for 2 minutes more. Serve the warm sauce over bread pudding.

Nutrition facts per serving: 247 calories, 9 g protein, 37 g carbohydrate, 8 g total fat (3 g saturated fat), 105 mg cholesterol, 163 mg sodium, 1 g fiber. Daily values: 12% vitamin A, 19% vitamin C, 12% calcium, 10% iron.

International Origin

Cherry Clafouti

The area surrounding Limoges, France, is famous not only for its fine porcelain, but also for its cherry flan or clafouti.

- **1 teaspoon butter or margarine**
- **2 cups pitted fresh tart red or sweet cherries**
- **2 tablespoons granulated sugar**
- **2 egg yolks**
- **1 cup half-and-half or light cream**
- **⅓ cup all-purpose flour**
- **¼ cup granulated sugar**
- **¼ teaspoon almond extract**
- **2 tablespoons powdered sugar**

1 Butter a 9-inch glass pie plate with the butter. Toss cherries with the 2 tablespoons granulated sugar. Cover the bottom of the pie plate with cherries; set pie plate aside.

2 In a medium mixing bowl use a rotary beater or wire whisk to beat together egg yolks, cream, flour, ¼ cup granulated sugar, and almond extract. Pour mixture over the cherries.

3 Bake in a 375° oven for 25 minutes or until a knife inserted near the center comes out clean. Cool on a wire rack for 10 minutes. Sprinkle with the powdered sugar. Serve at once. Makes 6 to 8 servings.

Nutrition facts per serving: *138 calories, 2 g protein, 21 g carbohydrate, 5 g total fat (3 g saturated fat), 66 mg cholesterol, 20 mg sodium, 1 g fiber. Daily values: 17% vitamin A, 6% vitamin C, 3% calcium, 3% iron.*

Orange Bread Pudding with Maple Sauce

Add orange marmalade to the custard mixture and serve it with a maple sauce and you have an old-time favorite with a new twist. This pudding goes together in a snap— just mix, pour, and bake.

3 **eggs**
2 **egg whites**
1¾ **cups milk**
⅓ **cup orange marmalade**
¼ **cup granulated sugar**
½ **teaspoon ground cinnamon**
½ **teaspoon vanilla**
4 **slices dry bread (white or wheat), cut into 2-inch strips (about 3 cups)**
⅓ **cup raisins**
Maple Sauce
Orange slices, halved (optional)

1 In a medium mixing bowl use a wire whisk or rotary beater to beat together whole eggs, egg whites, milk, orange marmalade, sugar, cinnamon, and vanilla. Set egg mixture aside.

2 Place the bread strips in an ungreased 2-quart square glass baking dish. Sprinkle raisins over bread and pour egg mixture evenly over the top.

3 Bake in a 325° oven for 35 to 40 minutes or until a knife inserted near the center comes out clean. Cool slightly on a wire rack. Serve warm with Maple Sauce. If desired, garnish with orange slices. Makes 6 servings.

Maple Sauce: In a small saucepan combine 1 tablespoon cornstarch and ¼ teaspoon finely shredded orange peel. Stir in ¾ cup orange juice and ⅓ cup maple syrup. Cook and stir the mixture until thickened and bubbly. Cook and stir for 2 minutes more. Remove the saucepan from heat and stir in 2 teaspoons butter or mar-

Up to Scratch

Nothing tops off a freshly baked bread pudding, crisp, or betty quite like a stirred custard sauce made from scratch. And making such a sauce is unbelievably quick and easy.

In a heavy, medium saucepan combine 3 eggs; 2 cups milk, half-and-half, or light cream; and ¼ cup sugar. Cook and stir over medium heat until mixture just coats a metal spoon; remove from heat. Stir in 1 teaspoon vanilla or 2 to 3 tablespoons amaretto, orange liqueur, coffee liqueur, rum, or brandy.

Quickly cool the custard mixture by placing the saucepan in a sink or bowl of ice water for 1 to 2 minutes, stirring constantly. Pour custard into a bowl. Cover the surface with clear plastic wrap and chill until serving time. Makes 3 cups.

garine. Serve the warm sauce over bread pudding.

Nutrition facts per serving: *301 calories, 9 g protein, 56 g carbohydrate, 6 g total fat (3 g saturated fat), 115 mg cholesterol, 194 mg sodium, 1 g fiber. Daily values: 11% vitamin A, 29% vitamin C, 11% calcium, 10% iron.*

International Origin

French Apple Soufflé

Follow the baking time carefully to avoid overbaking or the soufflé will water out and easily could collapse.

Butter or margarine
Granulated sugar
½ **cup chunk-style applesauce**
2 **tablespoons apple brandy or apple juice**
1 **tablespoon lemon juice**
2 **tablespoons butter or margarine**
3 **tablespoons all-purpose flour**
¾ **cup milk**
4 **beaten egg yolks**
4 **egg whites**
½ **teaspoon vanilla**
¼ **cup granulated sugar**

1 Butter the sides of a 1½-quart soufflé dish. Sprinkle sides of dish with a little sugar. Set dish aside.

2 In a small mixing bowl stir together applesauce, apple brandy, or apple juice, and lemon juice. Set aside.

3 In a small saucepan melt 2 tablespoons butter. Stir in flour. Add milk all at once. Cook and stir over medium heat until thickened and bubbly. Remove from heat.

4 Gradually stir thickened milk mixture into beaten egg yolks. Stir in applesauce mixture. Set aside.

5 In a large mixing bowl beat egg whites and vanilla with an electric mixer on medium speed until soft peaks form (tips curl). Gradually add the ¼ cup sugar, about 1 tablespoon at a time, beating on medium to high speed until stiff peaks form (tips stand straight).

6 Fold about 1 cup of the beaten whites into apple mixture. Then fold apple mixture into remaining beaten whites. Carefully transfer mixture to the prepared soufflé dish.

7 Bake in a 350° oven about 35 minutes or until a knife inserted near center comes out clean. Serve soufflé at once. Makes 6 servings.

Nutrition facts per serving: *190 calories, 6 g protein, 19 g carbohydrate, 9 g total fat (5 g saturated fat), 158 mg cholesterol, 109 mg sodium, 0 g fiber. Daily values: 28% vitamin A, 3% vitamin C, 4% calcium, 4% iron.*

French Apple Soufflé

Chocolate-Peanut Soufflé

When serving a delicate baked soufflé, use two forks to gently divide the mixture into individual portions.

8   egg whites
    Butter or margarine
**3   tablespoons finely chopped
    unsalted peanuts**
½   cup chunky peanut butter
½   cup granulated sugar
**1   ounce semisweet or
    unsweetened chocolate,
    melted and cooled**

1 Place egg whites in a large mixing bowl, and allow them to stand at room temperature for 30 minutes. Preheat oven to 450°.

2 Generously butter the sides of a 1½-quart soufflé dish. Sprinkle bottom and sides of dish with chopped peanuts. Set dish aside.

3 Place the peanut butter in a medium mixing bowl. In a separate mixing bowl beat the egg whites with an electric mixer on medium-high speed until frothy. Gradually add the sugar and beat on high speed until soft peaks form (tips curl).

4 Stir about 1 cup of the beaten egg whites into peanut butter; stir until smooth and even colored. Gently fold the peanut butter mixture into remaining beaten egg whites, being careful not to overmix. Turn mixture into the prepared soufflé dish.

5 Drizzle melted chocolate on top of the soufflé mixture. Run a knife through the mixture to create a marbled effect, being careful not to scrape peanuts from sides of the dish.

6 Place soufflé dish in center of preheated oven and immediately reduce oven temperature to 375°. Bake for 20 to 25 minutes or until a knife inserted near center comes out clean. Do not overbake. Serve soufflé at once. Makes 6 to 8 servings.

Nutrition facts per serving: *263 calories, 11 g protein, 26 g carbohydrate, 14 g total fat (3 g saturated fat), 0 mg cholesterol, 178 mg sodium, 2 g fiber. Daily values: 0% vitamin A, 0% vitamin C, 1% calcium, 4% iron.*

To help your soufflé climb the sides of the soufflé dish, coat the dish with nuts or sugar. Sprinkle finely chopped nuts over the bottom of the generously buttered soufflé dish. Tilt and tap the dish, rotating it as necessary to evenly distribute the nuts.

To fold one mixture into another, cut down through the mixture, move across the bottom, and come up and over the top. Give the bowl a quarter turn and repeat the motion until the two mixtures are blended.

Strawberry Soufflé

For a double-berry treat, serve the soufflé with a delicately sweetened sauce that contains strawberry cream cheese.

    Butter or margarine
    Granulated sugar
4 **egg whites**
1 **teaspoon vanilla**
¼ **cup granulated sugar**
1 **8-ounce container soft-style cream cheese with strawberries**
2 **tablespoons lemon juice**
4 **egg yolks**
    Red food coloring (optional)
    Strawberry Coulis

1 Butter the sides of six 1-cup soufflé dishes or a 1½-quart soufflé dish. Sprinkle sides of dishes with a little sugar. Set dishes aside.

2 In a large mixing bowl beat egg whites and vanilla with an electric mixer on medium speed until soft peaks form (tips curl). Gradually add the ¼ cup sugar, about 1 tablespoon at a time, beating on medium to high speed until stiff peaks form (tips stand straight).

3 In a medium mixing bowl beat cream cheese and lemon juice until combined. Beat egg yolks, two at a time, into cream cheese mixture until smooth. If desired, tint mixture with a few drops of red food coloring.

4 Fold the cream cheese mixture into the beaten whites. Carefully transfer into the prepared dishes.

5 Bake in a 350° oven about 25 minutes (about 35 minutes for 1½-quart dish) or until a knife inserted near center comes out clean. Serve soufflés at once with chilled Strawberry Coulis. Makes 6 servings.

Strawberry Coulis: Place 2 cups fresh or frozen strawberries (if frozen, thaw first) in a blender container or food processor bowl. Cover and blend or process until berries are puréed. Then press berries through a fine-mesh sieve; discard seeds. In a small bowl combine sieved berries with 2 tablespoons granulated sugar and, if desired, 1 tablespoon kirsch. Chill before serving.

Nutrition facts per serving: *254 calories, 6 g protein, 24 g carbohydrate, 16 g total fat (9 g saturated fat), 179 mg cholesterol, 135 mg sodium, 1 g fiber. Daily values: 27% vitamin A, 50% vitamin C, 3% calcium, and 4% iron.*

Tin-Collar Worker

Soufflés have so much hot air that when baked they rise above the top of the dish. To keep soufflés from going over the edge, you need to make a collar for the dish.

    Measure the dish's circumference and add 6 inches. Cut a 12-inch-wide piece of foil the measured length. Fold the piece lengthwise into thirds. Lightly butter and sugar one side of the foil (except 3 inches on one end). Attach the foil, sugared side in, around the outside of the dish so that the foil extends about 2 inches above the dish, taping the unbuttered end to the outside. Then add the soufflé mixture and bake as directed. When done, remove the collar and serve the soufflé immediately.

Notes

Fudge Brownies
(see recipe, page 188)

Pistachio Balls
(see recipe, page 315)

Mantecados
(see recipe, page 201)

Raspberry-Filled Hearts
(see recipe, page 317)

Maple Leaves
(see recipe, page 316)

Hazelnut-Orange Bûche de Noël
(see recipe, page 312)

Home for The Holidays

There is no doubt that food plays a big part in all our holiday celebrations. Whether you're gathering with family and friends in honor of a religious or secular commemoration, special baked goods can set the tone for the occasion.

❦

In this chapter we've gathered all the best festive cookies, biscuits, cakes, tarts, pies, and puddings for you to bake and share.

❦

Whether you're playing host or relaxing as a guest, there's sure to be a recipe that will help make your holiday get-together a joy, not a chore.

Sweet Dessert Popovers

Serve these popovers with a custard, fruit filling, or your favorite ice cream. The combinations are endless, and they all taste great with the hot fudge sauce.

1 tablespoon shortening or
 nonstick spray coating
2 eggs
½ cup milk
½ cup strong coffee
1 tablespoon cooking oil
1 cup all-purpose flour
1 tablespoon granulated sugar
¼ teaspoon salt
1 pint coffee ice cream
 Fudge Sauce

1 Using ½ teaspoon of shortening for each cup, grease the bottoms and sides of six 6-ounce custard cups or the cups of a popover pan. Or, spray cups with nonstick coating. Place the custard cups on a 15x10x1-inch baking pan; set aside.

2 In a medium mixing bowl beat the eggs, milk, coffee, and cooking oil together with a wire whisk or rotary beater until combined. Add the flour, sugar, and salt. Beat until the mixture is smooth.

3 Fill the prepared cups half full with batter. Bake in a 400° oven about 40 minutes or until very firm.

4 Immediately after removing the popovers from the oven, use the tines of a fork to prick each popover to let the steam escape. Turn off oven. For crisper popovers, return popovers to oven 5 to 10 minutes or until they reach the desired crispness. Remove from cups; cool. Split popovers open and spoon in ice cream (⅓ cup per popover). Drizzle with Fudge Sauce. Makes 6.

Fudge Sauce: In a heavy saucepan heat ½ cup semisweet chocolate pieces and 2 tablespoons butter or margarine until melted. Add ⅓ cup granulated sugar. Gradually stir in ⅓ cup evaporated milk. Bring mixture to boiling. Reduce heat and boil gently over low heat for 8 minutes, stirring frequently. Remove from heat. Serve warm.

Nutrition facts per popover: 401 calories, 8 g protein, 50 g carbohydrate, 20 g total fat (8 g saturated), 106 mg cholesterol, 210 mg sodium, 1 g fiber. Daily values: 14% vitamin A, 1% vitamin C, 11% calcium, 10% iron.

Sweet Potato Biscuits

To cook a sweet potato, first wash and peel it. Cut off any woody portions and both ends, then cut it into quarters or cubes. Cook, covered, in enough boiling salted water to cover for 25 to 35 minutes or until tender.

1½ cups all-purpose flour
1 tablespoon baking powder
2 teaspoons brown sugar
¼ teaspoon salt
 Dash ground nutmeg
¼ cup shortening
⅓ cup chopped pecans or walnuts
 (optional)
½ cup milk
1 medium sweet potato, peeled,
 cooked, and mashed
 (about ⅔ cup), or ⅔ cup
 mashed vacuum-packed
 sweet potatoes

1 In a medium mixing bowl stir together flour, baking powder, brown sugar, salt, and nutmeg. Using a pastry blender, cut in shortening until mixture resembles coarse crumbs. If desired, stir in nuts. Make a well in center of dry mixture; set aside.

2 In a small mixing bowl, stir milk into mashed sweet potato. Add potato mixture all at once to dry mixture. Using a fork, stir just until moistened (dough will be soft).

3 Turn dough out onto a lightly floured surface. Quickly knead dough by folding and pressing dough gently for 10 to 12 strokes or until it is nearly smooth. Pat or lightly roll dough to ½-inch thickness. Using a 2½-inch biscuit cutter dipped into flour between cuts, cut into rounds.

4 Place dough rounds 1 inch apart on an ungreased baking sheet. Bake in a 450° oven for 10 to 12 minutes or until golden. Remove biscuits from baking sheet. Serve warm. If desired, serve with flavored butter. Makes about 12.

Nutrition facts per biscuit: 156 calories, 3 g protein, 19 g carbohydrate, 8 g total fat (2 g saturated), 1 mg cholesterol, 170 mg sodium, 1 g fiber. Daily values: 0% vitamin A, 3% vitamin C, 10% calcium, 7% iron.

Shortcut

Prepare Sweet Potato Biscuits as directed, except increase milk to ⅔ cup. Do not knead, roll, or cut dough. Drop dough from a tablespoon 1 inch apart onto an ungreased baking sheet. Bake and serve as directed. Makes 10 to 12 biscuits.

To Make Ahead

Prepare and bake biscuits as directed; cool completely. Place biscuits in a freezer container or bag and freeze for up to 3 months. Before serving, wrap the frozen biscuits in foil and bake in a 300° oven 20 minutes or until warm.

Cranberry Ring

For a totally different taste, use the same amount of dried tart red cherries or chopped dried apricots in place of the dried cranberries.

- 2 **3-ounce packages cream cheese, softened**
- 1 **egg**
- ⅓ **cup granulated sugar**
- 1½ **cups all-purpose flour**
- 2 **teaspoons baking powder**
- ¼ **teaspoon salt**
- ½ **cup granulated sugar**
- ½ **cup butter or margarine**
- 1 **egg**
  Few drops almond extract
- ¾ **cup milk**
- ¾ **cup dried cranberries (about 3 ounces)**
  Powdered Sugar Glaze or powdered sugar (optional)

1 Grease a 6-cup fluted pan or a 6½-cup ring mold; set aside.

2 In a small mixing bowl beat together cream cheese, 1 egg, and the ⅓ cup sugar with an electric mixer on medium speed until well blended. Set cream cheese mixture aside.

3 In a medium mixing bowl stir together flour, baking powder, and salt. Set flour mixture aside.

4 In a large mixing bowl beat together the ½ cup sugar, butter, 1 egg, and almond extract with an electric mixer on medium speed until fluffy. Add flour mixture and milk alternately, beating just until blended after each addition. Fold in cranberries.

5 Pour half the batter into the prepared pan. Spread cream cheese mixture evenly over batter. Spoon remaining batter over cream cheese layer. Bake in a 350° oven for 50 to 55 minutes for 6-cup fluted pan (about 35 minutes for 6½-cup ring mold) or until a wooden toothpick inserted near the center comes out clean. Cool in pan on a wire rack for 10 minutes. If necessary, remove ring from pan. Cool completely on wire rack. If desired, drizzle with Powdered Sugar Glaze or sprinkle with powdered sugar. Cover and refrigerate for up to 3 days. Makes 1 ring (12 servings).

Powdered Sugar Glaze: Stir together ½ cup sifted powdered sugar, 2 to 3 drops almond extract, and enough milk (2 to 3 teaspoons) to make a glaze that is easy to drizzle.

Nutrition facts per serving: 266 calories, 4 g protein, 32 g carbohydrate, 14 g total fat (8 g saturated), 73 mg cholesterol, 244 mg sodium, 1 g fiber. Daily values: 15% vitamin A, 0% vitamin C, 8% calcium, 7% iron.

To Make Ahead

Prepare and bake as directed; cool completely. Do not glaze. Place in a freezer container or bag and freeze for up to 3 months. Before serving, thaw overnight in the refrigerator. If desired, before serving, drizzle with glaze or sprinkle with powdered sugar.

Spring Brunch Of Breads

There's nothing like a morning brunch to celebrate spring—a new day, a new season. Everything's fresh and everyone's feeling fine. What better excuse to get together with friends, neighbors, family, or even the gang at work. Combine a selection of these breads (or your own favorites) with lots of hot steaming coffee and tea, a variety of fresh fruits and juices, and perhaps some flavored butters or cream cheese spreads.

Walnut Easter Bread
Cranberry Ring
Holiday Prune Butter Bread
Apricot-Pistachio Fruitcake

Candied Fruit Coffee Cake

Candied fruit and peel are all that tie this to the holidays. For an any-time taste, substitute ½ cup miniature semisweet chocolate pieces or chopped pecans.

1½ **cups all-purpose flour**
2 **teaspoons baking powder**
¼ **teaspoon salt**
2 **3-ounce packages cream cheese, softened**
1 **egg**
⅓ **cup granulated sugar**
½ **teaspoon vanilla**
½ **cup granulated sugar**
½ **cup butter or margarine, softened**

½ **teaspoon vanilla**
1 **egg**
¾ **cup milk**
½ **cup chopped mixed candied fruit and peels**
Brandied Glaze (optional)

1 Grease a 6-cup fluted tube pan or a 6½-cup ring mold. In a bowl combine flour, baking powder, and salt. Set pan and flour mixture aside.

2 Beat together cream cheese, 1 egg, the ⅓ cup sugar, and ½ teaspoon vanilla with an electric mixer on medium speed until fluffy. Set aside.

3 In a large mixing bowl beat together the ½ cup sugar, butter, and ½ teaspoon vanilla with an electric mixer on medium speed until light and fluffy. Beat in 1 egg. Add flour mixture and milk alternately, beating just until blended after each addition. Fold in the candied fruit and peels.

4 Pour half the batter into prepared pan. Pour cream cheese mixture evenly over batter. Spoon remaining batter over cream cheese layer. Bake in a 350° oven 50 to 55 minutes for the 6-cup fluted pan (about 35 minutes for the 6½-cup ring mold) or until a wooden toothpick inserted near center comes out clean. Cool in pan on a wire rack 10 minutes. Remove from pan. If desired, spoon Brandied Glaze over warm cake. Cool cake completely. Cover and store in the refrigerator up to 3 days. Makes 12 servings.

Brandied Glaze: Stir together ¾ cup sifted powdered sugar and 1 tablespoon brandy or milk. Stir in 2 or 3 teaspoons additional milk to make a glaze that is easy to drizzle.

Nutrition facts per serving: 225 calories, 6 g protein, 31 g carbohydrate, 9 g total fat (5 g saturated), 58 mg cholesterol, 203 mg sodium, 0 g fiber. Daily values: 9% vitamin A, 0% vitamin C, 7% calcium, 6% iron.

To Make Ahead

Prepare and bake coffee cake as directed, except do not glaze; cool completely. Place in a freezer container or bag and freeze for up to 3 months. Before serving, wrap the frozen coffee cake with foil and heat in a 300° oven about 25 minutes or until warm. If desired, before serving, spoon or brush glaze over warm cake.

Baker's Bonus

Getting It Together

Begin your entertaining plan with the guest list. Big groups lend themselves to potlucks, where everyone brings a dish, or a buffet, which can be prepared well in advance. Smaller groups suit elaborate sit-down dinners or brunches that require more last-minute preparation.

Invite your guests well in advance. Be sure to provide all the necessary information: date, time, place, type of party, attire (if special), address, and phone number, and request a reply so you'll know how many people to expect.

Plan a menu that blends foods you're comfortable preparing with one or two new foods. Try to include foods that have different textures and tastes and that provide a contrast for each other, such as sweet and salty foods or bland and spicy ones. The more you can prepare ahead, the better.

It's easy, elegant, and relatively inexpensive to create a festive atmosphere using seasonal flowers and plants. Or, the food itself can be a wonderful centerpiece. Accent your decor with color-coordinated napkins, some appropriate background music, and plenty of chairs in which your guests can relax.

Holiday Prune Butter Bread
(see recipe, page 300)

Candied Fruit Coffee Cake

Mom's Holiday Bread

Twenty years after moving away from home, I still wake up every Christmas and Easter morning and smell Mom's holiday bread. Unfortunately, for most of the past 20 years, I have been only dreaming, rather than actually enjoying the aroma of this special bread from an unbelievably great cook.
—Tom Wierzbicki—

- 4 **cups all-purpose flour**
- ¼ **cup granulated sugar**
- 1 **teaspoon salt**
- 1 **cup butter or margarine**
- 1 **envelope active dry yeast**
- ¼ **cup warm water (105° to 115°)**
- 1 **cup warm milk (105° to 115°)**
- 3 **egg yolks, beaten**
- 3 **egg whites**
- 1 **cup granulated sugar**
- 1 **cup chopped nuts**
- 2 **teaspoons ground cinnamon**
- 1 **recipe Powdered Sugar Icing (see page 151)**

1 In a large mixing bowl sift together flour, the ¼ cup sugar, and salt. Cut in the butter until mixture is the size of small peas; set aside.

2 In a small mixing bowl dissolve yeast in the warm water. Let stand for 5 to 10 minutes to soften. In another small mixing bowl combine the 1 cup warm milk with beaten egg yolks. Stir in the softened yeast.

3 Add the yeast mixture to flour mixture. Using a wooden spoon, beat the mixture by hand until a soft dough forms. Cover the dough with oiled waxed paper and then plastic wrap and refrigerate overnight.

4 Divide dough into 2 parts. On a lightly floured surface, roll each dough portion into a 9x14-inch rectangle (¼ inch thick).

5 Beat egg whites with an electric mixer on high speed until stiff peaks form (tips stand straight). In a small mixing bowl combine 1 cup sugar, nuts, and cinnamon. Fold into the beaten egg whites. Spread each rectangle with half of the egg white mixture. Tightly roll up each rectangle, jelly-roll style, starting from one of the short sides. Seal with fingertips as you roll. Place the shaped dough on a greased 15x10x1-inch baking pan. Cover and let rise in a warm place until nearly double in size (about 45 minutes).

6 Bake in a 350° oven for 35 to 40 minutes or until loaves sound hollow when you tap the tops with your fingers; cool slightly. Drizzle with Powdered Sugar Icing. Serve warm. Cover and store any leftovers at room temperature for up to 3 days. Makes 2 loaves (32 servings).

Nutrition facts per serving: 184 calories, 3 g protein, 24 g carbohydrate, 9 g total fat (4 g saturated), 36 mg cholesterol, 135 mg sodium, 0 g fiber. Daily values: 8% vitamin A, 0% vitamin C, 1% calcium, 6% iron.

To Make Ahead
Prepare and bake the bread as directed; cool completely. Place in a freezer container or bag and freeze for up to 3 months. Before serving, wrap the frozen bread in foil and bake in a 300° oven about 25 minutes or until warm. Drizzle the warm bread with glaze and serve.

Holiday Prune Butter Bread

Swirls of honey-flavored prune butter earn this wheat bread top honors.

- 1 **cup lightly packed, pitted prunes (about 8 ounces)**
- 1 **teaspoon lemon juice**
- ¾ **cup water**
- 2 **tablespoons honey**
- 3 **to 3½ cups all-purpose flour**
- 1 **package active dry yeast**
- 1 **teaspoon ground cardamom**
- 1 **cup milk**
- ½ **cup butter or margarine**
- ⅓ **cup granulated sugar**
- ¾ **teaspoon salt**
- 3 **eggs**
- 1 **teaspoon vanilla**
- 2 **cups whole wheat flour**
- 1 **cup chopped walnuts**
- 2 **teaspoons ground cinnamon**
- 1 **tablespoon butter or margarine, melted**

1 For prune butter, in a saucepan combine prunes, lemon juice, and water. Bring mixture to boiling; reduce

Walnut Easter Bread

heat. Cover and simmer for 40 minutes. Remove from heat and stir in honey; cool. Place in a blender container or food processor bowl. Cover and blend or process until smooth. Cover and chill until ready to use.

2 In a large mixing bowl stir together 2 cups of the all-purpose flour, yeast, and cardamom; set aside.

3 In a medium saucepan heat and stir the milk, the ½ cup butter, the sugar, and salt just until warm (120° to 130°) and butter almost melts. Add the milk mixture to flour mixture. Then add eggs and vanilla. Beat with an electric mixer on low to medium speed for 30 seconds, scraping the sides of the bowl constantly. Then beat on high speed for 3 minutes. Using a wooden spoon, stir in the whole wheat flour and as much of the remaining all-purpose flour as you can.

4 Turn the dough out onto a lightly floured surface. Knead in enough of the remaining all-purpose flour to make a moderately soft dough that is smooth and elastic (6 to 8 minutes total). Shape the dough into a ball. Place dough in a lightly greased bowl, turning once to grease the surface of the dough. Cover and let rise in a warm place until dough is double in size (about 1 hour).

5 Punch dough down. Turn dough out onto a lightly floured surface. Divide dough in half. Cover and let rest for 10 minutes. Grease two 8x4x2-inch loaf pans; set aside.

6 Roll each half of the dough into a 12x7-inch rectangle. Spread each rectangle with ½ cup of the prune butter to within 1 inch of edges. Sprinkle with nuts and cinnamon. Tightly roll up, jelly-roll style, starting from one of the short sides. Seal with fingertips as you roll. Place loaves, seam down, in prepared loaf pans. Cover and let rise in a warm place until double in size (30 to 40 minutes).

7 Bake in a 350° oven for 30 to 35 minutes or until bread sounds hollow when you tap the top with your fingers (if necessary, cover loosely with foil the last 10 minutes of baking to prevent overbrowning). Immediately remove bread from pans and place on a wire rack. Brush loaves with the melted butter; cool. Serve with remaining prune butter. Place in an airtight container or bag and store at room temperature or in the refrigerator for up to 3 days. Makes 2 loaves (32 servings).

Nutrition facts per serving: *156 calories, 4 g protein, 22 g carbohydrate, 6 g total fat (2 g saturated), 29 mg cholesterol, 44 mg sodium, 2 g fiber. Daily values: 5% vitamin A, 0% vitamin C, 2% calcium, 8% iron.*

To Make Ahead

Prepare and bake bread as directed; cool completely. Place in a freezer container or bag and freeze for up to 3 months. Before serving, thaw the frozen wrapped bread overnight in the refrigerator.

Finishing Touches

If you find yourself long on holiday spirit and short on time, here are some quick ways to creating a wonderful selection of festive treats based on ready-made cookies and pretzels.

Melt together 6 ounces semisweet chocolate, white or tinted baking bars, or candy coating with 2 teaspoons shortening.

Dip half or all of each cookie or pretzel in the shortening mixture. Cookies can be dipped twice—first in white or tinted coating, then in chocolate. Once cookies or pretzels have been dipped, sprinkle with crushed peppermint candy, colorful decorating sprinkles, or finely chopped nuts, or drizzle them with melted chocolate or candy coating.

Or, make a fabulous citrus frosting. Stir together 2 cups sifted powdered sugar, 2 tablespoons softened butter or margarine, 1 teaspoon finely shredded orange or lemon peel, and ½ teaspoon vanilla until blended. Stir in milk, ½ teaspoon at a time, until mixture is spreadable.

Thin the frosting to drizzle it on dipped cookies or pretzels. Or, sandwich cookies together with the citrus frosting or peanut butter. Then drizzle them with frosting, or top them with frosting and sprinkle with crushed candies, colorful decorating sprinkles, finely chopped nuts, or grated chocolate.

Walnut Easter Bread

If you use two baking sheets, refrigerate one loaf while the other bakes. Baking one at a time ensures that each loaf bakes evenly.

  6 to 6½ **cups all-purpose flour**
  2 **packages active dry yeast**
1⅔ **cups milk**
 ⅔ **cup butter or margarine**
 ½ **cup granulated sugar**
 ½ **teaspoon salt**
 ½ **teaspoon ground nutmeg**
  1 **egg**
 ¾ **cup finely chopped walnuts**
 10 **walnut halves**
  1 **beaten egg yolk**
  1 **tablespoon water**

1 In a large mixing bowl stir together 3 cups of the flour and the yeast. Set the flour-yeast mixture aside.

2 In a medium saucepan heat and stir the milk, butter, sugar, salt, and nutmeg just until warm (120° to 130°) and butter almost melts. Add the milk mixture to the flour mixture. Then add the whole egg. Beat with an electric mixer on low to medium speed for 30 seconds, scraping the sides of bowl constantly. Beat on high speed for 3 minutes. Using a wooden spoon, stir in the chopped walnuts and as much of the remaining flour as you can.

3 Turn the dough out onto a lightly floured surface. Knead in enough of the remaining flour to make a moderately soft dough that is smooth and elastic (6 to 8 minutes total). Shape the dough into a ball. Place dough in a lightly greased bowl, turning once to grease the surface of the dough. Cover and let rise in a warm place until double in size (about 1 hour).

4 Punch the dough down. Turn the dough out onto a lightly floured surface. Divide the dough into 3 portions. Cover and let dough rest for 10 minutes. Grease 1 large or 2 small baking sheets; set aside.

5 Shape 2 of the dough portions into balls. Place on the prepared baking sheet(s), allowing 4 inches between balls. Flatten each ball to a 5½ inch in diameter. Divide the remaining portion of dough into 16 pieces. Roll each piece into a 10-inch-long rope. Loosely twist 2 ropes together. Repeat with remaining ropes, making 8 twisted ropes total.

6 Place two of the twisted ropes in a cross atop each flattened ball of dough; tuck rope ends under balls. Place two more twisted ropes around the base of each ball, stretching the ropes if necessary so ends will meet. Brush ends with water and pinch together to seal. Brush centers and ends of crossed ropes with water. Press a walnut half in the center and at the ends of the crossed ropes. Cover and let rise in a warm place until nearly double in size (about 30 minutes).

7 In a small mixing bowl beat the egg yolk and water with a fork. Brush loaves with some of the egg mixture. Bake in a 350° oven for 45 to 50 minutes or until bread sounds hollow when you tap the top with your fingers (if necessary, cover loosely with foil the last 20 minutes of baking to prevent overbrowning). Remove bread from pan(s) and cool on wire racks. Place in an airtight container or bag and store at room temperature or in the refrigerator for up to 3 days. Makes 2 loaves (32 servings).

Nutrition facts per serving: *162 calories, 4 g protein, 21 g carbohydrate, 7 g total fat (3 g saturated), 25 mg cholesterol, 81 mg sodium, 1 g fiber. Daily values: 5% vitamin A, 0% vitamin C, 2% calcium, 8% iron.*

To Make Ahead

Prepare and bake bread as directed; cool completely. Place bread in a freezer container or bag and freeze for up to 3 months. Before serving, thaw frozen bread overnight in the refrigerator.

Notes

Gingerbread

*The spicy smell of gingerbread baking
heralds the fall season for me.
Some in my family preferred it with
a tart lemon sauce, some with whipped
cream or ice cream; my mother
indulged us all. Now my son indulges our
family with this cold-weather treat.
—Betty Rice—*

2½ **cups all-purpose flour**
1½ **teaspoons baking soda**
 1 **teaspoon ground ginger**
 1 **teaspoon ground cinnamon**
 ½ **teaspoon salt**
 ½ **cup butter or margarine**
 1 **cup molasses (light)**
 ½ **cup granulated sugar**
 1 **egg**
 1 **cup hot water**

1 Grease a 13x9x2-inch baking pan;
set aside.

2 In a small mixing bowl stir together
flour, baking soda, ginger, cinnamon,
and salt; set aside.

3 In a large mixing bowl beat the butter with an electric mixer on medium
to high speed about 30 seconds or
until softened. Add molasses and sugar
and beat until combined. Add egg and
beat until combined.

4 Alternately add the flour mixture
and hot water to the molasses mixture,
beating on low to medium speed after
each addition just until combined.

5 Pour the batter into the prepared
baking pan. Bake in a 350° oven for 35
minutes or until a wooden toothpick
inserted near the center of the cake
comes out clean. Cool cake in pan for
30 minutes. Serve warm. Cover and
store any leftovers at room temperature or in the refrigerator for up to 3
days. Makes 12 to 15 servings.
  *Nutrition facts per serving: 260 calo-
ries, 3 g protein, 44 g carbohydrate, 8 g
total fat (5 g saturated), 38 mg cholesterol,
334 mg sodium, 1 g fiber. Daily values: 7%
vitamin A, 0% vitamin C, 4% calcium,
16% iron.*

Apricot-Pistachio Fruitcake

*Dried fruits, coconut, and pistachio
nuts replace the traditional candied fruit
and pecans in this fruitcake.*

 1 **cup snipped dried apricots**
 ½ **cup snipped dried pears or
    apples**
 ½ **cup light raisins**
 ½ **cup raisins**
 1 **teaspoon finely shredded
    orange peel**
 ⅓ **cup apricot brandy or nectar**
1¾ **cups all-purpose flour**
 ½ **teaspoon baking powder**
 ¼ **teaspoon baking soda**
 ⅓ **cup butter or margarine,
    softened**
 ½ **cup granulated sugar**
 2 **eggs**
 ½ **cup buttermilk**
 1 **cup coarsely chopped pistachio
    nuts**
 ½ **cup coconut**
 ¼ **cup apricot brandy or nectar
    Apricot brandy or nectar**

1 In a small bowl combine apricots,
pears, raisins, orange peel, and ⅓ cup
brandy. Let stand 2 hours at room
temperature, stirring occasionally.

2 Grease a 9x5x3-inch loaf pan. Line
the loaf pan with parchment paper;
grease paper. In a medium bowl combine flour, baking powder, and baking
soda. Set pan and flour mixture aside.

3 In a large mixing bowl beat the butter with an electric mixer on medium
to high speed about 30 seconds or
until softened.

4 Add sugar and beat until fluffy. Add
eggs, one at a time, beating on medium speed after each addition until
combined. Alternately add flour mixture and buttermilk, beating on low to
medium speed after each addition just
until combined. Stir in the undrained
fruit, pistachio nuts, and coconut.

5 Pour batter into prepared pan. Bake
in a 300° oven for 1 hour 15 minutes to
1 hour 20 minutes or until a wooden
toothpick inserted near center of the
cake comes out clean. Cool cake in pan
on a wire rack 10 minutes. Remove
cake from pan, place on rack, and peel
off paper. Turn cake right side up.

6 Using a pastry brush, brush the ¼ cup apricot brandy over top and sides of warm cake. Cool completely. Wrap cake in brandy- or fruit juice-moistened 100% cotton cheesecloth. Overwrap with foil. Place in a plastic bag and seal. Store in the refrigerator for 2 to 8 weeks to mellow flavors. Remoisten cheesecloth with brandy or juice once a week or when dry. Makes 16 servings.

Nutrition facts per serving: 262 calories, 5 g protein, 38 g carbohydrate, 9 g total fat (4 g saturated fat), 37 mg cholesterol, 90 mg sodium, 3 g fiber. Daily values: 10% vitamin A, 4% vitamin C, 3% calcium, 13% iron.

Eggnog Layer Cake

A luscious cake filled with the flavors of the classic yuletide drink. Try garnishing it with marzipan fruit or sugared cranberries.*

2⅓ **cups all-purpose flour**
  1 **tablespoon baking powder**
 ½ **teaspoon nutmeg**
 ¼ **teaspoon salt**
 ⅔ **cup butter or margarine, softened**
1½ **cups granulated sugar**
  3 **egg yolks**
  1 **cup dairy eggnog**
  3 **egg whites**
    Creamy Eggnog Frosting

1 Grease and lightly flour two 9x1½-inch or 8x1½-inch round baking pans. In a medium mixing bowl stir together flour, baking powder, nutmeg, and salt. Set pans and flour mixture aside.

2 In a large mixing bowl beat the butter with an electric mixer on medium to high speed about 30 seconds or until softened.

3 Add the sugar to butter and beat until well combined. Add the egg yolks, one at a time, beating on medium speed after each addition until combined. Alternately add flour mixture and eggnog, beating on low to medium speed after each addition just until combined.

4 Thoroughly wash beaters. In a medium mixing bowl beat egg whites until stiff peaks form (tips stand straight). Gently fold the beaten egg whites into the batter.

5 Pour the batter into prepared pans. Bake in a 350° oven for 25 to 30 minutes for 9-inch cake pans (30 to 35 minutes for 8-inch cake pans) or until a wooden toothpick inserted near the center of each cake comes out clean. Cool cakes in pans on wire racks for 10 minutes. Remove cakes from pans and completely cool on the wire racks. Fill and frost with Creamy Eggnog Frosting. Cover and store in the refrigerator for up to 3 days. Let stand at room temperature for 30 minutes before serving. Makes 12 servings.

Creamy Eggnog Frosting: In a medium saucepan combine ⅔ cup granulated sugar, 3 tablespoons all-purpose flour, and ¼ teaspoon ground nutmeg. Whisk in 1 cup dairy eggnog. Cook and stir over medium heat until mixture is thickened and bubbly. Remove from heat. Gradually stir hot mixture into 2 beaten egg yolks. Return mixture to saucepan. Bring to a gentle boil. Cook and stir for 2 minutes more. Remove from the heat. Add 1 tablespoon rum (or, add 1 tablespoon milk or eggnog and ¼ teaspoon rum extract). Pour mixture into a bowl. Cover the surface with clear plastic wrap. Cool to room temperature. Do not stir. In a medium mixing bowl beat 1 cup softened butter (no substitutes) with an electric mixer on medium to high speed about 30 seconds or until fluffy. Add the cooled cooked mixture, one-fourth at a time, beating on low speed after each addition until smooth.

*Note: To make sugared cranberries, dip cranberries in lightly beaten egg white, then roll in granulated sugar. Set aside to dry.

Nutrition facts per serving: 511 calories, 6 g protein, 58 g carbohydrate, 29 g total fat (17 g saturated fat), 169 mg cholesterol, 422 mg sodium, 1 g fiber. Daily values: 39% vitamin A, 0% vitamin C, 11% calcium, 10% iron.

To Make Ahead

Prepare and bake cakes as directed; cool completely. Do not fill and frost. Place cakes on a baking sheet and freeze until firm. Once firm, place cakes in 2-gallon freezer bags and freeze up to 3 months. Before serving, thaw at room temperature for several hours. Fill and frost as directed.

Red Waldorf Cake

Red Waldorf Cake

*As I was growing up, the holidays
were special times when my family would
get together with all my aunts, uncles,
and cousins on my mom's side. Besides
having a fun time with my relatives,
the other thing that comes to mind is the
feasting we did. The day before most
of these family gatherings my mom would
be in the kitchen making her specialty—
Red Waldorf Cake—from a recipe that was
handed down to her by my dad's mom.*
—Margie Schenkelberg—

½ **cup unsweetened cocoa powder**
2 **ounces red food coloring
(¼ cup)**
2¼ **cups sifted cake flour**
½ **teaspoon salt**
½ **cup shortening**
1½ **cups granulated sugar**
1 **teaspoon vanilla**
2 **eggs**
1 **cup buttermilk**
1 **teaspoon baking soda**
1 **teaspoon vinegar
Creamy Frosting
Red cinnamon candies and
heart-shaped candies
(optional)**

1 Grease and flour two 9x1½-inch
round baking pans or one 13x9x2-
inch baking pan. In a small bowl stir
together cocoa powder and food coloring. In a small mixing bowl stir
together flour and salt. Set pans, cocoa
mixture, and flour mixture aside.

2 In a large mixing bowl beat shortening with an electric mixer on medium to high speed about 30 seconds or
until softened. Add sugar and vanilla
to shortening and beat until well combined. Add eggs, one at a time, beating
on medium speed after each addition
until combined. Beat in cocoa mixture. Alternately add flour mixture and
buttermilk, beating on low to medium
speed after each addition just until
combined. Stir together baking soda
and vinegar. Add to batter, mixing
until combined.

3 Pour batter into prepared pans.
Bake in 350° oven for 30 to 35 minutes
(about 30 minutes for 13x9x2-inch
pan) or until wooden toothpick
inserted near the center of each cake
comes out clean. Cool cake layers in
pans for 10 minutes. Remove cake layers from pans and completely cool on
the wire racks. If using 13x9x2-inch
pan, do not remove from pan.
Completely cool it in pan on a wire
rack. Frost with Creamy Frosting. If
desired, decorate with candies. Cover
and store in the refrigerator for up to 3
days. Makes 12 servings.

Creamy Frosting: In a medium
saucepan, using a whisk, blend 1 cup
milk into 3 tablespoons all-purpose
flour. Cook and stir over medium heat
until thickened and bubbly. Reduce
heat; cook and stir 2 minutes more.
Cover surface with plastic wrap. Cool
to room temperature (do not stir). In a
mixing bowl beat 1 cup softened butter (no substitutes), 1 cup granulated
sugar, and 1 teaspoon vanilla with an
electric mixer on medium speed until
light and fluffy. Add the cooled cooked
mixture ¼ cup at a time, beating on
low speed after each addition until
smooth.

Nutrition facts per serving: *499 calories, 5 g protein, 63 g carbohydrate, 26 g
total fat (12 g saturated fat), 79 mg cholesterol, 390 mg sodium, 0 g fiber. Daily values: 17% vitamin A, 0% vitamin C, 8%
calcium, 13% iron.*

To Make Ahead
Prepare and bake layer cakes as directed; cool completely. Do not frost. Place
the cakes on a baking sheet and freeze
until firm. Once firm, place cakes in 2-
gallon freezer bags and freeze up to 3
months. Before serving, thaw at room
temperature several hours. Fill and
frost as directed.

Baking with Buttermilk

*Why bake with buttermilk?
Because buttermilk has more lac-
tic acid, which reacts with baking
soda to produce carbon dioxide for
leavening. It also produces a product with a lighter, more tender
crumb and a rich flavor.*

*If you don't have any butter-
milk on hand, you can substitute
soured milk. For each cup of
soured milk, in a glass measuring
cup combine 1 tablespoon lemon
juice or vinegar and enough milk
to make 1 cup total. Stir well and
let stand 5 minutes before using.*

Royal Christmas Cake

I remember licking the sweet marzipan filling from the Father Christmas figurine that always adorned our Christmas cake. Because it just wasn't Christmas without them, my mother wrote home for the family Christmas cake recipe and her figurine soon after she emigrated from England.
—Julia Malloy—

2   **cups all-purpose flour**
1   **teaspoon ground cinnamon**
½   **teaspoon baking powder**
¼   **teaspoon baking soda**
¼   **teaspoon ground nutmeg**
¼   **teaspoon ground cloves**
1½ **cups currants**
1½ **cups dark or light raisins**
1½ **cups diced mixed candied
      fruits and peels**
1   **cup candied red and/or green
      cherries**
½   **cup ground almonds
      (2 ounces)**
4   **eggs**
1   **cup granulated sugar**
¾   **cup butter or margarine,
      melted**
½   **cup rum, brandy, or orange
      juice**
3   **tablespoons lemon juice,
      Rum, brandy, or orange juice**
1   **8-ounce can almond paste
      Royal Icing**

1 Grease two 9x1½-inch round baking pans. Line bottom and sides with parchment or waxed paper; grease the paper. Set pans aside.

2 In a large mixing bowl stir together the flour, cinnamon, baking powder, baking soda, nutmeg, and cloves. Stir in the currants, raisins, candied fruits and peels, candied cherries, and almonds; set aside.

3 In a small mixing bowl beat the eggs slightly with a fork. Add the sugar, butter, ½ cup rum, and lemon juice; stir until combined. Pour the egg mixture into the flour mixture and stir until well mixed.

4 Pour the batter into the prepared pans. Bake in a 300° oven for 1¼ to 1½ hours or until a wooden toothpick inserted near the center of each cake comes out clean. (Cover pans loosely with foil after 1 hour of baking to prevent overbrowning.) Completely cool cakes in pans on a wire rack.

5 Remove cooled cake from pans. Wrap layers separately in rum-, brandy-, or juice-moistened 100% cotton cheesecloth. Overwrap with foil. Store in the refrigerator for 1 to 2 weeks to mellow flavors. Remoisten cheesecloth with rum, brandy, or juice every 3 or 4 days or when dry.

6 To assemble, place one cake layer, top side down, on a serving plate. Spread with half of the almond paste. (Or, if paste is too thick to spread, divide into 2 balls. Place each ball between two sheets of waxed paper; flatten slightly. With a rolling pin, roll each portion from center to edges until 10 inches in diameter; trim to form a 9-inch circle. Remove one sheet of paper from one circle; invert onto cake. Peel off remaining paper.)

7 Spread some of the Royal Icing over almond paste on first cake layer. Add second cake layer, top side up; top with remaining paste. Frost top and sides of cake with remaining Royal Icing. Cover and store in the refrigerator for up to 1 week. Makes 16 servings.

Royal Icing: In a large mixing bowl combine 4 cups sifted powdered sugar, ½ cup water, ¼ cup meringue powder, and 1 teaspoon vanilla. Beat with an electric mixer on high speed for 7 to 10 minutes or until very stiff. Use immediately, covering icing in bowl with a damp paper towel.

Nutrition facts per serving: 577 calories, 8 g protein, 101 g carbohydrate, 16 g total fat (6 g saturated fat), 76 mg cholesterol, 148 mg sodium, 3 g fiber. Daily values: 10% vitamin A, 4% vitamin C, 7% calcium, 15% iron.

Cranberry Pecan Pound Cake

*Create the perfect ending to
a holiday brunch.*

2   **cups all-purpose flour**
2   **teaspoons baking powder**
¼   **teaspoon salt**
¾   **cup butter (no substitutes)**
1½ **cups granulated sugar**

3 **eggs**
¼ **cup milk**
1 **tablespoon finely shredded orange peel (set aside)**
¼ **cup orange juice**
2 **cups coarsely chopped cranberries**
1 **cup coarsely chopped pecans, toasted**
1 **recipe Powdered Sugar Icing (see page 151)**

1 Grease and lightly flour a 10-inch fluted tube pan. Combine flour, baking powder, and salt. Set aside.

2 Beat butter with an electric mixer on medium to high speed 30 seconds. Gradually add sugar to butter, 2 tablespoons at a time, beating on medium to high speed 6 minutes or until very light and fluffy. Add eggs, one at a time, beating 1 minute after each addition, scraping bowl often. Alternately add flour mixture with milk and juice, beating on low to medium speed after each addition until combined. Stir in cranberries, pecans, and orange peel.

3 Spoon batter into prepared pan. Bake in a 350° oven 60 to 65 minutes or until a wooden toothpick inserted near centercomes out clean. Cool cake in pan on a wire rack 10 minutes. Remove cake from pan and completely cool on wire rack. Drizzle with Powdered Sugar Icing. Serves 18.

Nutrition facts per serving: 262 calories, 3 g protein, 36 g carbohydrate, 13 g total fat (5 g saturated), 56 mg cholesterol, 161 mg sodium, 1 g fiber. Daily values: 9% vitamin A, 6% vitamin C, 4% calcium, 6% iron.

To Make Ahead

Prepare and bake cake as directed; cool completely. Do not ice. Place cake on a baking sheet and freeze until firm. Place cake in a freezer bag and freeze up to 3 months. Before serving, thaw at room temperature several hours. Drizzle with icing as directed.

Genoise Cake in Strawberry Champagne Sauce

6 **eggs**
¾ **cup granulated sugar**
⅓ **cup extra-light or light olive oil (not extra-virgin olive oil)**
1⅓ **cups sifted cake flour or 1¼ cups sifted all-purpose flour**
Strawberry Champagne Sauce

1 Allow eggs to stand at room temperature 30 minutes. Grease bottom and sides of a 9-inch springform pan. Line bottom with parchment paper; grease paper. Sprinkle with sugar, then dust with flour. Set pan aside.

2 In a large mixing bowl combine the eggs and sugar. Beat with an electric mixer on high speed 15 minutes. After 15 minutes, with mixer running, gradually add olive oil in a thin, steady stream (this will take 1½ to 2 minutes). Turn off mixer immediately after all of the oil has been added.

3 Sift the flour over the egg mixture. Carefully fold in flour until no lumps remain. Pour batter into the prepared pan. Place pan on a baking sheet.

4 Bake in a 350° oven 35 minutes or until cake springs back when lightly touched. Cool completely in pan.

5 To assemble, remove cake from pan. Remove and discard the parchment paper. Sift powdered sugar atop cake. Cut cake into wedges. Place wedges on plates or in shallow bowls. Pour Strawberry Champagne sauce around cake wedges. Cover any leftover cake and store at room temperature up to 3 days. Refrigerate any remaining sauce. Serves 10 to 12.

Strawberry Champagne Sauce: In a blender container combine 5 cups strawberries, ¾ cup champagne or sparkling white wine, and ¼ cup granulated sugar. (Or, for a food processor, combine half of the ingredients at a time.) Cover and blend or process until smooth. Cover and chill for several hours or overnight.

Nutrition facts per serving: 281 calories, 5 g protein, 40 g carbohydrate, 11 g total fat (2 g saturated fat), 128 mg cholesterol, 39 mg sodium, 2 g fiber. Daily values: 5% vitamin A, 70% vitamin C, 2% calcium, 12% iron.

To Make Ahead

Prepare and bake cake as directed; cool completely. Place cake on a baking sheet and freeze until firm. Once firm, place cake in a 2-gallon freezer bag and freeze for up to 3 months. Before serving, thaw at room temperature for several hours. Serve as directed.

Pumpkin-Praline Cheesecake

Don't reserve pumpkin-flavored desserts just for Thanksgiving. Your guests are sure to appreciate them throughout the year.

Pecan-Praline Powder and
    Pieces*
⅓ cup butter (no substitutes)
¼ cup packed brown sugar
1 cup all-purpose flour
3 8-ounces packages cream
    cheese, softened
¾ cup packed brown sugar
2 tablespoons all-purpose flour
1 16-ounce can pumpkin
1 teaspoon vanilla
½ teaspoon ground cinnamon
½ teaspoon ground ginger
½ teaspoon ground nutmeg
3 eggs
1 8-ounce carton dairy sour
    cream
1 tablespoon granulated sugar
    Pecan halves (optional)

1 Prepare the Pecan-Praline Powder and Pieces; set aside.

2 For crust, in a medium mixing bowl beat butter with an electric mixer on medium to high speed about 30 seconds or until softened. Add the ¼ cup brown sugar and beat until fluffy. Add the 1 cup flour. Beat on low to medium speed just until combined.

3 Pat dough onto bottom and 1½ inches up the sides of a 9-inch spring-form pan. Bake in a 375° oven about 10 minutes or until lightly browned. Cool crust on a wire rack while preparing filling.

4 For filling, in a large mixing bowl beat cream cheese, the ¾ cup brown sugar, and 2 tablespoons flour with an electric mixer on medium to high speed until combined. Add the pumpkin, vanilla, cinnamon, ginger, and nutmeg. Beat until combined. Add eggs all at once. Beat on low speed just until combined. Stir in the coarsely broken Pecan-Praline Pieces, reserving the powder for the topping.

5 Pour filling into the crust-lined springform pan. Place the springform pan in a shallow baking pan on the oven rack. Bake in a 375° oven for 45 to 50 to 55 minutes or until center appears nearly set when shaken. Meanwhile, in a small bowl combine sour cream and granulated sugar. Spread over top of cheesecake.

6 Remove springform pan from baking pan. Cool cheesecake in springform pan on a wire rack for 15 minutes. Use a small metal spatula to loosen crust from sides of pan. Cool 30 minutes more. Remove sides of the springform pan. Cool for 1 hour, then cover and chill for at least 4 hours.

7 Just before serving, sprinkle the Pecan-Praline Powder over sour cream topping in center of cheesecake and garnish with pecan halves, if desired.. Makes 12 to 16 servings.

*Pecan-Praline Powder and Pieces:** Line a large baking sheet with foil; set aside. In a heavy skillet place ½ cup granulated sugar. Cook over medium-high heat, shaking skillet occasionally until sugar begins to melt. Do not stir. Reduce heat to low. Stir in ½ cup chopped pecans, and cook about 3 minutes more or until sugar is golden brown and pecans are toasted, stirring occasionally. Then pour the mixture onto the prepared baking sheet, spreading with a wooden spoon as thin as possible. Cool. Break or chop the cooled praline into ¼-inch pieces. Set half of it aside. Place remaining broken pieces in a blender container or food processor bowl. Cover and blend or process until ground.

Note: Be extremely careful when working with the hot sugar mixture for the Pecan-Praline Powder and Pieces. Total attention must be given as things move quickly when the sugar reaches the proper temperature to caramelize. Store praline powder in an airtight container until serving time. If desired, the praline powder also can be used as an ice-cream topping.

Nutrition facts per serving: 479 calories, 8 g protein, 39 g carbohydrate, 34 g total fat (19 g saturated fat), 138 mg cholesterol, 254 mg sodium, 2 g fiber. Daily values: 119% vitamin A, 3% vitamin C, 8% calcium, 15% iron.

Pumpkin-Praline Cheesecake, top, and Maple Leaves (see recipe, page 316), bottom

International Origin

Hazelnut-Orange Búche de Noël

A wonderfully different version of the traditional Búche de Noël, this makes an ideal finale for your holiday meal. (Pictured on page 294.)

1½	**cups toasted hazelnuts (filberts)**
¼	**cup all-purpose flour**
6	**egg yolks**
⅔	**cup packed brown sugar**
2	**teaspoons finely shredded orange peel**
6	**egg whites**
¼	**teaspoon cream of tartar**
	Powdered sugar
	Caramel-Orange Buttercream
	Sugared cranberries*
	(optional)

1 Grease and lightly flour a 15x10x1-inch jelly roll pan; set aside. In a food processor bowl combine the nuts and flour. Process until nuts are finely ground; set aside.

2 In a medium mixing bowl beat the egg yolks with an electric mixer on high speed about 6 minutes or until thick and the color of lemons. Gradually add ⅓ cup of the brown sugar, beating on medium speed about 5 minutes or until sugar is almost dissolved. Stir in orange peel; set aside.

3 Thoroughly wash beaters. In a large mixing bowl beat egg whites and cream of tartar on medium speed until soft peaks form (tips curl). Gradually add the remaining ⅓ cup brown sugar, about 2 tablespoons at a time, beating until stiff peaks form (tips stand straight). Fold the yolk mixture into the beaten egg whites. Sprinkle flour mixture into egg mixture and gently fold in by hand.

4 Spread batter evenly into prepared pan. Bake in a 350° oven 15 to 20 minutes or until top springs back when lightly touched. Immediately loosen cake from pan. Invert onto a towel sprinkled with powdered sugar. Roll up warm cake and towel, jelly-roll style, starting from a short side. Cool.

5 Gently unroll the cake. Spread 1¼ cups Caramel Orange Buttercream on cake to within ½ inch of the edges. Roll up cake without towel, jelly-roll style, starting from one of the short sides. Cut a 2-inch diagonal slice from one end of cake. Place the slice at the side of the "log" to form a "branch." Frost with the remaining buttercream. Using the tines of a fork, score the cake lengthwise to resemble tree bark. If desired, garnish with sugared cranberries. Cover and store in the refrigerator for up to 3 days. Makes 10 servings.

Caramel-Orange Buttercream: In a medium saucepan stir together ⅓ cup packed brown sugar and 2 tablespoons cornstarch. Stir in 1¼ cups half-and-half or light cream. Cook and stir over medium heat until thickened and bubbly. Reduce heat, then cook and stir 2 minutes more. Gradually stir about half of the mixture into 2 slightly beaten egg yolks; return to remaining hot mixture. Bring to a gentle boil. Cook and stir for 2 minutes. Remove from heat. Stir in 2 teaspoons finely shredded orange peel. Cover surface with clear plastic wrap. Cool to room temperature. Do not stir. In a mixing bowl beat ¾ cup softened butter (no substitutes), ¾ cup sifted powdered sugar, and 1 tablespoon orange liqueur or orange juice with an electric mixer on medium speed until light and fluffy. Add cooled cooked mixture, ¼ cup at a time, beating on low speed after each addition until smooth.

*Note: To make sugared cranberries, dip cranberries in lightly beaten egg white, then roll in granulated sugar. Set aside to dry.

Nutrition facts per serving: *443 calories, 8 g protein, 33 g carbohydrate, 32 g total fat (13 g saturated fat), 218 mg cholesterol, 196 mg sodium, 2 g fiber. Daily values: 42% vitamin A, 2% vitamin C, 8% calcium, 10% iron.*

Make a diagonal cut about 2 inches from one end of the log. Place the slice with the newly cut side against the "log" to form a branch.

Delicious Memories

Toffee Squares

My mother made these cookies when I was a child, and they were one of my favorites. I made these cookies for my kids (they're now "twenty-somethings"), but because they didn't like nuts, I left about half of the bars "nutless" and made the rest extra nutty. This is one of the few cookie recipes that I still make.
—Susan Yinger—

> 1 cup shortening
> 1 cup packed brown sugar
> 1 egg
> 1 teaspoon vanilla
> 2 cups all-purpose flour
> ¼ teaspoon salt
> 1 6-ounce package (1 cup) semisweet chocolate pieces
> ½ cup chopped walnuts or pecans

1 In a large mixing bowl, beat the shortening with an electric mixer on medium to high speed for 30 seconds. Add the brown sugar, egg, and vanilla. Beat until fluffy. Beat in flour and salt until combined.

2 Spread batter in a 15x10x1-inch baking pan. Bake in a 350° oven for 18 to 20 minutes or until golden. Remove from oven and immediately sprinkle chocolate pieces over the hot cookie base. Let stand about 2 minutes or until chocolate is melted; spread evenly. Cut into bars while still hot. Then sprinkle with walnuts or pecans. Cool completely. Place in an airtight container and store at room temperature for up to 3 days. Makes 48.

Nutrition facts per bar: *95 calories, 1 g protein, 10 g carbohydrate, 6 g total fat (1 g saturated), 4 mg cholesterol, 14 mg sodium, 0 g fiber. Daily values: 0% vitamin A, 0% vitamin C, 0% calcium, 2% iron.*

Minty Meringues

Light and airy, these puffs of cookies explode with the coolness of mint.

> 3 egg whites
> 2 teaspoons white crème de menthe or 1 teaspoon vanilla
> ½ teaspoon cream of tartar
> 1 cup granulated sugar
> 40 miniature chocolate-covered peppermint patties (two 1.6-ounce packages)

1 Let egg whites stand at room temperature for 30 minutes in a large mixing bowl. Meanwhile, line 2 large baking sheets with parchment paper, foil, or plain brown paper; set aside.

2 Add the crème de menthe or vanilla and cream of tartar to the egg whites. Beat with an electric mixer on medium speed until soft peaks form (tips curl). Gradually add sugar, 1 tablespoon at a time, beating on high speed until stiff peaks form (tips stand straight) and sugar is almost dissolved.

3 Drop meringue mixture by tablespoons 2 inches apart onto the prepared baking sheets. Press 1 mint patty into each meringue. With a knife or narrow spatula, bring meringue up and over candy and swirl the top.

4 Bake in a 300° oven for 20 minutes. Turn off oven. Let meringues dry in the oven with the door closed for 30 minutes. Peel the meringues from paper. Place in an airtight container and store in a cool, dry place for up to 1 week. Makes about 40.

Nutrition facts per meringue: *31 calories, 0 g protein, 7 g carbohydrate, 0 g total fat (0 g saturated), 0 mg cholesterol, 5 mg sodium, 0 g fiber. Daily values: 0% vitamin A, 0% vitamin C, 0% calcium, 0% iron.*

Noel!

Even if you're expecting a warm Christmas this year, you still can enjoy a traditional yule log. Folklore says burning a log on Christmas Eve burns away all bad luck and old wrongs. The French Christmas log, the Bûche de Noël, is the continental answer to a rich fruitcake. Underneath the buttercream "bark" is a chocolate sponge roll that sometimes is filled with a chestnut cream. The log is traditionally decorated with small gnomes dressed as woodchoppers, but you can use anything you like—ivy, meringue mushrooms, or even a tiny Santa and reindeer.

Butter Rum Cookies

Butter Rum Cookies

With the cookie shaping directions, you can turn this buttery dough into a variety of shapes, sizes, and flavors. If you run short on time, shape some cookies now and freeze the remaining dough for later use.

2⅔ cups all-purpose flour
1 teaspoon baking powder
1 teaspoon ground nutmeg
¼ teaspoon salt
1 cup butter (no substitutes)
⅔ cup packed brown sugar
1 egg
1 teaspoon rum extract or vanilla
1 recipe Confectioner's Icing, made with vanilla (see page 196) (optional)
1 recipe Decorator Frosting, made with milk and vanilla (see page 196) (optional)
Red cinnamon candies, multi-colored decorative candies, and colored sugar (optional)

1 In a medium mixing bowl stir together flour, baking powder, nutmeg, and salt; set aside.

2 In a large mixing bowl beat the butter with an electric mixer on medium to high speed for 30 seconds or until softened. Add brown sugar and beat until fluffy. Add egg and rum extract. Beat until combined. Gradually add flour mixture, beating until combined. If necessary, cover and chill the dough about 1 hour or until easy to handle. Shape the cookies as desired (see shaping directions, below).

3 To bake, place the dough shapes 1 inch apart on an ungreased cookie sheet. Bake in a 350° oven for 8 to 10 minutes or until slightly brown around the edges. Remove cookies from cookie sheet and cool on a wire rack. Place cookies in layers separated by waxed paper in an airtight container and store at room temperature for up to 3 days.

Nutrition facts per plain Butter Rum Cookie: *68 calories, 1 g protein, 8 g carbohydrate, 4 g total fat (2 g saturated), 14 mg cholesterol, 58 mg sodium, 0 g fiber. Daily values: 3% vitamin A, 0% vitamin C, 0% calcium, 2% iron.*

Shaping Directions for Butter Rum Cookies

Pistachio Balls: Roll dough into 1-inch balls. Place about 1 cup finely chopped pistachio nuts in a shallow bowl. Roll dough balls in chopped nuts, coating thoroughly. Bake as directed and cool.

Bite-Size Tarts: Roll dough into 1-inch balls. Place balls in 1¾-inch muffin pans. With your fingers, press dough to cover bottom and sides of cups. Fill each muffin cup with about 1 teaspoon cherry or apricot preserves. Bake as directed; cool. If desired, drizzle the tarts with Confectioner's Icing.

Pinwheels: On a lightly floured surface, roll half of the chilled dough into a 15x12½-inch rectangle. Cover and chill remaining dough until needed. With a sharp knife, cut rectangle into thirty 2½-inch squares. Arrange squares ½ inch apart on an ungreased cookie sheet. Place a scant teaspoon cherry or seedless raspberry preserves in the center of each square. Cut 1-inch slits diagonally from each corner toward filling. Fold every other tip over to cover filling, forming a pinwheel. Press the center lightly to seal. If desired, repeat with remaining half of dough or use it to make another cookie shape. Bake as directed and cool.

Christmas Cutouts: On a lightly floured surface, roll half of the dough at a time to ⅛-inch thickness. Cover and chill remaining dough until needed. With cookie cutters dipped in flour, cut dough into desired shapes. Reroll dough scraps to make more cookies. Use a thin spatula to transfer cutouts to baking sheet. If desired, repeat with remaining dough or use it to make another cookie shape. Bake as directed and cool. If desired, drizzle with Confectioner's Icing or decorate cookies with tinted Decorator Frosting, red cinnamon candies, small multicolored decorative candies, and colored sugar.

Shortcut
Prepare dough for Butter Rum Cookies as directed. Wrap dough in clear plastic wrap and place in a freezer container or bag and freeze for up to 1 month. Before using, thaw in the refrigerator overnight. Shape cookies and bake as directed.

Maple Leaves

These maple-sweetened cookie leaves are a perfect way to usher in fall's arrival. Cut them into different shapes and they'll be a perfect year-round pleaser. (Pictured on pages 294 and 311.)

½   **cup butter (no substitutes)**
⅔   **cup packed brown sugar**
½   **teaspoon baking soda**
¼   **teaspoon salt**
 1   **egg**
¼   **cup maple syrup or maple-flavored syrup**
 1   **teaspoon vanilla**
 1   **cup whole wheat flour**
1½ **cups all-purpose flour**
     Maple Frosting

1 In a mixing bowl beat butter with an electric mixer on medium to high speed 30 seconds. Add brown sugar, soda, and salt. Beat until combined. Beat in egg, maple syrup, and vanilla. Beat in whole wheat flour and as much of the all-purpose flour as you can with the mixer. Stir in any remaining flour. Divide dough in half. Cover; chill 3 hours or until easy to handle.

2 On a lightly floured surface, roll each portion of dough to ⅛-inch thickness. Using 2½- to 3-inch leaf cookie cutters dipped in flour, cut into leaf shapes. Place 1 inch apart on an ungreased cookie sheet. Bake in a 375° oven 7 to 8 minutes or until edges are firm. Remove from cookie sheet and cool on a wire rack. Frost with Maple Frosting. Let frosting set. Place in an airtight container; store at room tem-

perature up to 3 days. Makes about 54.

Maple Frosting: Beat together 1½ cups sifted powdered sugar and 2 tablespoons softened butter or margarine. Beat in enough maple syrup or maple-flavored syrup (about 2 tablespoons) to make easy to spread.

Nutrition facts per cookie: 64 calories, 1 g protein, 10 g carbohydrate, 2 g total fat (1 g saturated), 10 mg cholesterol, 45 mg sodium, 0 g fiber. Daily values: 2% vitamin A, 0% vitamin C, 0% calcium, 2% iron.

To Make Ahead

Bake cookies as directed; cool completely. Do not frost. Place in a freezer container or bag and freeze for up to 1 month. Before serving, thaw for 15 minutes. Frost with Maple Frosting.

Kid Appeal

May Flower Cookies

 1   **20-ounce roll refrigerated sugar cookie dough**
½   **cup almond paste**
     Food coloring
     Colored sugars, coarse sugar, or edible glitter

1 Divide cookie dough among 4 small mixing bowls. Add 2 tablespoons almond paste and desired food coloring to each bowl of dough.

2 Using clean beaters for each bowl, beat dough wtih an electric mixer on

medium speed until color is well mixed. Break off small pieces of different colors of dough and shape them into flowers (see directions below), or create your own flower shapes. If desired, sprinkle flowers with colored sugars, coarse sugars, or edible glitter.

3 Place flowers 2 inches apart on ungreased cookie sheets. For 2½- to 3-inch cookies, bake in a 375° oven for 8 to 10 minutes or until the edges are light brown. Remove cookies from cookie sheet and cool on a wire rack. Place in an airtight container and store at room temperature for up to 3 days. Makes about 24.

Pansies: Shape colored dough into ¼- to ½-inch balls. Use the balls for the flower centers and petals. Or, flatten the balls to make petals. If desired, overlap the petals around the center.

Tulips: Roll colored dough into 2½-inch-long logs. Place 5 logs side by side; pinch the logs together at one

Form flower petals as directed in the recipe. Arrange the pieces on a cookie sheet so the flower cookies are about 2 inches apart.

end to make the flower stem base. Curl out the tips at the other end to look like open petals.

aisies: Roll colored dough into 2-inch ropes. Place 6 or 7 ropes pinwheel fashion from a center and curl in the tips. Top center with a small ball of another color of dough.

Nutrition facts per cookie: *133 calories, 2 g protein, 18 g carbohydrate, 6 g total fat (1 g saturated), 7 mg cholesterol, 99 mg sodium, 0 g fiber. Daily values: 0% vitamin A, 0% vitamin C, 2% calcium, and 3% iron.*

Raspberry-Filled Hearts

Decorate and bake the small center cutouts for marvelous miniature cookies. (Pictured on page 294.)

½ cup butter (no substitutes)
1 cup granulated sugar
1 teaspoon baking powder
¼ teaspoon baking soda
　 Dash salt
½ cup dairy sour cream
1 egg
1 teaspoon vanilla
2½ cups all-purpose flour
1 slightly beaten egg white
　 Pearl sugar, red-colored sugar, or granulated sugar
　 Seedless red raspberry jam

1 In a large mixing bowl beat the butter with an electric mixer on medium to high speed 30 seconds. Add the sugar, baking powder, baking soda, and salt. Beat until combined. Beat in sour cream, whole egg, and vanilla until combined. Beat in as much of the flour as you can with the mixer. Stir in any remaining flour. Divide dough in half. Cover and chill 2 to 3 hours or until dough is easy to handle.

2 On a well floured surface, roll half of the dough to a ⅛-inch thickness. Using a 2½- to 3-inch heart-shape cutter dipped in flour, cut dough into hearts. Place cutouts on an ungreased cookie sheet. Bake in a 375° oven 7 to 8 minutes or until edges are firm and bottoms are lightly browned. Remove from cookie sheet; cool on a wire rack.

3 Roll out remaining dough. Cut hearts as directed above. Place shapes on cookie sheet. Using a ½- to ¾-inch circle or heart-shape cutter, cut out and remove center from each larger heart. Brush cookies with egg white; carefully sprinkle with desired sugar. Bake and cool as directed. Place in an airtight container and store at room temperature for up to 3 days.

4 Before serving, spoon ½ teaspoon of jam on each whole cookie. Top the cookie with the heart-shape cutout. Makes about 30.

Nutrition facts per cookie: *111 calories, 1 g protein, 18 g carbohydrate, 4 g total fat (2 g saturated), 17 mg cholesterol, 63 mg sodium, 0 g fiber. Daily values: 3% vitamin A, 0% vitamin C, 1% calcium, 3% iron.*

Baker's Bonus

Shades of the Holidays

It's easy to add festive colors to cookies and pastries with food coloring. You can choose between paste food coloring, which comes in tubes or small plastic cups, or liquid food coloring, which comes in tiny bottles.

Paste coloring provides the widest color range. It works particularly well in frostings because it doesn't thin them. Use only paste to tint melted white baking bars and candy coating.

Liquid coloring tends to thin frosting so you may need to add additional powdered sugar to achieve the right consistency. Do not use liquid coloring to tint melted white baking bars or candy coating because it will cause graininess or clumping. Liquid food coloring comes in a limited range of colors, so you have to mix them to create the look you want.

To create some basic colors, follow these guidelines. You can change the hue by changing proportions. Once you get the color you want, intensify it by adding additional amounts of both colors in the same proportions.

Green—blue + yellow　　　Purple—blue + red
Orange—red + yellow　　　Pink—a small amount of red

International Origin

Spumoni Slices

And you thought pistachio, peppermint, and chocolate could only be had together in a scoop of ice cream. Here is that wonderful taste sensation all rolled into one cookie.

2½ **cups all-purpose flour**
1½ **teaspoons baking powder**
½ **teaspoon salt**
1 **cup butter (no substitutes)**
1½ **cups granulated sugar**
1 **egg**
1 **teaspoon vanilla**
¼ **teaspoon peppermint extract**
5 **drops red food coloring**
¼ **cup ground pistachio nuts or almonds**
5 **drops green food coloring**
1 **ounce unsweetened chocolate, melted and cooled**
   Granulated sugar (optional)

1 In a medium mixing bowl stir together flour, baking powder, and salt; set aside.

2 In a large mixing bowl beat butter with an electric mixer on medium to high speed about 30 seconds or until softened. Add the 1½ cups sugar. Beat until fluffy. Beat in the egg and vanilla just until combined. Slowly add the flour mixture, beating until combined.

3 Divide dough into 3 equal portions. To one portion of the dough, stir in peppermint extract and red food coloring. To the second portion of dough, stir in the pistachio nuts and green food coloring. To remaining portion of dough, stir in melted chocolate. Divide each portion of dough in half, for a total of 6 portions.

4 On a piece of waxed paper, shape each portion into a 10-inch roll. Lift and smooth the waxed paper to help shape the roll. Gently press 1 roll of the pistachio dough and 1 roll of the chocolate dough together lengthwise, keeping the round shapes intact. Gently press 1 roll peppermint dough atop lengthwise, for a shape that is similar to a triangle. Repeat with remaining 3 rolls. Wrap each tricolor roll in waxed paper or clear plastic wrap; chill for 2 to 48 hours or until firm enough to slice.

5 Using a thin-blade knife, slice a tricolor roll of dough into ¼-inch-thick slices. Rotate the roll as you slice to avoid flattening it. Place cutouts 1 inch apart on an ungreased cookie sheet. Sprinkle with sugar, if desired. Bake in a 350° oven for 10 to 12 minutes or until edges are firm and light brown. Cool cookies on the cookie sheet for 1 minute. Remove cookies from cookie sheet and cool on a wire rack. Repeat with the remaining tricolor roll. Place in an airtight container and store at room temperature for up to 3 days. Makes about 60.

Nutrition facts per cookie: 70 calories, 1 g protein, 9 g carbohydrate, 4 g total fat (2 g saturated), 12 mg cholesterol, 59 mg sodium, 0 g fiber. Daily values: 2% vitamin A, 0% vitamin C, 0% calcium, 2% iron.

Shortcut

Prepare tricolor dough as directed. Wrap dough in clear plastic wrap and place in a freezer container or bag and freeze for up to 1 month. Before using, thaw in the refrigerator overnight. Slice and bake as directed.

To Make Ahead

Bake cookies as directed; cool completely. Place in a freezer container or bag and freeze for up to 1 month. Before serving, thaw for 15 minutes.

Delicious Memories

Kringla

This Norwegian treat made a big impact on me as a child. I remember when I was 5, eating Kringla with lots of butter and a small cup of strong coffee. Needless to say, I learned to make Kringla at a very young age.
—Lisa Mannes—

1 **cup whipping cream**
1 **8-ounce carton dairy sour cream**
3 **cups all-purpose flour**
2 **teaspoons baking powder**
   Dash salt
1⅓ **cups granulated sugar**
2 **tablespoons shortening**
1 **egg yolk**
1 **teaspoon baking soda**
½ **teaspoon vanilla**

1 In a small mixing bowl stir together whipping cream and sour cream until well blended. Cover and refrigerate overnight or for up to 24 hours. When ready to use, let stand at room temperature for 1 hour. In a medium mixing bowl stir together the flour, baking powder, and salt; set aside.

2 In a large mixing bowl beat the sugar and shortening with an electric mixer until well combined. Beat in the egg yolk.

3 Add the baking soda and vanilla to the whipping cream-sour cream mixture. Mix well. Add the whipping cream mixture to the sugar mixture and beat together until combined. Add the flour mixture and beat until combined. Cover and chill overnight.

4 On a well-floured pastry cloth, drop 2 rounded tablespoons of dough for each cookie. With your hands, roll dough into an 8x½-inch rope. Form the rope into a circle, placing one end looped under the other end. Place on an ungreased cookie sheet. Bake in a 475° oven about 5 minutes or until lightly brown. Remove cookies from cookie sheet and cool slightly on a wire rack. Serve warm, if desired. Place in an airtight container and store at room temperature for up to 3 days. Makes about 24.

Nutrition facts per cookie: *162 calories, 2 g protein, 23 g carbohydrate, 7 g total fat (4 g saturated), 27 mg cholesterol, 98 mg sodium, 0 g fiber. Daily values: 8% vitamin A, 0% vitamin C, 4% calcium, 5% iron.*

To Make Ahead

Bake cookies as directed; cool completely. Place in a freezer container and freeze for up to 1 month. Before serving, thaw for 15 minutes.

International Origin

Minted Spritz Cookies

The coolness of fresh mint is so refreshing in these rich, buttery Scandinavian cookies. You'll need a cookie press to create the traditional shape.

¾ **cup butter (no substitutes)**
½ **cup granulated sugar**
1 **tablespoon finely snipped fresh mint or 1 teaspoon dried mint, crushed**
½ **teaspoon baking powder**
1 **egg yolk**
1 **teaspoon vanilla**
1¾ **cups all-purpose flour**
1 **6-ounce package (1 cup) semi-sweet chocolate pieces (optional)**
2 **tablespoons shortening (optional)**

1 In a large mixing bowl beat the butter with an electric mixer on medium to high speed about 30 seconds or until softened. Add the sugar, mint, and baking powder. Beat until combined. Add egg yolk and vanilla. Beat until combined. Beat in as much of the flour as you can with the mixer. Using a wooden spoon, stir in the remaining flour. Do not chill dough.

2 Pack dough into a cookie press. Force the dough through the press onto an ungreased cookie sheet. Bake in a 375° oven for 8 to 10 minutes or until edges are firm but not browned. Remove cookies from cookie sheet and cool on a wire rack.

3 If desired, in a heavy small saucepan heat chocolate and shortening over low heat just until melted, stirring occasionally. Remove from heat. Dip one end of each cookie into chocolate mixture. Let excess drip off. Transfer to a waxed-paper-lined cookie sheet. Let stand until chocolate is set. Place in layers separated by waxed paper in an airtight container and store at room temperature for up to 3 days. Makes about 48.

Nutrition facts per cookie: *50 calories, 1 g protein, 5 g carbohydrate, 3 g total fat (2 g saturated), 12 mg cholesterol, 33 mg sodium, 0 g fiber. Daily values: 3% vitamin A, 0% vitamin C, 0% calcium, 1% iron.*

To Make Ahead

Bake cookies as directed; cool completely. Do not dip in chocolate. Place cookies in a freezer container or bag and freeze for up to 1 month. Before serving, thaw for 15 minutes. If desired, dip cookies in chocolate as directed.

Santa's Sugarplum Gingerbread House

Remember when Christmas was as simple as writing a letter to Santa, hanging the stockings, and wishing for loads of presents to appear under the Christmas tree? Did "visions of sugarplums" dance in your head while you nestled in a warm bed, dreaming of Christmas day? Then you'll want to create a bit of your own Christmas magic with this whimsical gingerbread house. In the land of the sugarplums there is a Santa Claus and Christmas can be anything you want it to be. Best of all, you can create it together with your family and make it last for more than just one day.

Gingerbread Cookie Dough

You'll need two batches of this cookie dough for the Sugarplum House. Do not try to make both batches at the same time because it is too much for most mixing bowls.

½ **cup shortening**
½ **cup granulated sugar**
1 **teaspoon baking powder**
1 **teaspoon ground ginger**
½ **teaspoon baking soda**
½ **teaspoon ground cinnamon**
½ **teaspoon ground cloves**
½ **cup molasses**
1 **egg**
1 **tablespoon vinegar**
2½ **cups all-purpose flour**

In a mixing bowl beat shortening with an electric mixer on medium to high speed about 30 seconds. Add sugar, baking powder, ginger, baking soda, cinnamon, and cloves; beat until combined. Beat in molasses, egg, and vinegar. Beat in as much flour as you can. Stir in any remaining flour. Cover; chill 3 hours or until easy to handle. Cut and bake dough as directed.

Royal Icing

Make the icing just before you are ready to decorate the house and trees.

3 **egg whites**
1 **16-ounce package powdered sugar, sifted**
1 **teaspoon vanilla**
½ **teaspoon cream of tartar**

In a large bowl combine egg whites, powdered sugar, vanilla, and cream of tartar. Beat with an electric mixer on high speed for 7 to 10 minutes or until very stiff. Keep icing covered with plastic wrap at all times to prevent it from drying out. May be refrigerated overnight in tightly covered container; stir before using. Makes 3 cups.

Cutting and Baking the Pieces

Enlarge the patterns (opposite) as directed. Grease the back of a 15x10x1-inch baking pan. On the prepared pan, roll out one-fourth of the dough to ¼-inch thickness. Place the pattern pieces 1 inch apart on dough. Cut around pieces. Carefully remove excess dough.

Leave cookie pieces on pan. Bake in a 375° oven 10 to 12 minutes or until edges are browned. Remove from oven; place pattern pieces on cookie pieces and recut if necessary to form straight edges. Let cool 5 minutes on pan. Carefully transfer pieces to wire racks; cool completely. Repeat with remaining dough and patterns until all

Gingerbread Colonial House
Materials

◆ 2 recipes Gingerbread Cookie Dough
◆ 1 or 2 recipes Royal Icing (depending on how elaborate your decorations are)
◆ Candy canes
◆ Assorted nonpareils and sprinkles
◆ Small, round candies
◆ Waffle ice-cream cones (optional)

◆ Graham crackers
◆ Small, hard, ribbon candies
◆ Fruit-flavored circle candies
◆ Jelly beans
◆ Pastry bags and decorating tips
◆ Graph paper
◆ Frosted bite-size shredded wheat biscuits
◆ Colored sugars (optional)

house pieces are baked. For the base, roll half a recipe of gingerbread dough to about 16½x10 inches on a foil-lined extra-large baking sheet. Trim uneven edges.

Cool all gingerbread pieces completely before beginning to assemble the house. If you allow the pieces to dry overnight, they will be even firmer and better for construction.

Decorating the Pieces

Prepare Royal Icing. Use a pastry bag with a medium star tip; fill with icing. If icing begins to dry and plugs decorating tip, wipe it with a wet paper towel. Working on a waxed-paper-covered surface, outline the doors and windows on all four sides of the house. Use small amounts of icing to attach desired decorations.

Assembling

For the porch, cut one graham cracker square in half lengthwise. Cut another square in half diagonally. Decorate one triangle as desired (discard the other). Cement the porch roof on one side using the icing.

For house, assemble section A on one end of cookie's base; use a star tip to pipe icing on each of the edges that will join with another piece. Press pieces together. Assemble section B

next to section A; use a few dabs of icing to hold the end sections of A and B together. Let icing dry.

For roof, use a star tip to pipe icing on edges of side and end pieces of both sections of the house. Press roof pieces into position, placing notched ends of sections B at the outside edge.

For chimney, cement 3 chimney pieces together with icing; attach to end of house section B with icing, fitting chimney into notched area of roof. Spread a portion of chimney with icing. Place jelly beans in icing, allowing space between. Repeat until chimney is covered with jelly beans. Let dry.

For thatch, spread roof with icing; press the wheat biscuits into frosting, staggering the rows like shingles.

For trees, pipe icing on waffle cones; sprinkle with colored sugars.

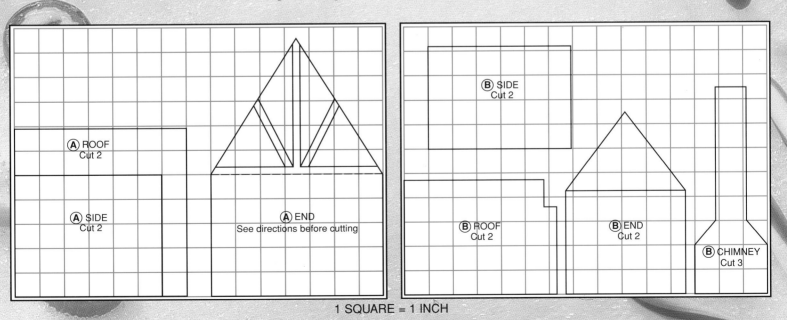

Ⓐ ROOF
Cut 2

Ⓐ SIDE
Cut 2

Ⓐ END
See directions before cutting

Ⓑ SIDE
Cut 2

Ⓑ ROOF
Cut 2

Ⓑ END
Cut 2

Ⓑ CHIMNEY
Cut 3

1 SQUARE = 1 INCH

Delicious Memories

Mom's Pumpkin Pie

What Thanksgiving would be complete without a pumpkin pie? You can always find three of these at my house during the holiday season—and there are never any leftovers.
—Lisa Mannes—

1 **recipe Pastry for Single-Crust Pie (see page 224)**
1 **cup canned pumpkin**
1 **cup half-and-half, light cream, or whipping cream**
2 **eggs**
1 **cup granulated sugar**
1 **teaspoon ground cinnamon**
¼ **teaspoon salt**
⅛ **teaspoon ground ginger**
⅛ **teaspoon ground allspice**

1 Prepare and roll out Pastry for Single-Crust Pie as directed. Line a 9-inch pie plate with pastry. Trim and flute edge of pastry. Do not prick shell.

2 For filling, in a large mixing bowl beat the pumpkin, cream, and eggs with an electric mixer on low speed until thoroughly combined. Add the sugar, cinnamon, salt, ginger, and allspice. Mix until thoroughly combined.

3 Pour filling into pastry shell. To prevent overbrowning, cover edge of pie with foil. Bake in a 375° oven for 25 minutes. Remove foil and bake 20 to 25 minutes more or until a knife inserted near the center comes out clean. Cool on a wire rack. Refrigerate within 2 hours; add cover for longer storage. Refrigerate any leftovers and use within 2 days. Makes 8 servings.

Nutrition facts per serving: 371 calories, 4 g protein, 42 g carbohydrate, 21 g total fat (9 g saturated), 94 mg cholesterol, 163 mg sodium, 1 g fiber. Daily values: 83% vitamin A, 2% vitamin C, 3% calcium, 10% iron.

Shortcut

Prepare pie as directed, except use half of a 15-ounce package folded, refrigerated, unbaked piecrust (1 crust) for the pastry. Let stand at room temperature according to package directions before fitting into pie plate.

Apple-Mincemeat Pie With Rum Sauce

Sliced peaches or pears can be substituted for the apples.

1 **recipe Pastry for Double-Crust Pie (see page 224)**
3 **cups thinly sliced, peeled, cooking apples (about 1 pound)**
1 **27- or 28-ounce jar (2⅔ cups) mincemeat**
½ **cup chopped walnuts or pecans**
½ **cup packed brown sugar**
½ **cup water**
1 **tablespoon cornstarch**
2 **tablespoons orange marmalade**
1 **tablespoon rum or ¼ teaspoon rum flavoring**

1 Prepare and roll out Pastry for Double-Crust Pie as directed. Line a 9-inch pie plate with half of the pastry.

2 For filling, in a large mixing bowl stir together the apples, mincemeat, and nuts. Transfer the apple mixture to the pastry-lined pie plate. Trim bottom pastry to ½ inch beyond edge of pie plate. Top with lattice crust. Seal and flute edge.

3 To prevent overbrowning, cover the edge of the pie with foil. Bake in a 375° oven for 25 minutes. Remove foil. Bake 25 to 30 minutes more or until top is golden. Cool on a wire rack.

4 For sauce, in medium saucepan combine the brown sugar, water, and cornstarch. Cook and stir over medium heat until mixture is slightly thickened and bubbly. Reduce heat. Cook and stir for 2 minutes more. Stir in orange marmalade and rum.

5 To serve, spoon rum sauce over slices of warm pie. Cover aand refrigerate any leftovers and use within 2 days. Makes 8 servings.

Nutrition facts per serving: 583 calories, 5 g protein, 91 g carbohydrate, 23 g total fat (5 g saturated), 0 mg cholesterol, 420 mg sodium, 2 g fiber. Daily values: 0% vitamin A, 1% vitamin C, 4% calcium, 22% iron.

Shortcut

Prepare pie as directed, except use one 15-ounce package folded, refrigerated, unbaked piecrust (2 crusts) for the pastry. Let stand at room temperature according to package directions before fitting bottom crust into pie plate.

Coconut Cream Napoleons

Most likely the name "napoleon" came from the large, elaborately decorated, and alternately layered cakes known as "napolitains" that were featured center-pieces of grand French buffets.

½ **of 1 portion Quick Puff Pastry (see page 262) or ½ of a 17¼-ounce package (1 sheet) frozen puff pastry, thawed**
½ **cup granulated sugar**
2 **tablespoons all-purpose flour**
2 **tablespoons cornstarch**
1¼ **cups milk**
1 **beaten egg yolk**
½ **cup coconut**
½ **teaspoon vanilla**
½ **cup sifted powdered sugar**
2 **to 3 teaspoons hot water**
¼ **teaspoon vanilla**
1 **ounce semisweet chocolate, melted and cooled**
    Toasted coconut (optional)

1 On a lightly floured surface, roll half of a portion of dough into an 8x7-inch rectangle. Or, if using purchased pastry, unfold pastry sheet and trim into an 8x7-inch rectangle. Using a sharp knife, cut pastry into eight 3½x2-inch rectangles.

2 Transfer pastry rectangles to an ungreased baking sheet. Using the tines of a fork, prick pastry several times. Bake in a 425° oven about 16 minutes (about 12 minutes for purchased pastry) or until golden. Remove from baking sheet and cool on a wire rack.

3 For filling, in a heavy medium saucepan stir together the sugar, flour, and cornstarch. Gradually stir in milk. Cook and stir over medium heat until thickened and bubbly. Reduce heat. Cook and stir for 2 minutes more. Remove from heat. Gradually stir about half of mixture into the beaten egg yolk. Return egg mixture to the saucepan. Bring to a gentle boil. Cook and stir 2 minutes more. Remove from heat. Stir in coconut and ½ teaspoon vanilla. Cover surface with plastic wrap, then chill without stirring. Just before using, gently stir.

4 For glaze, in a medium mixing bowl stir together the powdered sugar and enough hot water to make a glaze that is easy to spread. Stir in ¼ teaspoon vanilla; set aside.

5 To assemble, using the tines of a fork, separate each pastry rectangle horizontally into three layers. Spread a rounded tablespoon of filling on each bottom layer. Replace middle pastry layers and spread another rounded tablespoon of filling on each. Replace top layers. Spread glaze over the tops. Drizzle with chocolate. If desired, sprinkle tops with toasted coconut. Serve immediately or cover and chill for up to 1 hour. Makes 8.

Nutrition facts per napoleon: 305 calories, 4 g protein, 39 g carbohydrate, 16 g total fat (10 g saturated), 60 mg cholesterol, 205 mg sodium, 1 g fiber. Daily values: 16% vitamin A, 0% vitamin C, 4% calcium, 7% iron.

To Make Ahead

Napoleons are best consumed within an hour of being assembled. To simplify serving, prepare, bake, and separate pastry into layers early in the day. Store in airtight container. Have filling and glaze prepared and assemble just before serving.

Notes

Ultimate Nut and Chocolate Chip Tart

Ultimate Nut And Chocolate Chip Tart

Mixed nuts and chocolate add richness to the caramel custard filling.

1   recipe **Pastry for Single-Crust Pie** (see page 224)
3   eggs
1   cup light corn syrup
½   cup packed brown sugar
⅓   cup butter (no substitutes), melted and cooled
1   teaspoon vanilla
1   cup coarsely chopped salted mixed nuts
½   cup miniature semisweet chocolate pieces
⅓   cup miniature semisweet chocolate pieces
1   tablespoon shortening
    Vanilla ice cream (optional)
    Fresh currants
    White chocolate leaves

1 Prepare Pastry for Single-Crust Pie as directed. On a lightly floured surface, flatten dough with your hands. Roll pastry from the center to the edge, forming a circle about 12 inches in diameter. Ease pastry into an 11-inch tart pan with removable bottom. Trim pastry even with the rim of the pan. Do not prick pastry.

2 For filling, in a large mixing bowl beat eggs slightly using a rotary beater or fork. Stir in the corn syrup. Add the brown sugar, butter, and vanilla, stirring until sugar is dissolved. Stir in the nuts and the ½ cup chocolate pieces.

3 Place the pastry-lined tart pan on a baking sheet on the oven rack. Carefully pour filling into pan. Bake in a 350° oven about 40 minutes or until a knife inserted near the center comes out clean. Cool on a wire rack.

4 For glaze, in a small, heavy saucepan place the ⅓ cup chocolate pieces and the shortening. Heat over very low heat, stirring constantly, until it begins to melt. Immediately remove from heat and stir until smooth. Cool slightly. Transfer chocolate mixture to a clean, small, heavy plastic bag.

5 To serve, cut the tart into wedges and transfer wedges to dessert plates. Snip a very small hole in one corner of the bag of melted chocolate. Drizzle the melted chocolate in zigzag lines across each tart wedge and onto the plate. If desired, serve with vanilla ice cream and garnish with currants and chocolate leaves. Cover and refrigerate any leftover tart and use within 2 days. Makes 8 to 10 servings.

Nutrition facts per serving: *622 calories, 8 g protein, 76 g carbohydrate, 35 g total fat (9 g saturated), 100 mg cholesterol, 204 mg sodium, 2 g fiber. Daily values: 10% vitamin A, 0% vitamin C, 4% calcium, 18% iron.*

Shortcut

Prepare tart as directed, except use half of a 15-ounce package folded, refrigerated, unbaked piecrust (1 crust) for the pastry. Let stand at room temperature according to package directions before fitting into pan.

Cookie Swap

Time is at a premium, particularly during the holidays. If you want to have a variety of cookies but can't find time to bake them, why not organize a cookie swap? It's the perfect way to have your cookies and eat them, too, all while enjoying the company of friends.

Determine how many people you comfortably can host. Remember, you'll need enough space to display all the cookies. Four or five friends are plenty, but for a large variety of cookies you may want to invite 10 or 12 people. Schedule the swap for sometime in late November or early December to give your guests time to bake before the holiday rush and to ensure they'll have plenty of cookies on hand for surprise visitors.

Ask each friend to bring six dozen cookies and an empty container. It's also a nice idea to ask each one to bring enough copies of his or her recipe so that everyone can take one home. When your friends arrive, arrange all the cookie containers (marked with the type of cookie and the baker's name) on a long table or counter. Divide 72 (six dozen) by the number of guests to determine the number of each type of cookie each guest may take. Give your guests an opportunity to fill their empty containers. (You might have extra containers on hand, just in case someone forgets to bring one.)

Pistachio Cream Éclairs

If you don't have a decorating bag, use two spoons to drop and shape the dough.

 1   **recipe Cream Puff Pastry (see page 258)**
 ½   **cup granulated sugar**
 ⅓   **cup all-purpose flour**
 1½ **cups half-and-half or light cream**
 2   **slightly beaten egg yolks**
 1   **teaspoon vanilla**
 ½   **cup whipping cream**
 ½   **cup chopped salted pistachio nuts**
 2   **ounces semisweet chocolate, finely chopped**
 1   **tablespoon butter**
 1   **tablespoon light corn syrup**
 ½   **cup sifted powdered sugar**
 1   **tablespoon water**
     Chopped pistachio nuts (optional)

1 Grease a baking sheet; set aside.

2 Prepare Cream Puff Pastry as directed. Spoon cream puff dough into a decorating bag fitted with a large, plain, round tip (a ½- to 1-inch opening). Slowly pipe 12 strips of dough 3 inches apart on the prepared baking sheet; make each about 4½ inches long, 1 inch wide, and ¾ inch high. Bake in a 400° oven for 30 to 35 minutes or until golden and set. Remove puffs from the baking sheet and cool on a wire rack.

3 For pistachio filling, in a heavy, medium saucepan stir together sugar and flour. Gradually stir in cream. Cook and stir over medium heat until thickened and bubbly. Reduce heat. Cook and stir for 2 minutes more. Remove from heat. Gradually stir about 1 cup of the hot filling into the beaten egg yolks. Return the egg yolk mixture to the filling in the saucepan. Bring to a gentle boil. Cook and stir 2 minutes more. Remove from heat. Stir in vanilla. Cover surface with plastic wrap, then chill without stirring.

4 In a small mixing bowl beat the whipping cream with an electric mixer on medium speed until soft peaks form. Fold the whipped cream and ½ cup pistachio nuts into the cold filling. Serve immediately or cover and chill for up to 2 hours.

5 For chocolate glaze, in a small, heavy saucepan combine chocolate, butter, and corn syrup. Cook and stir over low heat until the chocolate is melted. Stir in powdered sugar. If necessary, stir in a little hot water to make a glaze that is easy to drizzle. Keep warm while assembling the éclairs.

6 To assemble, horizontally cut off the tops of the éclairs. Using a fork, remove any soft dough from inside. Spoon a scant ⅓ cup of the chilled pistachio filling into each éclair. Replace tops. Drizzle chocolate glaze over the tops. If desired, sprinkle with chopped pistachio nuts. Cover and chill for up to 1 hour. Makes 12.

Nutrition facts per éclair: *338 calories, 6 g protein, 30 g carbohydrate, 22 g total fat (12 g saturated), 154 mg cholesterol, 172 mg sodium, 1 g fiber. Daily values: 24% vitamin A, 1% vitamin C, 5% calcium, 10% iron.*

To Make Ahead

Prepare, bake, and cool the puffs as directed. Place puffs in a freezer container and freeze for up to 2 months. Before serving, thaw for 15 minutes. Fill as directed.

Eggnog Bread Pudding

Serve this dessert during the holidays when time is short—it's so easy to toss together. Use either the dried or candied fruit for a festive touch.

 4   **eggs**
 2   **cups canned or dairy eggnog**
 ⅓   **cup granulated sugar**
 ¼   **cup rum or eggnog**
 ¾   **teaspoon ground nutmeg**
 6   **cups dry French bread cubes (about 8 slices)***
 ½   **cup dried cranberries or dried cherries or chopped candied cherries**
     Sifted powdered sugar

1 Lightly grease a 2-quart square glass baking dish. Set baking dish aside.

2 In a large mixing bowl use a rotary beater or wire whisk to beat together eggs, eggnog, sugar, rum, and nutmeg. Add bread cubes and dried fruit. Let stand 10 to 15 minutes or until bread is softened, stirring once or twice.

3 Pour softened bread mixture into prepared dish. If desired, sprinkle with additional ground nutmeg.

4 Bake in a 325° oven for 35 to 40 minutes or until a knife inserted near the center comes out clean. Sprinkle with powdered sugar before serving. Serve warm. Makes 6 servings.

   Note: To make dry bread cubes, cut bread into ½-inch cubes. Spread bread cubes in a single layer in a shallow baking pan. Bake in a 300° oven for 10 to 15 minutes or until dry, stirring twice during baking. Or, let bread cubes stand, covered, at room temperature for 8 to 12 hours.

   Nutrition facts per serving: *349 calories, 9 g protein, 49 g carbohydrate, 11 g total fat (1 g saturated fat), 142 mg cholesterol, 300 mg sodium, 1 g fiber. Daily values: 9% vitamin A, 0% vitamin C, 8% calcium, 9% iron.*

Amaretti Soufflé

The secret to a successful soufflé is twofold—beating the egg whites properly and serving the soufflé immediately. In fact, it's wise to have your guests seated before you begin baking. Guests should wait on the soufflé, not the soufflé on the guests!

   Butter or margarine
   Granulated sugar
 6 amaretti cookies, crumbled
    (¼ cup)
 1 tablespoon amaretto (optional)

 2 tablespoons butter or
    margarine
 3 tablespoons all-purpose flour
 ¾ cup milk
 ½ of an 8-ounce can almond paste
 4 egg yolks
 4 egg whites
 ½ teaspoon vanilla
 ¼ cup granulated sugar

1 Butter the sides of a 1½-quart soufflé dish. Sprinkle sides of dish with a little sugar. Set dish aside.

2 For collar on soufflé dish, measure enough foil to wrap around the top of the dish plus 3 inches. Fold the foil into thirds lengthwise. Lightly grease one side with butter or margarine and sprinkle with sugar. Attach foil, sugar side in, around the outside of the soufflé dish with the foil extending about 2 inches above the dish. Tape the ends of the foil together. Sprinkle the crumbled amaretti cookies over the bottom of the soufflé dish. If desired, sprinkle the amaretto liqueur over the amaretti crumbs. Set dish aside.

3 In a small saucepan melt 2 tablespoons butter. Stir in flour. Add milk all at once. Cook and stir over medium heat until thickened and bubbly. Remove from heat.

4 In a small mixing bowl beat almond paste until crumbly. Beat in egg yolks, one at a time, until smooth. Gradually stir thickened milk mixture into almond mixture; set aside.

5 Wash beaters. In a large mixing bowl beat egg whites and vanilla with an electric mixer on medium speed until soft peaks form (tips curl). Gradually add the ¼ cup sugar, about 1 tablespoon at a time, beating on medium to high speed until stiff peaks form (tips stand straight).

6 Fold about 1 cup of the beaten egg whites into the almond mixture. Then fold almond mixture into the remaining beaten whites. Carefully, t+ransfer mixture to the prepared soufflé dish.

7 Bake in a 350° oven for 40 to 45 minutes or until a knife inserted near center comes out clean. Serve soufflé at once. Makes 6 servings.

   Nutrition facts per serving: *322 calories, 9 g protein, 33 g carbohydrate, 18 g total fat (5 g saturated fat), 158 mg cholesterol, 115 mg sodium, 0 g fiber. Daily values: 28% vitamin A, 0% vitamin C, 8% calcium, 8% iron.*

Notes

Metric Cooking Hints

By making a few conversions, cooks in Australia, Canada, and the United Kingdom can use the recipes in *Better Homes and Gardens® Complete Book of Baking* with confidence. The charts on this page provide a guide for converting measurements from the U.S. customary system, which is used throughout this book, to the imperial and metric systems. There also is a conversion table for oven temperatures to accommodate the differences in oven calibrations.

Volume and Weight: Americans traditionally use cup measures for liquid and solid ingredients. The chart (top right) shows the approximate imperial and metric equivalents. If you are accustomed to weighing solid ingredients, here are some helpful approximate equivalents.
♦ 1 cup butter, caster sugar, or rice = 8 ounces = about 250 grams
♦ 1 cup flour = 4 ounces = about 125 grams
♦ 1 cup icing sugar = 5 ounces = about 150 grams
 Spoon measures are used for smaller amounts of ingredients. Although the size of the tablespoon varies slightly among countries, for practical purposes and for recipes in this book, a straight substitution is all that's necessary.
 Measurements made using cups or spoons should always be level, unless stated otherwise.

Product Differences: Most of the ingredients called for in the recipes in this book are available in English-speaking countries. However, some are known by different names. Here are some common American ingredients and their possible counterparts:
♦ Sugar is granulated or caster sugar.
♦ Powdered sugar is icing sugar.
♦ All-purpose flour is plain household flour or white flour. When self-rising flour is used in place of all-purpose flour in a recipe that calls for leavening, omit the leavening agent (baking soda or baking powder) and salt.
♦ Light corn syrup is golden syrup.
♦ Cornstarch is cornflour.
♦ Baking soda is bicarbonate of soda.
♦ Vanilla is vanilla essence.

Useful Equivalents: U.S. = Aust./Br.

⅛ teaspoon = 0.5 ml	⅔ cup = ½ cup = 5 fluid ounces = 150 ml
¼ teaspoon = 1 ml	¾ cup = ⅔ cup = 6 fluid ounces = 180 ml
½ teaspoon = 2 ml	1 cup = ¾ cup = 8 fluid ounces = 240 ml
1 teaspoon = 5 ml	1¼ cups = 1 cup
1 tablespoon = 1 tablespoon	2 cups = 1 pint
¼ cup = 2 tablespoons = 2 fluid ounces = 60 ml	1 quart = 1 litre
⅓ cup = ¼ cup = 3 fluid ounces = 90 ml	½ inch = 1½ centimetre
½ cup = ⅓ cup = 4 fluid ounces = 120 ml	1 inch = 2½ centimetres

Baking Pan Sizes

American	Metric
8x1½-inch round baking pan	20x4-centimetre cake tin
9x1½-inch round baking pan	23x3.5-centimetre cake tin
11x7x1½-inch baking pan	28x18x3-centimetre baking tin
13x9x2-inch baking pan	30x20x3-centimetre baking tin
2-quart rectangular baking dish	30x20x3-centimetre baking tin
15x10x2-inch baking pan	38x25x2-centimetre baking tin (Swiss roll tin)
9-inch pie plate	22x4- or 23x4-centimetre pie plate
7- or 8-inch springform pan	18- or 20-centimetre springform or loose-bottom cake tin
9x5x3-inch loaf pan	23x13x7-centimetre or 2-pound narrow loaf tin or paté tin
1½-quart casserole	1.5-litre casserole
2-quart casserole	2-litre casserole

Oven Temperature Equivalents

Fahrenheit Setting	Celsius Setting*	Gas Setting
300°F	150°C	Gas Mark 2 (slow)
325°F	160°C	Gas Mark 3 (moderately slow)
350°F	180°C	Gas Mark 4 (moderate)
375°F	190°C	Gas Mark 5 (moderately hot)
400°F	200°C	Gas Mark 6 (hot)
425°F	220°C	Gas Mark 7
450°F	230°C	Gas Mark 8 (very hot)
Broil		Grill

Electric and gas ovens may be calibrated using Celsius. However, increase the Celsius setting 10 to 20 degrees when cooking above 160°C with an electric oven. For convection or forced-air ovens (gas or electric), lower the temperature setting 10°C when cooking at all heat levels.